The Units of Evolution

The Units of Evolution

Essays on the Nature of Species

edited by Marc Ereshefsky

A Bradford Book
The MIT Press
Cambridge, Massachusetts
London, England

This book was set in Palatino by Asco Trade Typesetting Ltd., Hong Kong, and was printed and bound in the United States of America.

Library of Congress Cataloging-in-Publication Data

The Units of evolution : essays on the nature of species / edited by
Marc Ereshefsky.
     p.   cm.
"A Bradford book."
Includes bibliographical references and index.
ISBN 0-262-05044-7.—ISBN 0-262-55020-2 (pbk.)
  1. Species (Biology) I. Ereshefsky, Marc.
QH380.U54   1992
574'.012—dc20
                                                                    91-4097
                                                                        CIP

Contents

Preface

A number of people helped me at various stages in the development of this anthology. Elliott Sober, David Hull, Michael Ruse, and Richard Burian provided initial support and encouragement for the project. Suggestions for contents were kindly offered by the above as well as Joel Cracraft, Michael Donoghue, Douglas Futuyma, John Kirsch, Philip Kitcher, Allan Larson, and Brent Mishler. Unfortunately space limitations prevented the reprinting of many excellent papers. I owe a special thanks to David Hull, Allan Larson, Brent Mishler, Michael Ruse, Elliott Sober, and Richard Watson for reading and commenting on drafts of the introductions. Finally, I am grateful to Ayala Roudstein, Betty Stanton, and Joanna Poole for their help in the production of this book. A hearty thanks to all of the above, and may the resultant anthology be worthy of their efforts.

Contributors

John Beatty
Department of Ecology, Evolution,
    and Behavior
University of Minnesota
Minneapolis, Minnesota 55455

Joel Cracraft
Department of Anatomy and Cell
    Biology
University of Illinois-Chicago
Chicago, Illinois 60680

Theodore Crovello
Department of Biology
University of Notre Dame
Notre Dame, Indiana 46206

Michael Donoghue
Department of Ecology and
    Evolutionary Biology
University of Arizona
Tucson, Arizona 85721

Paul Ehrlich
Department of Biology
Stanford University
Stanford, California 94305

Marc Ereshefsky
Department of Philosophy
University of Calgary
Calgary, Alberta, T2N 1N4, Canada

Michael Ghiselin
California Academy of Sciences
Golden Gate Park, San Francisco
California 94118

David Hull
Department of Philosophy
Northwestern University
Evanston, Illinois 60201

Philip Kitcher
Department of Philosophy
University of California-San Diego
La Jolla, California 92093

Ernst Mayr
Museum of Comparative Zoology
Harvard University
Cambridge, Massachusetts 02138

Brent Mishler
Department of Botany
Duke University
Durham, North Carolina 27706

Hugh Paterson
Department of Entomology
University of Queensland
St. Lucia, Queensland 4067,
    Australia

Peter Raven
Missouri Botanical Garden
St. Louis, Missouri 63166

Michael Ruse
Departments of History and
    Philosophy
University of Guelph
Guelph, Ontario, N1G 2W1,
    Canada

Elliott Sober
Department of Philosophy
5185 H. C. White Hall
University of Wisconsin
Madison, Wisconsin 53706

Robert Sokal
Department of Ecology and
    Evolution
State University of New York
Stony Brook, New York 11794

Alan Templeton
Department of Biology
Washington University
St. Louis, Missouri 63130

Leigh Van Valen
Department of Biology
University of Chicago
Chicago, Illinois 60637

Edward Wiley
Museum of Natural History
University of Kansas
Lawrence, Kansas 66045

Introduction

The processes of biological evolution have produced an amazing diversity of organisms. Much of that diversity falls into discrete clusters of organisms rather than forming a continuum. Consider the organisms one might see on a stroll in the country. The squirrel darting out of a bush and the deer further afield differ in size, color, and other morphological traits. The song sparrow, cardinal, and chickadee in a meadow each have a distinctive coloration, beak, and call. The taxonomy of such organic diversity is structured according to the framework handed down from Linnaeus (1707–1778). Species are the basal taxonomic groups of organisms. Groups of species form more inclusive taxonomic units called higher taxa. Together, species and higher taxa form a taxonomic hierarchy of the organic world. For example, the species wolf, dog, dingo, and coyote comprise the genus *Canis*. That genus and other genera form the family Canidae. That family belongs to the order of carnivores, which in turn belongs to the class of mammals.

Biological systematists attempt to provide a taxonomy of the world's organic diversity. Evolutionary biologists attempt to explain why that diversity exists. Species often are viewed as *the* evolutionary units of the organic world. The members of a species are exposed to common evolutionary processes that cause those organisms to evolve in step with one another or maintain a common evolutionary stasis. When such processes are disrupted, a new species may form. Higher taxa lack such processes. Thus any stability that a higher taxon has is the result of processes occurring at the species level. Similarly, any change that occurs in a higher taxon is due to a disruption of species-level processes. Species are active agents in the evolutionary process, while higher taxa are passive aggregates consisting of species (Eldredge and Cracraft 1980, 249–250; Wiley 1981, 75).

Because species are the units of evolution, and because they are the base units of biological systematics, a proper understanding of species is crucial for the success of evolutionary biology and biological systematics. Given

Unless otherwise noted, all references are to chapters within this volume.

their importance, is there a generally accepted definition of species among biologists? Before answering this question, a distinction should be made. The term "species" refers to two types of entities: species taxa and the species category (Mayr 1982, 253–4). *Species taxa* are groups of organisms. Dog is a species taxon and chickadee is another. The *species category*, on the other hand, is the class of all species taxa. Our concern is with a definition of the species category: what do all species taxa have in common such that they are members of the species category?

Biologists disagree widely on how to define the species category. This disagreement has significant ramifications for constructing a taxonomy of the organic world. The use of different definitions of the species category can give rise to incompatible taxonomies. Consider a simple example. Suppose we collect insect specimens from a ten-square-meter plot of land. The specimens fall into four morphologically distinct clusters. In two of those clusters the organisms reproduce sexually—two adults of opposite sex must interbreed. In the other two clusters the organisms are partheno-genetic—only females are required for reproduction. How many species are present in the plot? According to a species definition based on overall similarity (Sokal and Crovello chapter 2), four species are present. According to a definition that excludes asexually reproducing organisms from forming species (Ghiselin chapters 13 and 17), two species are present. This problem is compounded when additional species concepts are considered. An ecological species concept (Van Valen chapter 4) and a definition based on phylogenetic relations (Mishler and Donoghue chapter 7) may add two more incompatible taxonomies of our plot. Because biologists disagree on the proper definition of the species category, they disagree on the proper taxonomy of the biological world.

This is no small disagreement, nor is it a transitory one. Since Linnaeus, biologists have disagreed on the nature of species. In a letter to the botanist Joseph Hooker, Darwin writes, "it is really laughable to see what different ideas are prominent in various naturalists' minds, when they speak of 'species'; in some, resemblance is everything and descent of little weight— in some, resemblance seems to go for nothing, and creation the reigning idea—in some, sterility an unfailing test, with others it is not worth a farthing" (F. Darwin 1887, vol. 2, p. 88). The controversy surrounding the species category has not diminished. In the last twenty-five years, well over a hundred books and articles have appeared on the nature of species. Those publications offer more than twenty definitions of the species category. Part I of this volume provides a glimpse of this literature. Nine prominent essays on the species category are reprinted. In those essays, eight definitions of the category are offered.

The debate concerning the nature of species has both empirical and philosophical dimensions. Most proponents of a definition of the species category have a common goal—to cite the biological factor unique to all species taxa. In philosophical jargon, they attempt to provide the essential property of the species category—a property found in all and only species taxa. Most of these proponents consider the species problem an unfinished debate in which the proper definition needs to be weeded from the improper ones. But others argue that the variety of species definitions used by biologists indicates that there is no unique factor common to all species (Kitcher chapter 15, Mishler and Donoghue chapter 7). This latter possibility raises a philosophical question. If the species category lacks a single defining characteristic, then it is a heterogeneous category consisting of different types of species taxa. But then is the species category a real category of nature? Kitcher and Mishler and Donoghue argue that the species category is both heterogeneous and real. Others, however, maintain that such a pluralistic stance towards species is the one to avoid and that we should continue searching for the factor that unifies all species taxa (if it has not already been found) (Ghiselin chapter 17; Hull 1987; Sober 1984). So the debate concerning the species category is complicated by both empirical and philosophical questions. Do all species taxa share a common defining property? Must real categories have such defining properties?

The question of realism arises at a different level as well. Not only is there concern over the reality of the species category but also over whether species taxa exist. Early evolutionists such as Lyell and Lamarck believed that if species are real taxonomic units, then their members must share species-specific essences—properties found in all and only the members of a species taxon (Hull chapter 10). But their conception of species as evolving entities conflicts with this essentialist requirement. Rarely are traits found that occur in all and only the members of a particular species taxon. Furthermore, even if such traits did occur, the forces of evolution can destroy their uniqueness or universality (Hull chapter 10; Sober 1984). Wedded to an essentialist criterion of existence, Lyell, Lamarck, and other early evolutionists doubted the reality of species taxa (Hull chapter 10; Mayr 1982, 263–264). Ghiselin (chapter 13) and Hull (chapter 14), however, have responded that the reality of species taxa does not turn on the existence of such essential properties. Membership in a species, they contend, depends on the organisms of a species having certain spatiotemporal relations to one another rather than on their sharing a common essential property. So again, the question of realism turns on both empirical and philosophical questions. Do the members of a species taxon share a common essential property? Does the existence of species taxa depend on the existence of such properties?

The authors of the essays in part II of this volume discuss the philosophical questions concerning species. They also investigate the philosophical implications that follow from the nature of species. Consider the debate concerning the structure of scientific theories and the nature of evolutionary theory in particular. According to the view accepted by many philosophers, scientific theories consist of universal laws that refer to natural kinds and their essential properties. For example, chemical theory contains universal laws that refer to the elements and their atomic weights. Such laws are used to explain and predict the properties associated with those elements. A number of philosophers contend that evolutionary theory conflicts with this view of science. Species taxa evolve and lack species-specific essences; consequently, no universal laws exist for explaining and predicting the behavior of the members of a particular species. For some philosophers (for example, Smart 1963, 1968), the lack of such laws implies that evolutionary theory is not a scientific theory. Evolutionary theory is merely a localized case study of what has happened on earth, in contrast to the unrestricted and universal laws of chemistry and physics. Other philosophers (for example, Beatty 1981 and Lloyd 1988) argue that evolutionary theory is a scientific theory. They maintain that the traditional view of scientific theories should be replaced with a new approach to theories (in particular, the semantic view advocated by van Fraassen (1980) and others).

The nature of species affects the status of evolutionary theory and our general approach to scientific theories. And, of course, a proper understanding of species is vital for biological systematics and evolutionary biology. The species problem is a prime example of an interdisciplinary problem. Philosophical questions concerning the nature of taxonomy affect our choice of a definition of the species category. Empirical and theoretical considerations from evolutionary biology affect our view of scientific theories. Philosophers often strain to be practical; biologists enjoy a relevant philosophical discussion. The species problem satisfies both of these desires. It is an instance of practical metaphysics.

References

Beatty, J. (1981), "What's Wrong with the Received View of Evolutionary Theory?" In P. Asquith and R. Giere (eds.), *PSA 1980*, vol. 2. East Lansing: Philosophy of Science Association.

Darwin, F. ed. (1887), *The Life and Letters of Charles Darwin, including an Autobiographical Chapter*. London: John Murray.

Eldredge, N., and Cracraft, J. (1980), *Phylogenetic Patterns and the Evolutionary Process*. New York: Columbia University Press.

Hull, D. (1987), "Genealogical Actors in Ecological Roles," *Biology and Philosophy* 2:168–183.

Lloyd, E. (1988), *The Structure and Confirmation of Evolutionary Theory*. New York: Greenwood Press.

Mayr, E. (1982), *The Growth of Biological Thought*. Cambridge, Mass.: Harvard University Press.

Smart, J. J. C. (1963), *Philosophy and Scientific Realism*. London: Routledge and Kegan Paul.
Smart, J. J. C. (1968), *Between Philosophy and Science*. London: Routledge and Kegan Paul.
Sober, E. (1984), "Sets, Species, and Evolution: Comments on Philip Kitcher's 'Species'," Philosophy of Science 51:334–341.
van Fraassen, B. (1980), *The Scientific Image*. New York: Oxford University Press.
Wiley, E. (1981), *Phylogenetics*. New York: Wiley.

Part I
Biological Concepts

Introduction to Part I: Biological Concepts

The biological literature contains a wide variety of definitions of the species category. The essays in part I of this volume contain eight definitions. The first essay presents Mayr's biological species concept, the most popular and influential species definition of the last fifty years. Despite its prominence, many biologists contend that the biological species concept is an inadequate definition of the species category. The remaining essays of part I contain criticisms of the biological species concept and provide seven alternative definitions.

Mayr offers several versions of the biological species concept. The most widely accepted one appears in Mayr (1963): "species are groups of interbreeding natural populations that are reproductively isolated from other such groups." A species is a group of organisms that interbreed and produce fertile offspring. That group can consist of a single local population or a number of populations connected by at least occasional interbreeding. The members of different species, however, are prevented from producing fertile offspring. Their members are separated by "isolating mechanisms" that either prevent interbreeding from ever occurring or prevent the production of fertile offspring if interbreeding does occur (see Mayr 1970, 55ff., for a discussion of such mechanisms). The biological species concept is defined explicitly in terms of reproductive mechanisms, but the concept is motivated largely by the idea that species taxa form a unique and important type of genetic system. "A species is the most inclusive Mendelian population" (Dobzhansky 1970, 357). It is "a field for gene recombination" (Carson 1957). From a genetic perspective, each biological species is a distinct gene pool whose genetic material is recombined in every generation. The boundaries of that pool are determined by which organisms can combine genetic material through interbreeding and produce fertile offspring.

The biological species concept defines species by the reproductive mechanisms that mark their boundaries. But more importantly, those mechanisms are responsible for the existence of species. According to Mayr,

Unless otherwise noted, all references are to chapters within this volume.

"every new species is an ecological experiment, an attempt to occupy a new niche" 1970, 357). If a species is to survive, it must consist of organisms with relatively adaptive phenotypes. Furthermore, a species will continue to succeed only if it is protected from the incursion of genetic material that may cause its members to become maladaptive. Mayr writes, "the major biological meaning of reproductive isolation is that it provides protection for a genotype adapted for the utilization of a species niche" (1982, 275; also Mayr chapter 1). Species are stable gene pools, protected from the incursion of foreign genetic material by isolating mechanisms. A species' stability arises from interbreeding as well. A mutation that enhances the adaptedness of an organism may take hold within a subpopulation of a species, causing that population to diverge from the rest of the species. Interbreeding between that population and the rest of the species may spread the new trait, thereby preserving the unity of the species (Mayr 1970, 298, 300). Species are genetic fortresses, protected by isolating mechanisms and held together by interbreeding.

In his *Systematics and the Origin of Species*, Mayr offers a slightly different version of the biological species concept: "species are groups of actually or potentially interbreeding natural populations which are reproductively isolated from other such groups" (1942, 120). The difference between this early version of the biological species concept and the one cited above is the "potentially interbreeding" clause. Mayr explains why he dropped the clause: 'the actual vs. potential' distinction is unnecessary since 'reproductively isolated' refers to the possession of isolating mechanisms, and it is irrelevant for species status whether or not they are challenged at a given moment" (Mayr 1982, 273). Mayr eliminated the reference to potential interbreeding because he thought it was redundant with the notion of reproductive isolation: a group of populations that potentially interbreed *is* reproductively isolated from all other groups.

Mayr first presented the biological species concept in his essay "Speciation Phenomena in Birds" (1940). Dobzhansky introduced an earlier version in his *Genetics and the Origin of Species* (1937). But the history of the biological species concept goes back much further. Buffon presented a strikingly similar definition: "we should regard two animals as belonging to the same species if, by means of copulation, they can perpetuate themselves and preserve the likeness of the species; and we should regard them as belonging to different species if they are incapable of producing progeny by the same means" (Buffon 1749, 10; quoted in Lovejoy 1959, 93). Other biologists who used reproductive criteria for defining species include John Ray (1686), Cuvier (1815), Poulton (1903), and K. Jordon (1905); see Mayr 1982, 270ff. and Dobzhansky 1970, 353ff. for discussions of the history and development of the biological species concept.

In the last twenty-five years, numerous objections have been launched against the biological species concept. Sokal and Crovello (chapter 2), for example, argue that the concept has methodological flaws. The biological species concept defines species by the processes responsible for their existence: interbreeding and reproductive isolation. Still, the organisms in a species display a pattern of phenotypic similarity and covariation. For proponents of the biological species concept, these phenotypic patterns are secondary attributes; species are identified first and foremost by the causal processes responsible for them. Sokal and Crovello charge that while the biological species concept is designed to identify species by the processes responsible for them, the identification of species as interbreeding groups is performed by essentially phenetic means. Thus the biological species concept is nonoperational: it fails to provide the procedures needed for identifying species.

Sokal and Crovello illustrate this charge by considering the steps required for identifying a group of organisms as a biological species. The members of a biological species must be physiologically capable of interbreeding, that is, they must be interfertile. But according to Sokal and Crovello, the first cue that a group may consist of interfertile organisms is their phenotypic similarity. Only after observing that the organisms have certain phenotypic similarities are they then collected for interfertility tests or for field observations of reproduction. Additional phenotypic considerations are needed as well. Suppose the organisms sampled are shown to be interfertile. Given the limited time and resources available, tests for interfertility are restricted to small samples of the group in question. Whether the entire group forms an interfertile population of organisms is settled by the phenotypic similarity between the sampled and unsampled organisms in that group.

Sokal and Crovello also charge that the biological species concept subjectively colors and consequently hinders our investigations of species. "If we assume a priori that all organisms can be put into some biological species, then we of necessity concentrate on finding such classes .... The emphasis [should] be on unbiased description of the variety of evolutionary patterns that actually exist among organisms in nature." Sokal and Crovello believe that this can be achieved by adopting an overtly phenetic species concept. Accordingly, they propose that species are simply those groups of organisms that have the most overall phenotypic similarity. Such phenetic groups are found by the methods of phenetic taxonomy. A number of organisms are assembled; their similarities and dissimilarities are recorded. Given enough data, and the use of statistical methods, a pattern should develop with certain groups having the most overall similarity among their members. Those groups are species taxa. For Sokal and Crovello, the phenetic species concept is an improvement over the biological species concept in two ways: it avoids the bias of the biological species concept; and, unlike the biological species concept, it provides operational criteria for identifying species taxa. (For a critical review of the phenetic species concept and Sokal and Crovello's charges against the biological species concept, see Hull 1970.)

Ehrlich and Raven (chapter 3) and Van Valen (chapter 4) also object to the biological species concept. But their concern is with the empirical adequacy of the concept rather than its methodological basis. Ehrlich and Raven, and Van Valen suggest that the biological species concept misidentifies the processes responsible for the existence of species taxa. Ehrlich and Raven consider the first half of the concept—the claim that "species are groups of interbreeding natural populations." They argue that interbreeding is neither necessary nor sufficient for the existence of species. It is not necessary because many species consist of organisms or populations that do not interbreed. Asexual organisms form species taxa, yet they do not interbreed. And, many species of sexual organisms consist of geographically separated populations that exchange little, if any, genetic material through interbreeding. For example, the sand crab *Emerita analoga* consists of disjunct populations located in the Northern and Southern Hemispheres, and the butterfly *Clarkia rhomboidea* consists of disjunct populations separated by mountain ranges in the Great Basin of North America (Ehrlich and Raven chapter 3).

Two factors count against the sufficiency of the interbreeding criterion. First, Ehrlich and Raven cite examples of differentiated populations that preserve their distinctiveness despite widespread interbreeding among them. Second, Van Valen and Templeton argue that a number of species form multispecies: groups of species that remain distinct despite their members frequently exchanging genetic material and producing fertile offspring. A classic example is North American oaks. The Canadian species *Quercus macrarpa* and *Q. bicolor* often exchange genetic material; still, those species remain distinct (Van Valen chapter 4). Other examples include some species of Hawaiian *Drosophila*, and North American coyotes and wolves (Templeton chapter 9).

As an alternative to interbreeding, Ehrlich and Raven suggest that natural selection is the primary force preserving species taxa. Species consisting of geographically isolated populations are unified by their organisms being exposed to similar sets of selection forces (what they call "common selection regimes"). Species consisting of asexual organisms are unified in the same fashion. Ehrlich and Raven allow that interbreeding may be an important factor in maintaining the unity of some species, but they contend that in most it is not. Ehrlich and Raven relegate the effectiveness of interbreeding to local populations of sexual organisms—groups of organisms far smaller then those commonly recognized as species taxa.

Van Valen presents a similar case against the biological species concept. Interbreeding is neither necessary nor sufficient for the existence of species taxa. Instead, Van Valen suggests that "species are maintained for the most part ecologically." Consequently, he offers an ecological definition of the species category. "A species is a lineage ... which occupies an adaptive zone minimally different from that of any other lineage in its range and evolves separately from all lineages outside its range." A lineage is an ancestral-descendant sequence of populations. "An adaptive zone is some part of the resource space together with whatever predation and parasitism occurs on the group considered." For Van Valen, each species taxon occupies its own distinctive adaptive zone, or "niche," and the distinct set of selective forces in each zone is responsible for the maintenance of species as distinct taxonomic units.

Mayr has offered a version of the biological species concept that incorporates an ecological component: "a species is a reproductive community (reproductively isolated from others) that occupies a specific niche in nature" (1982, 273). But the motivations underlying this version of the biological species concept and Van Valen's ecological species concept are different. For Mayr, a species survives only if it succeeds in its own ecological niche (1970, 357). The processes of interbreeding and reproductive isolation ensure that the organisms of a species remain adapted to their niche (1982, 275; also Mayr chapter 1). The role of a species' niche is quite different for Van Valen (and Ehrlich and Raven). A species does not survive because reproductive processes ensure that its members are adapted to their niche. Instead, the ecological forces of a species' niche are the primary forces responsible for the preservation and distinctness of that species. (For criticisms of the ecological species concept, see Wiley chapter 5, Ghiselin chapter 17, and Rosenberg 1985. The latter two pieces also contain criticisms of Mayr's recent version of the biological species concept.)

The biological and ecological species concepts highlight specific processes responsible for the existence of species taxa. But a number of authors propose species definitions that are neutral concerning those processes. These definitions include the evolutionary species concept (Simpson 1961; Wiley chapter 5) and the phylogenetic species concepts (Cracraft chapter 6, Mishler and Donoghue chapter 7, Mishler and Brandon 1987). Consider Wiley's version of the evolutionary species concept. "A species is a single lineage of ancestral descendant populations of organisms which maintains its identity from other such lineages and which has its own evolutionary tendencies and historical fate." Species taxa are lineages with their own evolutionary tendencies despite the different types of processes responsible for those tendencies. In many species, interbreeding and reproductive isolation are responsible for those tendencies. For example, two populations may have the same evolutionary tendencies as the result of extensive interbreeding among their members. Indeed, for Wiley and Simpson, taxa whose evolutionary tendencies are due to reproductive processes constitute "the most important special case" of species taxa (Simpson 1961, 154). But species consisting of geographically isolated populations or asexual organisms owe their unique tendencies to other sorts of processes. The tendencies of such taxa are due to their organisms being exposed to common selection pressures or having similar developmental constraints.

Simpson first introduced the evolutionary species concept to overcome what he saw as the overly restrictive nature of the biological species concept (1961, 153ff.). The biological species concept does not apply to asexual species, nor does it apply to species consisting of geographically isolated populations. Furthermore, according to Simpson, it does not apply to extinct species whose fossils lack information concerning their ability to interbreed. The evolutionary species concept is applicable in such cases because it highlights a more fundamental aspect of species than the biological species concept. Asexual species, species with geographically disjunct populations, extinct species, and good biological species, are all lineages with their own "evolutionary tendencies." Thus all form species on the evolutionary species concept. (For criticisms of the evolutionary species concept see Ghiselin chapter 17 and Templeton chapter 9.)

Cracraft also rejects the biological species concept. He agrees with Simpson and Wiley that the concept is flawed because it cites only one of the processes responsible for species taxa. But he sees a more fundamental problem. Species are the "basic taxonomic units of evolution," where "the basic taxonomic units of evolution are those populations characterized by one or more evolutionary novelties" (Cracraft chapter 6). However, biological species often consist of a number of populations each characterized by one or more evolutionary novelties. In other words, many biological species are "polytypic" rather than "monotypic." Consequently, many biological species do not form basic taxonomic units. This problem gives rise to another. Monotypic species form basic taxonomic units; polytypic species consist of one or more such taxonomic units. The category defined by the biological species concept consists of both types of taxa. Thus the biological species concept defines a category consisting of incompatible types of taxa.

Dobzhansky and Mayr see the polytypic nature of the biological species concept as an asset rather than a detriment. "At the beginning of the current century, some taxonomists succumbed to the temptation of assigning species names to every local race" (Dobzhansky 1970, 356). The result was a "pandemonium" of species designations. The biological species concept reduces the number of species by combining races that form single reproductive units into single species. Mayr (1969, 38) notes that "the greatest benefit derived from the recognition of polytypic [biological] spe-

cies is that . . . it has led to a considerable simplification of the classification."
For Cracraft, this move of "convenience" obscures the basic patterns of
nature. Each population (or set of populations) characterized by one or
more evolutionary novelties should be recognized as a distinct basal taxonomic unit. Accordingly, Cracraft offers a species concept that defines a
species taxa as "the smallest diagnosable cluster of individual organisms
within which there is a parental pattern of ancestry and descent." Species
are simply those lineages whose members share a unique set of novel
characteristics. (For criticisms of Cracraft's phylogenetic species concept,
see Mishler and Brandon 1987 and Ereshefsky 1989.)

Mishler and Donoghue also reject the biological species concept for
its singular reliance on reproductive processes. Moreover, they criticize the
concept for not producing species taxa that are "useful for cladistic analysis."
Cladistic analysis, or "cladism," is one of the three general schools of
biological systematics. Evolutionary taxonomy and phenetic taxonomy are
the other two. (See Ridley 1986 and Futuyma 1986 for introductions to
these schools). For cladists, biological classification should be based strictly
on propinquity of descent. Each taxonomic group should contain all and
only the descendants of a particular ancestor. In other words, taxa should
be "monophyletic." Usually cladists reserve the criterion of monophyly for
only higher taxa. But Mishler and Donoghue want to bring the species
category in line with cladism and require that species taxa form monophyletic groups. The problem with the biological species concept is that
biological species may form nonmonophyletic taxa (Mishler and Donoghue
chapter 7, de Queiroz and Donoghue 1988). Consider a group of interbreeding populations that are reproductively isolated from other such
groups, yet whose members do not include all the descendants of a common ancestor. That group forms a species on the biological species concept. But because it does not contain all the descendants of a common
ancestor, it is not monophyletic. Due to such considerations, Mishler and
Donoghue suggest that the biological species concept be replaced with a
definition that requires that species form monophyletic groups.

This requirement of monophyly constitutes only half of their species
definition. Monophyletic groups occur up and down the evolutionary
hierarchy. For cladists, all real taxa—genera, families, orders, even all life
on this planet (assuming a common origin)—form monophyletic groups.
So Mishler and Donoghue's definition also contains criteria for distinguishing which monophyletic taxa should be ranked as species: "Species ranking
criteria could include group size, gap size, geological age, ecological and
geographical criteria, degree of intersterility, tradition and possibly others."
Ranking criteria vary among species. Some taxa are ranked as species
because of interbreeding among their members. Other taxa are ranked as
species because of common ecological and developmental factors affecting

their organisms. Still other taxa are ranked as species on the basis of morphological gaps between their organisms and those of other species (Mishler and Brandon 1987, 406). (For criticisms of Mishler and Donoghue's phylogenetic species concept, see Sober 1988, de Querioz and Donoghue 1988, and Ereshefsky 1989.)

Thus far we have focused on the forces that maintain species. But what of the forces responsible for their creation? In other words, how does speciation occur? Mayr argues (and his views are widely accepted) that the prominent form of speciation among sexual organisms begins with geographic isolation. Suppose a small population or group of migrants is geographically cut off from the main body of a species such that no gene flow occurs between it and the main body. That population may be exposed to different ecological factors, causing it to diverge genetically from the main body of the species. The isolated population also will be exposed to mutations and instances of genetic drift (random genetic sampling) different than those found in the main body of the species, providing further chances for divergence. If the isolated population were connected by gene flow to the main body, such divergence would be opposed by the influx of genetic material from the main body. But because it is not, the isolated population is vulnerable to genetic change. Consequently, the population may undergo a genetic revolution—a drastic genetic restructuring required to survive in its new ecological and genetic environments.

In Mayr's model of geographic speciation, two factors must be met for speciation to occur. An isolated population must be genetically restructured so that it survives in its new ecological and genetic environments. Second, it must develop reproductive isolating mechanisms to protect its adapted gene pool from the incursion of genetic material from other species. An important question remains: How do such isolating mechanisms develop? According to Mayr, isolating mechanisms "arise as an incidental by-product of genetic divergence in isolated populations" (1970, 327). There is no selection for reproductive isolating mechanisms within geographically isolated populations because such populations are already isolated. Such mechanisms are merely the by-product of the organisms in an isolated population becoming adapted to new ecological and genetic environments.

The link between the biological species concept and Mayr's model of geographic speciation should be evident. According to the concept, "species are groups of interbreeding natural populations that are reproductively isolated from other such groups." In Mayr's model of geographic speciation, a speciation event is initiated only when interbreeding between a geographically isolated population and the main body of a species is interrupted. Furthermore, geographic speciation is completed only when an incipient species becomes reproductively isolated from other species. (For detailed discussions of geographic speciation, see Mayr 1970 and Futuyma 1986.)

Paterson agrees with Mayr on the importance of geographic speciation, but argues that Mayr's model of geographic speciation is incorrect. According to Mayr's model, the rise of isolating mechanisms is merely an accidental by-product of an isolated population's genetic reconstruction. Paterson, however, contends that there are forces directly responsible for the existence of isolating mechanisms. We just need to view isolating mechanisms differently. Rather than treating them as mechanisms that prevent reproduction among species, they should be viewed as mechanisms that promote successful interbreeding within species. Paterson agrees with Mayr that if an isolated population is to become a new species, it must adjust to a new way of life (both ecologically and genetically). But Paterson suggests that the organisms in an isolated population must develop mechanisms for recognizing mates who have also adapted to that way of life. If they do not develop such mechanisms, their newly acquired adaptations will be diluted by genetic information from organisms outside of the population. So there is selection within isolated populations for organisms that recognize each other as appropriate mates. That selection causes their members to acquire what Paterson calls "specific-mate recognition systems." The characteristics of such systems are diverse: many conspecific birds use calls and songs to recognize their appropriate mates; moths, bees, and wasps use chemical signals; fireflies light their lights; and peacocks display their plumage.

Both Paterson's and Mayr's models of geographic speciation allow that the organisms of a species acquire mechanisms for discriminating among prospective mates. But according to Paterson, only his model provides an adaptational explanation of why organisms develop those mechanisms. Therefore Paterson contends that his model of geographic speciation should be accepted in place of Mayr's. Paterson believes that this indicates a weakness in Mayr's biological species concept. Mayr defines species as "groups of interbreeding natural populations that are reproductively isolated from other such groups." Because there is no adaptational explanation for the existence of purely reproductive isolating mechanisms, Paterson argues that the second half of Mayr's definition should be eliminated. Paterson proposes that a species is "that most inclusive population of individual biparental organisms which share a common fertilization system" (Paterson chapter 8). This is very much in line with promoters of the biological species concept who contend that a species is "a field for gene recombination" (Carson 1957; also see Dobzhansky 1970, 357). Paterson calls his definition "the recognition concept of species" because of the importance he attaches to mate recognition systems for conspecific interbreeding. (For responses to Paterson's work on species, see Templeton chapter 9; Mayr 1988; and Coyne, Orr, and Futuyma 1988.)

Templeton views the recognition species concept as an improvement over the biological species concept. But he contends that both concepts have the same fundamental difficulty: they assert that all and only groups of interbreeding populations form species. Like Ehrlich and Raven (as well as a number of other authors in this volume), Templeton argues that many species consist of populations that do not interbreed—for example, species consisting of geographically isolated populations or asexual organisms. Furthermore, he argues that some species form multispecies—groups of distinct species that freely interbreed. Templeton is sympathetic to the general approach of the biological and recognition concepts, namely their attempt to define species by the genetic mechanisms that are responsible for species. However, he believes that a genetic approach to species should not be limited to reproductive mechanisms. As an alternative to the biological and recognition concepts, Templeton offers the cohesive species concept: "the cohesion species is the most inclusive population of individuals having the potential for phenotypic cohesion through intrinsic cohesion mechanisms."

For Templeton, a species is an evolutionary lineage in which "the genetic essence of an evolutionary lineage is that a new mutation can go to fixation within it." Three forces can cause a mutation to go to fixation within a lineage: gene flow, genetic drift, and natural selection. Cohesion mechanisms, on the other hand, determine how far mutations can spread. There are two types of cohesion mechanisms. The first determines "genetic exchangeability: the factors that define the limits of spread of new genetic variants through gene flow" (Templeton chapter 9). These are mechanisms that govern interbreeding within a species, such as common fertilization and mate recognition systems. Cohesion mechanisms of the second type determine "demographic exchangeability." These are environmental pressures that limit the spread of genetic novelties. The more similar the organisms of a species are in their ability to survive and reproduce in various environments, the higher the probability that a genetic novelty will go to fixation. In short, species are genetic channels in which gene flow, genetic drift, and natural selection may cause mutations to go to fixation. Cohesion mechanisms determine the boundaries of those channels.

The cohesion concept defines species in terms of the genetic processes responsible for species cohesion. But unlike the biological and recognition concepts, it describes cohesion processes that occur in asexual species, multispecies, as well as biological species. The cohesion concept also allows that species may have varying degrees of genetic and demographic exchangeability, thereby allowing species to have varying degrees of genetic cohesiveness. "Good species" have high degrees of genetic and demographic exchangeability. "Good higher taxa," on the other hand, lack both genetic and demographic exchangeability (Templeton chapter 9). Thus on the cohesion concept a continuum exists between good species and good higher taxa.

The number of species definitions outlined in this introduction may leave the reader feeling dizzy. But one controversy dominates the debate and is worth highlighting. The biological species concept, as well as Paterson's and Ghiselin's definitions, require that species taxa consist of interbreeding populations. None of the other species definitions of part I impose this requirement. Reaching a conclusion over whether or not species taxa must consist of interbreeding populations will have significance for biological systematics and evolutionary biology. In systematics, it will determine whether a taxonomy of the organic world will consist of species of asexual organisms. Indeed, it will determine whether any groups of asexual organisms form any Linnaean taxonomic units. In evolutionary biology, the outcome of this controversy will determine the nature of the base units of evolution. Are they the result of reproductive processes (Mayr, Paterson, and Ghiselin) or ecological forces (Ehrlich and Raven, and Van Valen)? Or, are they governed by various types of evolutionary processes but manifest a similar phylogenetic pattern (Wiley, Cracraft, and Mishler and Donoghue)? Philosophical issues are tied to this controversy as well. Do species form causally cohesive wholes whose members are connected by interbreeding, or do species form sets of spatiotemporally scattered members? Even the reality of species taxa is affected. According to Ghiselin (chapter 17), a species taxon must form an interbreeding unit, otherwise it would not exist. So empirical issues concerning species spill over into philosophical ones. These philosophical issues are the subject of part II.

References

Carson, L. (1957), "The Species as a Field for Genetic Recombination." In *The Species Problem*, Mayr (ed.), pp. 23–38. Washington D.C.: American Association for the Advancement of Science.

de Queiroz, K., and Donoghue, M. (1988), "Phylogenetic Systematics and the Species Problem," *Cladistics* 4:317–338.

Dobzhansky, T. (1937), *Genetics and the Origin of Species*. New York: Columbia University Press.

Dobzhansky, T. (1970), *Genetics and the Evolutionary Process*. New York: Columbia University Press.

Ereshefsky, M. (1989), "Where's the Species? Comments on the Phylogenetic Species Concepts", *Biology and Philosophy* 4:89–96.

Futuyma, D. (1986), *Evolutionary Biology*, 2 edition. Sunderland, Mass.: Sinauer Assoc.

Coyne, J., Orr, H., and Futuyma, D. (1988), "Do We Need a New Species Concept?", *Systematic Zoology* 37:190–200.

Hull, D. (1970), "Contemporary Systematic Philosophies." *Annual Review of Ecology and Systematics* 1:19–54.

Lovejoy, A. (1959), "Buffon and the Problem of Species." In *Forerunners of Darwin*, B. Glass, O. Temkin, and W. Straus (eds.), pp. 84–113. Baltimore: Johns Hopkins University Press.

Mayr, E. (1940), "Speciation Phenomena in Birds," *American Naturalist* 74:249–278.

Mayr, E. (1942), *Systematics and the Origin of Species*. Cambridge, Mass.: Harvard University Press.

Mayr, E. (1963), *Animal Species and Evolution*. Cambridge, Mass.: Harvard University Press.

Mayr, E. (1969), *Principles of Systematic Zoology*. Cambridge, Mass.: Harvard University Press.

Mayr, E. (1970), *Populations, Species, and Evolution*. Cambridge, Mass.: Harvard University Press.

Mayr, E. (1982), *The Growth of Biological Thought*. Cambridge, Mass.: Harvard University Press.

Mayr, E. (1988), "The Why and How of Species," *Biology and Philosophy* 3:431–442.

Mishler, B., and Brandon, R. (1987), "Individuality, Pluralism, and the Phylogenetic Species Concept," *Biology and Philosophy* 2:397–414.

Ridley, M. (1986), *Evolution and Classification: The Reformation of Cladism*. London: Longman.

Rosenberg, A. (1985), *The Structure of Biological Science*. Cambridge: Cambridge University Press.

Simpson, G. (1961), *The Principles of Animal Taxonomy*. New York: Columbia University Press.

Sober, E. (1988), *Reconstructing the Past: Parsimony, Evolution, and Inference*. Cambridge, Mass.: MIT Press.

Chapter 1
Species Concepts and Their Application
Ernst Mayr

Darwin's choice of title for his great evolutionary classic, *On the Origin of Species*, was no accident. The origin of new "varieties" within species had been taken for granted since the time of the Greeks. Likewise the occurrence of gradations, of "scales of perfection" among "higher" and "lower" organisms, was a familiar concept, though usually interpreted in a strictly static manner. The species remained the great fortress of stability, and this stability was the crux of the anti-evolutionist argument. "Descent with modification," true biological evolution, could be proved only by demonstrating that one species could originate from another. It is a familiar and often-told story how Darwin succeeded in convincing the world of the occurrence of evolution and how—in natural selection—he found the mechanism that is responsible for evolutionary change and adaptation. It is not nearly so widely recognized that Darwin failed to solve the problem indicated by the title of his work. Although he demonstrated the modification of species in the time dimension, he never seriously attempted a rigorous analysis of the problem of the multiplication of species, of the splitting of one species into two. I have examined the reasons for this failure (Mayr 1959a) and found that foremost among them was Darwin's uncertainty about the nature of species. The same can be said of those authors who attempted to solve the problem of speciation by saltation or other heterodox hypotheses. They all failed to find solutions that are workable in the light of the modern appreciation of the population structure of species. An understanding of the nature of species, then, is an indispensable prerequisite for the understanding of the evolutionary process.

Species Concepts

The term *species* is frequently used to designate a class of similar things to which a name has been attached. Most often this term is applied to living organisms, such as birds, fishes, flowers, or trees, but it has also been used for inanimate objects and even for human artifacts. Mineralogists speak of species of minerals, physicists of nuclear species; interior decorators consider tables and chairs species of furniture. The application of the same term both to organisms and to inanimate objects has led to much confusion and an almost endless number of species definitions (Mayr 1963, 1969); these, however, can be reduced to three basic species concepts. The first two, mainly applicable to inanimate objects, have considerable historical significance, because their advocacy was the cause of much past confusion. The third is the species concept now prevailing in biology.

The Typological Species Concept

The typological species concept, going back to the philosophies of Plato and Aristotle (and thus sometimes called the essentialist concept), was the species concept of Linnaeus and his followers (Cain 1958). According to this concept, the observed diversity of the universe reflects the existence of a limited number of underlying "universals" or types (*eidos* of Plato). Individuals do not stand in any special relation to one another, being merely expressions of the same type. Variation is the result of imperfect manifestations of the idea implicit in each species. The presence of the same underlying essence is inferred from similarity, and morphological similarity is, therefore, the species criterion for the essentialist. This is the so-called morphological species concept. Morphological characteristics do provide valuable clues for the determination of species status. However, using degree of morphological difference as the primary criterion for species status is completely different from utilizing morphological evidence together with various other kinds of evidence in order to determine whether or not a population deserves species rank under the biological species concept. Degree of morphological difference is not the decisive criterion in the ranking of taxa as species. This is quite apparent from the difficulties into which a morphological-typological species concept leads in taxonomic practice. Indeed, its own adherents abandon the typological species concept whenever they discover that they have named as a separate species something that is merely an individual variant.

The Nominalistic Species Concept

The nominalists (Occam and his followers) deny the existence of "real" universals. For them only individuals exist; species are man-made abstractions. (When they have to deal with a species, they treat it as an individual on a higher plane.) The nominalistic species concept was popular in France in the eighteenth century and still has adherents today. Bessey (1908) expressed this viewpoint particularly well: "Nature produces individuals and nothing more ... species have no actual existence in nature. They are mental concepts and nothing more ... species have been invented in order that we may refer to great numbers of individuals collectively."

Any naturalist, whether a primitive native or a trained population geneticist, knows that this is simply not true. Species of animals are not human constructs, nor are they types in the sense of Plato and Aristotle; but they are something for which there is no equivalent in the realm of inanimate objects.

From the middle of the eighteenth century on, the inapplicability of these two medieval species concepts to biological species became increasingly apparent. An entirely new concept, applicable only to species of organisms, began to emerge in the later writings of Buffon and of many other naturalists and taxonomists of the nineteenth century (Mayr 1968).

The Biological Species Concept
This concept stresses the fact that species consist of populations and that species have reality and an internal genetic cohesion owing to the historically evolved genetic program that is shared by all members of the species. According to this concept, then, the members of a species constitute (1) *a reproductive community*. The individuals of a species of animals respond to one another as potential mates and seek one another for the purpose of reproduction. A multitude of devices ensures intraspecific reproduction in all organisms. The species is also (2) *an ecological unit* that, regardless of the individuals composing it, interacts as a unit with other species with which it shares the environment. The species, finally, is (3) *a genetic unit* consisting of a large intercommunicating gene pool, whereas an individual is merely a temporary vessel holding a small portion of the contents of the gene pool for a short period of time. These three properties raise the species above the typological interpretation of a "class of objects" (Mayr 1963, 21). The species definition that results from this theoretical species concept is: *Species are groups of interbreeding natural populations that are reproductively isolated from other such groups.*

The development of the biological concept of the species is one of the earliest manifestations of the emancipation of biology from an inappropriate philosophy based on the phenomena of inanimate nature. The species concept is called biological not because it deals with biological taxa, but because the definition is biological. It utilizes criteria that are meaningless as far as the inanimate world is concerned.

When difficulties are encountered, it is important to focus on the basic biological meaning of the species: A species is a protected gene pool. It is a Mendelian population that has its own devices (called isolating mechanisms) to protect it from harmful gene flow from other gene pools. Genes of the same gene pool form harmonious combinations because they have become coadapted by natural selection. Mixing the genes of two different species leads to a high frequency of disharmonious gene combinations; mechanisms that prevent this are therefore favored by selection. Thus it is quite clear that the word "species" in biology is a relational term.

A is a species in relation to *B* or *C* because it is reproductively isolated from them. The biological species concept has its primary significance with respect to sympatric and synchronic populations (existing at a single locality and at the same time), and these—the "nondimensional species"—are precisely the ones where the application of the concept faces the fewest difficulties. The more distant two populations are in space and time, the more difficult it becomes to test their species status in relation to each other, but also the more irrelevant biologically this becomes.

The biological species concept also solves the paradox caused by the conflict between the fixity of the species of the naturalist and the fluidity of the species of the evolutionist. It was this conflict that made Linnaeus deny evolution and Darwin the reality of species (Mayr 1957). The biological species combines the discreteness of the local species at a given time with an evolutionary potential for continuing change.

The Species Category and Species Taxa

The advocacy of three different species concepts has been one of the two major reasons for the "species problem." The second is that many authors have failed to make a distinction between the definition of the species category and the delimitation of species taxa (for fuller discussion see Mayr 1969).

A *category* designates a given rank or level in a hierarchic classification. Such terms as "species," "genus," "family," and "order" designate categories. A category, thus, is an abstract term, a class name, while the organisms placed in these categories are concrete zoological objects.

Organisms, in turn, are classified not as individuals, but as groups of organisms. Words like "bluebirds," "thrushes," "songbirds," or "vertebrates" refer to such groups. These are the concrete objects of classification. Any such group of populations is called a *taxon* if it is considered sufficiently distinct to be worthy of being formally assigned to a definite category in the hierarchic classification . *A taxon is a taxonomic group of any rank that is sufficiently distinct to be worthy of being assigned to a definite category.*

Two aspects of the taxon must be stressed. A taxon always refers to specified organisms. Thus *the* species is not a taxon, but any given species, such as the robin (*Turdus migratorius*) is. Second, the taxon must be formally recognized as such, by being described under a designated name.

Categories, which designate a rank in a hierarchy, and taxa, which designate named groupings of organisms, are thus two very different kinds of phenomena. A somewhat analogous situation exists in our human affairs. Fred Smith is a concrete person, but "captain" or "professor" is his rank in a hierarchy of levels.

The Assignment of Taxa to the Species Category

Much of the task of the taxonomist consists of assigning taxa to the appropriate categorical rank. In this procedure there is a drastic difference between the species taxon and the higher taxa. Higher taxa are defined by intrinsic characteristics. Birds is the class of feathered vertebrates. Any and all species that satisfy the definition of "feathered vertebrates" belong to the class of birds. An essentialist (typological) definition is satisfactory and sufficient at the level of the higher taxa. It is, however, irrelevant and misleading to define species in an essentialistic way because the species is not defined by intrinsic, but by *relational* properties.

Let me explain this. There are certain words that indicate a relational property, like the word "brother." Being a brother is not an inherent property of an individual, as hardness is a property of a stone. An individual is a brother only with respect to someone else. The word "species" likewise designates such a relational property. A population is a species with respect to all other populations with which it exhibits the relationship of reproductive isolation—noninterbreeding. If only a single population existed in the entire world, it would be meaningless to call it a species.

Noninterbreeding between populations is manifested by a gap. It is this gap between populations that coexist (are sympatric) at a single locality at a given time which delimits the species recognized by the local naturalist. Whether one studies birds, mammals, butterflies, or snails near one's home town, one finds each species clearly delimited and sharply separated from all other species. This demarcation is sometimes referred to as the species delimitation *in a nondimensional system* (a system without the dimensions of space and time).

Anyone can test the reality of these discontinuities for himself, even where the morphological differences are slight. In eastern North America, for instance, there are four similar species of the thrush genus *Catharus* (Table 1.1), the veery (*C. fuscescens*), the hermit thrush (*C. guttatus*), the olive-backed or Swainson's thrush (*C. ustulatus*), and the gray-cheeked thrush (*C. minimus*). These four species are sufficiently similar visually to confuse not only the human observer, but also silent males of the other species. The species-specific songs and call notes, however, permit easy species discrimination, as observationally substantiated by Dilger (1956). Rarely do more than two species breed in the same area, and the overlapping species, $f + g$, $g + u$, and $u + m$, usually differ considerably in their foraging habits and niche preference, so that competition is minimized with each other and with two other thrushes, the robin (*Turdus migratorius*) and the wood thrush (*Hylocichla mustelina*), with which they share their geographic range and many ecological requirements. In connection with their different foraging and migratory habits the four species

Table 1.1
Characteristics of four eastern North American species of *Catharus* (from Dilger 1956)

Characteristic compared	C. fuscescens	C. guttatus	C. ustulatus	C. minimus
Breeding range	Southernmost	More northerly	Boreal	Arctic
Wintering area	No. South America	So. United States	C. America to Argentina	No. South America
Breeding habitat	Bottomland woods with lush under-growth	Coniferous woods mixed with deciduous	Mixed or pure tall coniferous forests	Stunted northern fir and spruce forests
Foraging	Ground and arboreal (forest interior)	Ground (inner forest edges)	Largely arboreal (forest interior)	Ground (forest interior)
Nest	Ground	Ground	Trees	Trees
Spotting on eggs	Rare	Rare	Always	Always
Relative wing length	Medium	Short	Very long	Medium
Hostile call	*veer* *pheu*	*chuck* *seeeep*	*peep* *chuck-burr*	*beer*
Song	Very distinct	Very distinct	Very distinct	Very distinct
Flight song	Absent	Absent	Absent	Present

differ from one another (and from other thrushes) in the relative length of wing and leg elements and in the shape of the bill. There are thus many small differences between these at first sight very similar species. Most important, no hybrids or intermediates among these four species have ever been found. Each is a separate genetic, behavioral, and ecological system, separated from the others by a complete biological discontinuity, a gap.

Difficulties in the Application of the Biological Species Concept

The practicing taxonomist often has difficulties when he endeavors to assign populations to the correct rank. Sometimes the difficulty is caused by a lack of information concerning the degree of variability of the species with which he is dealing. Helpful hints on the solution of such practical difficulties are given in the technical taxonomic literature (Mayr 1969).

More interesting to the evolutionist are the difficulties that are introduced when the dimensions of time and space are added. Most species taxa do not consist merely of a single local population but are an aggregate of numerous local populations that exchange genes with each other to a greater or lesser degree. The more distant that two populations are from each other, the more likely they are to differ in a number of characteristics. I show elsewhere (Mayr 1963, ch. 10 and 11) that some of these populations are incipient species, having acquired some but not all characteristics of species. One or another of the three most characteristic properties of species taxa—reproductive isolation, ecological difference, and morphological distinguishability—is in such cases only incompletely developed. The application of the species concept to such incompletely speciated populations raises considerable difficulties. There are six wholly different situations that may cause difficulties.

1. *Evolutionary continuity in space and time*   Widespread species may have terminal populations that behave toward each other as distinct species even though they are connected by a chain of interbreeding populations. Cases of reproductive isolation among geographically distant populations of a single species are discussed in Mayr 1963, ch. 16.

2. *Acquisition of reproductive isolation without corresponding morphological change*   When the reconstruction of the genotype in an isolated population has resulted in the acquisition of reproductive isolation, such a population must be considered a biological species. If the correlated morphological change is very slight or unnoticeable, such a species is called a sibling species (Mayr 1963, ch. 3).

3. *Morphological differentiation without acquisition of reproductive isolation* Isolated populations sometimes acquire a degree of morphological divergence one would ordinarily expect only in a different species. Yet some such populations, although as different morphologically as good species, interbreed indiscriminately where they come in contact. The West Indian snail genus *Cerion* illustrates this situation particularly well (fig. 1.1).

4. *Reproductive isolation dependent on habitat isolation*   Numerous cases have been described in the literature in which natural populations acted toward each other like good species (in areas of contact) as long as their habitats were undisturbed. Yet the reproductive isolation broke down as soon as the characteristics of these habitats were changed, usually by the interference of man. Such cases of secondary breakdown of isolation are discussed in Mayr 1963, ch. 6.

5. *Incompleteness of isolating mechanisms*   Very few isolating mechanisms are all-or-none devices (see Mayr 1963, ch. 5). They are built up step by step, and most isolating mechanisms of an incipient species are imperfect and incomplete. Species level is reached when the process of speciation has

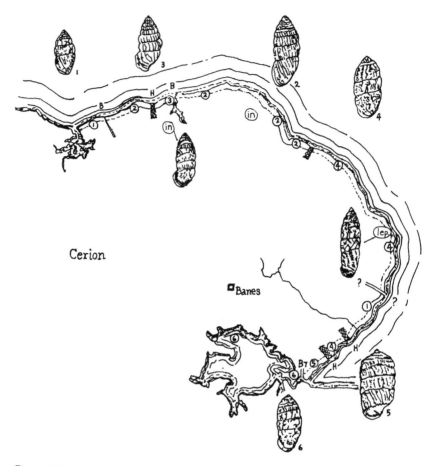

Figure 1.1
The distribution pattern of populations of the halophilous land snail *Cerion* on the Banes Peninsula in eastern Cuba. Numbers refer to distinctive races or "species." Where two populations come in contact (with one exception) they hybridize (*H*), regardless of degree of difference. In other cases contact is prevented by a barrier (*B*). *In* = isolated inland population.

become irreversible, even if some of the secondary isolating mechanisms have not yet reached perfection (see Mayr 1963, ch. 17).

6. *Attainment of different levels of speciation in different local populations*   The perfecting of isolating mechanisms may proceed in different populations of a polytypic species (one having several subspecies) at different rates. Two widely overlapping species may, as a consequence, be completely distinct at certain localities but may freely hybridize at others. Many cases of sympatric hybridization discussed in Mayr 1963, ch. 6, fit this characterization (see Mayr 1969, for advice on handling such situations).

These six types of phenomena are consequences of the gradual nature of the ordinary process of speciation (excluding polyploidy; see Mayr 1963, 254). Determination of species status of a given population is difficult or arbitrary in many of these cases.

Difficulties Posed by Uniparental Reproduction

The task of assembling individuals into populations and species taxa is very difficult in most cases involving uniparental (asexual) reproduction. Self-fertilization, parthenogenesis, pseudogamy, and vegetative reproduction are forms of uniparental reproduction. The biological species concept, which is based on the presence or absence of interbreeding between natural populations, cannot be applied to groups with obligatory asexual reproduction because interbreeding of populations is nonexistent in these groups. The nature of this dilemma is discussed in more detail elsewhere (Mayr 1963, 1969). Fortunately, there seem to be rather well-defined discontinuities among most kinds of uniparentally reproducing organisms. These discontinuities are apparently produced by natural selection from the various mutations that occur in the asexual lines (clones). It is customary to utilize the existence of such discontinuities and the amount of morphological difference between them to delimit species among uniparentally reproducing types.

The Importance of a Nonarbitrary Definition of Species

The clarification of the species concept has led to a clarification of many evolutionary problems as well as, often, to a simplification of practical problems in taxonomy. The correct classification of the many different kinds of varieties (phena), of polymorphism (Mayr 1963, ch. 7), of polytypic species (ibid. ch. 12), and of biological races (ibid. ch. 15) would be impossible without the arranging of natural populations and phenotypes into biological species. It was impossible to solve, indeed even to state precisely, the problem of the multiplication of species until the biological species concept had been developed. The genetics of speciation, the role of species in large-scale evolutionary trends, and other major evolutionary problems could not be discussed profitably until the species problem was settled. It is evident then that the species problem is of great importance in evolutionary biology and that the growing agreement on the concept of the biological species has resulted in a uniformity of standards and a precision that is beneficial for practical as well as theoretical reasons.

The Biological Meaning of Species

The fact that the organic world is organized into species seems so fundamental that one usually forgets to ask why there are species, what their meaning is in the scheme of things. There is no better way of answering these questions than to try to conceive of a world without species. Let us think, for instance, of a world in which there are only individuals, all belonging to a single interbreeding community. Each individual is in varying degrees different from every other one, and each individual is capable of mating with those others that are most similar to it. In such a world, each individual would be, so to speak, the center of a series of concentric rings of increasingly more different individuals. Any two mates would be on the average rather different from each other and would produce a vast array of genetically different types among their offspring. Now let us assume that one of these recombinations is particularly well adapted for one of the available niches. It is prosperous in this niche, but when the time for mating comes, this superior genotype will inevitably be broken up. There is no mechanism that would prevent such a destruction of superior gene combinations, and there is, therefore, no possibility of the gradual improvement of gene combinations. The significance of the species now becomes evident. The reproductive isolation of a species is a protective device that guards against the breaking up of its well-integrated, coadapted gene system. Organizing organic diversity into species creates a system that permits genetic diversification and the accumulation of favorable genes and gene combinations without the danger of destruction of the basic gene complex. There are definite limits to the amount of genetic variability that can be accommodated in a single gene pool without producing too high a proportion of inviable recombinants. Organizing genetic diversity into protected gene pools—that is, species—guarantees that these limits are not overstepped. This is the biological meaning of species.

References

Bessey, C. E., 1908, The taxonomic aspect of the species. *American Naturalist* 42:218–224.

Cain, A. J., 1958, Logic and memory in Linnaeus's system of taxonomy. *Proc. Linn. Soc.,* London, 169:144–163.

Mayr, E., 1957, Species concepts and definitions. *Amer. Assoc. Adv. Sci.*, Publ. No. 50:1–22, Washington, D.C.

Mayr, E., 1959a, Darwin and the evolutionary theory in biology. In *Evolution and Anthropology: A Centennial Approach*, Anthropological Society of America, Washington, D.C.

Mayr, E., 1963, *Animal Species and Evolution*, Cambridge: Harvard University Press.

Mayr, E., 1968, Illiger and the biological species concept. *J. Hist. Biol.* 1:163–178.

Mayr, E., 1969, *Principles of Systematic Zoology*. New York: McGraw-Hill.

Mayr, E., 1976, Is the Species a Class or an Individual? *Systematic Zoology* 25:192.

Mayr, E., 1987, The Ontological Status of Species: Scientific Progress and Philosophical Terminology. *Biology and Philosophy* 2:145–166.

Mayr, E., 1987, Answers to These Comments. *Biology and Philosophy* 2:212–220.

Mayr, E., 1988, The Species Category. In E. Mayr, *Toward a New Philosophy of Biology*. Cambridge, Harvard University Press, 315–334.

Mayr, E., 1988, The Why and How of Species. *Biology and Philosophy* 3:431–442.

Mayr, E., and L. Short, 1970, *Species Taxa of North American Birds*. Cambridge: Nuttall Ornithological Club, Publication Number 9.

Chapter 2

The Biological Species Concept: A Critical Evaluation

Robert R. Sokal and Theodore J. Crovello

A species concept has been a central tenet of biological belief since the early origins of biology as a science. The implications of this term have changed over the years: the fixed, immutable, and sharply distinct entities of the Linnaean period gave way to the more variable and intergrading units of the post-Darwinian era. For many taxonomists before and after Darwin, the species has simply implied the recognition of groups of morphologically similar individuals that differ from other such groups.

Through much of biological history there has been controversy regarding the existence of species in nature. Are species real units in nature? Can the species category be defined objectively? Given an affirmative answer to the above two questions, can real organisms be assigned to one of the nonoverlapping species so delimited? Darwin's work contributed to the recognition of species as real entities. The very title of his book, *On the Origin of Species*, stressed this category. But as Mayr (1959) has pointed out, Darwin himself was so impressed by the variability and intergradation in the material he studied that he considered the term "species" to be arbitrary, not differing in essential features from "variety." Argument regarding these questions has persisted through changing concepts of the biological universe and with increasing insights into the genetic and ecological mechanisms governing the behavior of individuals and populations. The history of these ideas and controversies is reviewed by Mayr (1957), and we shall not enlarge upon it here. Some have considered species as man-made, arbitrary units either because of their philosophical orientation or because of the difficulty of interpreting variable material from widely ranging organisms as consisting of one or more species. These arguments have been countered by evidence of the common-sense recognition of discontinuities in nature even by lay observers (see Mayr 1963, 17 for an account of species recognition by New Guinea natives, but see Berlin, Breedlove, and Raven 1966 for a contrary view) and also of species recognition, presumably instinctive, by other organisms. Such discontinuities are most easily noted by naturalists who study local faunas and floras, and the species concept derived from such situations has been called the "nondimensional species concept" by Mayr (1963). But in some taxa, such as in willows, groups generally assigned generic or sectional rank are more easily recognized by local naturalists than are the species.

The apparent necessity to accommodate within one species concept several aspects of organisms led to the development of the so-called biological species concept (hereafter abbreviated BSC). These aspects include the variation of characteristics over large geographic areas, changes in these characteristics as populations adapt to environmental challenges or interact with other populations, and the integration of individuals into populations to form gene pools through direct processes, as well as indirectly through their ecological interactions. We shall not trace the development of the concept during the 1930s. Ernst Mayr, recognized as its foremost advocate, has called the BSC a "multidimensional concept" (Mayr 1963) because it deals with populations that are distributed through time and space, interrelated through mutual interbreeding, and distinguished from others by reproductive barriers.

Since its formulation there have been objections to the BSC from a variety of sources and motives. Many taxonomists have ignored it for practical reasons. Some workers (e.g., Blackwelder 1962, Sokal 1962) have charged that the employment of the BSC is misleading in that it imbues species described by conventional morphological criteria with a false aura of evolutionary distinctness and with unwarranted biosystematic implications. In fairness we point out that some supporters of the BSC (e.g., Simpson 1961, 149) state clearly the difficulties of correlating phenetic and genetic species criteria even in the same taxonomic group but especially across diverse taxa. Nevertheless, such caveats do not generally affect either taxonomic practice or teaching as it filters down to the level of the introductory courses. These critics also point out that the actual procedures employed even by systematists with a modern outlook are quite different from those implied or required by the BSC. Recent trends toward quantification in the biological sciences and especially emphasis on operationalism in systematic and taxonomic procedures (Ehrlich and Holm 1962, Ehrlich and Raven 1969, Sokal 1964, Sokal and Camin 1965, Sokal and Sneath 1963) have raised fundamental questions about the BSC to discover whether it is operational, useful, and/or heuristic with relation to an understanding of organic evolution.

The general purposes of this paper are: (1) to show, by means of a detailed flowchart, that the BSC is largely a phenetic concept; (2) given the above, to show that the BSC should be at least as arbitrary as phenetic taxonomic procedure; and (3) to explore the value of the BSC to evolution by posing a set of specific questions. Specifically, we shall first review the definition of the BSC and enumerate those of its attributes that require extended discussion and analysis. Next we shall discuss three operations required for making decisions about actual populations with respect to these attributes of the BSC. Armed with an understanding of these operations, we shall then consider a flowchart of the detailed steps necessary to determine which of a set of organisms under study can be considered to form a biological species.

As a next step we shall note the difficulties of applying the BSC even in the optimal case of complete knowledge regarding the material under study, and examine how problems multiply as knowledge of the organisms diminishes.

Finally, given the difficulties of the BSC as a workable concept for the practicing taxonomist, we shall briefly examine the necessity for such a concept in evolutionary theory, its heuristic value, and the evidence for the existence of biological species in spite of the difficulty of their recognition and definition.

Although our philosophical attitude in systematics is that of empiricism and consequently we are not committed to the existence of biological species, we have approached our task with as open minds as has been possible. We recognize, as must any observer of nature, that there are discontinuities in the spectrum of phenetic variation. The question we have asked ourselves, one which we believe must be asked by every biologist concerned with problems of systematics and of evolution, is whether there is a special class of these discontinuities that delimits units (the biological species) whose definition and description should be attempted because they play an especially significant role in the process of evolution or help in understanding it.

I The Biological Species Concept

The number of species definitions that have been proposed since the advent of the New Systematics and that fall within the general purlieus of the BSC is very large, but an extended review and discussion of these definitions would serve little useful purpose here. Many are but minor variants of the one to be discussed below, and they share in most ways the problems that we shall encounter with it. We shall employ the classical definition of biological species as restated by Mayr (1963, 19) in his definitive treatise. The definition is:

Groups of	(1)
actually	(2)
or potentially	(3)
interbreeding	(4)
populations,	(5)

which are reproductively isolated   (6)

from other such groups.   (7)

We have deliberately arranged the definition in the above manner to emphasize those terms or phrases which make separate and important contributions to the overall definition. Let us briefly go through these. We are dealing with *populations* (line 5) whose members *interbreed* (line 4) *actually* (line 2) or *potentially* (line 3). The difficulties of the latter term will be taken up in the next section. There usually is more than one such population (line 1). This group of populations will not exchange genes (line 6) with other interbreeding groups (line 7). This phenomenon is referred to as *reproductive isolation*.

According to Mayr (1963, 20) there are three aspects of the BSC: "(1) Species are defined by distinctness rather than by difference." By this he means reproductive gaps rather than phenetic differences (Mayr, personal communication). "(2) Species consist of populations rather than of unconnected individuals; and (3) species are more unequivocally defined by their relation to nonconspecific populations ('isolation') than by the relation of conspecific individuals to each other. The decisive criterion is not the fertility of individuals but the reproductive isolation of populations."

Thus to discover whether a given set of individuals is a biological species in the sense of the above definition we must have information about three essential components of the BSC: (1) that some individuals lack distinctness (*sensu* Mayr) from other individuals and join these in comprising biological populations of interbreeding individuals (this is the meaning by implication of the term "population" in the definition of the BSC); (2) that there is a group of such populations among which interbreeding does, or could, take place (this follows from the "actually or potentially interbreeding" clause of this definition); (3) that this group lacks gene flow with other groups of populations (this covers the "reproductively isolated" portion of the definition). These three aspects of the biological species are worked into the flowchart (fig. 2.1) that follows.

II Fundamental Operations

To ascertain whether a given assemblage of organisms belongs to one or more biological species, three types of operations for grouping organisms and population samples will be found necessary (although only the third is directly implied by the definition given above). The first operation groups organisms by geographic contiguity; the second, by phenetic relationships; and the third, by reproductive relationships. In all these cases there will be some difference in the procedure when the initial grouping is of individuals into subsets (populations), and when these subsets are the basic units being grouped into more inclusive sets (species).

All grouping procedures will of necessity be based on samples of organisms and populations. Only in a minuscule number of instances will we have knowledge of all the individuals about which inferences are being made. This is not necessarily an unsatisfactory state of affairs, but it is important to specify the size of the samples required to estimate parameters of the populations with a desired level of confidence. Also, the use of samples necessitates that some assumptions be made about the spatiotemporal distribution of individuals and populations.

The grouping operations will frequently refer to the idea of *connectedness*. We shall consider two operational taxonomic units (OTUs; see Sokal and Sneath 1963, 121—individuals or population samples in this context) to be connected if there exists some definable relation between them (geographic contiguity, phenetic similarity, or interfertility, for example). *Minimally* connected sets of such OTUs have at least as many such relations as permit any two OTUs to be connected via any other members of the set. *Fully* connected sets have relations between every pair of members of the set. We use these terms by analogy with their employment in graph theory (Busacker and Saaty 1965).

We shall take up the three types of operations in the order in which they were introduced.

The first operation groups by *geographic contiguity*. In order to belong to one population, organisms must be within reach of some others, that is, have the possibility of encountering for reproductive purposes other organisms within the same spatiotemporal framework. A first prerequisite for individuals to belong to the same population is that they come from sites which would enable them to be within reach of each other, considering the normal vagility of these organisms or of their propagules. In many cases we can simply assume this when we have samples from one site containing numerous individuals such as are obtained by seining, light traps, or botanical mass collecting. In other cases (especially with large organisms) where single individuals are found at specific sites, we have to be reasonably certain that individuals from separate sites presumed to be within the same local population have intersecting home ranges. In developing a criterion of geographic connectedness among local populations we need to be concerned with the probability of members of one locality visiting members of another one to permit the necessary gene flow required by the model. Again, this will be a function of the distance between localities, the vagility of organisms, and the ecological conditions that obtain between points. Various techniques of locational analysis (see Haggett 1966) can be used for establishing these linkages. We note in passing that the essential information required for this operation is lacking for most taxa. For example, the pollen and seed ranges for most flowering plant taxa are unknown (Harper 1966).

A second operation is the establishment of *phenetic similarity* between individuals within population samples and between such samples from various areas. While the definition of the BSC does not invoke phenetic considerations, it will be shown in the next section that any attempt to apply the definition to an actual sample of organisms will need to resort to phenetics in practice. In the initial stages of a study it may be that sufficient estimates of phenetic similarity can be determined by visual inspection of the specimens. Clearly, when the material is very heterogenous such an initial sorting of the material into putatively conspecific assemblages can be profitable. When more refined analysis is indicated, a quantitative phenetic approach is necessary. Here again we need not concern ourselves with the technical details, which are by now well established through the techniques of numerical taxonomy (Sokal and Sneath 1963).

The third operation involves grouping *interbreeding individuals* into population samples and grouping *interbreeding population samples* into larger assemblages. Before discussing this in detail, a semantic digression is necessary. In most relevant texts the term "interbreeding" is not defined precisely or distinguished clearly from intercrossing, interfertility, mating, and similar terms. Recourse to a dictionary is not enlightening. The reader is aware that the very act of mating (i.e., copulation in animals with or without insemination, or pollination in plants, to name only two of the more common mechanisms of sexual reproduction) does not of itself insure the production of viable offspring and especially of fertile offspring. Clearly, the act of mating or the transfer of male gametes toward a female gamete is the single necessary precondition for successful interbreeding, but it does not in itself insure fertile offspring. We shall use the term "interbreeding" to mean crossing between individuals resulting in the production of fertile offspring, but we shall occasionally use the terms "interfertility" or simply "mating" in a similar context.

The only unequivocal, direct basis for forming interbreeding groups is to observe organisms interbreeding in nature. If we wanted to make the definition absurdly rigorous, we would wish to insist that an interbreeding population sample be one where a sufficient number of females from the local population sample is mated with a sufficient number of males in the same sample to insure reproductive connectedness to the required degree. Fertile offspring would have to result from all of these unions. Obviously such observations are unlikely. Even if we were to turn to experiments to answer the question, we could not insist on so complete a test of interfertility, both because the number of experiments would be far too great and because, in most cases such crosses would be impossible, since the biological nature of the organisms precludes more than a single mating (e.g., longevity of mating individuals, incompatibility toward further mates by an already mated female, developmental period of the young, etc.).

Thus, as noted earlier we shall have to resort to samples of field observations or of crossing experiments. The latter raise the often discussed issue of whether laboratory tests of interbreeding should be considered as evidence when contrasted with field observations. Clearly, first consideration must be given to observations of nature as it is. Success in crossing experiments might indicate "potential" interbreeding. In designing crossing experiments as criteria of interfertility, clear instructions must be given on what role these experiments will play and whether the definition to be tested will be satisfied by laboratory crossing experiments or whether field observations are required.

Added to these difficulties is the fact that most of the material systematists deal with is already dead at the time of study and cannot be brought into the laboratory or experimental garden for crossing purposes. Thus, extensive interbreeding tests are impractical, and one needs to resort to partial or circumstantial evidence on crossing for inference on interfertility. As direct evidence on interbreeding diminishes, the methods become increasingly phenetic. Phenetic information is of value in ascertaining interbreeding relationships only insofar as one may assume that phenetic similarity is directly related to ease of interbreeding. Yet we know that phenetics is an imperfect reflection of interfertility between organisms. In fact, this has been one of the main criticisms of numerical taxonomy by evolutionists.

The above arguments should not be interpreted as insistence on our part for "complete" knowledge of reproductive relationships. Just as one samples in phenetic studies to obtain estimates of phenetic structure of a larger population, so it is entirely justified to test reproductive relationships among only a sample of individuals and make inferences about a larger population. However, both sampling procedures are based on prior phenetic sorting out of specimens and populations. Thus we test reproductive relationships only among organisms likely to be interfertile, and the only way we can recognize these is on a phenetic basis. Therefore, except for the absurdly extreme reproductive test of each organism against every other one—biologically and experimentally infeasible, as well as destructive of the original taxa if it were possible to carry out such a test—reproductive tests based on samples reflect phenetic considerations in choosing the individuals to be tested. Furthermore, we must stress that even if we carried out some crossing experiments we would still need to employ phenetic inference to reason from the results of our limited number of crosses to the larger population sample, to the entire local population living today, and to the entire local population both living and dead.

Depending on the set of reproductive properties chosen by a given scientist, interbreeding will range continuously from complete interbreeding through intermediate stages to total lack of interbreeding. The two properties most often considered are connectedness and success of reproduction. If every individual in a group could interbreed with every other one of the opposite sex, *connectedness* would be complete. But the total number of possible combinations will likely be reduced; that is, some pairs may not be able to interbreed. This could be so for a variety of reasons, directly and indirectly genetic, such as sterility genes, reproductive incompatibilities, behavioral differences, seasonal isolation, etc. We are prepared to accept a sample as connected within itself if each individual is capable of interbreeding with one or more of the opposite sex in such a way that the reproductive relationships would yield a minimally connected graph (Busacker and Saaty 1965) (with $n + m - 1$ edges, where n is the number of one sex and m that of the other), with terminal members being connected to one mate only. Such a minimal interbreeding relationship is unlikely in a large biological sample because it would imply a very complex system of mating types and intersterilities; yet even such a system practiced over many generations would insure genetic connectedness among its members. A sample whose reproductive relations are less than a minimal connected set should be separated into those subsets which are connected.

But the ability to mate is clearly not enough. Fertile offspring, which have a nonzero probability of survival and of leaving new offspring, must result from such a union. This consideration leads us directly to the second property characterizing interbreeding.

Success of reproduction can be expressed as the percentage of fertile offspring resulting from a given mating measured in terms of percentage of eggs hatched, percentage of seed set, litter size, and similar criteria in the F_1 or later generations. The standards set for such criteria and acceptable levels of success will vary with the investigator.

Therefore, members of a local population sample may be considered to interbreed either if they are completely interfertile as defined above or if they are partially interfertile. In the latter case, only samples whose members show at least minimal connectedness and whose average success of reproduction is greater than an arbitrarily established value would qualify.

If organisms are apomicts or obligate selfers, then by their very nature they cannot form biological species (as has indeed been pointed out by proponents of the BSC, e.g., Simpson 1961, 161 or Mayr 1963, 27). If these biological facts are not known to us, they might be suggested by all individuals forming a disjoint set in this step (i.e., no individuals will reproduce with any other individual in the sample). Technically, we should no longer process such samples through the flowchart. However, a useful classification could be arrived at if we ran the individuals of each local sample through the phenetic pathways of the flowchart. We infer this because taxonomists have had no apparent difficulty in describing species by conventional methods in these forms.

Once it has been demonstrated that the individuals *within* each local population sample interbreed, we need only show that there is some gene flow among the samples studied in order to establish interbreeding among them. Once genes from population *A* enter population *B*, (and those from *B* enter *A*), interbreeding among the members of *A* and *B* provides an opportunity for the establishment of the new genes in both populations.

We can conceive of several partially interfertile population samples as a connected set. It would follow that in order to be considered actually interbreeding the several population samples would have to represent at least a minimally connected set of reproductive relationships. Therefore, not every population sample needs to be directly reproductively connected to every other population sample in the study. A *Rassenkreis* is an example of such a situation. These relationships may be somewhat difficult to represent because the paths of connection will have to pass through either the offspring or parents of mates in a zigzag fashion. However, in populations among which there is substantial gene flow, it should be possible to make a chain of connection between any two organisms by going through relatively few ancestral and descendant generations.

The term "potentially interbreeding," which is included in some definitions of the biological species, has never really been defined, let alone defined operationally. It appears to us that the only possible answer one could get to the question of whether two samples are potentially interbreeding is "don't know." At best, one would be reduced to inferences about potential interfertility from phenetic evidence (and we have already seen that this is not too reliable). It is interesting to note that in his latest work, Mayr (1969) has dropped "potentially interbreeding" from his biological species definition.

III Flowchart for Recognizing Biological Species

The actual flowchart is shown in figure 2.1. The various steps in this figure are listed in this section, each followed by an explanatory account of the reasons for the step, the manner in which it could be carried out, and inherent difficulties.

1. *Assemble phenetically similar individuals.*   This preliminary step is important because unless the individuals used for the study are "relatively" similar, it is not reasonable to suppose that they interbreed. Lacking such a procedure, one would be forced to carry out a vast amount of fruitless testing for interfertility. Cottonwoods, aphids, and field mice could all be

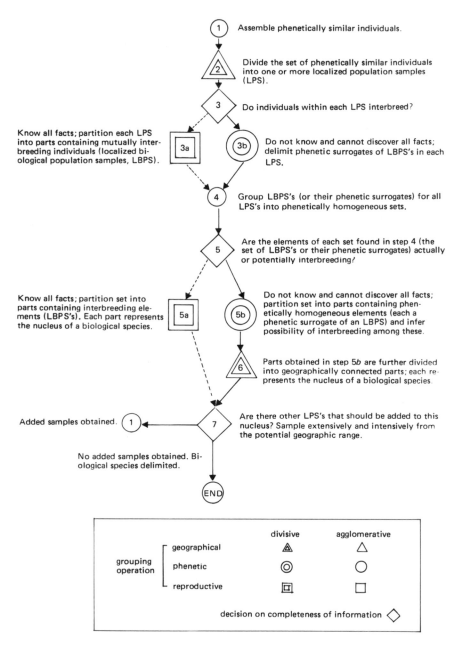

Figure 2.1
Flowchart for determining biological species. For explanation, see text.

obtained in samples from the same locality, and, while the subsequent logic of the flowchart should ensure their separation into independent biological species (if we can determine that they are not actually or potentially interbreeding populations), a large amount of unnecessary and most likely impractical work would have to be done to test for fertility between cottonwoods and field mice, for example.

Systematists have appropriately decided not to trouble about this point but to use the relatively great phenetic dissimilarity of such groups of organisms to infer that they would be intersterile if an attempt at artificial crossing were made. Substantial evidence is available, especially from plants, that individuals allocated to different orders, families, or genera are usually intersterile. However, in the vast majority of organisms we may state with certainty that decisions about the presumptive intersterility of two dissimilar individuals or populations are based on phenetics alone. But since phenetic similarity is a continuous variable (as is reproductive interrelationship), it is difficult to designate anything but arbitrary similarity levels above which individuals and populations are potentially interbreeding and hence potentially conspecific and therefore need further testing and below which they are phenetically so different that the likelihood of interbreeding (hence of conspecificity) is small enough to be neglected. In the absurdly extreme instance of cottonwoods and field mice, this phenetic comparison is made instantaneously by the taxonomist without the need for more precise and sophisticated phenetic methods. This step is stressed here mainly to make the logic of the flowchart complete. When assembling similar individuals, dimorphisms and polymorphisms may give rise to practical difficulties, and relational criteria based on knowledge of the biology of the organisms involved may be invoked. Thus, knowing that given caterpillars give rise to given butterflies, we shall associate them, and in cases of marked sexual dimorphism we would wish to associate males and females that appear to form sexual pairs. This can sometimes be done by refined biometric techniques, but where previous knowledge or simple observations suffice these should surely be preferred.

A second point is that step 1 should not be carried out so finely that potential candidates for conspecific status are excluded. Thus the grouping should err by inclusion rather than by exclusion. Otherwise, since the flowchart will not cycle through the original sample again, some of the initial sample of organisms that also belong to the same biological species would be excluded.

2. *Divide the set of phenetically similar individuals into one or more localized population samples.*   The procedure leading to localized population samples is that of grouping by geographical contiguity as defined in section II. Since we are at the moment concerned with the grouping of individuals to form

population samples, we would be unlikely to encounter fixed geographic points from which we can create an interconnected network. Rather, we are likely to obtain a scattering of incidental collection sites from which we must draw inferences about the potential for geographic overlap of the lifetime movement ranges of the individuals concerned.

We shall define a *localized population sample* (LPS) in terms of the natural vagility of the organism. The need for such a definition stems from the biological attributes of populations as integrated gene pools which require that the members of a population be within the geographic range making such integration possible. We use the term "localized," following the conventions of the statistical geographers (Haggett 1966), rather than the more common "local" population which has certain biological, genetic, and ecological connotations that, although hard to define, nevertheless are generally invoked in the minds of systematists. By localized population sample we mean to imply only connection by an external relationship, largely spatial but also temporal and ecological. Unless otherwise qualified, this does not necessarily imply genetic or phenetic similarity among its members.

Gametes or propagules will differ in the distances they travel. A distribution of such distances, if known, could serve as a measure of vagility. The ninety-ninth percentile, V, gives a near upper limit to the distances travelled. If the largest observed distance between any two members of a cluster being formed is less than kV, where k is an arbitrary constant, we may define this cluster as a localized population sample. Problems might arise with uniformly spaced individuals, but such instances invite arbitrary decisions by any procedure. Also, while the samples are likely to be phenetically similar following step 1, we have no assurance that each sample represents one and the same species. Hence the vagilities of the individuals within each sample are potentially heterogeneous as well. Percentiles other than the ninety-ninth might be employed.

Many times one will not have a distribution of exact locations at which individual specimens have been obtained because the sample will have been collected at one spot or because the collection records for the entire sample refer to one spot or to a broad area. In the former case we are clearly dealing with a sample from a localized population; in the latter we have to make a judicious definition of the area sampled. For instance, if a botanist furnishes only county records and the sample may be from anywhere within a county, the maximum straight-line distance within the county will have to stand for the greatest distance between any two members of the sample.

Of course, in most instances we will not know enough about the biology of the organisms studied to make a useful estimate of V. We therefore may have to guess at this value by analogy with known similar organisms.

The definition for localized samples given above should perhaps also include other criteria, such as time and ecological factors. The biological species definition as generally stated does not specifically refer to synchronous populations; yet, as has been repeatedly pointed out, the delimitation of species becomes much more complicated if chronistic aspects are also considered. One might very well impose an analogous criterion of chronistic connectedness on the definition and obtain samples localized in both space and time. Restriction to a given general habitat such as crowns of trees or leaf litter could also be imposed to restrict the possibility further, but we do not pursue this subject here.

Each resulting LPS is not necessarily a local population in the conventional biological sense. To be that it would have to be connected not only in the geographical sense but also by interbreeding relationships. The next step in the flowchart will impose this added constraint.

3. *Is each localized population sample, defined by geographic contiguity in step 2, also interbreeding within itself; that is, do its individual members interbreed among themselves?*   Localized populations that are not interfertile within themselves cannot make up the elements of a biological species population. In its rigid interpretation, we would have to ascertain whether there is either actual or potential interbreeding within each localized population sample. We have two choices in answering this question: we can either claim to know or hope to find out what the actual interbreeding relations among the organisms are—this leads us to step 3a—or we may decide that the question cannot be answered fully or at all in terms of interbreeding relationships and proceed to make inferences about these from other evidence, usually phenetics (step 3b).

3a. Knowing all the facts about interbreeding interrelationships within each LPS, we may partition it into parts containing mutually interbreeding elements. Each such part represents a *localized biological population sample* (LBPS) .

The general criteria for recognizing interbreeding have been given in the previous section and will not be repeated here. The difficulties of testing even within a limited sample the interbreeding of a sufficient number of members are considerable, and in fact step 3a is, for all intents and purposes, impracticable. Even if all necessary crosses were feasible in theory, we have seen that sampling based on phenetics will be required sooner or later for inferences about potential interfertility of some untested members of each LPS and of the larger local population. For this reason a broken arrow leads to and from the grouping operation based strictly on reproductive criteria, 3a, to indicate that this is *not* the usual path.

3b. When we do not know and cannot discover all the facts regarding interbreeding, we have to delimit at least some phenetically homogeneous subsets in each LPS and infer interbreeding of members of each subset (we may call these subsets phenetic surrogates of an LBPS).

We may assume that markedly dissimilar organisms have already been eliminated in step 1. When eliminating grossly different organisms, one should also take care that polymorphic forms representing sexes, genetic polymorphs, or different ontogenetic or cyclomorphic stages are not excluded. If no obvious differences are present, the establishment of the homogeneity of the individuals within the sample may require sophisticated biometrical analysis. Even then, homogeneity cannot ever be proven. It can only be established that for the set of characters which has been measured the individuals appear to be homogeneous. If a heterogeneity is discovered, as, for example, in the form of a bimodality of a given character or a constriction or discontinuity in character hyperspace, we need to allocate the sampled individuals to the two or more subpopulations thus defined. Intergrades will be troublesome in this context, and final decisions on boundaries of the phenetic groups are bound to be arbitrary.

Another method for grouping the subsamples within the original LPS would be to cluster the organisms by one of the methods of numerical taxonomy. As before, such a procedure is quite arbitrary in terms of the choice of a criterion of homogeneity.

4. *Group the LBPSs (or their phenetic surrogates) for all LPSs into phenetically homogeneous sets.*   This is an agglomerative phenetic grouping procedure and is necessary as a preliminary to the rigorous test by the defined criteria for the BSC. This is so because, following the strict guidelines of the biological species definition of "actually or potentially interbreeding populations," one would have to test all samples obtained at the various localities for mutual interbreeding. As will be seen later, this is a formidable, if not impossible, task even when the samples are homogeneous within and among LBPSs, so that one may presume that they all belong to the same species. However, at this point in our procedure for determining whether a group of populations constitutes a biological species, we do not as yet know that the separate subsets in the various LBPSs defined in step 3 are similar to such a degree. All we know is that they are homogeneous *within* LBPSs. This does not necessarily mean that they are homogeneous *among* LBPSs.

Markedly different populations will already have been eliminated in step 1 of the flowchart. Thus we would no longer find one LBPS of drosophila and another LBPS of field mice. However, there might well be several species of drosophila, from the same locality, each in a single LBPS, formed by a partition of one original LPS during step 3. We now must take all LBPSs (subsets from different LPSs) and combine them to form one or more sets whose elements are phenetically closely related LBPSs, regardless of the LBP from which they originated. It should be understood here that LBPSs in this step include not only those samples defined by step 3*a*, when this is possible, but must often include their phenetic surrogates established in step 3*b*.

When the LBPSs comprise two or more phenetically closely related but reproductively isolated groups of samples, this admixture becomes a problem. In most cases, techniques like numerical taxonomy should be able to cluster the populations correctly into those that are phenetically alike and therefore candidates for becoming a biological species, subject to further tests in this flowchart. The criterion of phenetic similarity to be employed is necessarily arbitrary, and for this step to be operational we have to establish phenetic limits. One situation where such an analysis might result in clusters undesirable for the present purpose is with marked geographic variation, possibly related to adaptation to ecological differences. Suppose there were two sibling species distributed over the area. It may well be that samples from reproductively isolated populations showing parallel ecological adaptations may cluster before joining with freely interbreeding samples from ecologically different areas. In such cases, some other form of multivariate analysis that removed the effect of ecological differences from a series of morphological variables would reveal the correct situation.

In summary, in most instances of testing for biological species the preliminary test (step 1) is carried out automatically, often already by the collector who does not bother to pick up animals other than those of the species group he is interested in. Nevertheless, it must be clearly recognized that unless the *phenetic* decisions of steps 1 and 4 are taken, one cannot in practice proceed with the determination of the specific status of these populations.

5. *Are the elements of each set found in step 4, the set of LBPSs or their phenetic surrogates, actually or potentially interbreeding among themselves?*   This question refers to the most important criterion of the BSC. In its rigid interpretation in terms of the definition, we would have to ascertain whether there is either actual or potential interbreeding among individuals of all the population samples obtained for our study. We have two choices in answering this question: we can either claim to know or hope to find out what the actual interbreeding relations among the organisms are—this leads us to step 5*a*—or, we may decide that the question cannot be answered fully or at all in terms of fertility relationships and proceed to make inferences about these from other evidence, usually phenetics (step 5*b*).

5*a*. Knowing all of the facts about interbreeding interrelationships among elements of this set, we may partition it into parts containing mutually interbreeding elements (LBPSs). Each such part represents the nucleus of a biological species.

As has been pointed out repeatedly by proponents as well as opponents of the biological species definition, it is impracticable to ascertain these facts in most real situations. The difficulties encountered are of many kinds. The only kind of evidence that would unequivocally answer the question posed is direct observations of marked individuals and of their dispersal (or that of their gametes or offspring), plus observations on mating and success of the progeny in the field. Laboratory experiments on interfertility could be carried out but would indicate neither whether such interbreeding would take place in the field nor whether the offspring of such unions would be viable and reproduce under field conditions.

Even if we were to admit the evidence of laboratory tests, or of crossing experiments by botanists in experimental gardens, the number of crosses required would be formidable. With only two reciprocal crosses for any pair of population samples, we would need a^2 tests for a samples (including controls within samples). Thus, for 10 local populations (a far from adequate number in most modern studies of speciation), 100 crosses would have to be made. Yet, we have no assurance that a single representative of each local sample would suffice to establish the necessary facts. After all, if an incomplete sterility barrier exists between these populations, then certain genotypes representing the population might not be able to cross while others would do so successfully. Doubtless, a more representative subsample of each population sample is needed to arrive at a decision on this matter.

On the other hand, since it was demonstrated—or inferred—in step 3 that the individuals within each sample interbreed, we have already stressed in section II that we need only show that there is *some* gene flow among the samples being compared in order to establish interbreeding. Again, we need to distinguish between complete interbreeding, which would mean total panmixia or swamping among all population samples (an unlikely occurrence if the samples are reasonably far apart), and partial interbreeding. The latter, again, could depend on *connectedness* between some individuals in different LBPSs, which will govern the amount of gene flow, and *success of reproduction*, which refers to the percentage of fertile offspring from such crosses and the success of these offspring, evaluated by some standard. Arbitrary levels for these parameters must be designated to make the definition operational. We shall not suggest such levels here. In any event, the amount of experimental work and of field observations necessary to obtain answers for step 5a would become staggering and is clearly not practical. Sampling and inferences for the larger population are again phenetically based. For this reason there is once more (as in step 3a) a broken arrow leading to and from this operation.

5*b*. We do not know and cannot discover reproductive relationships among all of the elements (LBPSs) of this set. We therefore partition it into parts containing phenetically homogeneous elements (phenetic surrogates of LBPSs) and infer the possibility of interfertility among these.

This is a phenetic grouping procedure. The type of phenetic connectedness that should reflect whether samples (LBPSs) are actually interbreeding includes a high degree of overall phenetic similarity or the presence of intermediaries (introgression). Both kinds of phenetic evidence are subject to the same arbitrariness associated with the degree to which isolating mechanisms must be present before one can call two samples the same biological species. Here, we have to decide what degree of phenetic similarity must be present before considering two samples members of the same biological species. This will vary, of course, with the particular group under study and most of all with the characters chosen for analysis. As Davis and Heywood (1963), as well as critics of numerical taxonomy (e.g., Stebbins 1963), point out, morphological similarity is not a very accurate reflection of the evolutionary status of biological species. Also, overall similarity may not be the most critical phenetic relationship to be established. Phenetic evidence of introgression may be considered a more important criterion. We shall not discuss the possible procedures in detail here, since our main point is to point out the necessity of inference from phenetic evidence.

Had we been able to follow through on step 5*a* and define parts containing mutually interfertile elements, we could have bypassed step 6 below because we would have met the requirements of the biological species definition. Since we could not rigidly proceed by step 5*a* and had to resort to phenetic evidence in step 5*b*, we should strengthen our inferences by determining the geographical connectedness of these elements as shown in step 6.

6. *The parts of homogeneous sets of phenetic surrogates of LBPSs obtained in step 5b are further divided into one or more parts by geographic contiguity.*   This is done to increase our accuracy in the delimitation of biological species. Criteria of geographic proximity should reflect the likelihood of gene flow occurring between any two populations. Thus localities will be considered connected if some members of one LBPS at one locality have an opportunity to join a similar LBPS at the other locality. Geographical distances in such a model would be modified into ecological distances expressing the probability of propagules from one population entering the other population. We are now in a position to make joint judgments about the biological status of the resulting parts, which are phenetically homogeneous and geographically connected sets, constructed by a technique analogous to that of Gabriel and Sokal (1969) for geographic variation analysis.

It will be obvious that, since the level of phenetic homogeneity designated for assigning LBPSs to the same biological species is arbitrary, as is the accepted degree of geographic connectedness, decisions on membership in a biological species are arbitrary as well. That is, we may occasionally decide to include within the same biological species phenetically homogeneous populations that are not fully geographically connected; and, conversely, we may include populations that are phenetically distinct but seem to be fully geographically connected. Since these criteria do not, in any case, meet the formal definition of the BSC, their exact interpretation is not at issue here, unless we wish to infer "potential interbreeding" from them.

Following steps 5b and 6 we obtain the intersection of the parts resulting from these procedures. We infer that the elements in such an intersection (LBPSs or their phenetic surrogates) can represent the nucleus of a biological species. If we are prepared to accept the concept of potentially interbreeding populations, then we may simply use phenetic similarity as a criterion and bypass step 6, which implies actual gene flow in the geographic connections defined by its operations. To avoid confusion, this alternative is not shown in figure 3.1.

We now must ask ourselves whether the delimitation of this particular biological species can be extended to include other local populations. This is done by the final step, which follows.

7. *Are there other LPSs that should be added to the above nucleus?*   This step tests the adequacy of sampling. This question can be answered by further sampling of organisms from newly studied LPSs, starting with step 1 and repeating the entire procedure.

We define two kinds of additional sampling. *Extensive sampling* gathers further samples beyond the spatial limits of previous samples. *Intensive sampling* seeks to sample areas within the spatial limits of previous samples that have not been sampled before. This step will involve phenetic and geographic criteria, since it would be even more impractical to employ fertility criteria here as well. There is little point in going back through the flowchart, since the same information (phenetics and contiguity in distribution) will be used. In this step, as in steps 1, 3b, 4, and 5b, phenetic considerations will in the end largely delimit the biological species.

IV Phenetic Bottlenecks

We now can examine the flowchart as a whole and imagine ourselves running some organisms through it to determine into how many biological species they should be divided. Let us design the optimal case for the systematic study of these organisms by the BSC criteria. Therefore we assume unlimited quantities of live material available from suitably positioned locations throughout the range of the organisms. Since tests of fertility would still require an enormous amount of experimentation, we shall imagine ourselves equipped with an all-knowing computer of unlimited capacity which will provide correct answers for meaningful questions asked of it, obviating experimental tests for interbreeding between pairs of individuals within and between locality samples. To make the situation correspond more closely to the real world about which we wish to make inferences, we shall restrict the computer's performance as follows. It cannot be queried simultaneously about the interbreeding of all individuals of interest, but it will provide correct replies to sequential questions about relationships between each and every pair of individuals.

Given the above (and assuming that we have agreed on a criterion of interbreeding as discussed in section II), we should be able to eliminate all steps in the flowchart except those that make critical tests of interbreeding, namely, 3a and 5a. But we would find that even our phenomenal computer would soon be running overtime providing answers to the millions of questions about interbreeding results of the possible combinations of individuals which we would have to ask. Hence, even in this utopian case we would wish to avail ourselves of steps 1 and 4 for purposes of grouping individuals and populations initially by phenetic likeness so as to cut down on the number of questions about interbreeding that need to be asked. (Thus we shall avoid asking whether an individual cottonwood would cross with an individual aphid.) However, even this timesaving device would not be sufficient. We would still have so many questions to ask about interbreeding, that our patience, if not that of a computer, would soon be exhausted, and we would take certain shortcuts, that is, ask questions about interbreeding of some of the individuals while resorting to phenetic similarities of these with other untested individuals for conclusions about the entire sample. But, having made this concession (i.e., having taken the path of the solid arrows in figure 2.1), we are back at steps 3b and 5b, which we call the *phenetic bottlenecks* because limitations of time will force all studies, even the imaginary optimal study just discussed, into these operations.

Hence, while the definition of the BSC does not involve phenetics, the actual determination of a biological species always will do so, even in the optimal case. As soon as we permit less favorable (and more realistic) conditions to obtain, such as more limited material and no omniscient computer but a hard-working scientist with limited resources and facilities, establishment of biological species from fertility characteristics is entirely quixotic. We are left with what is essentially a phenetic criterion of homogeneous groups that show definite aspects of geographic connectedness and in which we have any evidence at all on interbreeding in only a minuscule proportion of cases.

The above is true for all animal organisms and for most plant organisms, as well. But even in those plant groups where crossing tests (the so-called experimental taxonomy) have been applied, the basic definition of the species is of necessity phenetic because the statements that are made rest on phenetic inferences from the relatively few crosses that have actually been carried out in these groups.

Phylogenetically oriented systematists have pointed out in the past that there are practical difficulties in determining the potentiality of interbreeding in given cases. But, as we have shown here, the concept cannot be used even under optimal circumstances. Simpson (1961, 150) has called this a pseudoproblem. He feels that the difficulty of ascertaining whether the definition is met in a given case with a sufficient degree of probability is different from the validity of the concept as such. Yet, as will be discussed below, there is serious question that the concept is evolutionarily meaningful.

V Discussion

The BSC is imprecise in its formulation and inapplicable in practice.   An obvious conclusion from the preceding flowchart and analysis is that in practice phenetics plays an essential role at several crucial points in the delimitation of a biological species. This leads to the critical question of the degree to which phenetics reflects interbreeding among individuals and populations. But many examples are known (see Davis and Heywood 1963) where phenetics can only mislead the biosystematist who is seeking the biological species. This ranges from simple polyploidy without phenotypic change and cryptic species, on the one hand, to problems of reactions to the environment, on the other. For example, small flowers are a result of dryness but can also be produced by mutation (Grant 1954). Without subjecting his material to experimental analysis the practicing systematist could not distinguish between these two causes. In other words, the inductive inference that is necessary here is often unwarranted.

Our study of the operations necessary to delimit a biological species revealed considerable arbitrariness in the application of the concept. This is in direct conflict with the claims of nonarbitrariness by proponents of the BSC. We use the terms "arbitrary" and "nonarbitrary" here in the sense of Simpson (1961, 115), where "a group is nonarbitrary as to inclusion if all its members are continuous by an appropriate criterion, and nonarbitrary as to exclusion if it is discontinuous from any other group by the same criterion. It is arbitrary as to inclusion if it has internal discontinuities and as to exclusion if it has an external continuity." The degree of sterility required in any given cross and the number of fertile crosses between members of populations, not to mention the necessarily arbitrary decisions proper to the hidden phenetic components of the BSC, make this concept no less arbitrary than a purely phenetic species concept, and perhaps even more so, since phenetics is but one of its components.

Relevant at this point is a contradiction in the use of the BSC regarding hybridization. This is a confusing term because at one extreme some authors call successful crosses between members of two strains a hybrid, while at the other extreme only crosses between members of two species, or between two genera, are hybrids. If a hybrid is produced in nature from two species and there is *any* backcrossing at all, then by a strict application of the BSC the two parents should belong to the same species, even if such hybrids appear in only a small part of the range of the species. But such an application is not usually made, since the investigator has some arbitrary level of frequency of crossing that he will tolerate before assigning the parents to the same species.

One of the prime complaints of the opponents of a phenetic taxonomy has been that it is typological (Inger 1958, Mayr 1965, Simpson 1961). Whether empirical or statistical typology is an undesirable approach for a classificatory procedure is not at issue here. This question is discussed in some detail by Sokal (1962). In his most recent work on systematics Mayr (1969, 67) describes essentialist ideology as synonymous with typology in the following terms: "This philosophy, when applied to the classification of organic diversity, attempts to assign the variability of nature to a fixed number of basic types at various levels. It postulates that all members of a taxon reflect the same essential nature, or in other words that they conform to the same type. ... The constancy of taxa and the sharpness of the gaps separating them tend to be exaggerated by [the typologist]. The fatal flaw of essentialism is that there is no way of determining what the essential properties of an organism are." However, it should be pointed out that, whether this is desirable or not, the BSC as advanced by its proponents is in itself a typological concept in the above sense. It is typological because it is defined by strict genetic criteria which are rarely tested, and which may not be met by its members (individuals or local populations). We shall examine below the question of whether populations in nature correspond to the biological species type erected by the new systematists. It may well be that the BSC does not reflect a widespread phenomenon in nature but rather represents a theoretical ideal to which existing situations are forced to fit as closely as possible.

It might be claimed that other variants of the biological species definition than the one employed by us could have been shown not to involve unwarranted inferences. However, a careful study of a great variety of such definitions shows this not to be the case. The definition by Emerson (1945)—"evolved (and probably evolving), genetically distinctive, reproductively isolated, natural population"—and that by Grant (1957)—"a community of cross-fertilizing individuals linked together by bonds of mating and isolated reproductively from other species by barriers to mating"—are both prone to the same difficulties. Simpson (1961, 153) defined "evolutionary species" as "a linkage (an ancestral-descendant sequence of populations) evolving separately from others and with its own unitary evolutionary role and tendencies." This is so vague as to make any attempt at operational definition foredoomed to failure.

Some plant biosystematists consider the BSC definition we have chosen to be genetic, and not necessarily evolutionary. Some, for example, would maintain that two populations belong to two biological species if they differ in at least one qualitative character and if there exists a certain amount of sterility between them. But this and similar definitions contain the same drawbacks of necessary phenetic inferences and arbitrariness as the concept we have discussed. It still is based in large part on phenetic inferences that may be unwarranted, and it still distorts relationships among populations by lumping them into a smaller number of biological species. The same comments apply to the definition of a biological species as a set of individuals sharing a common gene pool. This last definition may appear to have one advantage over previous ones. It does not demand that local populations be erected during the process of species delimitation. In terms of our flowchart, steps 2 and 3 would be deleted and subsequent steps reworded. Although this has the "advantage" of reducing the number of necessary steps in the process, this is more than outweighed by the increased amount of inference about gene-pool membership that now must be made from only phenetic evidence, as opposed to inferences made previously from both phenetic and geographic information.

Some essential questions about the BSC   From the above conclusions drawn about the BSC, we see that only in rare instances, such as a species consisting entirely of one small endemic population, is the concept even partly operational in practice. But a nonoperational concept may still be of value. For example, it may be used to generate hypotheses of evolutionary importance. We shall examine several relevant questions for systematists and evolutionists concerned with the BSC. At this time we can do little more than to ask the questions and to suggest possible answers.

1. Is the BSC necessary for practical taxonomy? By practical taxonomy we mean the straightforward description of the patterns of variation in nature for the purpose of ordering knowledge. This is phenetic taxonomy, or perhaps simply taxonomy as Blackwelder (1967)

sees it. The BSC is not a necessary part of the theory of practical taxonomy, although the category "species" is. The answer to question one is no.

2. Is the BSC necessary (or useful) for evolutionary taxonomy? This is a more difficult question to answer, since different workers attach different meanings to the term "evolutionary taxonomy." It may mean the relatively less complex task of putting all members believed to be derived from the same ancestral stock into the same taxon, say at the genus, or family, level. Or it may involve detailed (usually phenetically inferred) description of cladistic relationships among taxa at some categorical level. The property of interbreeding may or may not be possessed by all members of the group currently under study. Most evidence for decisions in evolutionary taxonomy (and all evidence above the level of classification where crossing is not possible, e.g., between members of two families) is based not on interbreeding, but on phenetics and homologies, whether they are morphological, behavioral, physiological, serological, or DNA homologies. Most work to date, especially on DNA homologies, has involved very dissimilar taxa, such as wheat, corn, pigs, monkeys, and man. Since the biological species does not play an essential role in any of the above work, the answer to question 2 also would appear to be no.

3. Is the BSC valuable as a unique, heuristic concept from which hypotheses valuable for evolutionary theory can be generated at a high rate? It would appear that any evolutionary hypothesis generated in terms of the BSC can also be generated in terms of the less abstract localized population and perhaps generated more easily. Significantly, population genetics, both theoretical and practical, in nature and in the laboratory, concerns itself with the localized population, or a small number of adjacent localized biological populations. There are few if any insights supposedly obtained from species that cannot be better interpreted at the population level. In fact, some would say that they can be interpreted only at the population level. Nothing is gained by additional abstraction to the species level (except perhaps in efficiency of names), but much is lost, namely, accuracy, for no two localized biological populations are alike. By forcing a large series of them into one biological species we lose the resolution of their differences. The answer to question 3 appears to be no.

4. Is the BSC necessary (or useful) for evolutionary theory? That is, does the general theory of evolution, or any particular evolutionary process, require, or use, the BSC? With respect to the general theory, the answer appears to be no. If we examine the evolutionary situation within some ecosystem, we can generate the same theory based on localized biological populations without grouping sets of interbreed-

ing populations into more abstract biological species. Parenthetically, we may point out that what are probably the most important and progressive books on evolutionary theory that have been published within the last year or so essentially do not refer to the biological species at all. MacArthur and Wilson (1967) in their study of island biogeography, Wallace (1968) in his analysis of evolutionary mechanisms, and Levins (1968) in his theory of evolution in changing environments base their entire discussions on Mendelian populations and hardly mention the BSC. Williams (1966, 252) believes that the species is "a key taxonomic and evolutionary concept but [it] has no special significance for the study of adaptation. It is not an adapted unit and there are no mechanisms that function for the survival of the species."

Let us turn to evolution over geological time and consider the birth and death of a presumed biological species. Assume that a certain phenetic form appeared at time i in the fossil record, subsequently became abundant, and then became extinct at time j. What does this mean? It means only that certain populations that possessed the given phenotype were able to survive from time i to time j. Ignoring polytopic origins, this means that this favorable character combination was transmitted among several localized biological populations. Nowhere does such a process demand that this set of populations be put into one group and that it be called a biological species. This can be done, but it is not essential to evolutionary theory. Of course, it is done for convenience of reference. It orders our knowledge in a certain way, as does grouping organisms into taxonomic species, then into genera, then families, etc. Thus it would seem to us that the biological species is an arbitrary category, which may be useful in given situations but is not a fundamental unit of evolution, except possibly in a case in which there is only one local biological population, and therefore the biological species as a class has only one member.

Furthermore, if we assume a priori that all organisms can be put into some biological species, then we of necessity concentrate on finding such classes. Could it be that the occurrence of well-circumscribed biological species is *not* the rule but the exception, in biology? Although Stebbins (1963) says that 70%–80% of higher plant species conform well to the BSC, other evolutionists, upon the accumulation of more and more evidence (e.g., Grant 1963, 343ff.) recognize the frequent occurrence of borderline situations.

We do not in any of the above statements imply that reproductive barriers are either nonexistent or unimportant in evolution. Quite clearly they are of fundamental significance. But we do question whether they can be employed to define species and whether emphasis in evolutionary theory should be based on phenomena (including reproductive barriers) pertaining to the species category or to a lower category, the local population.

The answer to question 4 appears to be unclear at best.

Conclusions   If our contention that the BSC is neither operational nor necessary for evolutionary theory is granted, what consequences result for general evolutionary theory? There would be few changes if any in terms of our understanding of speciational mechanisms. For example, the numerous important principles outlined by Mayr (1963) in his treatise on the species would still be relevant even if the term "species" as such were removed and replaced by others referring to phenetically different populations, or reproductively isolated populations, or populations with both properties. The positive aspect of such a procedure would be that evolutionary theory and research would concern themselves more with discovering and describing mechanisms bringing about population changes than with trying to bring organic diversity into an order conforming to an abstract ideal. The emphasis would be on unbiased description of the variety of evolutionary patterns that actually exist among organisms in nature, and of the types of processes bringing about the different varieties of population structure. We believe that in the long run this approach would lead to greater and newer insights into the mechanisms of evolution. Fundamentally this would be so because such an approach would free hypothesis construction in evolution from the language-bound constraint imposed by the species concept. (See Kraus 1968 for a lucid exposition of some of these issues and especially the role of the Whorfian hypothesis.) Even if the Whorfian hypothesis is only partially correct, the very fact that we need no longer put our major emphasis on species definition and description would have a liberating effect on evolutionary thinking. By not tying the variation of individuals and populations to abstract ideals or relating it to a one-dimensional nomenclatural system incapable of handling the higher dimensionality of the variation pattern, we would be led to new ways of looking at nature and evolution.

Having decided that the BSC is neither operational nor heuristic nor of practical value, we conclude that the phenetic species as normally described and whose definition may be improved by numerical taxonomy is the appropriate concept to be associated with the taxonomic category "species," while the local population may be the most useful unit for evolutionary study.

In advocating a phenetic species concept we should stress that, in concert with most numerical taxonomists, we conceive of phenetics in a very wide sense. All observable properties of organisms and populations are considered in estimating phenetic similarities between pairs of OTUs. These would include not only traditional morphological similarity but also physiological, biochemical, behavioral similarity, DNA homologies (Reich et al. 1966), similarities in amino acid sequences in proteins (Eck and Dayhoff 1966, Fitch and Margoliash 1967), ecological properties (Fujii 1969), and even intercrossability (Morishima 1969). Critics of a phenetic taxonomy have claimed that such a wide definition of phenetics makes the term meaningless, since all possible relationships among organisms are then by definition phenetic. But this is not necessarily so. Similarities over the set of all known properties are surely different from similarities based solely on the ability to produce fertile offspring.

Insistence on a phenetic species concept leads inevitably to a conceptualization of species as dense regions within a hyperdimensional environmental space in the sense of Hutchinson (1957, 1969). Current trends in evolutionary thinking do, in fact, consider this approach to species definition as a more useful and heuristic concept, and, as already mentioned, the existence of apparently "good" asexual species supports this view. However, the establishment of such an environmentally bounded species concept, an idea whose germs can be found in numerous recent papers, is beyond the scope of the present article, which limits itself to pointing out the weaknesses of the generally promulgalted BSC.

Summary

The term "species" has been a central tenet of biological belief since the early days of biology. But the concepts attached to the term have varied and often were not defined rigorously. The purpose of this paper is to investigate the biological species concept (BSC): to consider its theoretical aspects, how one would actually delimit a biological species in nature, whether such species exist in nature, and whether the concept is of any unique value to the study of evolution.

The classical definition of the BSC is partitioned into its essential components, and some of their aspects and problems are discussed. Three fundamental operations necessary for the delimitation of biological species in nature are described in detail. These are operations based on criteria of: (1) geographic contiguity, (2) phenetic similarity, and (3) interbreeding. Two properties of interbreeding, connectedness and success of reproduction, are defined and discussed.

A flowchart for recognizing biological species is constructed from the definition as given by Mayr. Each step involves one of the three operations mentioned above. Reasons are given for including each step, as well as the inherent difficulties of each. It can be seen that most steps are either largely or entirely phenetic, even in theory. The necessary phenetic steps are termed "phenetic bottlenecks." To test the flowchart, we assume the unrealistic but optimal situation of total knowledge about the interbreeding relations among sampled organisms. The phenetic bottlenecks remain in this optimal case, and the degree of reliance on phenetic information for the delimitation of biological species increases as we depart from the optimal situation and make it more realistic.

The BSC is found to be arbitrary (*sensu* Simpson) when attempts are made to apply it to actual data in nature, and not only because arbitrary phenetic decisions are a necessary part of the delimitation of biological species in nature.

On asking some essential questions about the value of the BSC to taxonomy and evolution, we find that the BSC is not necessary for practical taxonomy, is neither necessary nor especially useful for evolutionary taxonomy, nor is it a unique or heuristic concept necessary for generating hypotheses in evolutionary theory. Most of the important evolutionary principles commonly associated with the BSC could just as easily be applied to localized biological populations, often resulting in deeper insight into evolution.

Having decided that the BSC is neither operational nor heuristic nor of any practical value, we conclude that the phenetic species as normally described is the desirable species concept to be associated with the taxonomic category "species," and that the localized biological population may be the most useful unit for evolutionary study.

Acknowledgments

We have been fortunate to have benefitted from a critical reading of an earlier draft of this paper by several esteemed colleagues, representing considerable diversity in their attitudes to the "species problem." Paul R. Ehrlich, Richard W. Holm, and John A. Hendrickson, Jr., of Stanford University, James S. Farris of the State University of New York at Stony Brook, David L. Hull of the University of Wisconsin at Milwaukee, and Arnold G. Kluge of the University of Michigan contributed much constructive criticism and helped us remove numerous ambiguities and obscurities. A similar function was performed by many members of the Biosystematics Luncheon Group at the University of Kansas. We are much in the debt of all of these individuals, even in those rare instances where we have chosen not to follow their advice.

Collaboration leading to this paper was made possible by grant no. GB-4927 from the National Science Foundation and by a Research Career Award (no. 5-KO3-GM22021) from the National Institute of General Medical Sciences, both to Robert R. Sokal.

References

Berlin, B., D. E. Breedlove, and P. H. Raven. 1966. Folk taxonomies and biological classification. Science 154:273–275.

Blackwelder, R. E. 1962. Animal taxonomy and the new systematics. Survey Biol. Progress 4:1–57.

Blackwelder, R. E. 1967. Taxonomy. Wiley, New York, 698 p.

Busacker, R. G., and T. L. Saaty. 1965. Finite graphs and networks: an introduction with applications. McGraw-Hill, New York, 294 p.

Davis, P. H., and V. H. Heywood. 1963. Principles of angiosperm taxonomy. Oliver & Boyd, London. 558 p.

Eck, R. B., and M. O. Dayhoff. 1966. Atlas of protein sequence and structure. Nat. Biomed. Res. Found, Silver Spring, Md. 215 p.

Ehrlich, P. R., and R. W. Holm. 1962. Patterns and populations. Science 137:652–657.

Ehrlich, P. R., and P. H. Raven. 1969. Differentiation of populations. Science 165:1228–1232.

Emerson, A. E. 1945. Taxonomic categories and population genetics. Entomol. News 56: 14–19.

Fitch, W. M., and E. Margoliash. 1967. Construction of phylogenetic trees. Science 155: 279–284.

Fujii, K. 1969. Numerical taxonomy of ecological characteristics and the niche concept. Syst. Zool. 18:151–153.

Gabriel, K. R., and R. R. Sokal. 1969. A new statistical approach to geographic variation analysis. Syst. Zool. 18:259–278.

Grant, V. E. 1954. Genetic and taxonomic studies in *Gilia*. IV. *Gilia achilleaefolia*. Aliso 3:1–18.

Grant, V. E. 1957. The plant species in theory and practice, p. 39–80. *In* E. Mayr [ed.], The species problem. Amer. Ass. Advance. Sci. Pub. 50.

Grant, V. E. 1963. The origin of adaptions. Columbia Univ. Press, New York, 606 p.

Haggett, P. 1966. Locational analysis in human geography. St. Martin's, New York. 310 p.

Harper, J. L. 1966. The reproductive biology of the British poppies, p. 26–39. *In* J. G. Hawkes [ed.], Reproductive biology and taxonomy of vascular plants. Pergamon, New York.

Hutchinson, G. E. 1957. Concluding remarks. Cold Spring Harbor Symp. Quant. Biol. 22:415–427.

Hutchinson, G. E. 1969. When are species necessary? p. 177–186. *In* R. C. Lewontin [ed.], Population biology and evolution. Syracuse Univ. Press, Syracuse, N.Y.

Inger, R. F. 1958. Comments on the definition of genera. Evolution 12:370–384.

Kraus, R. M. 1968. Language as a symbolic process in communication. Amer. Sci. 56:265–278.

Levins, R. 1968. Evolution in changing environments. Princeton Univ. Press, Princeton, N.J. 120 p.

MacArthur, R. H., and E. O. Wilson. 1967. The theory of island biogeography. Princeton Univ. Press, Princeton, N.J. 203 p.

Mayr, E. 1957. Species concepts and definitions, p. 1–22. *In* E. Mayr [ed.], The species problem. Amer. Ass. Advance. Sci. Publ. 50.

Mayr, E. 1959. Isolation as an evolutionary factor. Amer. Phil. Soc., Proc. 103:221–230.

Mayr, E. 1963. Animal species and evolution. Harvard Univ. Press, Cambridge, Mass. 797 p.

Mayr, E. 1965. Numerical phenetics and taxonomic theory. Syst. Zool. 14:73–97.

Mayr, E. 1969. Principles of systematic zoology. McGraw-Hill, New York. 428 p.

Morishima, H. 1969. Phenetic similarity and phylogenetic relationships among strains of *Oryza perennis*, estimated by methods of numerical taxonomy. Evolution 23:429–443.

Reich, P. R., N. L. Somerson, C. J. Hybner, R. M. Chanock, and S. M. Weissman. 1966. Genetic differentiation by nucleic acid homology. I. Relationship among *Mycoplasma* species of man. J. Bacteriol. 92:302–310.

Simpson, G. G. 1961. Principles of animal taxonomy. Columbia Univ. Press, New York. 237 p.

Sokal, R. R. 1962. Typology and empiricism in taxonomy. J. Theoretical Biol. 3:230–267.

Sokal, R. R. 1964. The future systematics, p. 33–48, *In* C. A. Leone [ed.], Taxonomic biochemistry and serology, Ronald, New York.

Sokal, R. R., and J. H. Camin. 1965. The two taxonomies: areas of agreement and conflict. Syst. Zool. 14:176–195.

Sokal, R. R., and P. H. A. Sneath 1963. Principles of numerical taxonomy. Freeman, San Francisco. 359 p.

Stebbins, G. L. 1963. Perspectives. I. Amer. Sci. 51:362–370.

Wallace, B. 1968. Topics in population genetics. Norton, New York. 481 p.

Williams, G. C. 1966. Adaptation and natural selection. Princeton Univ. Press, Princeton, N.J. 307 p.

Chapter 3

Differentiation of Populations

Paul R. Ehrlich and Peter H. Raven

Most contemporary biologists think of species as evolutionary units held together by gene flow. For instance Mayr (1) writes "The nonarbitrariness of the biological species is the result of ... internal cohesion of the gene pool." Merrell (2) states "The species is a natural biological unit tied together by bonds of mating and sharing a common gene pool." This idea is founded in the pioneering work of Dobzhansky, Mayr, Stebbins, and others integrating the theory of population genetics with laboratory and field experiments and observations to produce the neo-Darwinian or synthetic theory of evolution. These workers quite logically concluded that differentiation of populations would be prevented by gene flow, and they focused their discussions of speciation on various means of interrupting that flow. In other words, they emphasized the role of mechanisms isolating populations from one another. Until quite recently there has been little reason to question this view. In the past few years, however, growing evidence from field experiments has led us to reevaluate the processes leading to organic diversity, and to conclude that a revision of this section of evolutionary theory is in order.

In this paper we suggest that many, if not most, species are not evolutionary units, except in the sense that they (like genera, families, and so forth) are products of evolution. We will argue that selection is both the primary cohesive and disruptive force in evolution, and that the selective regime itself determines what influence gene flow (or isolation) will have. Threefold evidence is presented for this. We will show that (i) gene flow in nature is much more restricted than commonly thought; (ii) populations that have been completely isolated for long periods often show little differentiation; and (iii) populations freely exchanging genes but under different selective regimes may show marked differentiation.

We finally reiterate the point (3) that a vast diversity of evolutionary situations is subsumed under the rubric "speciation," and that this diversity tends to be concealed by an extension of a taxonomic approach from the products of evolution to the processes leading to the differentiation of populations. *Euphydryas editha* and *Festuca rubra* are both species to the taxonomist, but knowing this does not tell us if they are evolutionary units or how they evolved. Nor does it permit us to guess how similar are their evolutionary pasts, in what way they are similar today, or to predict anything about their evolutionary futures.

Gene Flow in Nature

To what extent do populations considered to be conspecific ordinarily share a common gene pool? Mayr (4) estimated that "genetic exchange per generation ... due to normal gene flow is at least as high as 10^{-3} to 10^{-2} for open populations that are normal components of species." He considered that gene flow was the principal source of genetic variation in natural populations, and we would agree that the introduction of genetic novelties into natural populations, even at a low level, may be important in supplying raw material for selection (5). The problem of testing Mayr's estimates and the conclusions to be drawn from them is complex. First, we must ascertain how much gene flow ordinarily occurs in nature. Second, we must determine the amount of gene flow at which significant sharing occurs. That is, we must find the amount at which subpopulations of a species affect the evolution of other subpopulations. Both questions are difficult to answer, but at least a general picture of patterns of gene flow in nature has started to emerge recently.

Movement and Gene Flow in Animals

For many animals there is information on the movement of individuals. For instance, butterflies (except those few species which are migratory) seem to be quite sedentary as compared with what one might expect in view of their powers of movement (6). Birds also often seem to show less movement than they are capable of—the young of migratory species often nest near the parental nest site (7). There also is some evidence that birds may be stopped by "psychological barriers" (8). Similar restriction of movement not associated with insurmountable physical barriers has been observed in many nonaerial organisms, such as the rusty lizard (9). Twitty's (10) studies demonstrate that California newts show great perseverance and navigating ability in returning precisely to a particular stretch of stream to breed. Individuals displaced several miles in mountainous country have successfully returned to their "home pool." And, of course, the great accuracy with which salmon return to their birthplace to breed is well documented (11).

On the other hand, there also is abundant evidence in the literature that individuals may travel very long distances, such as in Bishopp and Laake's (12) release-recapture experiments with flies in which individuals were recovered as far as 17 miles (27 km) from the point of release. Small wind-dispersed terrestrial organisms may travel tremendous distances, as may some mammals (13). It is also clear (14) that extremely careful work covering the entire life history under a variety of weather conditions is necessary before reasonably definitive statements on amounts of individual movement may be made.

Of course, movement of individuals does not necessarily indicate gene flow. Anderson (15) has shown that the presence of wandering individuals of *Mus musculus* as emigrants from granary populations does not indicate significant gene flow, since in general the granary demes do not admit immigrants. Ehrlich and his coworkers (16) have produced evidence indicating that the reproductive success of emigrant *Euphydryas editha* individuals is less than that of stay-at-homes, a situation which also probably pertains among small mammal populations (17).

Even reproduction by migrants or propagules may not constitute evolutionarily significant gene flow. Only if the migrants are carriers of alleles or arrangements of alleles not represented in the recipient population has gene flow occurred. In addition, if a new allele is to be passed from population to population by gene flow, one must consider the probability of its spread in each new population and its possibility of being included in the genome of migrant individuals leaving that population. Its fate in the first instance will presumably be governed by the kind of gloomy odds facing mutant genes (18); in no small part it will rest with its fitness in that population. One would normally expect selective barriers to the movement of genetic novelties.

Movement and Gene Flow in Plants

In plants, we have some actual estimates of gene flow between populations. Here the chances of crossing diminish rapidly with distance. In wind-pollinated species, on might expect a great deal of gene flow even between well-separated populations, but this assumption is not borne out by the available data. In *Zea mays* and *Beta vulgaris*, whose pollen is carried far and wide by wind, measurements have been made of contamination because of their agricultural importance. At distances greater than 60 feet (18.3 m), contamination by distant outcrossing in *Zea* was only 1 percent. In *Beta* plants separated by 200 meters, contamination was only 0.3 percent (19). Colwell (20) studied the dispersal of pollen of Coulter pine (*Pinus coulteri*) labeled with radioactive phosphorus. The bulk of the dispersal was within 10 to 30 feet (3 to 9 m) downwind from the source, with very little beyond 150 feet (46 m). It is obvious that, although pollen can be dispersed great distances at times, the chances of its falling on a receptive stigma at any great distance are slight. On the other hand, a given plant normally will be completely pollinated, even in an outcrossing species, with pollen from nearby sources. A very short distance therefore will form the basis for nearly complete genetic discontinuity, even in a wind-pollinated plant.

In insect-pollinated species, Bateman (21) found that beyond 50 feet (15 m) there was less than 1 percent contamination between two varieties of turnips or radishes. Similarly, Roberts and Lewis (22) cite examples in several species of the herbs of the genera *Clarkia* and *Delphinium* where no more than 50 feet (15 m) seems to be an effective barrier. In *Linanthus parryae* the pattern of variation suggests that a very short distance effectively isolates these insect-pollinated plants (23). On the other hand, insects may occasionally carry pollen to somewhat greater distances. Because of their relative specificity, they actually may do so at a much higher frequency than occurs in plants whose pollen is carried by wind. An interesting demonstration of this is provided by Emerson's (24) studies of *Oenothera organensis*. This species is a local endemic of the Organ Mountains in New Mexico, where it occurs in isolated small colonies in the bottom of several steep-walled canyons. The colonies are separated by high ridges and are from 600 feet (183 m) to about 3 miles (5 km) apart. Emerson was able to demonstrate that this species had a system of self-sterility (S) alleles, the majority of which occurred in more than one colony, and some of which occurred in all of the colonies. Wright's (25) analysis of these data led to the conclusion that intergroup crossing had to have occurred about 2 percent of the time to account for this distribution. The plants are pollinated by strong-flying hawkmoths (Sphingidae), and Gregory (26) believes that this figure is consistent with the known behavior and power of flight of these insects.

In tropical rain forest, trees of a given species are often separated by considerable distances. Here it would appear that either strong-flying selective pollinators must actively seek out individuals or self-pollination must be prevalent. It is of interest to distinguish between these two possibilities, but little is understood of the structure of tree populations in the tropical rain forest at present.

In plants, therefore, there is considerable evidence that distances of from 50 feet (15 m) to a few miles (several kilometers) may effectively isolate populations, and there is no evidence of longer-range gene flow. Beyond these limits, there is no suggestion of gene flow at or near the amounts suggested as "normal" by Mayr (4).

The possibilites of gene flow between natural populations of most species are sharply limited by their wide separation. Both plants and animals are usually highly colonial, the populations being separated by relatively great distances. For example, colonies of the butterfly *Euphydryas editha* occur scattered throughout California, many of them separated by distances of several kilometers and some by gaps of nearly 200 kilometers. It has been demonstrated that there is almost no gene flow in this species over gaps of as little as 100 meters (27). For this reason, there seems no possibility that gene flow "holds together" its widely scattered populations. The cave-dwelling collembolan *Pseudosinella hirsuta* occurs in a series of populations in the southeastern United States. There is no gene flow between them (28), yet they resemble one another. *Clarkia rhomboidea* occurs in the Great Basin of the western United States as a disjunct series of similar populations in widely separated mountain ranges. These are separated by gaps of scores or hundreds of kilometers and they are genetically highly differentiated (29). Gene flow can have no bearing on their evolution under present conditions, and we suggest that these three examples are representative of the vast majority of plant and animal distributions.

What then is the evidence for gene flow as a cohesive force holding together plant and animal species? Basically, the evidence seems to be that they are "held together"—populations considered to belong to a given species resemble one another. But the taxonomic decision to consider them members of one species is inevitably based on the fact that they do resemble one another and does not in itself provide an explanation for the resemblance. It may be that in certain continuously distributed species—if there are such—the regular exchange of genes between populations prevents differentiation in the face of different kinds of selection pressures at different places. But such a situation has never, to our knowledge, been demonstrated convincingly in either plants or animals.

One can see that, at the very least, it is unwise to view species of sexual organisms in general as the largest group of organisms sharing a common gene pool, although it may be true in particular instances. Yet this notion is important in the history of evolutionary biology, because it has promoted the idea that a species is an evolutionary unit, and that gene flow among its populations makes it such a unit. It led also to the conclusion that sharing the gene pool gives a species "cohesion" which must be broken if further speciation is to occur.

It is appropriate now to consider what processes are critical to the multiplication of species. There is an abundance of inferential evidence indicating that, at least in many cases, gene flow is of little or no importance in maintaining many of the phenetic units we call "species." Some of the strongest evidence, of course, comes from the wide variety of organisms with asexual reproduction. When this is obligate there is, by definition, no gene flow either within or between populations. And yet these organisms tend to occur as phenetic species—presumably groups of individuals being kept similar by their continued existence under similar selective regimes. And, as Mayr (30) points out, the existence of groups of sibling species indicates that gene flow is not necessarily the cause of phenotypic uniformity.

It is not necessary, however, to turn to asexual organisms (with, presumably, sharply restricted genetic variability) or sibling species to find evidence of selection rather than gene flow maintaining phenetic units. This is clearly what is happening in *Euphydryas editha* in California as well as in many other butterflies with populations that are totally isolated from one another. *Erebia theano* populations in Alaska are only slightly differentiated from those isolated in Colorado, indeed from those in Europe. Yet we would be greatly surprised if the Colorado populations (occurring as scattered isolates) receive a gene originating in Alaska once per hundred millennia. *Lycaena phlaeas* remains *Lycaena phlaeas* in the Sierra Nevada of California, although almost certainly no alleles from its European or eastern American relatives have reached this area for thousands of generations. The sand crab *Emerita analoga* has a strongly disjunct Northern-Southern Hemisphere distribution with apparently no possibility of significant gene flow (31). In spite of this the two populations are not obviously differentiated. This is just one of many cases of a phenomenon known to marine biogeographers as "bipolarity" (32). Similarly, many species of plants have disjunct ranges in temperate North and South America, with varying amounts of differentiation despite a distributional gap of thousands of kilometers (33). Another case in point is the extreme resemblance of the marine faunas of the east and west sides of the Isthmus of Panama, which includes organisms considered to occur as pairs of relatively undifferentiated "twin species" (32). The close resemblance of the faunas remains, although the organisms on either side of the isthmus (that is, those which are restricted to warm seas) have presumably not exchanged genes for two million generations or more. Similarly, reef fishes often are remarkably similar throughout tropical seas, although gene flow among their populations is probably very reduced. The same can be said for plants on the numerous low atolls scattered through the Pacific. The plants which occcur on them are identical everywhere, as contrasted with the plants on the high islands which present different selective regimes. Similar examples of lack of obvious differentiation in the absence of gene flow we suspect will prove to be common in all groups of organisms, just as will examples of rapid and prominent local differentiation (34) with or without gene flow.

In view of these considerations, we should reexamine the commonly observed situation in which island populations are more different from mainland populations than mainland populations are from one another. This difference is usually attributed to interruption of gene flow, but may more often be a function of a very different selective regime—for example, a milder climate—on the islands. Similar reasoning might be applied to other instances of differentiation on islands, for example, the case of the Galápagos finches (35). Isolation is always assumed to play the major role in this case, and indeed it may. But the islands, although superficially similar, are ecologically very different and had depauperate faunas at the time of the original invasion (that is, there were many empty niches). Furthermore, the higher islands also show great internal diversification. If this explanation is correct, then we might expect relatively slow differentiation in the future, since much of the "ecological opportunity" is gone, and the various species have now spread over the islands.

A word is necessary here about the function of isolating mechanisms, which have received so much attention from evolutionists (36). There is now no reason whatever to believe that such mechanisms evolved to somehow "protect" the genetic integrity of species. Incompatibility arises because two populations are subjected to differing selective regimes, and it is often reinforced by selection operating against hybrids. It is a common but not universal result, not a cause, of the process of speciation.

The similarity of populations that are obviously isolated from one another is conventionally attributed to their existence under similar selective regimes. But similarity where isolation is thought not to have been of long duration, or where isolation is not obvious, is almost always attributed to gene flow. This assumption seems untenable in the light of our knowledge of how rapidly differentiation can occur, gene flow or no, when selection promotes it. *Biston betularia* in England in 1825 would doubtless have been considered to be uniform in appearance because its populations were exchanging genes. We now know how fallacious that conclusion would have been, since whatever level of gene flow existed was insufficient to prevent dramatic local differentiation when the selective situation changed (37). Similarly the butterfly *Maniola jurtina* maintains stable genetic configurations selectively over vast areas (38) and maintains sharp borders between the different types in spite of strong gene flow (39). Genetic "area effects" are also well known in *Cepaea* populations (40) with boundaries not coinciding with barriers to gene flow.

The formation of very local races of plants and animals is commonplace even in extreme outcrossers such as the self-incompatible wind-pollinated grasses *Festuca rubra* and *Agrostis tenuis* (41). Such races, which may be sharply differentiated genetically, may occupy areas in nature only a meter or so in diameter—with these races surrounded by plants of another race. The differentiation of such localized populations dependent on the interplay between natural selection, the breeding system, and gene flow, has been analyzed (42). The advantage of particular genotypes in reproducing under a particular, often extremely local, set of conditions may be such that recombinants and other variants are systematically eliminated. In spite of the opportunity for high levels of gene flow, the selection pressures determined experimentally in such cases seem theoretically adequate to explain the very local patterns of differentiation found, for example, in *Agrostis stolonifera* (43).

The increasingly refined methods of genetic analysis that are being applied to natural populations are revealing more and more instances of unexpectedly local differentiation even when the organisms concerned are highly mobile and the populations appear to be continuous. In *Drosophila aldrichi*, Richardson (44) analyzed three populations within a 40-mile (64 km) radius of Austin, Texas, for the frequencies of six alleles concerned with a particular esterase system. The frequencies differed slightly from locality to locality but remained constant at each locality during a year. Using a similar approach, Selander (45) showed "microgeographic" variation between populations of the house mouse (*Mus musculus*) in a single large barn.

Thus, there is increasing evidence of extremely local patterns of differentiation in both plants and animals. We predict that such patterns may prove to be the rule, rather than the exception, for most populations of organisms.

Evidence from natural populations is supported by experimental work such as that of Thoday and his coworkers (46) which indicates that selection can override the effects of gene flow even when the amount of that flow is greater than would ever occur in nature. Evidence of this sort would undermine arguments about "gene flow" as a cohesive force binding together all the populations of some widespread species into a genetic entity, even if such binding were not patently impossible for most organisms on purely distributional grounds. Indeed, gene flow eventually might be discovered to play a rather insignificant role in evolution as a whole. There is substantial evidence that populations can be changed rapidly by selection. Similarly there is evidence that selection often resists such change—presumably in part because of genetic homeostasis. The most basic forces involved in the differentiation of populations may be antagonistic selective strategies, one for close "tracking" of the environment and one for maintaining "coadapted" genetic combinations—combinations which have high average fitness in environments which are inevitably variable through time.

Of course final answers about the relative evolutionary roles of selection and gene flow will not come until we have more thorough studies of natural situations. Some of the cases commonly presented as showing gene flow preventing differentiation need careful reexamination, for example, those of Hooper (47) and others on the development of dark-lava races in mice. If this, indeed, is a case of gene flow swamping selection, then we must learn the magnitude of both factors. In cases such as that of *Euphydryas editha*, laboratory and field experiments must be devised to determine the exact selective regimes which produce relative uniformity among populations along with temporal variability within populations, in the absence of gene flow. In this, and virtually all other situations cited in this paper, further genetic analysis is needed to determine how well phenetic uniformity or variability reflects genetic uniformity or variability. It is well known that there is no one-to-one relationship (48), but in general we are profoundly ignorant of the degree of overall genetic similarity, however defined (49), at all levels of phenetic differentiation.

Our suspicion is that, eventually, we will find that, in some species, gene flow is an important factor in keeping populations of the species relatively undifferentiated, but that in most it is not. As this becomes widely recognized we will see the disappearance of the idea that species, as groups of actually or potentially interbreeding populations, are evolutionary units "required" by theory. Modern evolutionary theory requires local interbreeding populations, far smaller groups than those normally called species, as evolutionary units in sexual organisms. It recognizes that such units will vary greatly in their genetic properties and may have a vast diversity of relationships with other such units. The evolution of larger phenetic clusters—the species, genera, orders, and so forth, of taxonomists—is easily derived from the theory, but it seems unwise to consider any of these as evolutionary units except in those cases where they can be shown to react to evolutionary pressures as units.

Summary

Evidence is presented from a variety of sources which indicates that species should not be thought of as evolutionary units held together by the cohesive force of gene flow. Gene flow in nature is much more restricted than commonly thought and experimental evidence is badly needed to document the extent to which it does occur. Selection itself is both the primary cohesive and disruptive force in evolution; the selective regime determines what influence gene flow has on observed patterns of differentiation. Populations will differentiate if they are subjected to different selective forces and will tend to remain similar if they are not. For sexual organisms it is the local interbreeding population and not the species that is clearly the evolutionary unit of importance.

References and Notes

We thank the members of the Population Biology Group of the Department of Biological Sciences, Stanford University, and numerous colleagues at other institutions for discussing and criticizing the ideas presented here. Supported in part by NSF grants GB-8038 and GB-8174 (P.R.E.) and GB-7949X (P.H.R.). A version of this paper was presented in the symposium "Ecology and the Origin of Species" at the 1968 annual meeting of the AAAS at Dallas.

   1. E. Mayr, *Animal Species and Evolution* (Harvard Univ. Press, Cambridge, Mass., 1963), p. 21.
   2. D. J. Merrell, *Evolution and Genetics* (Holt, Rinehart & Winston, 1962), p. 293.

3. P. H. Raven, *Univ. Calif. Publ. Bot.* 34, 1 (1962); P. R. Ehrlich and R. W. Holm, *Science* 137, 652 (1962); P. R. Ehrlich, *Syst. Zool.* 13, 109 (1964).
4. E. Mayr, *Animal Species and Evolution* (Harvard Univ. Press. Cambridge, Mass., 1963), pp. 521 and 177.
5. More work like that of H. L. Carson [*Evolution* 15, 496 (1961)] on the possible effects of single migrants or small groups of migrants is badly needed.
6. P. R. Ehrlich, *Science* 154, 108 (1961).
7. M. N. Nice, *Trans. Linn. Soc. N.Y.* 4, 1 (1937).
8. E. Mayr, *Systematics and the Origin of Species* (Columbia Univ. Press, New York, 1942).
9. W. F. Blair, *The Rusty Lizard, a Population Study* (Univ. of Texas Press, Austin, 1960).
10. V. C. Twitty, *Science* 130, 1735 (1959).
11. F. Neave, J. I. Manzer, H. Godfrey, R. J. Brasseur, *Fish Res. Bd. Can. Rep. No. 563* (1962).
12. F. C. Bishopp and E. W. Laake, *J. Agr. Res.* 21, 729 (1921).
13. See, for example, N. P. Naumov, *Proc. Symposium Thereologicum* (Prague, 1960), p. 221.
14. See, for example, W. G. Wellington, *Can. J. Zool.* 38, 289 (1960).
15. P. K. Anderson, unpublished data.
16. P. R. Ehrlich, unpublished data; P. Labine, *Evolution* 20, 580 (1966).
17. P. L. Errington, *Muskrat Populations* (Iowa State Univ. Press, Ames. 1963).
18. R. A. Fisher, *The Genetical Theory of Natural Selection* (Clarendon Press, Oxford, 1930).
19. A. Archimowitsch, *Bot. Rev.* 15, 613 (1949); A. J. Bateman, *Heredity* 1, 235 (1947).
20. R. N. Colwell, *Amer. J. Bot.* 38, 511 (1951).
21. A. J. Bateman, *Nature* 157, 752 (1946).
22. M. R. Roberts and H. Lewis, *Evolution* 9, 445 (1955).
23. C. Epling, H. Lewis, F. M. Ball, *ibid.* 14, 238 (1960).
24. S. Emerson, *Genetics* 23, 190 (1938); *ibid.* 24, 524 (1939).
25. S. Wright, *ibid.*, p. 538.
26. D. P. Gregory, *Aliso* 5, 385 (1964).
27. P. R. Ehrlich, *Evolution* 19, 327 (1965); and unpublished data.
28. K. Christiansen and D. Culver, *Evolution* 22, 237 (1968).
29. T. Mosquin, *ibid.* 18, 12 (1964).
30. E. Mayr, *Animal Species and Evolution* (Harvard Univ. Press, Cambridge, Mass., 1963), p. 521.
31. L. Eickstaedt, personal communications.
32. S. Ekman, *Zoogeography of the Sea* (Sedgwick and Jackson, London, 1953).
33. P. H. Raven, *Quart. Rev. Biol.* 38, 151 (1963).
34. See, for example, R. F. Johnson and R. K. Selander, *Science* 144, 548 (1964); E. Stodard, *CSIRO (Commonw. Sci. Ind. Res. Organ.) Wildlife Res.* 10, 73 (1966); G. C. Packard, *Syst. Zool.* 16, 73 (1967); A. D. Bradshaw, *Nature* 169, 1098 (1952); A. P. Nelson, *Brittonia* 17, 160 (1965)
35. V. Lack, *Darwin's Finches* (Cambridge Univ. Press, Cambridge, 1947).
36. See, for example, Th. Dobzhansky, *Genetics and the Origin of Species* (Columbia Univ. Press, New York, ed. 2, 1951).
37. H. B. D. Kettlewell, *Heredity* 12, 51 (1958).
38. W. H. Dowdeswell and K. McWhirter, *ibid.* 22, 187 (1967).
39. E. R. Creed, W. H. Dowdeswell, E. B. Ford, J. G. McWhirter, *ibid.* 17, 237 (1962).
40. A. J. Cain and C. Currey, *ibid.* 18, 467 (1963); C. B. Goodhart, *ibid.*, p. 459.
41. A. Smith, *Scot. Plant Breed. Sta. Rec.* 1965, 163 (1965).
42. S. K. Jain and A. D. Bradshaw, *Heredity* 22, 407 (1966).
43. J. L. Aston and A. D. Bradshaw, *ibid.* 21, 649 (1966).
44. R. H. Richardson, *Proc. Int. Congr. Genet.* 2, 155 (1968).

45. R. Selander, "Behavior and genetic variation in wild populations," a paper presented in a symposium "Ecology and the Origin of Species" at the 1960 annual meeting of the AAAS at Dallas.

46. See, for example, J. M. Thoday, *Heredity* 13, 187 (1959); — and T. B. Boam, *ibid.*, p. 205; J. M. Thoday and J. B. Gibson, *Nature* 193, 1164 (1962); J. B. Gibson and J. M. Thoday, *Heredity* 17, 1 (1962).

47. E. T. Hooper, *Misc. Publ. Mus. Zool. Univ. Mich.* 51, 1 (1941).

48. See, for example, J. M. Rendel, *J. Theor. Biol.* 2, 296 (1962); see, however, J. L. Hubby and L. H. Throckmorton [*Amer. Nat.* 102, 193 (1968)], which indicates a high correlation between phenetic and "genetic" differentiation.

49. P. R. Ehrlich, *Syst. Zool.* 13, 109 (1964).

Chapter 4

Ecological Species, Multispecies, and Oaks

Leigh Van Valen

Muller (1952) and more directly Burger (1975) have shown that North American populations of oaks (*Quercus*) cut across the frame of reference of the now usual concept of species. This discordance may well be widespread among plants and microorganisms and seems to occur for some animals; oaks are merely conspicuous and well studied. I believe with Burger that the situation is sufficiently serious that a reconsideration of the nature of species is needed. I agree with his conclusions but go beyond them. My concern is with the nature of processes rather than terms for them, although the latter level is sometimes more convenient for discussion.

The usual concept of species can be stated as follows (Mayr 1970): "Species are groups of interbreeding natural populations that are reproductively isolated from other such groups." This concept is grandly called "the biological species concept." But that is an arbitrary appropriation of a term with a more general and earlier meaning. I will instead use the term "reproductive species concept."

Simpson (1961) proposed a modification of the reproductive species concept to fit it to the numerous cases where the two defining criteria are irrelevant: "An evolutionary species is a lineage (an ancestral-descendent sequence of populations) evolving separately from others and with its own unitary evolutionary role and tendencies." I will modify Simpson's concept, first stating the revised version formally and then justifying it.

My underlying framework is radical and includes the beliefs (1) that genes are of minor importance in evolution and should ordinarily be considered there in nearly the same degree (if often not for the same reasons) as other molecules, (2) that the control of evolution is largely by ecology and the constraints of individual development, and (3) that selection acts primarily on phenotypes, which are the building blocks of communities. A species is one kind of unit of evolution, although there are many other kinds, but how best to say so precisely?

The Ecological Species Concept

The following definition is a vehicle for conceptual revision, not a standing monolith.

A species is a lineage (or a closely related set of lineages) which occupies an adaptive zone minimally different from that of any other lineage in its range and which evolves separately from all lineages outside its range.

A lineage is a clone or an ancestral-descendent sequence of populations. A population is a group of individuals in which adjacent individuals at least occasionally exchange genes with each other reproductively, and in which adjacent individuals do so more frequently than with individuals outside the population.

Lineages are closely related if they have occupied the same adaptive zone since their latest common ancestor. If their adaptive zone has changed since then, they are closely related if the new adaptations have been transferred among the lineages rather than originating separately in each.

An adaptive zone (Van Valen 1971) is some part of the resource space together with whatever predation and parasitism occurs on the group considered. It is a part of the environment, as distinct from the way of life of a taxon that may occupy it, and exists independently of any inhabitants it may have. The word "zone," although entrenched, is perhaps unfortunate in suggesting the necessary existence of natural boundaries or subcontinuities in the resource space. The boundaries of an adaptive zone may be fixed and if so will remain the same whatever species are present, like apartments in an apartment house or a surface with basins separated by ridges. Alternatively there may be no such preexisting boundaries, as with an Iroquois long house or a flat surface, and yet subdivision can be imposed on it by the nature of the particular species that happen to be present together. Which of these intergrading alternatives on the modality of the resource space is most prevalent is an unresolved, in fact nearly unstudied, and important empirical question.

The degree of difference in adaptive zones required will vary from case to case. Dandelions (*Taraxacum officinale*) have sympatric clones that differ slightly as to the part of the resource space occupied (Gadgil and Solbrig 1972), and even if these do not in fact interbreed it is arbitrary whether they are placed in the same or different species.

"Range" is both geographical and temporal. In cases of geographic or temporal variation of the adaptive zone of a species, it may occasionally happen (I know of no real cases, but the possibility is usually ignored) that some other species in part A of the range may be more similar adaptively to the first species as it exists in part B of the range than is the first species as it exists in part A. This is a minor semantic complication which does not seem worth incorporating into the definition, although a real case would be interesting ecologically. Separate evolution is, as Simpson (1961) noted, the underlying reason for the importance of reproductive isolation. It therefore seems appropriate to use it directly. As is the case in the real world, this criterion has fuzzy boundaries.

For instance, it is arbitrary whether otherwise similar populations on isolated islands are called different species. I would not want to make such a splitting, because their evolution is still sufficiently similar and splitting would unnecessarily complicate biogeographic theory and practical systematics, but the decision seems to be one of taste rather than biology. The populations are, after all, separate. It is for us to determine, for our own purposes, whether their evolution is controlled by pressures sufficiently different that the evolution of these populations is also separate. I believe that this criterion is the one most commonly applied to such situations in practice, at least implicitly.

It may seem that sympatric but isolated populations with similar phenotypes (sib species) present a problem, but they would not persist together if they did not occupy minimally different adaptive zones.

An operational criterion for the occupation of different adaptive zones is a difference in the ultimately regulating factor, or factors, of population density (cf. Van Valen 1973). Some species thus occupy more than one low-level adaptive zone.

Reproductive isolation of allopatric populations is of minor evolutionary importance and needs little consideration. For instance, Zouros (1974) and others have found that ecological difference is more closely related to genic difference than is the occurrence of reproductive isolation. Schwarz (1974) gives other evidence and concludes that speciation occurs by ecological change, any reproductive isolation being incidental.

Ghiselin (1975) has made a useful advance by considering species to be "the most extensive units in the natural economy such that reproductive competition [for genes] occurs among their parts." However, such competition occurs simultaneously at many levels with different time scales. The "most extensive" might perhaps be entire trophic levels competing reproductively for free energy, and indirectly for the preservation of their genes. I therefore find this proposal incomplete.

Species are maintained for the most part ecologically, not reproductively. Completely asexual communities would perhaps be as diverse as sexual ones, with numerous subcontinuities and even discontinuities. This suggests but does not require that the main criterion of species be ecological. Heed (1963) found the phenotypic diversity for a group of *Drosophila* to be similar in different places, but in some places the morphs belonged to the same species and in some places to different species. A similar situation, where morphs and species are almost interchangeable in a community, may hold for the snail *Cepaea* (Clarke 1962) and for spruce (*Picea*; Stern and

Roche 1974, 132—138). Cases of character displacement and character release are evidence for a similar significance of continuous variation. It is the ultimatc regulatory factors of its population density that determine whether a phenotype will persist in a community.

Evolution and the Ecological Species

It may well be that *Quercus macrocarpa* in Quebec exchanges many more genes with local *Q. bicolor* than it does with *Q. macrocarpa* in Texas. Considering the easily detectable proportion of intermediate individuals ("hybrids") in Quebec and the short-range gene dispersal of most plants (cf. Ehrlich and Raven 1969; Levin and Kerster 1974), it would be surprising if this were not the case. The nature of the selection that keeps the two species largely discrete, whether based on a strong environmental subcontinuity or on developmental ("genomic") integration, is unknown. Stebbins (1970) gave evidence for the maintenance of such a situation over millions of years for another pair of species of *Quercus*. A set of broadly sympatric species that exchange genes in nature can be called a *multispecies*. (The "syngameon" of Grant 1957, 1971 is a similar concept although restricted to hybridization as a method of gene exchange. However, this term was originally defined by Lotsy 1925, 1931 as meaning any Mendelian population, as Dobzhansky 1951 noted, and Cuenot 1951 used it even more broadly for any set of potentially interfertile organisms, including specifically the entire genus *Canis*. Turesson's ecospecies and coenospecies are based on ability to hybridize, not on gene flow in nature, Stebbins 1950.)

The ecological species concept treats gene flow differently depending on whether it is sympatric or allopatric. This distinction is partly arbitrary but has a reason. *Q. macrocarpa* and *Q. bicolor* are evolutionarily and ecologically largely discrete, and their broad sympatry over most of their range precludes subspecific designation. Moreover, each varies geographically. The possibility of multispecies with widely dissimilar components, discussed below, accentuates the usefulness of a distinction. At the other extreme, subspecies of the deermouse *Peromyscus maniculatus* are allopatric and often differ in major aspects of habitat use, yet they do intergrade and something coinciding with the reproductive species concept in this case seems useful. *Homo sapiens* has been a similar species.

Higher taxa may almost fit the definition of the ecological species concept, whence the word "minimally" with reference to the difference in adaptive zones. This delimits species from higher taxa and, as the end of a possible continuum, is why species are less arbitrary taxa than are those in higher categories. It is also why the species category itself is the least arbitrary category. However, the ecological species concept is similar to ecological interpretations of higher taxa (Simpson 1953; Van Valen 1971) and so helps in conceptually unifying all categories. A symposium published in the December, 1973, issue of *Systematic Zoology* shows an apparent consensus that evolutionary taxonomy is a simple combination of cladistics and resemblance. The addition of another dimension by the explicit use of adaptation, however, makes classification closer to the actual processes of evolution.

The apparent fact that species can originate from intermediate individuals (this seems to have happened in oaks: *Q. alvordiana* as discussed by Tucker 1952) permits the possibility that some such species have a multiple origin, from geographically separate intermediates expanding with the expansion of an intermediate environment. The lack of reproductive isolation between the more extreme species makes interbreeding of such expanding populations likely when they meet. Conversely, one species can expand and incorporate some or even all the surviving genes of another (the compilospecies of Harlan and de Wet 1963).

Ecotypes differ from species in being multiply derived from an ancestral stock and usually in being allopatric or parapatric to it. However, a geographically continuous ecotype regionally sympatric with its ancestor would be a species. Ecotypes restricted to small, unique areas of serpentine-derived or lead-polluted soil would be marginal cases and indicate a mechanism of origin for species if the edaphic conditions were more widespread.

Most importantly, however, incomplete reproductive isolation of species permits better evolutionary adaptation. Adaptations useful to only one species can easily be kept from the other, while adaptations useful to both can get to both wherever they originate (Brues 1964, 1973, 1974). This is true for adaptations useful to both species in only part of their range as well as for adaptations of general use. It would be desirable to survey *Q. macrocarpa* and *Q. bicolor* electrophoretically in different parts of their range to see how important this phenomenon has been. And the multispecies, more extensive than the ecological species, does not have all its seeds in one ecological basket. As Burger (1975) notes, the *Quercs* situation is relevant to the interspecific continuity of subspecies postulated by Coon (1962) (which even Dobzhansky 1970, 392 has accepted, without mentioning Coon), Freudenthal (1965, 1968, and personal communication), and Martin (1970), and discussed in terms of genetics by Van Valen (1966) and Brues (1964, 1973, 1974). It is difficult to see how such an advantageous situation could be selected for directly, however, and it is probably a byproduct of other phenomena.

There may be taxa without species. *Rubus*, *Crataegus*, and the Enterobacteriaceae are possible examples, and the dandelion case is conceptually similar. The problem resulting from this possibility would be nomenclatural and not scientific. Why, other than for names, must there always be species? And even names can be treated nontraditionally. It seems preferable to see whether there are in fact objectively bounded clusters more or less comparable in adaptive scope to those in other taxa, rather than starting from an assumption of the existence of species and then trying to find their boundaries (cf. Rahn 1929; Cowan 1962; Hutchinson 1968).

The *modality* of a broad adaptive zone can be defined as the degree to which it is partitioned when the effects of the included species on the adaptive zone itself are eliminated. In those parts of an adaptive zone which can suitably be represented by a multidimensional space, the modality is the density of clustering in this space of the images of points (or small regions) of the physical space in the part of the real world we are considering. For example, as a simple case with some applicability to herbivores, we can take the entire world with two dimensions of wetness and primary productivity. The wetness dimension will contain a strong subcontinuity in the region onto which bogs and marshes map, since they are rare in relation to waters and dry land, and there will perhaps be no marginal subcontinuity at all in the dimension of productivity although there are obvious interactions.

Statistically, I have defined (Van Valen 1974) the modality

$$M = \frac{\sum_i \sum_j d_{ij}^2 - (\text{uniform})}{N^2/2 - (\text{uniform})},$$

where d_{ij} is the Euclidean distance between any two points, and (*uniform*) is the value of the summation when the same number of points are distributed uniformly in a hypersphere with diameter equal to the distance between the extreme observed points. $N^2/2$ is the maximum value of the double summation and occurs when half the points are at each end of the diameter. M will then range from 0 for no modality to 1 for a clustering of all points into two. It can be negative when there is unimodality.

The variables should obviously be made equivalent, as by dividing each by its mean. But there is a serious problem in the application of M when measurements on different variables are best taken at physical points or different sizes of regions per unit, as with size of seeds and availability of holes for cover. There may be thousands of seeds, each representing one datum (perhaps weighted by nutritive value) to be plotted, in a region with one hole. A bird may need one hole but many seeds, so sampling one seed in the region is inadequate. M can be calculated independently for each variable, but their combination is awkward although relevant to the species that inhabit the adaptive zone.

The detailed pattern of natural variation itself, within perhaps more than among populations, phenotypic perhaps more than genotypic, is of considerable interest from the viewpoint of adaptation. "Difficult," predominantly asexual, taxa may be the best groups with which to study this. Even they confound (1) biologically relevant subcontinuities in the environment, (2) effects of competition, and (3) epistatic effects of different phenotypes and genotypes on fitness (isolated phenotypic and genotypic adaptive peaks in a uniform environment). But controls are possible and the discontinuities among sexual species limit the scope of their variation in a way that is irrelevant to this problem.

Just as at least some bacteriophage exchange genes with their prey, it may be that gene exchange occurs in other cases of intimate symbiosis, e.g. mycorrhizal associations. It is even conceivable that genes are transferred between insects and plants by means of those viruses which somehow grow in both (cf. Anderson 1970; Zhdanov and Tikchonenko 1974). A possible example has recently been described between carnivorans and primates (Todaro et al. 1974; Sherr and Todaro 1974; Benveniste and Todaro 1974). Such situations would be marginal examples of multispecies. In an important but obscurely published paper, Durden (1969) has proposed that there are often geographic clines between the extremes of one and two reproductive species, the intermediates being multispecies-like.

From the point of view of ecological interactions, and therefore with respect to the operation of (and to some extent the response to) natural selection, the species-level unit in a community is fuzzily bounded. The possibly mutualistic nature of chloroplasts and some other organelles is repeated by definitely mutualistic interactions that are less highly integrated (Margulis 1970). Lichens are commonly treated as species with a dual ancestry. Reef corals and many other organisms with a heterotroph ancestry are partly to wholely autotrophic (Odum 1971; Zucker 1973; Muscatine 1973, 1974) because of endosymbiotic algae which function as chloroplasts. Should such ecological units be considered species? The only important problems are the gradation of mutualism into occasional interactions of otherwise separate individuals, and the possibility of nontransitive mutualistic associations. A double genome is accepted for lichens. Mutualistic units compete with each other and with nonmutualistic species for a community's resources and in this respect behave as (suboptimal) coalitions in n-person zero-sum game theory.

It is unclear why multispecies seem to occur less commonly among metazoans than elsewhere. Burger (1975) suggests that the more complex structure (i.e., development) and more precise mating of many metazoans may be crucial. Additional possibilities are sharper delineation of adaptive zones, if this occurs, and the seemingly greater rarity of closely related sympatric species. Controls on these variables are possible and can help their evaluation. There may nevertheless be metazoan multispecies. Fischer-Piette (various papers reviewed by Van Valen 1969) has described a possible case in the limpet *Patella*, and others may occur in the rotifer *Polyarthra* (Pejler 1956), the abalone *Haliotis* (Owen, McLean, and Meyer 1971), the fish *Etheostoma* (Echelle et al. 1975), and the mussel *Mytilus* (Seed 1972). A theory that denies the possibility of multispecies inhibits their discovery.

Acknowledgments

W. Burger's analysis of oaks provided the stimulus for writing up these ideas. I thank him, N. Flesness, M. T. Ghiselin, H. W. Kerster, D. A. Levin, V. C. Maiorana, R. R. Sokal, V. Thompson, and W. Wimsatt for related discussions.

References

Anderson, N. G. 1970. Evolutionary significance of virus infection. Nature 227 : 1346–1347.

Benveniste, R. E., and G. J. Todaro 1974. Evolution of C-type viral genes: inheritance of exogenously acquired viral genes. Nature 252 : 456–459.

Brues, A. M. 1964. Selective factors in gene flow [abstract]. Amer. Jour. Phys. Anth. 22 : 507.

Brues, A. M. 1973. Models applicable to geographic variation in man. *In* Computer Simulation in Human Population Studies (B. Dyke and J. W. MacCluer, eds.), pp. 129–141. New York: Academic Press.

Brues, A. M. 1974. Models for evolution in a polytypic species [abstract]. Amer. Jour. Phys. Anth. 40 : 131–132.

Burger, W. 1975. The species-concept in *Quercus*. Taxon 24 : 45–50.

Clarke, B. 1962. Balanced polymorphism and the diversity of sympatric species. *In* Taxonomy and Geography (D. Nichols, ed.), pp. 47–70. London: Systematics Association (Publ. 4).

Coon, C. S. 1962. The Origin of Races. New York: Knopf.

Cowan, S. T. 1962. The microbial species—a macromyth? Symp. Soc. Gen. Microbiol. 12 : 433–455.

Cuenot, L. 1951. L'Évolution Biologique. Paris: Masson et Cie.

Dobzhansky, Th. 1951. Genetics and the Origin of Species. 3rd ed. New York: Columbia Univ. Press.

Dobzhansky, Th. 1970. Genetics of the Evolutionary Process. New York: Columbia Univ. Press.

Durden, C. J. 1969. Ecological aspects of the species concept. Armadillo Pap. 1 : 1–14.

Echelle, A. A., A. F. Echelle, M. H. Smith, and L. G. Hill 1975. Analysis of genic continuity in a headwater fish, *Etheostoma radiosum* (Percidae). Copeia (1975): 197–204.

Ehrlich, P. R., and P. H. Raven 1969. Differentiation of populations. Science 165 : 1228–1232.

Freudenthal, M. 1965. Betrachtungen über die Gattung *Cricetodon*. Koninkl. Nederlandse Akad. Wetensch. (B) 68 : 293–305.

Freudenthal, M. 1968. On the mammalian fauna of the *Hipparion*-beds in the Calatayud-Teruel Basin (Prov. Zaragoza, Spain). IV. The genus *Megacricetodon* (Rodentia). Koninkl. Nederlandse Akad. Wetensch. (B) 71 : 57–72.

Gadgil, M., and O. T. Solbrig 1972. The concept of r- and K-selection: evidence from wild flowers and some theoretical considerations. Amer. Nat. 106 : 14–31.

Ghiselin, M. T. 1975. A radical solution to the species problem. Syst. Zool. 23 (for 1974): 536–544.

Grant, V. 1947. The plant species in theory and practice. *In* The Species Problem (E. Mayr, ed.), pp. 39–80. Washington: Amer. Assoc. Adv. Sci.

Grant, V. 1971. Plant Speciation. New York: Columbia Univ. Press.

Harlan, J. R., and J. M. J. de Wet 1963. The compilospecies concept. Evolution 17 : 497–501.

Heed, W. B. 1963. Density and distribution of *Drosophila polymorpha* and its color alleles in South America. Evolution 17:502–518.

Hutchinson, G. E. 1968. When are species necessary? In Population Biology and Evolution (R. C. Lewontin, ed.), 177–186. Syracuse: Syracuse Univ. Press.

Levin, D. A., and H. W. Kerster 1974. Gene flow in seed plants. Evol. Biol. 7:139–220.

Lotsy, J. P. 1925. Species or Linneon? Genetica 7:487–506.

Lotsy, J. P. 1931. On the species of the taxonomist and its relation to evolution. Genetica 13:1–16.

Margulis, L. 1970. Origin of Eukaryotic Cells. New Haven: Yale Univ. Press.

Martin, R. A. 1970. Line and grade in the extinct *medius* species group of *Sigmodon*. Science 167:1504–1506.

Mayr, E. 1970. Populations, Species, and Evolution. Cambridge: Harvard Univ. Press.

Muller, C. H. 1952. Ecological control of hybridization in *Quercus:* a factor in the mechanism of evolution. Evolution 6:147–161.

Muscatine, L. 1973. Nutrition of corals. In Biology and Geology of Coral Reefs (O. A. Jones and R. Endean, eds.), vol. 2, 77–115. New York: Academic Press.

Muscatine, L. 1974. Endosymbiosis of cnidarians and algae. In Coelenterate Biology (L. Muscatine and H. M. Lenhoff, eds.), 359–395. New York: Academic Press.

Odum, E. P. 1971. Fundamentals of Ecology. 3rd ed. Philadelphia: Saunders.

Owen, B., J. H. McLean, and R. Meyer 1971. Hybridization in the eastern Pacific abalones (*Haliotis*). Bull. Los Angeles Co. Mus. Nat. Hist., Sci., 9:1–37.

Pejler, B. 1956. Introgression in planktonic Rotatoria with some points of view on its causes and conceivable results. Evolution 10:246–261.

Rahn, O. 1929. Contributions to the classification of bacteria. Zentralbl. Bakteriol. Parasitenk. Infektionskrank. (Abt. 2) 78:1–21.

Schwarz, S. S. 1974. Intraspecific variability and species-formation: evolutional and genetical aspects of the problem. Trans. First Int. Theriological Congress 2:136–139.

Seed, R. 1972. Morphological variations in *Mytilus edulis* Linnaeus and *M. galloprovincialis* Lamarck from the coasts of France. Cahiers Biol. Mar. 13:357–384.

Sherr, C. J. and G. J. Todaro 1974. Radioimmunoassay of the major group specific protein of endogenous baboon type C viruses. Virology 61:168–181.

Simpson, G. G. 1953. The Major Features of Evolution. New York: Columbia Univ. Press.

Simpson, G. G. 1961. Principles of Animal Taxonomy. New York: Columbia Univ. Press.

Stebbins, G. L. 1950. Variation and Evolution in Plants. New York: Columbia Univ. Press.

Stebbins, G. L. 1970. Variation and evolution in plants. In Essays in Evolution and Genetics (M. K. Hecht and W. C. Steere, eds.), 173–208. New York: Appleton-Century-Crofts.

Stern, K., and L. Roche 1974. Genetics of Forest Ecosystems. New York: Springer-Verlag.

Todaro, G. J., C. J. Sherr, R. E. Benveniste, M. M. Lieber, and J. L. Melnick 1974. Type C viruses of baboons: isolation from normal cell cultures. Cell 2:55–61.

Van Valen, L. 1966. On discussing human races. Persp. Biol. Med. 9:377–383.

Van Valen, L. 1969. Variation genetics of extinct animals. Amer. Nat. 103:193–224.

Van Valen, L. 1971. Adaptive zones and the orders of mammals. Evolution 25:420–428.

Van Valen, L. 1973. Pattern and the balance of nature. Evol. Theory 1:31–49.

Van Valen, L. 1974. Multivariate structural statistics in natural history. Jour. Theor. Biol. 45:235–247; 48:501.

Zhdanov, V. M., and T. I. Tikchonenko 1974. Viruses as a factor of evolution: exchange of genetic information in the biosphere. Adv. Virus Res. 19:361–394.

Zouros, E. 1974. Genic differentiation associated with the early stages of speciation in the *mulleri* subgroup of *Drosophila*. Evolution 27 (for 1973): 601–621.

Zucker, W. H. 1973. Fine structure of planktonic foraminifera and their endosymbiotic algae. Dissert. Abst. Int. (B) 34:1003.

Chapter 5

The Evolutionary Species Concept Reconsidered

E. O. Wiley

In all probability more paper has been consumed on the questions of the nature and definition of the species than any other subject in evolutionary and systematic biology. In my opinion this is because the species is usually viewed as an essential entity in the evolutionary process. A species, in the phylogenetic sense, may be viewed as the largest aggregate of individual organisms that evolve as a unit. There has been much investigation of the process, but the questions of what a species is and how species originate are far from solution. Sokal (1973) has suggested that there are two major problems, an adequate species definition, and the origin of species. I agree, but the two problems are not separate. The definition of the word species will be built on a species concept and the concept itself will profoundly affect the way in which investigators view the origin of the species they study. As Popper (1968), Eldredge and Gould (1972), and others have pointed out, the concepts and theories an investigator holds influence how that investigator views the "facts" of nature. This is as true for the species concept as it is for the concepts of relativity theory and quantum mechanics. I submit that the conceptual problems of species definitions are no worse than the conceptual problems of many other words in science.

The extensive literature regarding the histories of various species concepts has been reviewed by Mayr (1957, 1963, 1969), Simpson (1961), Dobzhansky (1970), Grant (1971), Sokal (1973), and Sneath and Sokal (1973), among others. An anthology of papers on species concepts has been compiled by Slobodchikoff (1976, see Platnick 1977 for significant omissions). Another historical review is unwarranted and I refer the interested reader to these works and references therein. Instead, I will attempt to resurrect and defend the species concept of Simpson (1961, see also Ghiselin 1969, Grant 1971) as best suited for dealing with the species and its origins.

Any species concept "adopted" in light of current knowledge must, in my opinion, fulfill several roles. (1) It must have as universal validity as current knowledge permits. This would be reflected in its applicability to species through time, to asexual as well as sexual species, to plants as well as to animals. (2) It should make possible the formulation of a hypothesis that a particular group of organisms either comprises a species or does not. The hypothesis must be testable in principle (cf. Hempel 1965). (3) It must subsume within its logical framework all valid special case definitions of species. (4) It must be capable of dealing with species as spatial, temporal, genetic, epigenetic, ecological, physiological, phenetic, and behavioral entities. (5) It must clearly specify what types of species origins are possible and what types are not possible. This final role is essential to the testability in principle of the concept itself, for if the concept permits everything and prohibits nothing, it is scientifically useless (Popper 1968).

Operationalism and Species Concepts

Some biologists (for example, Ehrlich 1961, Sneath and Sokal 1973) have argued that a species definition must be "operational" within the context of the philosophical school of operationalism espoused by Bridgmann (1945) among others. Operationalism has no doubt been beneficial in influencing scientists to clarify their concepts and definitions. However, Hull (1968) has argued that pure operationalism is not possible in science and that species concepts and definitions do not have to conform to operationalist philosophy to be scientific (see also Hempel 1966). In my opinion, operationalism has been found wanting because its "operational" definitions were either circular (Popper 1968) or failed to fulfill their set goal of separating, by definition, the cognitively meaningful from the cognitively meaningless. If "operational" definitions within an operationalist philosophy are flawed in these ways, then there can be little justification for criticizing various species definitions because they are not "operational." Furthermore, there can be little justification for applying pure operationalism to either systematic or evolutionary philosophy. It should be recognized that the critics of "nonoperational" species concepts (cf. Sokal and Crovello 1970, Sneath and Sokal 1973) have themselves been unable to supply an "operational" definition. Perhaps this is because the word "species" is a universal, and universals cannot be defined in an operational manner (Popper 1968).

Definition of the Evolutionary Species Concept

I propose that a simple modification of Simpson's (1961, 153) species definition fulfills the criteria discussed above. *A species is a single lineage of ancestral descendant populations of organisms which maintains its identity from other such lineages and which has its own evolutionary tendencies and historical fate.*[1] This definition implies that (1) species can be thought of as individuals rather than classes (cf. Ghiselin 1966, 1974, see discussion by Hull 1976, and comment by Mayr 1976), and (2) that species are historical, temporal, and spatial entities. The definition is empirical in that it permits hypotheses to be derived from it which can be tested in fact or principle (i.e., the concept of empiricism advocated by Hempel 1965). For example, we may frame the hypothesis, "these two populations (or groups of populations) maintain separate identifiable evolutionary lineages." Evidence used to test such a hypothesis can come from a variety of sources depending on the nature of the organism and the genetic, phenetic, spatial, temporal, ecological, biochemical, and/or behavioral evidence which is available to test the question. Whether a group of organisms is or is not a species then becomes an hypothesis to be tested.

Logical Corollaries of the Definition

Logical corollaries are those statements or implications which follow directly from an axiom, a definition, or a hypothesis. The evolutionary species concept has several logical corollaries which permit its evaluation. I do not suggest that the corollaries outlined below are the only corollaries possible.

Corollary 1   All organisms, past and present, belong to some evolutionary species. This corollary is logically evident from the observation that every organism belongs to a lineage including at least its parents (Vendler 1975). To deny this, one would have to invoke spontaneous generation. Evolutionary species differ from supraspecific taxa in that evolutionary species are lineages or continua whereas higher taxa are groups of separate lineages linked by past continua. Thus, higher taxa are historical constructs whose sole basis for existence is dependent on how accurately they document past continua whereas evolutionary species are the extinct or living continua themselves. In other words, evolutionary species make history, natural higher taxa (monophyletic groups) are history, and unnatural higher taxa (para- and polyphyletic groups) misrepresent history.

In terms of classification, as opposed to pattern and process, all organisms belong to a species, but not all species necessarily belong to a higher taxon such as a family or order (I exclude from this discussion the category genus because our system of nomenclature demands that every species belong to a genus). As Goldschmidt (1940), Schindewolf (1950), Løvtrup (1974) and others have asserted, phylogenetic evolution has proceeded from the apex to the base. Therefore, natural phylogenetic classification must also proceed from the apex to the base if it is to reflect the pattern of evolution.

No genus could have originated before the family in which it belongs originated. By this I do not mean that genera, families, or any other supraspecific taxa evolve. What I mean is that the stem species of a genus cannot originate before the stem species of the family to which that genus is a member. This is a logical corollary of the axiom of continuity of descent and simply a rejection of spontaneous generation. It is logically derived from the assertion that higher taxa originate concurrently with their stem species, i.e., that the family at the time of its origin was composed of a single evolutionary species (Hennig 1966, Wiley 1977, for another point of view see Platnick 1976, 1977). For example, the ancestral species of the gar family Lepisosteidae must have originated before either of the ancestral species of this family's included genera, *Lepisosteus* and *Atractosteus*. On the practical level of reconstructing phylogenies, the synapomorphies of the family Lepisosteidae are hypothesized to have originated before the synapomorphies of the genus *Lepisosteus*. On the theoretical level, when I make such a statement I mean that the characters which I hypothesize as synapomorphic for Lepisosteidae are those characters which are hypothesized to have arisen in the stem species of the family as autapomorphies and passed on to the descendants of that species (the ancestral stem species of *Lepisosteus* and *Atractosteus*). And, the stem species of these genera later developed their own sets of separate autapomorphies which were passed on modified or unmodified to their descendants. I do not wish to imply that any particular set of characters are "family characters" or that another set are "generic characters." The synapomorphies which characterize the stem species of Lepisosteidae do not make this taxon a family, the significance of Lepisosteidae lies in the fact that it is monophyletic and not on its particular categorical rank. When I look at a phylogram I perceive all branches as evolutionary species or higher taxa represented by their evolutionary stem species. Farris (1976) has recently discussed the relationships between categorical rank, taxa, and classification which I think makes these relationships clear and which is compatible with both the above discussion and the evolutionary species concept.

Corollary 2   Separate evolutionary lineages (species) must be reproductively isolated from one another to the extent that this is required for maintaining their separate identities, tendencies, and historical fates. This corollary covers the special case of the biological species definition (Mayr 1963, Dobzhansky 1970). The biological species concept stresses the community gene pool and reproductive isolation. Both are inherent in the evolutionary species concept (as Simpson 1961 concluded). And, in spite of the objections of Sokal and Crovello (1970) and of Ehrlich and Raven (1969), the biological species concept seems a testable special case definition covering the sympatric occurrence of sexually reproducing sister species (species that are each other's closest relatives). Thus, while the biological species concept may be valid it is not inclusive (see Hull 1971 for a detailed criticism of Sokal and Crovello 1970).[2]

Corollary 3   The evolutionary species concept does not demand that there be morphological or phenetic differences between species, nor does it preclude such differences. Therefore, any investigator may under- or over-estimate the true number of evolutionary species at one time plane or through several time planes when he or she bases that number on morphological or phenetic difference. The phenetic species concept (as discussed, if not explicitly defined, by Sneath and Sokal 1973) is a special case of this corollary when phenetic differences do occur between separately evolving lineages. The corollary specifically carries the connotation that real evolutionary lineages exist in nature outside man's ability to perceive these lineages (cf. the attitude taken by Dobzhansky 1970; Huxley 1940; Mayr 1963, 1969; Meglitsch 1954; Ghiselin 1974; but not Darwin 1859, or Gilmour 1940; see Meglitsch 1954 for a critique of Gilmour's attitude). The under- or over-estimation of the actual number of evolutionary species represents the observational error in the systems or methods employed to differentiate species. For example, it is possible that a fossil assemblage includes two sibling species with identical morphology in their preserved characters, but which operated as separate lineages when living. A paleontologist would conclude, on the basis of the evidence at hand, that only one lineage existed. Thus, he would under-estimate the actual number of evolutionary species. The same investigator might interpret a sexually dimorphic species as two species, an overestimation. A neontologist might recognize two evolutionary species as a single species because they hybridize at their zone of sympatry, while a future neontologist might conclude that this documented hybridization represented a sorting out and reinforcement of the two species' identities (Dobzhansky 1970) rather than a swamping of their identities. In practice, as Sokal and Crovello (1970), and others have pointed out, the morphological or phenetic differences between populations will usually determine the number of species recognized. But this does not require investigators to accept a phenetic species definition or a phenetic species concept (see Hull 1971 for discussion of this point). Rather, it requires that an investigator adopt the working hypothesis that sufficient morphological difference combined with geographic distribution are adequate evidence for separate evolutionary lineages. But what is "adequate" evidence? I suggest a clearly stated hypothesis with corroborating instances which are both relevant and parsimonious. What is adequate will change with increased knowledge of organisms studied and experience in dealing with similar problems. If this sounds rather vague, I suggest that no concept or method can guarantee a "correct" solution will follow from it. There is no guard against practicing "bad science" unless "bad" is defined in relation to some authoritarian standard. What is important is that the hypothesis be open to testing.

Corollary 4   No presumed separate, single, evolutionary lineage may be subdivided into a series of ancestral and descendant "species." This corollary is, perhaps, self-evident and would hardly be worth discussing if it were not for the rather common practice among some paleontologists of subdividing a single lineage into a number of "species." Simpson (1961) viewed this practice as necessary for escaping a kind of infinite regression in classification. He said (1961, 165): "If you start at any point in the sequence and follow the line backward through time, there is no point where the definition would cease to apply. You never leave an uninterrupted, separate, unitary lineage and therefore never leave the species with which you started unless some other criterion of definition can be brought in. If the fossil record were complete you could start with man and run back to a protist still in the species *Homo sapiens*. Such classification is manifestly both useless and somehow wrong in principle."

If this were true, then Simpson's definition and the modification presented here would be useless. However, evolution is composed of two geneological processes. One, the continuum, ties all of life together. The other, punctuations of the continuum, produces diversity, when accompanied by differentiation followed by divergence, by providing independence of lineages. As Bonde (1975, 294) has stated: "This continuum is subdivided in a non-arbitrary way by the *speciation process which delimits 'natural' species in the time dimension*." Every punctuation of the continuum followed by divergence results in a single evolutionary lineage being split into two or more evolutionary lineages. There is no doubt that one can run from man to protist in one classificatory taxon, but, in my opinion, that taxon would be Eucaryota, not species *Homo sapiens*. There was a genus *Homo* before there was a species *Homo sapiens*, just as there was a class Vertebrata before any of the Recent vertebrates evolved. Thus, we tie together increasingly ever larger taxa on the basis of the continuum they are hypothesized to have shared in the past, and if we adopt a truly natural classification, this classification will document past continua, not bury their reality or existence.

It is the punctuation of continua which is the first prerequisite that may lead to evolutionary diversity among species at any one time. These punctuations are for the most part what are termed allopatric speciation events (Mayr 1963 for discussion), but there is no conceptual reason to exclude sympatric speciation as a special case. In the case of the allopatric speciation model, one might expect that in most circumstances the ancestral species would become extinct at the time of speciation. This is because it is improbable that either of the two daughter species would have the same identity, role, and historical fate as the ancestral species. Thus, in most cases the methodological necessity of postulating extinction of ancestral species in phylogeny reconstruction as advocated by Hennig (1966) is biologically (as well as methodologically) sound. However, an implication of the evolutionary species concept would seem to be that if the ancestral species can lose one or more constituent populations without losing its historical identity or tendencies, then it can survive such a split. For example, there are herpetologists who recognize phenetically different partheno-genic "clones" of uniparental salamanders and lizards as species (Darevsky 1966, Wright 1967, Uzzell and Barry 1971). Darevksy (1966) recognized four uniparental species of *Lacerta* from the Caucasus and suggested their derivation from *L. saxicola*. The uniparental whiptail lizard *Cnemidophorus opatae* is said by Wright (1967) to be derived from the sexually reproducing species *C. tesselatus*. Does this derivation, probably caused by a fortunate mutation in a single female, require that *C. tesselatus* became extinct at the time this female's first brood hatched? I doubt that the origin of *C. opatae* has any more effect on the identity and evolutionary tendencies of *C. tesselatus* than did the death of any one other member of the population. One might argue that such "clones" are not species but variants of a single species (see Zweifel 1965). Yet, they do represent independent lineages (albeit perhaps of short duration) and thus do correspond to evolutionary species. Another example is the origin of a plant species by hybridization and subsequent polyploidy. This speciation mechanism would seem to have little effect on either parental species (except the waste of some ova and pollen) unless the hybrid successfully outcompeted its parents and caused their extinction, which would be possible only if the parental species survived the actual origin of the hybrid. It might even be reasonable to postulate that the allopatric separation of a peripheral isolate of a large population could occur without initially affecting that large population. The survival of the same species through more than a few of these "buds," however, would appear unlikely because it is unlikely that any one species could stand the loss of geographically or ecologically unique gene combinations without its role and tendencies being changed. The problem of determining the survival of a particular ancestral species in this situation is the practical testability of the situation. Engelmann and Wiley (1977) have argued that ancestor identification based on morphological or stratigraphic evidence is invalid. If so, it may not be possible at present to separate out those cases where peripheral budding results in extinction of the ancestral species from those cases where it does not. The point I would like to make is that both concepts are compatible whether or not we have the method-ological tools to discriminate between them at the present time.

Asexual Species and Allopatric Demes

Asexual species have been the bane of all proposed species definitions that are not overtly typological. Dobzhansky (1970) has termed the asexual species a pseudospecies. Yet, asexually reproducing lineages have existed and do exist. Phenetic taxonomists have, with justification, pointed to the difficulties of applying various biological species concepts to asexual species. Mayr (1963) concluded that his biological species definition was restricted to sexually reproducing species. Simpson (1961) suggested the evolutionary species concept covered asexual species. I suggest that asexual species can be accounted for under the evolutionary species concept in the same way we place allopatric demes into a single sexually reproducing species. We may ask, "why are the Siberian and North American populations of wolverines considered the same species?" (Kurtén and Rausch 1959). One might answer that we *assume* they would interbreed *if* they were brought into contact. This answer is impossible to evaluate because it assumes some future event. Anything could happen, but only what does happen can be used to corroborate a hypothesis. While such a statement might be considered a prediction, it cannot be used to justify the deduction. One might argue that there must be migration which keeps the populations from diverging morphologically. There is no evidence at hand for this, just the a priori assumption that they *must* diverge unless some other factor (such as migration) is present. I suggest that Siberian and North American wolverines are considered the same species because we have no corroborating evidence that they have reached a point of divergence where we can deduce that they are following separate evolutionary pathways. It is possible that 1,000 or 10,000 years from now an investigator will see differences and conclude that wolverines are following two independent evolutionary paths. It is possible that wolverines are already differentiated but we have examined the wrong characters for detecting that differentiation. I would suggest that whether wolverines are now differentiated or will differentiate in the future, the decisive factor in this process will be the geographic event which separated them and thus set up their potential independence. But at this time we have no corroboration that this particular geographic event will lead to separate evolutionary paths and thus we have no reason to recognize two evolutionary species. Meglitsch (1954) and Simpson (1961) argued that an evolutionary species definition can be applied to asexual organisms because the populations have retained the capacity to evolve as a unit if artificial (not man-made) barriers are removed, implying the assumption that uniparental lines are derived from biparental lines (Dougherty 1955, Pontecorvo 1956, Stebbins 1960). Perhaps so, but like potential interbreeding, this calls for evidence not at hand. My reasoning above would also apply to predominantly asexually reproducing species. It is not the evolution of asexual reproduction which "permits" us to consider genetically separate clones as a single species, but their lack of significant evolutionary divergence. Any species composed of allopatric demes or asexual clones has the potential for splitting into two or more separate independent evolutionary species, but it does not follow that any significant divergence *must* occur. Lack of differentiation is as valid a historical fate as differentiation and it may have real genetic, epigenetic, ecological, or other bases. We may hypothesize a lack of differentiation even if we cannot distinguish between truly undifferentiated populations and differentiated lineages whose nature has gone undetected. Failure to distinguish between the two represents an inadequacy of our systems of observation and method and not the inadequacy of the concept. In other words, we are faced with the same type I and type II errors that plague all systems of hypothesis testing, the chances of rejecting a true hypothesis and the chances of accepting a false hypothesis.

Ecology and the Evolutionary Species

Van Valen (1976, 233) recently offered a modification of Simpson's (1961) species definition: "A species is a lineage (or closely related set of lineages) which occupies an adaptive zone minimally different from that of any other lineage in its range and which evolves separately from all lineages outside its range."

Although there is much in this definition and Van Valen's subsequent discussion that I can agree with, the definition has certain logical difficulties. Any species is a component of its environment and must be at least minimally adapted to the biotic and abiotic factors of that environment if it is to survive. Species cannot be divorced from their environment any more than they can be divorced from their gene pools or their morphologies. But, species do not have to occupy minimally different niches or adaptive zones from other species within their ranges to be considered species.[3] It is possible for two species to share essentially the same niche within the same range. In the case where resources are not limiting, two such species could coexist. In the case where resources are limiting, one of the species could replace the other through interspecific competition from that portion of the range where they are sympatric, or, entirely via extinction. Indeed, *if* interspecific competition causes at least some extinctions, it can work only where the niches of the competing species are similar enough for competition to occur or where one species' niche completely overlaps the other's (MacArthur and Levins 1967).

This definition, applied to *successful* species, could be considered another special case definition of the evolutionary species concept as defined above. But, given the original definition of Van Valen (1976) one might argue that a species forced to extinction through interspecific competition was not a species at all. Interestingly, Pitelka (1951) presents exactly this argument in considering a hypothetical scenario involving blue jay evolution. Given the hypothetical situation where the Florida scrub jay and the Texas jay were

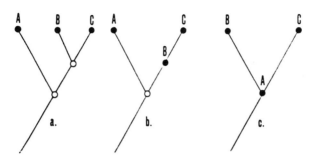

Figure 5.1
(a) One of four possible aspect-B statements of the phylogenetic relationships between species A, B, and C. (b) An aspect-A statement with "species" B considered the direct ancestor of "species" C. (c) An aspect-A statement with species A considered the ancestor of species B and C.

physiologically incapable of interbreeding, could the Florida jay be considered a species if it should fail to survive when it meets its ecological equivalent and sister species, the Texas jay? (Pitelka 1951, 379). Pitelka suggested that if the Florida scrub jay were eliminated, then it should not be considered a separate species, in spite of reproductive isolation, because the two jays are ecological equivalents. I would suggest that the elimination of one sister group by another through competition (and not swamping of the gene pool) is corroboration of separate lineages and therefore corroboration of separate species rather than the reverse. Both Van Valen's and Pitelka's discussions have merit, but it is my opinion that such concepts lead to an underestimation of the rates of extinction due to interspecific competition.

The Evolutionary Species and Phylogeny Reconstruction

Engelmann and Wiley (1977) argued that ancestor-descendant hypotheses based on morphological or stratigraphic evidence were unscientific because they could never be corroborated or refuted by valid tests. We addressed our discussions largely to alternate hypotheses such as those shown in figures 5.1a and 5.1b. Figure 5.1a represents what Nelson (1973) terms an aspect-B phylogeny in which only cladistic relationships are expressed and ancestral species remain hypothetical. Figure 5.1b represents Nelson's (1973) aspect-A phylogenetic hypothesis in which, for this example, species B is hypothesized the direct ancestor of species C. If an investigator adopts the evolutionary species concept, then figure 5.1b is logically impossible because "species" B and "species" C are part of the same unitary evolutionary lineage and thus B belongs to the same species as C. Thus, the problem collapses into a two-taxon problem whose relationships are already resolved since A must be the sister species of BC given no other taxa. Of course, population B could be considered ancestral to population C, given that BC is an evolutionary species, since it is a logical deduction that some individuals (sampled or unsampled) from population B are the populational ancestors of all of the individuals of population C (see Engelmann and Wiley 1977, 2 for a discussion of population ancestors).[4] I would conclude that much of the discussion we presented was directed toward a problem which does not exist under the evolutionary species concept and which we would not have discussed in the manner we did if we had adopted this concept. However, I would maintain that our analysis of the problem is applicable in cases where it is postulated that one species gave rise to two or more daughter species and itself became extinct (figure 5.1c). I would also submit that in a situation where an ancestral species is evolving phyletically (anagenic evolution) so that the autapomorphies which it will leave to its descendants as synapomorphies are fixed over a period of time, then the problem, on a morphological level, will never be resolved. This is because when the ancestor splits from its own ancestor it will presumably have few, if any, of the derived characters which will be fixed in its own populations at a later time (or times) and left to its descendants when it speciates and becomes extinct. Thus on a morphological level the analysis might result in a species being the primitive sister group of its descendants, plus the ancestor of its descendants, plus the third taxon in a trichotomy with its descendants depending on the rate of phyletic change and the number of samples from various stratigraphic levels available to the investigator. This is because at various times the ancestor might have none, part, or all of the shared derived characters of its descendants. Thus, even if we could identify one part of the lineage as the actual "ancestor," earlier parts of the same species would not be identifiable as the ancestor in question. Finally, with regard to stratigraphic criteria, if the ancestor can survive the split which produced one or more descendant species, then stratigraphic criteria cannot serve to falsify or corroborate an ancestor descendant hypothesis on the species level, since it is conceivable that an ancestor could postdate its descendants in the fossil record. But, if the ancestor cannot be established on morphological grounds, then perhaps that question is moot.

Acknowledgments

Earlier drafts of this paper were read by numerous reviewers whose comments are greatly appreciated. These include Drs. Richard Johnston, Robert Hoffmann, and Norman Slade and Messrs. Randall Moss, Gregory Pregill, and David Wiseman (University of Kansas); Drs. George Engelmann, Eugene Gaffney, Norman Platnick, Donn Rosen, and Bobb Schaeffer (American Museum of Natural History); and Dr. Michael Ghiselin (University of California at Berkeley). My special thanks to Dr. David Hull (Univ. of Wisconsin-Milwaukee) and Dr.

James S. Farris (State Univ. of New York, Stony Brook) for their extensive and penetrating comments which greatly strengthened the final draft. Ms. Debora Bennett prepared the figure. The conclusions drawn, and any mistakes in logic made, are my own responsibility.

Notes

1. Simpson's definition states: "*An evolutionary species is a lineage (an ancestral-descendant sequence of populations) evolving separately from others and with its own unitary evolutionary role and tendencies.*" Both definitions stress unity (as does Ghiselin's 1974) and both imply that the species is the most inclusive unit of evolution. My definition has the advantage of not implying that species must change (evolve). If species go through a rapid (or even saltatory) phase of evolutionary change and then settle down to a longer period of relative stasis (cf. Eldredge and Gould 1972), then "evolving" is not to be preferred over "maintaining identity" as species may maintain their identity relative to other species with or without changing. "Identity" as used here connotes individual identity and does not connote either stasis or change in morphology. As an analogy: I have maintained my own identity through the years in spite of the fact that my morphology has changed substantially from age 6 to present (also see Vendler 1975, for other discussions of individuality).
2. Rosen (1978, 1979, and pers. comm.) has argued that the biological species concept is simply invalid from the point of view of taxonomy and geographic analysis of monophyletic groups of taxa. This is because its premises are designed to sacrifice evidence of cladistic relationships in favor of real or imagined data on reproductive isolation when the two conflict. If so, one might ask if the concept should be used at all, at least by taxonomists and biogeographers.
3. I recognize that the term "adaptive zone" as used by Van Valen (1976) is not the exact equivalent to "niche," but the distinction is irrelevant to this discussion.
4. Of course it is impossible to verify (in the absolute sense) that B is a sample of the ancestral continuum leading to C. But this is, again, a fault of our system of observations and is common to all observational sciences. It is analogous to the wolverine problem and to the problem of "verifying" that similar features are homologous. One could corroborate the hypothesis by showing that a series of intermediate samples between B and C formed a statistically insignificant continuum (as a whole) and could refute the hypothesis by showing the opposite.

References

Bonde, N. 1975. Origin of "higher groups": view-points of phylogenetic systematics. Problèmes actuels de paléontologie—évolution des vertébrés. Coll. Internat. C.N.R.S., no. 218:293–324.

Bridgmann, P. W. 1945. Some general principles of operational analysis. Psychological Rev. 52:246–249.

Darevsky, I. S. 1966. Natural parthenogenesis in a polymorphic group of Caucasian rock lizards related to *Lacerta saxicola* Eversmann. J. Ohio Herpet. Soc. 5:115–152.

Darwin, C. 1859. On the origin of species by means of natural selection, or the preservation of favoured races in the struggle for life. John Murray, London.

Dobzhansky, T. 1970. Genetics of the evolutionary process. Columbia University Press, New York.

Dougherty, E. C. 1959. The origin of sexuality. Syst. Zool. 4:145–169.

Ehrlich, P. 1961. Has the biological species concept outlived its usefulness? Syst. Zool. 10:167–176.

Ehrlich, P. and P. H. Raven, 1969. Differentiation of populations. Science 165:1228–1231.

Eldredge, N., and S. J. Gould, 1972. Punctuated equilibria: an alternative to phyletic gradualism. In Schopf, T. J. M. (ed.), Models in paleontology, Freeman, Cooper, and Co., San Francisco, pp. 82–115.

Engelmann, G. F., and E. O. Wiley, 1977. The place of ancestor-descendant relationships in phylogeny reconstruction. Syst. Zool. 26:1–11.

Farris, J. S. 1976. Phylogenetic classification of fossils with recent species. Syst. Zool. 25:271–282.

Ghiselin, M. T. 1966. On psychologism in the logic of taxonomic controversies. Syst. Zool. 15:207–215.

Ghiselin, M. T. 1969. The triumph of the Darwinian method. University of California Press, Berkeley.

Ghiselin, M. T. 1974. A radical solution to the species problem. Syst. Zool. 23:536–544.

Gilmour, J. S. L. 1940. Taxonomy and philosophy. In Huxley, J. S. (ed.), The new systematics. Clarendon Press, London, pp. 461–468.

Goldschmidt, R. 1940. The material basis of evolution. Yale University Press, New Haven.

Grant, V. 1971. Plant speciation. Columbia University Press, New York.

Hempel, C. G. 1965. Aspects of scientific explanation and other essays in the philosophy of science. The Free Press, New York.

Hempel, C. G. 1966. Philosophy of natural science. Prentice-Hall, Inc., Englewood Cliffs, New Jersey.

Hennig, W. 1966. Phylogenetic systematics. University of Illinois Press, Urbana.

Hull, D. L. 1968. The operational imperative—sense and nonsense in operationalism. Syst. Zool. 17:438–457.

Hull, D. L. 1971. Contemporary systematic philosophies. Ann. Rev. Ecol. Syst. 1:19–54.

Hull, D. L. 1976. Are species really individuals? Syst. Zool. 25:174–191.

Huxley, J. S. 1940. Towards the new systematics. In Huxley, J. S. (ed.), The new systematics. Clarendon Press, London, pp. 1–46.

Kurten, B., and R. Rausch. 1959. Biometric comparisons between North American and European mammals. Acta Arctica, Fasc. IX E. Munksqaard, Copenhagen, pp. 1–44.

Løvtrup, S. 1974. Epigenetics, a treatise in theoretical biology. John Wiley and Sons, New York.

MacArthur, R. H., and R. Levins. 1967. The limiting similarity of convergence and divergence of coexisting species. Amer. Nat. 101:377–385.

Mayr, E. 1957. Species concepts and definitions. In Mayr, E. (ed.), The species problem. Amer. Assoc. Adv. Sci. Publ. 50:1–22.

Mayr, E. 1963. Animal species and evolution. Harvard University Press, Cambridge.

Mayr, E. 1969. Principles of systematic zoology. McGraw-Hill, New York.

Mayr, E. 1976. Is the species a class or an individual? Syst. Zool. 25:192.

Meglitsch, P. A. 1954, On the nature of the species. Syst. Zool. 3:49–65.

Nelson, G. J. 1973. Classification as an expression of phylogenetic relationships. Syst. Zool. 22:344–359.

Pitelka, F. A. 1951. Speciation and ecological distribution in American jays of the genus Aphelocoma. Univ. California Publ. Zool. 50:195–464.

Platnick, N. I. 1976. Are monotypic genera possible? Syst. Zool. 25:198–199.

Platnick, N. I. 1977. Monophyly and the origin of higher taxa: a reply to E. O. Wiley. Syst. Zool. 26:355–357.

Pontecorvo, G. 1958. Present trends in genetic analysis. Columbia University Press, New York.

Popper, K. R. 1968. The logic of scientific discovery. Harper Torch Books, New York.

Rosen, D. E. (1978). Vicariant patterns and historical explanation in biogeography. Syst. Zool. 27:159−188.

Rosen, D. E. (1979). Fishes from the uplands and intermontane basins of Guatemala. Bull. Amer. Mus. Nat. Hist. 162:267−376.

Schindewolf, O. H. 1950. Grundfragen der paläontologie. Schweizerbart'sche Verlagbuchhandlung, Stuttgart.

Simpson, G. C. 1961. Principles of animal taxonomy. Columbia University Press, New York.

Slobodchikoff, C. N. (ed.). 1976. Concepts of species. University of California Press, Berkeley.

Sneath, P. H. A., and R. R. Sokal. 1973. Numerical taxonomy. W. H. Freeman, San Francisco.

Sokal, R. R. 1973. The species problem reconsidered. Syst. Zool. 22:360−374.

Sokal, R. R., and T. J. Crovello. 1970. The biological species concept: a critical evaluation. Amer. Nat. 104:127−153.

Stebbins, R. C. 1960. The comparative evolution of genetic systems. In Tax, S. (ed.), The evolution of life. University of Chicago Press, Chicago, pp. 197−226.

Uzzell, T., and J. C. Barry. 1971. Leposoma percarinatum, a unisexual species related to L. quianense; and Leposoma ioanna, a new species from Pacific Coastal Colombia (Sauria: Teiidae.). Postilla 154:39 pp.

Van Valen, L. 1976. Ecological species, multispecies, and oaks. Taxon 25:233−239.

Vendler, Z. 1975. Possibility of possible worlds. Canadian J. Phil. 5:57−72.

Wiley, E. O. 1977. Are monotypic genera paraphyletic? A reply to Norman Platnick. Syst. Zool. 26:352−355.

Wright, J. W. 1967. A new uniparental whiptail lizard (Genus Cnemidophorus) from Sonora, Mexico. Arizona Acad. Sci. 4:185−193.

Zweifel, R. G. 1965. Variation in and distribution of the unisexual lizard Cnemidophorus tesselatus. Amer. Mus. Novitates 2235:49 pp.

Chapter 6

Species Concepts and Speciation Analysis

Joel Cracraft

Systematic biologists have directed much attention to species concepts because they realize that the origin of taxonomic diversity is the fundamental problem of evolutionary biology. Questions such as, what are the units of evolution and how do these units originate thus continually capture the attention of many. It is probably no exaggeration to say that most believe the "systematic" aspects of the problem have been solved to a greater or lesser extent, whereas the task before us now is to understand the "genetic" and "ecologic" components of differentiation, i.e., those aspects often perceived to constitute the "real mechanisms" of speciation:

> A study of speciation is, to a considerable extent, a study of the genetics and evolution of reproductive isolating mechanisms (Bush 1975, 339).
>
> ... a new mechanistic taxonomy of speciation is needed before population genetics, which deals with evolutionary mechanisms, can be properly integrated with speciation theory; that is, the various modes of speciation should be characterized according to the various forces and genetic mechanisms that underly [sic] the evolution of isolating barriers (Templeton 1980, 720).

Thus, in terms of the systematic component of speciation, it is now widely accepted, especially within vertebrate zoology, that the units of evolution are "biological" species, characterized by their *reproductive discontinuity* from other such units, and that their origins can be analyzed in terms of their geographic pattern (see summaries in Mayr 1963, Bush 1975). Ornithologists have contributed substantially to the development of this view. One only has to invoke the pivotal contributions of Stresemann, Rensch, Mayr, Miller, and others to appreciate the impact of ornithological systematics on questions of species concepts and speciation analysis.

The interests of classification theory and those of systematic analysis have long been viewed as being in conflict with each other (Selander 1971, 99), with "species" as classificatory units functioning in ways different from "species" as units of evolution. In fact, because these two conceptions of "species" often do not correspond, and this can be shown to be true in ornithology as well, it can be argued that the functions of both are being compromised. The problem, Selander (1971, 99) believes, is that "our typologically based system of nomenclature cannot adequately deal with speciation phenomena...." But is the "typologically based system of nomenclature" the real problem? I suggest the answer is no, the problem lies elsewhere. Indeed, the problem can be posed as the mirror image of that identified by Selander. Our classificatory system is reasonably capable of dealing with the results of speciation, i.e., the hierarchical arrangement of taxic interrelationships; rather, it is speciation analysis which is incapable of accomodating the prevailing concept of species that is being forced upon it. In particular, the idiosyncratic nature of the polytypic species concept and the *definition* of species as *discontinuous reproductive units* rather than as *phylogenetic units* prevents an adequate assessment of the patterns and processes of speciation.

Speciation can be viewed as the phylogenetic deployment of differentiated taxonomic units through space and time. If reproductive discontinuity does not precisely correlate with this deployment, then any definition of these taxonomic units solely in terms of that discontinuity will logically result in phylogenetic history (speciation) being reconstructed incompletely, at best, or incorrectly, at worst. There is abundant evidence, of course, that the pattern of reproductive disjunction among taxa does not necessarily correlate with the history of their differentiation (see especially Rosen 1979), yet the implications of this have not been fully appreciated by many workers interested in the broad area of speciation analysis. Moreover, allegiance to the polytypic-biological species concept hinders our understanding of speciation by focusing attention on unproductive problems (Is taxon X a species or a subspecies? How much genetic change must occur before a new species is formed? are two examples).

In this chapter, I first want to explore concepts of species. Unlike many previous discussions, I will be less concerned with definitions than with the analytical consequences of these definitions. I subscribe to the view that definitions within science are only meaningful to the extent that they can lead to growth in knowledge (Popper 1959, 1972), and thus my criterion of judgment is whether a particular species concept facilitates our understanding of the history of taxonomic diversification. Following this, I want to consider the research strategy we might adopt in developing hypotheses about the phylogenetic differentiation of taxa. The emphasis, therefore, is placed on how we might reconstruct the *pattern* of taxonomic diversification. The discussion focuses almost entirely on the literature of avian systematics, and I will suggest that pattern analysis has unfortunately been neglected by many previous workers. Because of this, ornithologists understand the history of avian diversification much less than heretofore realized.

Species Concepts

The "Biological Species" Concept
The polytypic-biological species concept (hereafter, BSC), as summarized by Mayr (1942, 1948, 1957a, 1957b, 1963, 1969), is without question the dominant view of species within ornithology. Indeed, it would be difficult to find any serious opposition to its acceptance, at least in principle, within the ornithological community.

According to this conception, species are defined as "groups of inter-breeding natural populations that are reproductively isolated from other such groups" (Mayr 1969, 26). If two or more groups are sympatric or parapatric, the presence or absence of reproductive isolation can usually be determined unambiguously. If groups are allopatric, on the other hand, then biological data must be evaluated in terms of whether it is thought individuals of these populations could interbreed were they to come into contact. Within the framework of the BSC, data on the extent of hybridization between populations are critical in determining their taxonomic status as species (Sibley 1957, Mayr 1969, Short, 1969).

Polytypic species include allopatric populations (often designated sub-species) assumed to be capable of interbreeding. It is important to realize that the polytypic species concept arose (Kleinschmidt 1900, Stresemann 1936, Mayr 1942, 110−113), not only to facilitate our understanding of taxonomic differentiation, but also as an attempt to come to grips with a classificatory problem, namely the propensity of many nineteenth century systematists to apply species names to every variation within local populations. Faced literally with many thousands of species names, the classificatory problems appeared real indeed, and a reaction against this situation developed. Yet, it is instructive to remember that classificatory "convenience" remains a major justification for the polytypic species concept (Mayr 1969, 38).

There is a tendency for those in vertebrate systematics to assume that the BSC is widely accepted and applied within biology. Speaking of the "morphological" species concept, Mayr (1963, 16−17), for example, remarks that "In recent years most systematists have found this typological-morphological concept inadequate and have rejected it... Where the taxonomist applies morphological criteria, he uses them as secondary indications of reproductive isolation." Many biologists consider this assessment to be false, for not only have the vast majority of plant systematists ignored or rejected the BSC, but most zoological systematists probably have done likewise, at least when dealing with the practical problems of describing the earth's biota. The list of the critics of the BSC is long (see summaries by Ehrlich 1961, Sokal and Crovello 1970, Raven 1970, Rosen 1978, Cronquist 1978, Levin 1979, Paterson 1981), and it is fair to say that their criticisms have not been answered satisfactorily. Importantly, the basis for this criticism does not lie entirely with the problem of classifying the taxonomic units of nature; in fact, the rejection of the BSC stems primarily from the realization that it does not function well in helping us to understand the pattern and process of taxonomic differentiation. If species are defined strictly in terms of known or presumed reproductive disjunction, these workers point out, then it compels biologists to consider the origin of reproductive isolation as the major problem of taxonomic differentiation, and such is not the case. A solution to the "species problem" does not lie, however, in adopting many different kinds of "species" (Scudder 1974), for to do so would be to abandon the search for general patterns of biotic diversification.

Are Biological Species the Units of Evolution?
Scientific theories direct attention to the relationships and interactions among things, or entities, thought to have an ontological status in nature. Theories themselves sometimes impart or predict the expectation of reality to things not known to exist. One only has to recall the predictions of particle physics or astronomy to appreciate this. Likewise, theories of evolution are theories about the descent and modification of entities. Biologists have traditionally called these entities "species," but it is essential to remember that the term "species" has been used in many different ways. Moreover, it is widely recognized that taxonomic species as such have not always been accepted as the "units of evolution" by many biologists. Indeed, these "units" have been postulated to be genes, gametes, individual organisms, local demes, populations, varieties, subspecies, "biological species," and even higher taxa (Lewontin 1970, Hull 1980). If this vast nomenclature signifies anything, perhaps it is the diversity of opinion that exists about the nature of the evolutionary process itself, for conceptions or theories about how nature is organized and has developed do influence opinions about the ontological status of the evolving entities. All of this is by way of introduction to the question of whether "biological species" (as in the BSC) can be defended as the "units of evolution."

Although it might be generally admitted that the BSC arose primarily as a classificatory concept its contemporary role in evolutionary analysis developed later (Mayr 1942, 1963, 1970; Cain 1954). "Biological species" are viewed by many biologists (in particular Mayr 1963, 1982) as the units of evolution, but this naturally implies that the origin of reproductive isolation is the most important component of taxonomic diversification. If, however, reproductive isolation is not the central issue of taxonomic differentiation, then logically a species concept based on isolation may not be necessary or desirable for systematic and evolutionary analysis. This would not imply, of course, that the phenomenon of reproductive isolation is uninteresting or lacking in general significance, only that its role in the description and explanation of patterns of evolutionary diversification has been exaggerated or misinterpreted.

A common theme runs through discussions of species concepts and speciation analysis, namely that the origin of taxa involves the differentiation of groups of individual organisms. The systematic status of these groups depends upon this differentiation first and foremost, and only secondarily upon the observation that individuals of each group interbreed with one another. Thus, it is the possession of unique phenotypes that permits us to recognize taxonomic units (Platnick 1977; Rosen 1978, 1979). Naturally, characters diagnostic of these differentiated units do not have to be morphological, but can include any intrinsic attribute, whether biochemical, physiological, or behavioral (in this sense, then, *a broad concept of "phenotype" is adopted throughout this paper*). Importantly, it is these intrinsic attributes of taxa that prevent interbreeding with other taxa, no matter how much they might generally resemble one another. All basic taxa (call them species) of birds, for example, can be distinguished from their close relatives by intrinsic characters alone, and I do not know of a single example in which data on reproductive cohesion or disjunction are the sole factors establishing taxonomic limits. Indeed, even with sibling species, phenotypic differences of some kind, e.g., behavioral or biochemical, are always the primary data that lead to their recognition as distinct taxa.

Given an isolated population that has evolved one or more apomorphous (derived) characters, most biologists would call it a "unit of evolution," in that the primary characteristic of evolution, i.e., the origin of a new taxon and the evolutionary modification of primitive characters, is satisfied. Following this line of thought, can this new taxon be equated with a "biological species" as conceived by advocates of the BSC? It might be, but avian systematics is replete with examples in which such taxa are not considered to be 'biological species," and as was mentioned earlier, the BSC arose as a methodological construct specifically designed under some circumstances to reject many of these differentiated taxa as "species." If so, then clearly many evolutionary taxonomic units would not be "biological species" to advocates of the BSC. Conversely, designated "biological species" (1) may be equivalent to a single evolutionary taxonomic unit, (2) may comprise two to many such taxonomic units, or (3) may contain a collection of evolutionary taxonomic units that, for one reason or the other, does not comprise a (strictly) monophyletic assemblage of related forms. Such a potpourri of possibilities is an inevitable outcome of the BSC itself and of the methodology recommended to identify "biological species" (see Mayr 1942, 1963, 1969). "Biological species" are, by and large, identified purely on a subjective assessment of phenotypic (usually morphological) distinctness (Sokal and Crovello 1970; Rosen 1978, 1979). If allopatric populations are not considered "sufficiently" distinct, they are lumped in the same polytypic species. If one or more of these populations are viewed as being distinct "enough," they are assigned to their own "biological species." In this manner, then, the BSC becomes a servant to classificatory philosophy (particularly that advocated by evolutionary systematists), rather than an instrument to analyze the pattern and process of taxonomic differentiation.

One might conclude from the foregoing that "biological species" are equivalent to the "units of evolution" only in cases in which they are monotypic. In the North American avifauna, approximately 59% of the "species" are monotypic (Mayr and Short 1970, 96), and according to Keast (1961, 393) about 44% of the Australian "species" are monotypic. But what about the polytypic species of these faunas? In actuality, both studies demonstrate that a substantial number of differentiated evolutionary units go unrecognized when "biological species" are accepted as the basis for systematic analyses of this kind. A polytypic "biological species" cannot logically constitute the lowest level taxonomic "unit of evolution" because these "species" may be composed of a variable number of evolutionary units, each possessing their own geographic, phenotypic, and (presumably) genetic integrity.

Differentiated taxonomic units as recognized by the methods of systematics constitute our only evidence about the kinds of evolutionary entities that exist in nature. At any one time, of course, our hypotheses may overestimate or underestimate their numbers. Nevertheless, comparative evolutionary analysis will be impossible without some general agreement among biologists over which taxonomic unit is to be considered equivalent to the "unit of evolution." In fact, biologists have traditionally adopted the concept of "species" as fulfilling that role. Because the BSC fails to designate the numbers of differentiated taxonomic units correctly, evolutionary analysis based on the BSC will inevitably lead to incorrect conclusions about evolutionary history. If the BSC is to be maintained, its defense will have to be based solely on an argument about taxonomic "convenience," i.e., its original rationale and an argument already rejected by many systematists, rather than on one about its efficacy for evolutionary analysis.

A Proposed Species Concept for Ornithology
This section will pursue the problem of formulating a species concept with widespread applicability within biology, including ornithology. Such a concept should be compatible with the two primary aims of systematic biology, namely the taxonomic recognition, description, and historical analysis of all potential evolutionary units, and then the expression of this information within the context of Linnaean hierarchical classifications.

Clearly, the BSC does neither entirely satisfactorily. As noted previously, "biological species" often do not represent evolutionary units, and as will be discussed shortly, assumptions underlying the identification and taxonomic ranking of "biological species" have the potential to obscure the analysis of taxonomic diversification when those "species' are then used as the elements of classification or as units of evolution.

Taxonomy: traditional methodology and its problems   Once differentiated taxonomic units have been recognized, a systematist is faced with the question of how to treat them within a Linnaean classification scheme, and, furthermore, how to interpret the pattern of differentiation historically. Traditional solutions to the former question will be considered here, and the latter will be postponed until the next section.

Our discussion can depart from three observations: (1) in terms of the formal rules of naming taxa, the International Code of Zoological Nomenclature recognizes only two categorical ranks, species and subspecies, which might be used when discussing speciation analysis, (2) there is no general agreement among avian systematists over whether species (of whatever kind) or subspecies are "units of evolution," and (3) in modern systematic practice, the distinction between species and subspecies ranking is almost always based on some subjective measure of the degree of phenotypic (in the broad sense) differentiation.

Traditionally, speciation analysis within ornithology has focused on a detailed description of geographic variation and its correlation with available knowledge about geography and climate, both of the present and in the past (Vuilleumier 1980). Many studies have elaborated the complexities of spatial variation in birds, and nearly all workers have confronted the difficulty of expressing these patterns of variation within the framework of conventional Linnaean classification. Because the International Code of Zoological Nomenclature recognizes only taxa of specific and subspecific rank, workers have typically found two taxonomic levels inadequate in actual systematic practice. Further complicating matters are not only different philosophies about what species and subspecies should mean but also how taxonomic rank should be assigned. Until recently a prevailing attitude has been that *somehow* all geographic variation must be expressed within classifications, and this has led to many taxa (especially subspecies) being defined arbitrarily. This may be one of the contributing factors to the decline in the perceived importance of the subspecies over the last several decades (see especially Wilson and Brown 1953). As Mayr notes:

> The taxonomist is an orderly person whose task it is to assign every specimen to definite category (or museum drawer!). This necessary process of pigeonholing has led to the erroneous belief among non-

taxonomists that subspecies are clear-cut units ... Such situations exist occasionally .... But subspecies intergrade almost unnoticeably in nearly all cases in which there is distributional continuity (Mayr 1942, 106).

Two systematic practices, therefore, have been particularly fundamental in shaping current attitudes toward the analysis of taxonomic differentiation. One is the long-standing ambivalence over the ontological status of subspecies. Are they merely subjective partitions of continuous variability, i.e., a taxonomic convenience, or do they represent real units of evolution? Logically, they cannot be both. For those viewing subspecies as units of evolution, i.e., as incipient species, there is an inclination to consider them as discrete taxa. But if subspecies are envisioned as mere tools of the descriptive taxonomist without any necessary connection to speciation, then they can become convenient, often arbitrary, designations of perceived patterns of variation. Because of the bewildering array of patterns of variation found in birds, it is not unusual to see systematists adopting both views.

The most influential book on speciation analysis was certainly Mayr's *Systematics and the Origin of Species* (1942). At one point he clearly assigns evolutionary status to subspecies:

Geographic speciation is thinkable only, if subspecies are incipient species. This, of course, does not mean that every subspecies will eventually develop into a good species. Far from it! All this statement implies is that every species that developed through geographic speciation had to pass through the subspecies stage (p. 155).

That there is an evolutionary continuum, expressed in terms of taxonomic rank, from isolated population to subspecies to species, and then to genus, is a reflection of Mayr's transformationist view of taxonomic differentiation (and his classificatory philosophy; see below); evolution generally tends to be slow and gradual (Mayr 1940, 1942, 159 *et seq.*; Mayr 1963, 24; see also below). Yet this attitude also permits the acceptance of subspecies as being entirely subjective:

Every subspecies that was ever carefully analyzed was found to be composed of a number of genetically, i.e., phenotypically, distinct populations. It is, in many cases, entirely dependent upon the judgment of the individual taxonomist how many of these populations are to be included in one subspecies. The limits of most subspecies are therefore subjective ... (Mayr 1942, 106).

In his later writings, Mayr's attitude toward the meaning of subspecies seems to harden, and they become taxonomic conveniences rather than a means to investigate taxonomic differentiation:

> The difficulties of the subspecies concept are intensified by persistent attempts to consider the subspecies not merely as a practical device of the taxonomist, but also as a "unit of evolution" ... the subspecies, which conceals so much of the inter- and intrapopulational variability, is an altogether unsuitable category for evolutionary discussions: the subspecies as such is not one of the units of evolution (1963, 347–348; see also 349).
>
> The primary use of subspecies is as a sorting device in collections, that is, as an index to populations that differ from each other "taxonomically" (1982, 595).

Opinions among other ornithologists also vary widely, and although some agree with Mayr that subspecies are primarily taxonomic conveniences, most recent commentary suggests a growing desire to see the subspecies concept applied to discrete taxonomic entities having status as evolutionary units (Gill 1982, Barrowclough 1982, Lanyon 1982, Johnson 1982, Zusi 1982, Monroe 1982, O'Neill 1982). Sympathy for subspecies as pigeon-holing devices seems to be waning.

The second major factor influencing speciation analysis is the practice of ranking geographic isolates according to their degree of differentiation. Evolution is thus taken to be relatively gradual, with the degree of differentiation paralleling the age of the taxon (Mayr 1942, 158–167, 173–176, 218–219; Mayr and Phelps 1967, 290). Ranking of these isolates is determined solely by a subjective assessment of the degree of differentiation. Have the isolates differentiated sufficiently to be classified as a distinct species?

It is customary now within much of vertebrate systematics, and certainly within ornithology, to allocate forms (allopatric or parapatric) showing low levels of differentiation to taxa of subspecific rank. Well-differentiated allopatric forms are generally given the rank of species and often are placed in a superspecies along with their hypothesized close relatives (Mayr 1942, Amadon 1966).

Although everyone would probably agree that the amount of differentiation must be related to age to some extent, to adopt this criterion for interspecific comparisons either within a genus or between genera necessitates the assumption that evolutionary rates among these taxa are equal. Few, if any, systematists would suggest that evolutionary rates of phenotypic characters are equal. Indeed, all would surely agree *prima facie* evidence for unequal rates. Yet, the underlying assumption of equality permeates discussions of taxonomic differentiation within the ornithological literature, from those about the age of isolates on islands (Mayr 1942, 158–162; Diamond and Marshall 1977) or mountains (Mayr and Phelps

1967) to the question of analyzing the relative ages of double invasions (Keast 1961, 396–398; Mayr 1963, 504–506).

At a theoretical level, at least, the errors that can be introduced by the assumption of equal evolutionary rates are easy to appreciate, but basically it confounds our attempts to understand the genealogical relationships of the taxa being studied. The assumption logically demands that the degree of similarity among taxa correlate with their recency of common ancestry. One could not claim, of course, that the workers cited above believe rates of character evolution are equal, and in fact many have explicitly denied this. Yet, the widespread adoption of equality in rates as an underlying working assumption cannot be denied. One major consequence of having taxonomic rank based on the degree of differentiation is that one cannot then use these systematic data to investigate the relative ages of lineages or faunas, two extremely important problems within speciation analysis and historical biogeography. An alternative approach to species is therefore essential.

The phylogenetic species concept   In order to study evolution, we must have a hypothesis about the identity of those entities thought to be evolving. And, if we want to develop theories about that evolution, then these entities must be named because scientific theories are class statements about processes acting on named entities (Ghiselin 1974; Hull 1976, 1977, 1978, 1980). The basic taxonomic units of evolution are those populations characterized by one or more evolutionary novelties, and, given the structure of Linnaean classifications, it follows that these basic taxonomic units have to be provided names with specific or subspecific rank. Most present approaches to the species question are in need of revision, because within the context of the BSC we do not now have a scientifically defensible alliance between classification theory on the one hand and evolutionary analysis on the other. Thus, if it is argued that subspecies should not be considered units of evolution, as recommended by some systematists, then we are left with only taxa of species-rank to designate those units. But this logically requires that the BSC as it is now conceived and applied be abandoned. A "biological species" simply does not refer to a single unit of evolution in many cases.

A solution to the above dilemma is forthcoming when we realize that a species concept is best formulated from the perspective of the *results* of evolution rather than from one emphasizing the processes thought to produce those results. Biologists have now come to believe that these processes are highly variable and often depend upon the group being studied. To have a number of species concepts, each possibly applying to a different group, obscures the potential discovery of common phylogenetic and evolutionary patterns from one taxon to another. The results of evolution appear to be more or less the same in all groups. Evolution produces taxonomic entities, defined in terms of their evolutionary differentiation from other such forms. These entities should be called species. By emphasizing the results of evolution, i.e., differentiated taxonomic units (species), comparisons among diverse groups of organisms become possible, even when different "processes" are thought to have produced those species. Thus, by defining species in terms of the resulting *pattern*, it allows us to investigate these processes, unbiased by a species concept that is derived from our preconceptions of those processes.

Accordingly, one possible definition of a species might be: *A species is the smallest diagnosable cluster of individual organisms within which there is a parental pattern of ancestry and descent.*

This *phylogenetic species concept* is not significantly different in content from those recommended by Eldredge and Cracraft (1980, 92) or Nelson and Platnick (1981, 12). It differs, however, from the definition of Eldredge and Cracraft (1980) in eliminating reference to reproductive disjunction from other species-level taxa (see following). Although most species will be defined by uniquely derived characters, this cannot be a component of a species definition (Rosen 1978, 1979), otherwise it would not be possible to recognize ancestral species, which must have primitive characters relative to their descendants (see Eldredge and Cracraft 1980, chapter 4). Species possess, therefore, only unique combinations of primitive and derived characters, that is, they simply must be diagnosable from all other species. Finally, as recognized by all workers, diagnostic characters must be passed from generation to generation, and must be taken to define a reproductive community, not simply males, females, parts of life cycles, or morphs. Hence, a species definition must include some concept of "parental ancestry and descent." This does not mean, however, that such a definition is predicated on reproductive *disjunction* as is the BSC, but only on an acknowledgment that *all* species definitions must have some notion of reproductive cohesion *within* some definable cluster of individual organisms.

The phylogenetic species concept has important advantages over the BSC, including:

1. The known diagnosable taxonomic units are by definition equivalent to the known evolutionary units. There no longer exists the problem of evolutionary units being arbitrarily ranked as either subspecies or as species. Consequently, evolutionary problems within groups are clarified, and two of the major questions of speciation analysis, What are the units of evolution? and, What are their relationships? are not encumbered by a subjective approach to taxonomic ranking.

2. The concept clarifies the distinction between recognizing species-taxa and the analysis of geographic variation. Because species are now defined in terms of diagnostic characters, their taxonomic status is seen to be independent of the patterns of variability that might be observed for nondiagnostic characters. Hence, incongruent patterns of clinal variation exhibited by different characters should no longer be considered a serious taxonomic problem (see Wilson and Brown 1953, 100–102). Because the phylogenetic species concept focuses attention on patterns of taxonomic differentiation, the concept thereby places a new perspective on the analysis of variation within a species. It is no longer necessary to interpret such variation from a taxonomic point of view. Because it is variation within the smallest taxonomic unit, it has no immediate taxonomic relevance. Instead, emphasis can be placed on investigating the dynamics of that variation, including elucidating the question of how character change takes place within populations.

3. The phylogenetic species concept clarifies the status and systematic role of subspecies. Subspecies cannot have ontological status as evolutionary units under a phylogenetic species concept. While it therefore can be argued that this renders subspecies superfluous for systematic and evolutionary analysis, their continued use might be thought defensible under some circumstances. If one so chose, subspecies names could be applied to populations showing clinal variation, and subspecies boundaries could then be determined by sharp gradients in character variation. In this context, however, subspecies are merely descriptors of variation seen in sometimes subjectively chosen, nondiagnostic characters and do not represent taxa having independent ontological status. Because of this, I would recommend that subspecies names not be used. Only objective taxonomic entities should be classified.

4. A major advantage of the phylogenetic species concept is that it places a new interpretation on the question of reproductive isolation, an interpretation not shared with any other species concept. The degree of reproductive isolation observed or presumed to exist between populations has always presented systematists with difficulties because (1) species are said to be defined in terms of reproductive disjunction, (2) species, however, are recognized only rarely by reproductive criteria, and (3) biologists have long realized that a definition based on reproductive criteria often obscures the pattern of differentiation in plants and many groups of animals. Unlike the BSC and the evolutionary species concept (Wiley 1978, 1981), the phylogenetic species concept does not use data on reproductive isolation, e.g., hybridization, in recognizing species taxa. Species are recognized

strictly in terms of their hypothesized status as diagnosable evolutionary taxa, which itself is revealed by shared character distributions within and between populations. Thus, even if two sister-taxa broadly hybridize, both can still be considered to be species if each is diagnosable as a discrete taxon (of course, it may not be possible to assign hybrids to one or the other species). The critical point is that both species have had a distinct phylogenetic and biogeographic history prior to hybridization. and the phylogenetic species concept merely acknowledges that history.

The phylogenetic species concept does not deny the importance of reproductive cohesion or disjunction when discussing ideas about the evolutionary process. It simply claims that incorporating reproductive criteria in a species concept, and using those criteria to determine the taxonomic status of populations, not only obscures the analysis of historical pattern but also impedes our understanding of the reproductive relationships themselves. Patterns of hybridization among taxa are discernible only when the taxa are defined independent of that hybridization and when we have a phylogenetic hypothesis for all those diagnosable taxonomic units (see Nelson and Platnick 1981).

Because the phylogenetic species concept emphasizes diagnosable taxa rather than those delimited by reproductive relationships, it will have broad applicability in botany and zoology alike. Rather than focusing on the processes producing taxa (Raven 1976, 293), we first need to identify the *results* of these processes (taxa), determine their interrelationships, and then attempt to decipher the possible causes for their phylogenetic and biogeographic pattern.

5. Another advantage of the phylogenetic species concept is that it directs more attention to the geographical history of species than does the BSC (discussed in more detail in the next section). The phylogenetic concept demands the recognition of all differentiated taxonomic (evolutionary) units, and as a consequence also leads us to ask where they are distributed, in other words, where they are endemic. The BSC, on the other hand, does not recognize all evolutionary taxonomic units, which might mean that some areas of endemism are not recognized, or only incompletely so. And, if this is the case, it is very easy to argue that common patterns of speciation will be hidden or lost altogether (next section). The phylogenetic species concept avoids these difficulties.

6. A phylogenetic species concept places a strong emphasis on character analysis, in particular, the search for diagnostic characters. Much of present-day speciation analysis is concerned with the quantitative description of variation at the expense, sometimes, of delimiting taxa on the basis of discrete characters. Both approaches are necessary, but

an interpretation of quantitative variation would seem possible only within the context of a hypothesis about species limits.

7. Finally, because the phylogenetic species concept seeks to identify all evolutionary taxonomic units, a much more accurate assessment of intra- and intercladal diversity patterns can be obtained than with the BSC. Many questions in species diversity analysis, or in the study of macroevolutionary patterns (Eldredge and Cracraft 1980), depend upon having a measure of the numbers of evolutionary taxa. It is clear that the BSC can greatly underestimate the numbers of these evolutionary units, whereas such will not be the case with a phylogenetic species concept.

Given these advantages we might ask what might be some potential difficulties with adopting a phylogenetic species concept. Clearly, one of the outcomes would be the recognition of many more species-level taxa. To some ornithologists, having a large number of species is apparently a disadvantage. Mayr (1969, 38, 1982, 290) believes, for example, that the BSC "led to a great clarification and simplification" as the numbers of avian species were reduced in various groups over the past 60 years or so. Precisely why avian species taxonomy should be considered "clarified" with this reduction has never been explained in detail, but I believe this perception is more illusory than real. We certainly do not have a better understanding of the numbers of evolutionary units as a consequence of the BSC. If we know more about the limits of avian taxa, surely it is merely a result of increased systematic work. Moreover, the number of taxonomic names in ornithology has not been reduced significantly, for most of those taxa no longer recognized as species are now named subspecies. And given the fact that some systematists (Mayr 1969, 1982) do not believe subspecies should be units of evolution, then the argument could be made that present species taxonomy is actually less "clarified," at least as far as that taxonomy reflects the results of evolution.

For conventional systematic practice within ornithology, the phylogenetic species concept should not increase the numbers of taxa already recognized. In general, the major effect will be to elevate some subspecies to species. In fact, depending upon one's philosophy toward the recognition of subspecies, under the phylogenetic species concept the total number of specific and subspecific taxa might actually decrease in some instances. This will certainly be true if efforts are made to eliminate subspecies based on subjectively chosen quantitative variation.

Why ornithologists should be uncomfortable with a family having 125 species under a phylogenetic species concept compared to that family having, say, 85 species under the BSC (to take an arbitrary example) is not clear. If those 125 species represent our best estimate of the number of real evolutionary taxa in the family, then 40 additional species seems a small price to pay, especially when most, if not all, of those taxa will already have been described and have valid names available.

The question will naturally arise about potential situations in which small isolated populations or demes can be defined by discrete biochemical characters. Are these groups to be treated taxonomically as distinct species? One approach to answering this question is first to make clear the structure of the pattern of variation. Are there really taxonomic characters diagnostic of these populations, and are they congruent or incongruent with other biochemical characters? If the populations are truly distinct, do they also possess a spatial unity that is distinct from other such groups? Finally, are we interested merely in describing these populations, or are we interested in their phylogenetic and distributional history? If the latter, then it seems clear that distinct units of evolution must be delimited, and naming them would not necessarily be inappropriate.

There is no evidence at present to conclude that cases such as the preceding are at all common in birds (Barrowclough 1983, personal communication). Indeed, local populations of birds do not seem diagnosable by present methods of genetic analysis. The conclusion therefore seems to be that presently known patterns of variation within avian populations are compatible with the phylogenetic species concept.

One, possibly unwelcome, outcome of adopting a phylogenetic species concept will be the necessity of revising much of our current species-level systematics. It is difficult to view this as a disadvantage to ornithology in that the evolutionary status of the species and subspecies of different groups would be reevaluated.

In summary, the phylogenetic species concept would be beneficial to ornithology because it places emphasis on the description and recognition of evolutionary taxonomic units. It would help bring species-level systematics of birds more in line with the practices of systematic botany and zoology as a whole, where tendencies to identify diagnosable taxa as species have always predominated thinking (Rosen 1978, Cronquist 1978). Finally, a phylogenetic species concept would encourage a more rigorous approach toward the phylogenetic and biogeographic analysis of avian diversification.

Speciation Analysis

Introduction

In ornithology, the methodology of speciation analysis has lain almost exclusively within the research program of evolutionary systematics (Mayr 1942, 1969). It has adopted the BSC, thereby emphasizing polytypic species and superspecies, and has viewed speciation primarily in terms of the ecological and genetic processes presumed to result in reproductive isolation. One could perhaps find no better characterization of this research program than that given by Vuilleumier (1980, 1298), who listed the following protocol:

1. Analyze population structure; document isolates and secondary contact zones.
2. Review literature on Plio-Pleistocene climatic and vegetational history; from this "reconstruct a spatio-temporal sequence of eco-geographical events."
3. Correlate these events with the postulated course of speciation.
4. Assign relative or absolute ages to the events of speciation "as a function of the amounts of differentiation of populations."
5. Describe the best speciation sequence.

Vuilleumier (1980, 1298–1299) also identified four assumptions found in most speciation papers: (1) relative amounts of morphologic and genetic differentiation are correlated with each other, (2) the amount of differentiation is proportional to age, (3) competition often determines the distribution of closely related species, and (4) following sympatry, competition often leads to character displacement. Although some might question details of Vuilleumier's protocol and assumptions, an examination of the literature would show that his is an accurate assessment (see Mayr 1942, 1963, 1969; Keast 1961; Selander 1971; Haffer 1969, 1974; Mayr and Short 1970). Yet another observation could be made. With few exceptions (notably Keast 1961, Haffer 1974), speciation analyses within birds have been noncomparative. Thus, most analyses attempt to reconstruct the speciation history of single groups (usually genera, occasionally families) rather than compare patterns of two or more groups sharing common areas of distribution. Studies of single groups are needed, but as will be discussed shortly, there are limits to the kinds of historical inferences that can be made when studies are not comparative.

The discussion of species in the preceding section partly exposes the conceptual interaction between viewpoints about the ontological status of species and the ways in which species are thought to evolve. And, within contemporary speciation analysis, the intellectual tension between these two has been especially apparent. The BSC, for instance, has obviously influenced methods of studying taxonomic differentiation. Witness the emphasis on the description of reproductive relationships among taxa. Likewise, one of the major goals of most speciation analyses has been to decide whether taxa are "good" species or not. I believe the adoption of the BSC has been an impediment to speciation analysis, and the problems inherent in the BSC, which have been documented here and by many other workers, should lead us to reexamine the goals and methods of contemporary speciation analysis. The questions we seek to ask of these investigations need to be reformulated, and alternative methods to answer these new questions need to be explicated. It is the purpose of this section to explore some of these questions and methods.

Some major questions about taxonomic differentiation can be derived from four established observations:

1. The organisms of nature can be clustered into diagnosable taxonomic units (called species).
2. These species have a hierarchical relationship with one another, as evidenced by congruence in their shared derived characters.
3. Each species is endemic to an area.
4. These areas of endemism are often seen to be congruent from group to group.

These observations pose a series of parallel questions, and taken together they form the core of a research program for speciation analysis: What species are there?, What are the interrelationships of these species?, Which areas of endemism exhibit a significant degree of congruence?, and What are the historical interrelationships of these areas? Such questions certainly do not exhaust the subject matter of taxonomic differentiation, but without some answers to each of them we cannot expect to understand the speciation of any group or be able to pursue other questions in any important detail. Unfortunately, except perhaps for the first of these questions, none have figured very prominently (if at all) in the current primary literature on speciation analysis (Mayr 1942, 1963, 1969; Cain 1954; Grant 1971; Bush 1975; White 1978). This is not to say, of course, that problems of phylogenetic relationships, or of endemism, have not received attention from systematics as a whole or from ornithology in particular. Nevertheless, their significance for speciation analysis, in ornithology as well as in other disciplines, has not been entirely appreciated.

Why do the above questions form the core of speciation analysis? The answer lies in the observations themselves. Taxonomic differentiation appears to be a spatial phenomenon, i.e., all taxa arise in a restricted area, and the geographical histories of different groups have elements in common, that is to say, they exhibit congruence. Accordingly, there are two ways to approach speciation studies. First, either by ignoring that congruence, in which case we can focus our attention on one group, define its taxa, formulate hypotheses about their interrelationships, and then interpret these results geographically in terms of earth history, climate, and/or ecology. Or we can investigate that congruence by directing attention to common patterns of spatial history across taxa and likewise interpret these results. Both approaches are necessary, but a comparative analysis of speciation should be our primary objective. Only through comparison can knowledge about the common elements of pattern shared from group to group be obtained, and thus only through comparison can those components of pattern that are unique to each group be isolated. It is the primary task of science to reveal and explain common patterns calling for general explanations. Unique events of history experienced by individual groups, if those events are considered of interest at all, must be explained by causes less general. Furthermore, it is likely that explanations based on noncomparative studies will require revision once they are placed in a comparative context.

How Are Areas of Endemism Determined?

As used here, areas of endemism are hypotheses about areas of origin. The area of endemism for a species is determined by mapping its known distribution, both that of the present and of the past. Because the area of origin itself is a changing entity (most species do not appear to arise spontaneously but over some period of time), areas of endemism, in that they represent those areas of origin, are abstractions. Fossils can rarely, if ever, help us locate the area of origin, because they are themselves nearly always distributed in only part of the range of a species, and thus they give us only a point in space and time. Fossils are, therefore, primarily useful in widening the known area of endemism. Whether the area of endemism is the same as the area of origin never can be determined for any species. Nevertheless, once the geographic ranges of many species sharing roughly the same area are known, it is possible to identify that which is unique in the distribution of each species (see below).

Many birds exhibit long-distance, seasonal migrations. What is their area of endemism, the breeding area, the nonbreeding area, or both? Until we understand the history of migratory movements, we may not be able to answer this question. Nevertheless, upon examining these distributions, the breeding areas of species exhibit a marked degree of congruence, and the little data that are available suggest these areas have had common histories as well (Mengel 1964). The breeding ranges, therefore, seem more important as estimators of area of origin than do nonbreeding ranges (especially in those species in which the two ranges are very widely separated), but this is a problem needing much more investigation.

Biologists have known for a very long time that areas of endemism exhibit congruence (see historical review in Nelson 1978, Nelson and Platnick 1981). To say that two or more species exhibit congruence does not mean their ranges are precisely the same. Each species has its own autecological characteristics and so ranges would not be expected to coincide exactly (except perhaps in cases in which obligatory coevolution might produce such coincidence). Congruence, then, simply means that species share some, usually significant part of their distributions. General areas of endemism are also abstractions of sorts, because determining the general (commonly shared) area of endemism will depend upon which species are examined and their distributions. Nevertheless, constructing hypotheses about general areas of endemism has not proved overly difficult for biologists.

What is the significance of these general areas of endemism? It is often suggested they represent coherent ecological entities, but this is true only when the ecological characteristics of species are described in superficial terms. Virtually all general areas of endemism are highly diverse ecologically, and species endemic in those areas are typically unlike one another in their detailed ecologies. General areas of endemism signify much more than common ecology, they signify common history. Areas of endemism represent biotas that are separated from other such biotas by geological barriers and/or by climatic—environmental extremes. These areas have significance for speciation analysis because the species inhabiting them comprise a biota and might be expected to share a common history of differentiation.

How Is the History of Areas of Endemism Determined?
The methods used to reconstruct the history of areas of endemism have been thoroughly discussed in the literature (Platnick and Nelson 1978; Rosen 1978; Nelson and Platnick 1981; Wiley 1980, 1981; Patterson 1981; Cracraft 1982, 1983), and it is therefore unnecessary to repeat them in detail here. Instead, a brief case study will be described to illustrate the relevance of a historical analysis of areas of endemism for deciphering avian speciation patterns.

The example concerns avian speciation patterns in northern and eastern Australia (Cracraft 1982, 1983). The method of analysis will be comparative, emphasizing the history of areas of endemism, and the results will then be used to identify and interpret some unique aspects of the speciation events in the taxa being studied.

In northern and eastern Australia, and in New Guinea, a number of well-defined areas of endemism can be recognized (figure 6.1). The question is whether the biotas of these areas have any general pattern of interrelationships with each other. Such a pattern would be an expression of the congruence observed in the phylogenetic relationships of different clades distributed in these areas. Accordingly, the phylogenetic relationships of some of these clades must be investigated (using methods outlined in Eldredge and Cracraft 1980; Nelson and Platnick 1981; Wiley 1981).

Figure 6.2 presents phylogenetic hypotheses for four lineages each with species endemic in three or more of these areas (detailed systematic data bearing on these hypotheses will be presented elsewhere, all differentiated forms are here treated as phylogenetic species): (A) some grassfinches

Figure 6.1
Areas of endemism for the birds of northern and eastern Australia (Keast 1961, Ford 1978, Cracraft 1982). These areas include: (1) a moist forest track in coastal southeastern Queens-land—eastern New South Wales, (2) the Cairns-Atherton rainforest area, (3) the Cape York Peninsula (the historical relationships between the northeast corner, here designated 3a, and the remainder of Cape York are uncertain), (4) the Arnhem Land plateau, and (5) the Kimberley plateau. For simplicity, New Guinea is considered as a single area of endemism (area 6), which is clearly not the case.

(*Poephila*) with six species (see also Goodwin 1982, 221—230; Cracraft 1983), (B) three species of wrens in the genus *Malurus*, (C) four species of robins, *Eopsaltria* (*Tregellasia*), and (D) four species of rifle-birds, genus *Ptiloris*.

Assuming the correctness of the phylogenetic hypotheses of figure 6.2, what information do they convey about the interrelationships of the areas of endemism? Based on these four clades, a single general area-cladogram can be hypothesized (figure 6.3). The simplest explanation of the area-cladogram itself is that a biota, once widespread in northern and eastern Australia and in New Guinea, became progressively subdivided. Because these avian lineages represent components of this biota, and have relation-ships exhibiting congruent cladistic pattern, they can be hypothesized to have shared a common history. Knowledge of this history is necessary if we are to explain the speciation patterns of individual taxa in any detail. The genus *Poephila* is a case in point. If a study had been re-stricted to the grassfinches, the pattern obtained in figure 6.2A would not be informative about the history of areas 1, 2, 3a, or 6. Based on comparisons with other clades, however, we might conclude that *P. leucotis*, *P. atropygialis*, and *P. cincta* failed to differentiate in these areas, whereas other taxa did respond to geologic and/or climatic events. In the absence of a comparison, we would not have an indication that the evolutionary history of *Poephila* is different in this regard. Consequently, we would not be led to ask why species of *Poephila* might be less responsive to isolating barriers than are some other species.

How Might General Area-Cladograms Be Explained?
To the extent that the history of differentiation of a group is congruent with the history of other groups, than an explanation for the general area-cladogram is also an explanation for those individual groups. In the preceding example it is evident that a remarkable amount of congruence exists, therefore developing a general explanation becomes especially important.

How might an area of endemism arise? Two answers can be readily suggested. First, a widespread biota can be subdivided into two or more units by development of geographic barriers, with subsequent differentiation defining them as areas of endemism (a vicariance explanation). A second possibility is that repeated dispersal across pre-existing barriers, already separating two areas, could lead to differentiation and an area of endemism (a long-distance dispersal explanation). There seem to be few other potential explanations. As Patterson (1981, 270) has expressed it, either the biota existed before the area of endemism did (vicariance) or the area existed before the endemic taxa (dispersal across a barrier). A choice between these two explanations in any given instance will depend upon the nature of the pattern itself. If patterns are highly congruent as in the Australian example, then vicariance of a widespread biota is the simplest explanation. If patterns are not highly congruent and if only a few taxa are endemic in the area in question, then perhaps those endemics arose following dispersal across a barrier.

Dispersalist biogeography has traditionally played a major role in avian speciation analysis. Part of this stems from the belief that birds, being winged creatures, are capable of reaching any isolated area given sufficient time. Dispersalist thinking also is characteristic of those methodologies which have not stressed the need for precise phylogenetic hypotheses and the search for congruence in the historical patterns of different groups. Moreover, the complex nature of dispersal has not always been understood, especially by those reacting negatively to vicariance explanations. Hence, the two major kinds of dispersal, range-expansion and long-distance, are not usually distinguished when vicariance biogeographers are incorrectly accused of dispensing with dispersal altogether. That species disperse and thereby increase or maintain their ranges is well known.

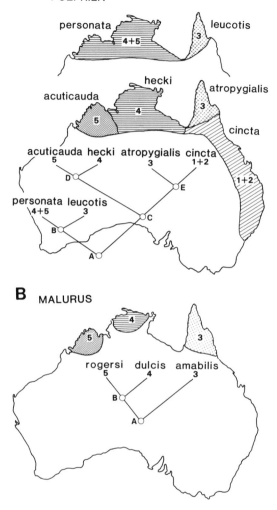

Figure 6.2
Phylogenetic hypotheses for the (phylogenetic) species of four genera having distributions in the areas of endemism shown in figure 6.1. (A) *Poephila*, postulated derived characters include: A, brown back, breast and belly buff, flanks with black band; B, yellow bill, black face pattern; C, extensive black throat, gray head; D, tail elongated, pointed; and E, bill black. Diagnostic characters of the species include: *personata* (face without white patch), *leucotis* (face with white patch), *acuticauda* (bill pink to red), *hecki* (bill yellow), *atropygialis* (upper tail coverts black), *cincta* (upper tail coverts white). (B) *Malurus*, postulated derived characters include: A, female with bluish back; B, males with lavender patch on flank. Diagnostic characters of the species include: *rogersi* (in females, lores and feathers near eye, white), *dulcis* (in females, lores and feathers near eye, chestnut), *amabilis* (males without lavender patch). (C) *Eopsaltria*, postulated derived characters include: A, small size, short broad bill; B, face white, head black; C, breast and belly pale yellow. Diagnostic characters of the species include: *leucops* (no white eye-ring), *albigularis* (white eye-ring), *nana* (lores and

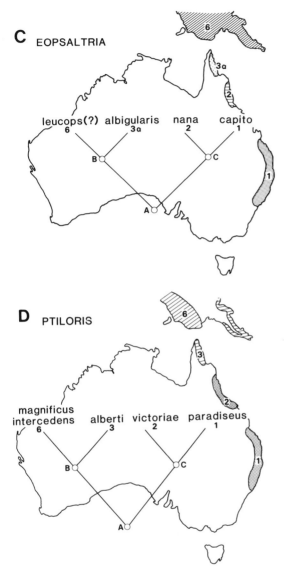

C EOPSALTRIA

leucops(?)   albigularis   nana   capito
6   3a   2   1

D PTILORIS

magnificus
intercedens   alberti   victoriae   paradiseus
6   3   2   1

eye-ring buff), *capito* (lores and eye-ring white). These species are often placed in the genus *Tregellasia*, which may prove more closely related to *Poecilodryas* than to *Eopsaltria*, species limits within *"albigularis"* and *"leucops"* are uncertain (to be discussed elsewhere), and *"albigularis"* may also occur in New Guinea where *"leucops"* is restricted. (D) *Ptiloris*, postulated derived characters include: A, males with green, blue, or blue-green crown, throat, and upper breast, and tail black with blue-green central feathers; B, in males, flank plumes filamentous, females vermiculated below; C, in males, feathers of abdomen and flanks black but edged with green. Diagnostic characters of the species include; *magnificus-intercedens* (in males, underparts with pink-purple gloss), *alberti* (in males, underparts with little or no pink-purple gloss), *victoriae* (much smaller than *paradiseus*), *paradiseus* (much larger than *victoriae*). Note: species taxa are not required to be characterized by derived characters (see text).

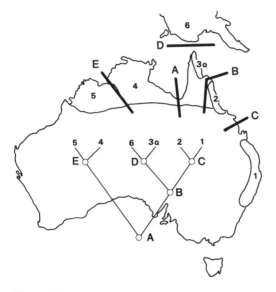

Figure 6.3
The general area-cladogram for the six areas of endemism shown in figure 6.1 based on the results shown in figure 6.2. Thick bars refer to geographic isolating events (see text).

Range-expansion dispersal is a phenomenon of populations, governed by the internal population dynamics of the species, by habitat availability, and by physical parameters of the environment. Long-distance dispersal, in contrast, is almost always a fortuitous event, typically involving very few individuals. One would not expect, therefore, that long-distance dispersal would play a significant role in establishing an area of endemism, particularly if (1) that area housed endemics from a broad taxonomic spectrum, and (2) the endemics of that area exhibited a high degree of congruence in their relationships to taxa endemic in other areas. This is not to say that long-distance dispersal might not establish an area of endemism, but demonstrating this in any instance is difficult and requires a phylogenetic analysis of each clade with endemic species in the area in question (Platnick and Nelson 1978, Nelson and Platnick 1981).

The areas of endemism in northern and eastern Australia are all defined by geologic or ecologic (climatic) barriers (figure 6.3). We can therefore postulate a historical sequence for the origin of these areas: (1) the northern area (4 + 5) was isolated from the eastern area (1 + 2 + 3 + 6), probably as a result of aridification in the region of the Gulf of Carpentaria (barrier A). (2) subsequent to this, areas 4 and 5 were isolated from each other by the development of the Victoria and Daly river valleys and by a more arid climatic regime (barrier E, see Ford 1978), (3) also subsequent to barrier A, the Cape York Peninsula and apparently New Guinea also were separated from eastern Australia (barrier B), possibly as a result of changes in topographic relief and aridification of the climate, (4) following barrier B, New Guinea and the Cape York Peninsula were isolated by a rise in sea-level (barrier D), and (5) following barrier B, areas 1 and 2 were separated by the origin of more arid, savannah-like vegetation (Keast 1961, barrier C). Data on the ages of these isolating barriers are not available, but when they are they can be used to date the origin of the areas and establish the maximum ages of their endemics.

Conclusions

This example suggests that one cannot expect to reconstruct accurately the history of speciation for a single group unless comparisons are made directly with historical patterns of other taxa. A comparative analysis is essential in order to reveal (1) whether areas of endemism are congruent and to what extent they differ from other species, (2) by the analysis of phylogenetic relationships, whether the areas of endemism are related in a nonrandom pattern, and (3) whether the origin of congruent areas of endemism can be explained by common geologic or ecologic factors. Moreover, one cannot recognize whether dispersal has led to endemism until it can be shown that a particular endemic is not part of a more general vicariance pattern.

Comparative studies are also necessary if we want to compare rates of differentiation from one group to the next (Cracraft 1981, 1982). The general area-cladogram is a hypothesis about the relative ages of areas of endemism. As a consequence, taxa endemic in the same area can be hypothesized to be the same age. Only in this way can rates of differentiation be studied. The traditional assumption that age is correlated with the degree of differentiation (and usually taxonomic rank) should be abandoned. It can lead to spurious conclusions about the ages of taxa and area of endemism and cannot serve as a methodological yardstick to compare evolutionary rates. Inasmuch as avian systematists have barely begun to define areas of endemism and understand their history, we can safely predict that speciation analysis will be an important subject for continuing research in ornithology.

Acknowledgments

I wish to thank David Hull, V. A. Funk, N. K. Johnson, Richard F. Johnston, and Norman Platnick for their helpful comments on the manuscript. I am also grateful to the National Science Foundation (through grant DEB79-21492) for supporting this research.

References

Amadon, D., 1966. The superspecies concept, *Syst. Zool.* 15:245–249.

Barrowclough, G. F., 1982. Geogeographic variation, predictiveness, and subspecies. *Auk* 99:601–603.

Barrowclough, G. F., 1983. Biochemical studies of microevolutionary processes, in: *Perspectives in Ornithology* (A. H. Brush and G. A. Clark. Jr., eds), Cambridge University Press, New York.

Bush, G. L., 1975. Modes of animal speciation, *Annu. Rev. Ecol. Syst.* 6:339–364.

Cain, A. J., 1954. *Animal Species and Their Evolution*, Hutchinson University Library, London.

Cracraft, J., 1981. Pattern and process in paleobiology: The role of cladistic analysis in systematic paleontology, *Paleobiol.* 7:456–468.

Cracraft, J., 1982. Geographic differentiation, cladistics, and vicariance biogeography: Reconstructing the tempo and mode of evolution, *Am. Zool.* 22:411–424.

Cracraft, J., 1983. Cladistic analysis and vicariance biogeography, *Am. Sci.* 71:273–281.

Cronquist, A., 1978. Once again, what is a species? *Beltsville Symp. Agric. Res.* 2:3–20.

Diamond, J., and Marshall, A. G., 1977. Niche shifts in New Hebridean birds, *Emu* 77:61–72.

Ehrlich, P. R., 1961. Has the biological species concept outlived its usefulness? *Syst. Zool.* 10:167–176.

Eldredge, N., and Cracraft, J., 1980. *Phylogenetic Patterns and the Evolutionary Process*, Columbia University Press, New York.

Ford, J., 1978. Geographical isolation and morphological and habitat differentiation between birds of the Kimberley and the Northern Territory, *Emu* 78:25–35.

Ghiselin, M. T., 1974. A radical solution to the species problem, *Syst. Zool.* 23:536–544.

Gill, F. B., 1982. Might there be a resurrection of the subspecies? *Auk.* 99:598–599.

Goodwin, D., 1982. *Estrildid Finches of the World*, Cornell University Press, Ithaca, New York.

Grant, V., 1971. *Plant Speciation*, Columbia University Press, New York.

Haffer, J., 1969. Speciation in Amazonian forest birds, *Science* 165:131–137.

Haffer, J., 1974. Avian speciation in tropical South America, *Publ. Nuttall Ornithol. Club* 14:1–390.

Hull, D. L., 1976. Are species really individuals? *Syst. Zool.* 25:174–191.

Hull, D. L., 1977. The ontological status of species as evolutionary units, in: *Foundational Problems in the Special Sciences* (R. Butts and J. Hintikka, eds.), D. Reidel, Dordrecht-Holland, pp. 91–102.

Hull, D. L., 1978. A matter of individuality, *Phil. Sci.* 45:335–360.

Hull, D. L., 1980. Individuality and selection, *Annu. Rev. Ecol. Syst.* 11:311–322.

Johnson, N. K., 1982. Retain subspecies—at least for the time being, *Auk* 99:605–606.

Keast, A., 1961. Bird speciation on the Australian continent, *Bull. Mus. Comp. Zool.* 123(8):303–495.

Kleinschmidt, O., 1900. Arten order Fomenkreise? *J. Ornithol.* 48:134–139.

Lanyon, W. E., 1982. The subspecies concept: Then, now, and always, *Auk* 99:603–604.

Levin, D. A., 1979. The nature of plant species, *Science* 204:381–384.

Lewontin, R. C., 1970. The units of selection, *Annu. Rev. Ecol. Syst.* 1:1–18.

Mayr, E., 1940. Speciation phenomena in birds. *Am. Natural.* 74:249–278.

Mayr, E., 1942. *Systematics and the Origin of Species*, Columbia University Press, New York.

Mayr, E., 1948. The bearing of the new systematics of genetical problems: The nature of species, *Adv. Genet.* 11:205–237.

Mayr, E., 1957a. Species concepts and definitions, in: *The Species Problem* (E. Mayr. ed.), Am. Assoc. Adv. Sci. Publ. No. 50, Washington, D.C., pp. 1–22.

Mayr, E., 1957b. Difficulties and importance of the biological species concept, in: *The Species Problem* (E. Mayr, ed.), Am. Assoc. Adv. Sci. Publ, No. 50, Washington. D.C., pp. 371–388.

Mayr, E., 1963. *Animal Species and Evolution*, Harvard University Press, Cambridge.

Mayr, E., 1969. *Principles of Systematic Zoology*, McGraw–Hill, New York.

Mayr, E., 1970. *Populations, Species and Evolution*, Harvard University Press, Cambridge.

Mayr, E., 1982. *The Growth of Biological Thought*, Harvard University Press, Cambridge.

Mayr, E., and Phelps, W. H., Jr., 1967. The origin of the bird fauna of the south Venezuelan highlands, *Bull. Am. Mus. Nat. Hist.* 136:269–328.

Mayr, E., and Short, L. L., 1970. Species taxa of North American birds, *Publ. Nuttall Ornithol. Club* 9:1–127.

Monroe, B. L., Jr., 1982. A modern concept of the subspecies, *Auk* 99:608–609.

Mengel, R. M., 1964. The probable history of species formation in some northern wood warblers (Parnulidae), *Living Bird* 3:9–43.

Nelson, G. J., 1978. From Candolle to Croizat: Comments on the history of biogeography, *J. Hist. Biol.* 11:269–305.

Nelson, G. J., and Platnick, N. I., 1981. *Systematics and Biogeography: Cladistics and Vicariance*, Columbia University Press, New York.

O'Neill, J. P., 1982. The subspecies concept in the 1980's, *Auk* 99:609–612.

Paterson, H. E. H., 1981. The continuing search for the unknown and unknowable: A critique of contemporary ideas on speciation, *S. Afr. J. Sci.* 77:113– 119.

Patterson, C., 1981. The development of the North American fish fauna—a problem of historical biogeography, in: *The Evolving Biosphere* (P. L. Forey, ed.), British Museum (Natural History), London, pp. 265–281.

Platnick, N. I., 1977. Review of *Concepts of Species* by C. N. Slobodchikoff, *Syst. Zool.* 26:96–98.

Platnick, N. I., and Nelson, G. J., 1978. A method of analysis for historical biogeography, *Syst. Zool.* 27:1–16.

Popper, K. R., 1959. *The Logic of Scientific Discovery*, Harper Torchbooks Edition (1968), Harper and Row, New York.

Popper, K. R., 1972. *Objective Knowledge*, Oxford University Press, London.

Raven, P. H., 1976. Systematics and plant population biology, *Syst. Botan.* 1:284–316.

Rosen, D. E., 1978. Vicariant patterns and historical explanation in biogeography, *Syst. Zool.* 27:159–188.

Rosen, D. E., 1979. Fishes from the uplands and intermontane basin of Guatemala: Revisionary studies and comparative geography, *Bull Am. Mus. Nat. Hist.* 162:267–376.

Scudder, G. G. E., 1974. Species concepts and speciation, *Can. J. Zool.* 52:1121–1134.

Selander, R. K., 1971. Systematics and speciation in birds, in: *Avian Biology*, Volume 1 (D. S. Farner and J. R. King, eds.), Academic Press, New York, pp. 57–147.

Short, L. L., 1969. Taxonomic aspects of avian hybridization, *Auk* 86:84–105.

Sibley, C. G., 1957. The evolutionary and taxonomic significance of sexual selection and hybridization in birds, *Condor* 59:166–191.

Sokal, R. R., and Crovello, T. J., 1970. The biological species concept: A critical evaluation, *Am. Natural.* 104:127–153.

Streseman, E., 1936. The formenkreis–theory, *Auk* 53:150–158.

Templeton, A. R., 1980. Modes of speciation and inferences based on genetic distances, *Evolution* 34:719–729.

Vuilleumier F., 1980. Reconstructing the course of speciation, in: *Proc. XVII Int. Ornithol. Cong.* Deutsch. Ornithol-Gesells., Berlin, pp. 1296–1301.

White, M. J. D., 1978. *Modes of Speciation*, W. H. Freeman & Co., San Francisco.

Wiley, E. O., 1978. The evolutionary species concept reconsidered, *Syst. Zool.* 27:17–26.

Wiley, E. O., 1980. Is the evolutionary species fiction?—A consideration of classes, individuals and historical entities, *Syst. Zool.* 29:76–80.

Wiley, E. O., 1981. *Phylogenetics: The Theory and Practice of Phylogenetic Systematics,* John Wiley and Sons, New York.

Wilson, E. O., and Brown, W. L., Jr., 1953. The subspecies concept and its taxonomic application, *Syst. Zool.* 2:97–111.

Zusi, R. L., 1982. Infraspecific geographic variation and the subspecies concept, *Auk* 99:606–608.

Chapter 7

Species Concepts: A Case for Pluralism

Brent D. Mishler and Michael J. Donoghue

We must resist at all costs the tendency to superimpose a false simplicity on the exterior of science to hide incompletely formulated theoretical foundations.
(Hull 1970, 37)

It has often been argued that it is empirically true and/or theoretically necessary that "species," as units in nature, are fundamentally and universally different from taxa at all other levels. Species are supposed to be unique because they are individuals (in the philosophical sense, as opposed to classes)—integrated, cohesive units, with a real existence in space and time (Ghiselin 1974, Hull 1978) Interbreeding among the members (parts) of a species and reproductive isolation between species are generally believed to account for their individuality. These reproductive criteria are supposed to provide the greater objectivity of the species category and have been suggested as *the* criteria by which species taxa are to be delimited in nature.

Wake (1980) has pointed out that this conception of species forms the basis upon which Eldredge and Cracraft (1980) have built their formulation of evolutionary process and phylogenetic analysis. In fact, this notion of species seems to underlie much of the recent and growing body of theory which, for convenience, could be called macroevolutionary theory (Eldredge and Gould 1979, Stanley 1975, Gould 1982). Moreover, most recent texts in systematics and ecology are predicated on the idea that species taxa are unique and fundamental (e.g., White 1978, Ricklefs 1979, Wiley 1981). It is therefore important to assess carefully any claim that species do or should possess the properties of individuals, and whether breeding criteria are adequate indicators of individuality.

The "species problem" has yielded an enormous quantity of literature, and it is not the purpose of this paper to provide a review (for which see Mayr 1957, Wiley 1978, and papers cited therein). Instead, we will (1) briefly characterize prevailing species concepts, (2) summarize some empirical observations that bear on the species problem, (3) consider the respects in which species taxa as currently delimited by systematists do and do not have the properties of individuals, (4) discuss several choices with which we are faced if all the criteria of individuality are not always met.

We will argue that current species concepts are theoretically oversimplified. Empirical studies show that patterns of discontinuity in ecological, morphological, and genetical variation are generally more complex than are represented by these concepts. Criteria for what constitutes "important" discontinuity appear to vary in response to the vast differences in biology between groups of organisms. In our view, no single and universal level of fundamental evolutionary units exists; in most cases species taxa have no special reality in nature. We urge explicit recognition and acceptance of a more pluralistic conception of species, one that recognizes the evident variety and complexity of "species situations." We will conclude by exploring important consequences of this view for ecology, paleontology, and systematics.

Prevailing Species Concepts

A consensus appears to have been reached that species are integrated, unique entities. The so-called biological species concept emphasizes that species are reproductive communities within which genes are (or can be) freely exchanged, but between which gene flow does not occur or at least is very rare (e.g., Mayr 1970). According to this view a species is a group of organisms with a common gene pool that is reproductively isolated from other such groups.

The evolutionary species concept (Simpson 1961, Grant 1971, Wiley 1978, 1981) is an important extension of the concept of biological species, an attempt to broaden the definition to include all sorts of organisms (not just sexually reproductive ones) and to portray the existence of species through time. According to this view species are separate ancestor-descendent lineages with their own evolutionary roles, tendencies, and fates. The ecological species concept of Van Valen (1976) is similar (but see Wiley 1981), however it emphasizes the "adaptive zone" occupied by a lineage.

Ghiselin (1974) and Hull (1976, 1978) have examined the status of species from a philosophical standpoint. They contend that if species are to play the role required of them in current systematic and evolutionary theory, they must be "individuals" (i.e., integrated and cohesive entities with a restricted spatiotemporal location) rather than "classes" (i.e., spatiotemporally unrestricted sets with defining characteristics). Hull (1980), Wiley (1980, 1981), and Ghiselin (1981) argue that species are fundamentally different from genera, families, and other higher taxa, because they are the most inclusive entities that are "actively evolving."

In general then, species are considered to be the most objectively defined taxonomic and evolutionary units. As Mayr (1970, 374) put it, they are "the real units of evolution, as the temporary incarnation of harmonious, well-integrated gene complexes." They differ from taxa at all other levels, which are considered to be arbitrarily defined and more subjective categories (e.g., Mayr 1969, 91).

For many workers, these views are not only theoretically satisfying but also seem sufficiently unproblematical in application. Many biologists (especially zoologists) seem to be satisfied that, with the exception of some sibling species complexes and rassenkreisse, the application of biological/evolutionary species concepts will yield the same sets of organisms that would be recognized as "species" by a competent taxonomist in a museum, or by a person on the street.[1]

It must be pointed out, however, that the prevailing species concepts are based on relatively few well-studied groups such as birds and *Drosophila*, groups in which discontinuities in the ability to interbreed are relatively complete, and discontinuities in morphological and ecological variation coincide well with the inability to breed in nature. It also must be pointed out that even though relatively few groups have been studied in detail, a correspondence between morphological, ecological, and breeding discontinuities is often simply assumed.

The acceptance of biological/evolutionary species concepts has not been universal. In particular, the botanical community has not wholeheartedly taken them up, and alternatives have been proliferated.[2] It seems clear that the group of organisms on which one specializes strongly influences the view of "species" that one develops. It also seems clear that in order to fully appreciate biological diversity (for purposes of developing general concepts), it is essential to study a variety of different kinds of organisms, or at least take seriously those who have.[3]

Numerous attacks have been leveled at the biological/evolutionary species concepts. Many of these have been concerned primarily with whether they are operational (e.g., Sokal and Crovello 1970). However, as Hull (1968, 1970) has pointed out, a concept cannot be completely operational and still be useful for the growth of science. The critical question is whether a concept is operational *enough* to be useful as a conceptual framework. Considerations of operationality, while certainly of interest, are not central to the argument developed below, which primarily concerns the theoretical adequacy of prevailing species concepts.

Empirical Considerations

In our view, a theoretically satisfactory species concept must bear some specifiable relationship to observed patterns of variation among organisms. It is *not* acceptable to adopt a definition of species simply because it conveniently fits into some more inclusive theory, e.g., a theory of evolutionary process. A species concept is, in effect, a low level hypothesis about the nature of that variation, itself subject to empirical tests. Therefore, in this section, we summarize some relevant empirical findings, many of which have not been generally recognized.

The Noncorrespondence of Discontinuities

The reason for discontent among botanists and other workers is not that they have been unable to perceive discontinuities in nature. Instead, it has become apparent that there are many kinds of discontinuities, all of which may be of interest (Davis and Heywood 1963, 91). The question is, how well do various discontinuities correspond; i.e., are the same sets of organisms delimited by discontinuities when we look at morphology, as when we look at ecology, or breeding? The answer appears to be that there is no necessary correspondence. Stebbins (1950), Grant (1957, 1971, 1981), Stace (1978) and many others have discussed hybridization, apomixis, polyploidy, and anomalous breeding systems in plants and have clearly documented the frequent noncorrespondence of different kinds of discontinuities. In some groups there is complete reproductive isolation between populations that would be recognized as one species on morphological grounds (i.e., "sibling species," as in some groups of *Gilia* (Grant 1964), and *Clarkia* (Small 1971)), and in many other groups of plants the interbreeding unit encompasses two to many morphological units (e.g., *Quercus* (Burger 1975)).

It has also become clear that discontinuities in morphological variation or in the ability to interbreed do not necessarily correspond to differences in ecology ("niche"?). The early work of Turesson (1922a, b) in Europe, and of Clausen, Keck, and Hiesey (1939, 1940) in North America, demonstrated that ecotypes "may or may not possess well-marked morphological differences which enable them to be recognized in the field" (Stebbins 1950, 49). The great extent to which local populations of the same biological or morphological species are physiologically differentiated and adapted to their particular environments is only now being realized (Mooney and Billings, 1961, Antonovics et al. 1971, Antonovics 1972, Bradshaw 1972, Kiang 1982).

If noncorrespondence is prevalent, then strict biological species will not necessarily have anything in common but reproductive isolation. It might be argued that a species concept that unambiguously reflects one aspect of variation may be preferable to one that ambiguously reflects several things. But why should we necessarily pin species names on sets of organisms delimited by reproductive barriers? Why not choose, for example, to name morphological units instead?

One argument for pinning species names on reproductively isolated groups is that breeding discontinuities are thought to be more clear-cut than morphological ones and therefore less arbitrary. However, Ornduff (1969) has summarized the complexity of the reproductive biology of flowering plants and pointed out the difficulty of applying rigid species delimitations based on interfertility. When variation in the ability to inter-breed is examined in detail, we find discontinuities of many different degrees and kinds. Groups of organisms range from completely interfertile to completely reproductively isolated. Hierarchies or networks of breeding groups vary in complex ways in space and time. Therefore, even if we were to decide that breeding discontinuities were theoretically the most important kind of discontinuity, and the ones that species names should reflect, the choice of what constitutes a significant discontinuity remains problematical.

A second argument for the importance of reproductive barriers is that gene flow prevents significant divergence while a lack of gene flow allows it. However, this now appears not to be the case. If a population is subjected to disruptive selection, there can be divergence even in the face of gene flow (Jain and Bradshaw 1966). In these instances it appears that some means of reproductive isolation will usually evolve, but such isolation follows initial divergence. Moreover, allopatric populations can remain morphologically similar for very long periods or they can diverge morphologically (see discussion of this point by Bremer and Wanntorp 1979a). This morphological divergence may or may not be accompanied by reproductive isolation, though it appears likely that eventually a reproductive barrier will result. The point is that morphological divergence and the attainment of means of reproductive isolation can be uncoupled events in time and space. Levin (1978, 288–289) concluded:

> If we adhere to the biological species concept—the integrated reproductive communities—described by Mayr, then speciation is capricious ... Isolating mechanisms are not the cause of divergent evolution, nor are they essential for it to occur.

A related, larger-scale argument for the importance of reproductive barriers is that groups that are reproductively isolated for long periods of time are at least evolutionarily independent (whether or not they diverge morphologically), making them effectively separate entities. Reproductive barriers indeed may often be important in this way, but other factors such as ecological role and homeostatic "inertia" are important as well. Because of the complex nature of variation in each of these factors, and because different factors may be "most important" in the evolution of different groups, a *universal* criterion for delimiting fundamental, cohesive evolutionary entities does not exist.

Questionable Internal Genetic Cohesion

The notion of integration and internal cohesion is central to biological/ evolutionary/individualistic species concepts. In this paper we will follow the common assumption that "cohesion" means genetic cohesion maintained via gene flow, a notion that has recently been explicitly formulated (Wiley and Brooks 1982). However, Hull (1978) has pointed out that other factors such as internal homeostasis and "external environment in the form of unitary selection pressures" (p. 344) may contribute to or confer cohesion. It seems to us likely that "cohesion," and the factors responsible for it, will differ from one group of organisms to another and from one level in the hierarchy to another.

Ehrlich and Raven (1969) pointed out that the extent of gene flow seems to be very limited in many organisms and may not account for the apparent integrity of the morphological units we recognize in nature. Bradshaw (1972, 42) suggested that "effective population size in plants is to be measured in meters and not in kilometers." Endler (1973) studied clinal variation and concluded that "gene flow may be unimportant in the differentiation of populations along environmental gradients" (p. 249). Levin and Kerster (1974) thoroughly reviewed and analyzed the literature concerning gene flow in seed plants and concluded that "the numbers [of individuals] within panmictic units are to be measured in tens and not hundreds" (p. 203). These same points were reiterated by Sokal (1973), Raven (1976), and Levin (1978, 1981). Levin (1979, 383) stated:

> The idea that plant species are Mendelian populations wedded by the bonds of mating is most difficult to justify given our knowledge about gene flow. Indeed a contrary viewpoint is supported. Populations separated by several kilometers may rarely, if ever, exchange genes and as such may evolve independently in the absence of strong or even weak selective differentials.

Lande (1980) has stressed that there has been an overemphasis on the genetic cohesion of widespread species and argued that "of the major forces conserving phenotypic uniformity in time and space stabilizing selection is by far the most powerful" (p. 467). Grant (1980, 167) suggested that "the homogeneity of species is due more to descent from a common ancestor than to gene exchange across significant parts of the species area."

Jackson and Pound (1979) critically reviewed much of this literature and rightly pointed out that there is little rigorous evidence in animals to support or to reject the generality of any statement about gene flow because detailed studies are rare. They concluded, however, that data "seem sufficient to indicate that gene flow in plants can be limited due to local or leptokurtic dispersal of pollen and seeds" (p. 78). It is important to keep in mind that population genetic theory predicts that a small amount of migration between populations may be sufficient to maintain genetic similarity in the absence of differential selection (Lewontin 1974, 212–216). Clearly, determining the relative importance of factors such as gene flow, developmental homeostasis, and selection in nature will require rigorous population genetic theory (e.g., Lande 1980) and careful quantification of empirical data, rather than qualitative, anecdotal arguments.

Evolutionary biologists are just beginning to understand gene flow in plants and animals, but have hardly begun to address the complicated patterns of gene exchange present in the fungi, bacteria, and "protists." A kind of chauvinism has so far restricted discussions of gene flow to comparisons of biparental sexual organisms and asexual ones. Complex patterns of sexuality are present in the fungi (Clémençon 1977); intricate incompatibility systems, as well as incompletely understood parasexuality cycles, make the simplistic application of the biological species concept impossible in most cases. The existence of discrete, integrated genetic lineages is even less likely in the "Monera" (Cowan 1962). There probably are very few absolute barriers to genetic exchange in bacteria, because of the phenomena of DNA-mediated transformation, phage-mediated transduction, and bacterial conjugation (Bodmer 1970).

Are Species Taxa Individuals?

In our view, the empirical considerations discussed above indicate that in many (perhaps most) major groups of organisms, actual patterns of variation are such that the species taxa *currently recognized* by taxonomists cannot be considered discrete, primary, and comparable individuals, integrated and cohesive via the exchange of genes, fundamentally different from taxa at other levels. Variation in morphology, ecology, and breeding is enormous and complex; there are discontinuities of varying degree in each of these factors and the discontinuities are often not congruent. There may often be roughly continuous reduction in the degree of cohesion due to gene flow as more inclusive groups of organisms are considered. The acquisition of reproductive isolating mechanisms appears in many cases to be fortuitous and such isolation is neither the cause of morphological or ecological divergence nor is it necessary for divergence to occur.

Although many currently recognized species do not meet one important criterion of "individuality," namely cohesion and integration of parts, another important criterion often is met, namely restricted spatiotemporal location (i.e., units united by common descent). These units are not strictly "individuals" or "classes," but clearly they can function in evolutionary theory and phylogeny construction. Wiley (1980) called such units "historical entities," but applied this term only to taxa above the species level.

We should mention, as a disclaimer, that although many species taxa (as currently delimited) cannot be considered unique, individualistic units, this does not mean that all species taxa are not. In some groups of organisms, biological species may conform in all respects to the philosophical concept of individual. We simply suggest that this condition is a special case, and that unwarranted extrapolations have been made from a very few groups of organisms to organisms generally.

Some Options

As discussed previously, in many plant and some animal groups, evolutionary processes (i.e., replication and interaction in the sense of Hull 1980) occur primarily on a small scale (even when extrapolated over many generations) relative to the traditional species level. In such groups, the units in nature that are more like individuals are actually interbreeding local populations, and therefore, the basal taxonomic unit (the species) is currently more inclusive than the basal evolutionary units (the populations). This means that many presently recognized species taxa are, at best, historical entities. If this is the case, and if we want species taxa that are more fully individuals, can we bring taxonomic practices in line with our theoretical desires, and at what cost? If we cannot, or if the costs are too great, are there any theoretically acceptable alternatives, and what would they entail?

We formulate here three options with which we are faced and reject the first two. In the next section we explore some implications of the third alternative.

> 1. Alter the usage of "species" to equal "evolutionary unit," i.e., attempt to locate all of the effectively isolated and independently evolving populations and apply species names to them.
> 2. Alter the usage of "species" to equal the "cenospecies" or "comparium" (see Stebbins 1950, Grant 1971), i.e., recognize as the basic taxonomic units only those taxa that are *completely* intersterile.
> 3. Apply species names at about the same level as we have in the past, and decouple the basal taxonomic unit from notions of "basic" evolutionary units.

We reject choice 1 for several reasons, some practical and some theoretical. In a practical sense, formally naming whatever the truly genetically integrated units turned out to be would be disastrous. There are certainly very many such units, they are at best very difficult to perceive even with the most sophisticated techniques and in the most studied organisms, and these units are continuously changing in size and membership from one generation to the next. At any one time we can never know which units will diverge forever.

Rosen (1978, 1979) has discussed and adopted a species concept quite similar to choice 1. While we would generally agree with him that populations with apomorphous character states are units of evolutionary significance (1978, 176), we could not agree that species should be "the smallest natural aggregation of individuals with a specifiable geographic integrity that can be defined by any current set of analytical techniques" (1979, 277). Since we could probably distinguish each individual organism, or very small groups of organisms, on the basis of apomorphies (if we looked hard enough), why shouldn't each of these units be given a Linnaean binomial?

There is a more important, theoretical reason for rejecting alternative 1, one that we have alluded to above. A pervasive confusion runs through much discussion of species: the erroneous notion that *a* single basal evolutionary unit is somewhere to be found among all the possible units that could be recognized. There are *many* evolutionary, genealogical units within a given lineage (Hull 1980)—a rough hierarchy or network of units, which may be temporally and spatially overlapping. Thus, in the search to find *the* evolutionary unit, one is on a very "slippery slope" indeed. Units all along this slope may be of interest to evolutionists, depending on the level of focus of the particular investigator. These units do require some sort of designation in order to be studied, but a formal, hierarchical Linnaean name is not necessary.

Option 2, in many instances, would represent the opposite extreme (an attempt to locate the "top" of the slippery slope). Absolute reproductive isolation would be used as the overriding ranking criterion. If two organisms could potentially exchange genes, either directly or through intermediates, they would be placed in the same species taxon. There are several reasons why we reject this alternative.

First, it is unclear that reproductive criteria necessarily provide species taxa that are useful for purposes of phylogeny reconstruction and historical biogeography. As Rosen (1978, 1979) and Bremer and Wanntorp (1979a) have pointed out, "biological species" may be paraphyletic assemblages of populations united only by a plesiomorphy, i.e., all those organisms that have not acquired a means of reproductive isolation. If reproductive criteria are to be useful for cladistic analysis, it is necessary to determine which modes of isolation arose as evolutionary novelties in a group.

Our second objection to option 2 has to do with the problem of measuring "potentiality." There have been numerous comments on the inadequacy of potential interbreeding as a ranking criterion, and even strong proponents of the biological species concept have rejected potential interbreeding as a part of their species definitions. Under certain conditions, very disparate organisms can be made to cross. If we adopted this option, the family Orchidaceae, with approximately 20,000 species at present (covering a great range of variation), might be lumped into just a few species because horticulturalists have produced so many bi- and pluri-generic hybrids. The universal application of any one criterion will undoubtedly obscure important patterns of variation in other parameters.

Species Like Genera

If we adopted alternative 3, what would happen to the species category? Would species taxa necessarily be theoretically meaningless entities? Are all alternatives to biological/evolutionary/individual species concepts devoid of theoretical interest as implied by Eldredge and Cracraft (1980, 94)?

We would agree that if species were simply phenetically similar groups of populations they might indeed be unsatisfactory for many purposes. The application of species concepts like those of Cronquist (1978) and of Nelson and Platnick (1981) may yield species taxa that are not useful from the standpoint of reconstructing phylogenies (see discussion by Beatty 1982).[4]

However, we think that one form of option 3 may provide theoretically meaningful units. In groups where the actually interbreeding units are small relative to the morphologically delimited units, species can be considered to be like genera or families or higher taxa at all levels. That is, they are assemblages of populations united by descent just as genera are assemblages of species united by descent, etc. If we required that species be monophyletic assemblages of populations (to the extent that this could be hypothesized), then they could play a role in evolutionary and phylogenetic theory just as monophyletic taxa at all levels can. Theoretical significance does not reside solely in the basal taxonomic units or in units that are "fully individuals."

If we recognize that species are like genera, and insist that they be monophyletic, then we are faced with the problems of assessing monophyly and of ranking, problems that plague systematists working at all levels. Several different concepts of monophyly have been employed by systematists, but none of them explicitly at the species level (see discussion by Holmes 1980). We favor Hennig's (1966) concept of monophyly (except explicitly applied at the species level) but are fully aware of the difficulties in its application at low taxonomic levels (Arnold 1981, Hill and Crane 1982). In particular, the difficulty posed by reticulation (hybridization) (Bremer and Wanntorp 1979b) may be especially acute at lower taxonomic levels. Using synapomorphy as evidence of monophyly requires that the polarity of character states be determined, and again this may be an especially difficult problem near the species level. Polarity assessments will be possible to a greater or lesser extent depending on the certainty with which out-groups are known (Stevens 1980b).

As noted previously, in order to use reproductive isolation as evidence of monophyly, it would be necessary to determine which means of reproductive isolation are apomorphies at a given level, and which are not. An example of the difficulty of applying a Hennigian concept of monophyly is the very real possibility of "paraphyletic speciation." If speciation by peripheral isolation happens frequently, then a population (geographically defined), which has developed some apomorphic feature (such as a morphological novelty or an isolating mechanism) with respect to its "parent" species, may often be cladistically more closely related to some part of the parent species than to the remainder (see discussion and example in Bremer and Wanntorp 1979a). In such a case, we would take the (perhaps controversial) position that if the population is to be recognizied as a formal species taxon, and if the phylogenetic relationships of the populations in the parent species can be resolved, then the taxonomist should not formally name the parent "species" (which has now been found to be a paraphyletic group), but instead name monophyletic groups discerned within it. Conversely, however, if cladistic structure within the parent species cannot be resolved, then in our view it would be acceptable to provisionally name it as a species (even if the populations included within shared no apomorphy).

This example illustrates the fact that even when monophyletic groups are delimited, the problem of ranking remains since monophyletic groups can be found at many levels within a clade. Species ranking criteria could include group size, gap size, geological age, ecological or geographical criteria, degree of intersterility, tradition, and possibly others. The general problem of ranking is presently unresolved, and we suspect that an absolute and universally applicable criterion may never be found and that, instead, answers will have to be developed on a group by group basis.

Some Consequences of Pluralism

We have outlined a concept of species (i.e., "species like genera") that may be appropriate for groups of organisms in which certain conditions obtain. However, we think that a variety of species concepts are necessary to adequately capture the complexity of variation patterns in nature. To subsume this variation under the rubric of any one concept leads to confusion and tends to obscure important evolutionary questions. As Hull (1970, see epigraph) has argued, we must resist the urge to superimpose false simplicity. If "species situations" are diverse, then a variety of concepts may be necessary and desirable to reflect this complexity.

Many theories in biology appear to lack the universality of theories in other natural sciences. Often the problem is to decide which one of several theories (not necessarily mutually exclusive) applies to a particular situation (for a specific application of this theoretical pluralism to evolutionary biology, see Gould and Lewontin 1979). A satisfactory general theory is one in which the number of subtheories is kept to a minimum, but not reduced to the point where important patterns and processes are obscured. The evaluation of how well a theoretical system "accounts for" patterns in the world is problematical, and we cannot offer any generally applicable criterion for making such an evaluation. However, in the case of species, we think that the search for a universal species concept, wherein the basal unit in evolutionary biology and in taxonomy is the same, is misguided. In our opinion, it is time for "species" to suffer a fate similar to that of the classical concept of "gene."[5]

We should recognize that species taxa have never been, and very probably cannot be made readily comparable units. This observation has a number of important theoretical implications. Ecologists must consider the extent to which "species" can be considered equivalent and comparable from one group of organisms to another. Population sizes and structures, gene flow, social organization, the nature of selective factors, and developmental constraints differ in multifarious ways. This means that it is imperative that systematists be explicit about the nature of variation in, and the properties of, the species that they recognize in the groups they study. In turn, the users of species names must at all times be aware that "species are only equivalent by designation, and not by virtue of the nature or extent of their evolutionary differentiation" (Davis and Heywood 1963, 92). As obfuscatory as this may seem, comparative biologists must not make inferences from a species name without consulting the systematic literature to see what patterns of variation the name purports to represent.

These considerations are also important to paleontologists, who make inferences about, and from, "fossil species," and imply correspondences between variation in morphology, ecology, and breeding. It is perplexing that some quite innovative paleontologists, such as Eldredge and Gould, have uncritically retained the biological species concept in their work. As we have shown, there are many reasons why species should not be treated as particles or quanta. Paleontologists should consider exactly what macroevolutionary theories require species to be. For many purposes they may not require species that are completely individuals, but simply monophyletic lineages. If units that are cohesive via gene flow are an absolute requirement, then fossils may not provide appropriate evidence.

Finally, what are the implications for the systematist of a pluralistic outlook on species? Systematists working on relatively little known organisms should not assume that concepts derived from other groups of organisms are necessarily applicable. Instead, in each group the systematist is obligated to study patterns of variation in morphology, ecology, and breeding, and to detail the nature of the correspondences among these patterns. It is essential that the ways in which names are applied to taxa at all levels be stated explicitly.

If we adopt a case-by-case approach and urge specialists to unabashedly develop concepts for their particular groups, are we saying that "anything goes"? Of course, the answer is no. We are only suggesting pluralism within limits. Taxa (including species) recognized by systematists must have a specifiable relationship to theoretically important variation, more specifically, we have argued that species taxa should be phylogenetically meaningful units. There may not be a *universal* criterion to arbitrate between conflicting species classifications of a given genus, but through the complex process that is science, the community of involved workers can and will hammer out criteria for making such decisions.

Acknowledgments

We are indebted to J. Beatty, E. Coombs, S. Fink, W. Fink, C. Hill, D. Hull, E. Mayr, N. Miller, P. Stevens, and five anonymous reviewers for criticizing this manuscript at one stage or another during its ontogeny; however, they are not to blame for its contents.

Notes

1. Gould (1979) and others have defended the biological species concept on the grounds that the same taxa recognized by western taxonomists are recognized by tribespeople in New Guinea, etc. There are several problems with this kind of argument. First, it is not clear that this finding constitutes an independent test because, after all, New Guinea tribespeople are human too, with similar cognitive principles and limitations of language. It should also be borne in mind that the observer is by no means neutral. Folk taxonomies have been collected by people with a knowledge of evolution and modern systematic concepts. Second, it is generally not a strong argument to show that a prescientific society has recognized something that modern science currently accepts. Surely a modern astronomer would not consider it very strong evidence that a primitive mythology supported one cosmological theory over another. Finally, the taxa recognized by western taxonomists (and often by natives at some level of their linguistic hierarchy) in these instances are not known to be biological species—for the most part they are morphological units that are *believed* to be reproductively isolated from other such units.

2. Initially, the biological species concept was embraced and promulgated by plant systematists interested in evolution (Stebbins 1950, Grant 1957). Cronquist (1978) detailed Grant's efforts (from 1956 to 1966) to apply the biological species concept in *Gilia* (Polemoniaceae). It very soon became apparent that the biological species concept was fraught with difficulties, but Grant chose to amend the concept (rather than abandon it altogether), first (1957) with the notion of the syngameon (i.e., the unit of interbreeding higher than the species), later (1971) by adopting an evolutionary species concept. Finally, in the second edition of his classic book on plant speciation, Grant (1981) treats species in a more flexible and pluralistic manner. Some botanists (e.g., Stebbins 1979, 25) continue to feel that the biological species concept, or some modification of it, is the only suitable framework for understanding plant diversity. However, many (perhaps most) botanical systematists remain rather skeptical about the general applicability of the concept in botany (Davis and Heywood 1963, Raven 1976, Cronquist 1978, Levin 1979, Stevens 1980a).

The different attitudes of zoologists and botanists towards the concept of species may be of interest to historians, sociologists, and philosophers of science. For organismic and evolutionary biology the "modern synthesis" of the 1930s and 1940s may have represented a revolution in the sense of Kuhn (1970). For systematists, the principal outcome was the biological species concept. Zoologists (especially vertebrate systematists) appear to have largely accepted the new paradigm and to have entered a period of "normal science," applying the concept in particular cases ("puzzle solving"). While problems like sibling species, semispecies, and subspecies have become apparent, these have generally not prompted a critical evaluation of the paradigm or a proliferation of alternatives. In contrast, in the botanical community the biological species concept was soon found to be inapplicable or of difficult application and likely to lead to confusion. This resulted in a groping for alternatives and a defense of older concepts. In this regard, the historical development of species concepts in botany seems to fit better Feyerabend's (1970) characterization of scientific change as the simultaneous practice of normal science and the proliferation of alternative theories.

3. The zoologists initially responsible for developing the biological species concept were aware of the difficulties in applying the concept in some groups of animals and many groups of plants. Dobzhansky (1937, 1972) consistently pointed out the diversity of "species situations" observable in nature. Mayr (1942, 122) was careful to point out differences between plants and animals, and difficulties in the practical application of the biological species concept in some cases. Particularly rigid versions of the biological species concept have been promulgated more recently, in attempted generalizations that have shown a startling lack of concern for the biology of the majority of organisms on earth. Mayr (1982) has examined the resistance of botanists to the biological species concept and concluded that "the concept does not describe an exceptional situation" (p. 280). But he grants some justification to the ideas of "certain botanists" who question "whether the wide spectrum of breeding systems that can be found in plants can all be subsumed under the single concept (and term) 'species'" (p. 278).

4. The species concepts of Cronquist and of Nelson and Platnick are as follows:
   Cronquist (1978, 15) "... the smallest groups that are consistently and persistently distinct, and distinguishable by ordinary means."
   Nelson and Platnick (1981, 12): "... the smallest detected samples of self-perpetuating organisms that have unique sets of characters."

5. Initially the "gene" was considered to be *the* unit of heredity, but the classical concept of gene has been replaced by several concepts which stand in a complex relation to one another (Hull 1965). The use of a disjunctive definition (Hull 1965) allows a single term to designate a complex of concepts. However, this can become so confusing that it may be desirable to replace (at least in part) an old terminology with a new set of terms with more precise meanings.

References

Antonovics, J. 1972. Population dynamics of the grass *Anthoxanthum oderatum* on a zinc mine. J. Ecol., 60:351–365.

Antonovics, J., A. D. Bradshaw, and R. G. Turner. 1971. Heavy metal tolerance in plants. Adv. Ecol. Res., 7:1–85.

Arnold, E. N. 1981. Estimating phylogenies at low taxonomic levels. Z. Zool. Syst. Evolut.-forsch., 19:1–35.

Beatty, J. 1982. Classes and cladists. Syst. Zool., 31:25–34.

Bodmer, W. F. 1970. The evolutionary significance of recombination in prokaryotes. Soc. Gen. Microb. Symp., 20:279–294.

Bradshaw, A. D. 1972. Some of the evolutionary consequences of being a plant. Evol. Biol., 5:25–47.

Bremer, K., and H.-E. Wanntorp. 1979a. Geographic populations or biological species in phylogeny reconstruction? Syst. Zool., 28:220–224.

Bremer, K., and H.-E. Wanntorp. 1979b. Hierarchy and reticulation in systematics. Syst. Zool., 28:624–627.

Burger, W. C. 1975. The species concept in Quercus. Taxon, 24:45–50.

Clausen, J., D. D. Keck, and W. M. Hiesey. 1939. The concept of species based on experiment. Amer. J. Bot., 26:103–106.

Clausen, J., D. D. Keck, and W. M. Hiesey. 1940. Experimental studies on the nature of species. I. The effect of varied environments on Western North American plants. Carnegie Inst. Wash., Publ. No. 520.

Clémençon, H. (ed.) 1977. The species concept in Hymenomycetes. J. Cramer, Vaduz, Liechtenstein.

Cowan, S. T. 1962. The microbial species—a macromyth? Soc. Gen. Microb. Symp., 12:433–455.

Cronquist, A. 1978. Once again, what is a species? Pp. 3–20, in Biosystematics in agriculture (J. A. Romberger, ed.). Allanheld & Osmun, Montclair, N. J.

Davis, P. H., and V. H. Heywood. 1963. Principles of angiosperm taxonomy. Oliver and Boyd, Edinburgh.

Dobzhansky, T. 1937. Genetics and the origin of species. Columbia Univ. Press, New York.

Dobzhansky, T. 1972. Species of Drosophila. Science, 177:664–669.

Ehrlich, P. R., and P. H. Raven. 1969. Differentiation of populations. Science, 165:1228–1232.

Eldredge, N., and J. Cracraft. 1980. Phylogenetic patterns and the evolutionary process. Columbia Univ. Press, New York.

Eldredge, N., and S. J. Gould. 1972. Punctuated equilibria: an alternative to phyletic gradualism. Pp. 82–115, in Models in paleobiology (T. J. M. Schopf, ed.). Freeman, Cooper and Co., San Francisco.

Endler, J. A. 1973. Gene flow and population differentiation. Science, 179:243–250.

Feyerabend, P. 1970. Consolations for the specialist. Pp. 197–230, in Criticism and the growth of knowledge (I. Lakatos and A. Musgrove, eds.). Cambridge Univ. Press, London.

Ghiselin, M. T. 1974. A radical solution to the species problem. Syst. Zool., 23:536–544.

Ghiselin, M. T. 1981. The metaphysics of phylogeny. [Review of Eldredge, N., and J. Cracraft. 1980. Phylogenetic patterns and the evolutionary process]. Paleobiology, 7:139–143.

Gould, S. J. 1979. A quahog is a quahog. Nat. Hist., 88:18–26.

Gould, S. J. 1982. Darwinism and the expansion of evolutionary theory. Science, 216:380–387.

Gould, S. J., and R. C. Lewontin. 1979. The spandrels of San Marco and the Panglossian paradigm: a critique of the adaptionist programme. Proc. Roy. Soc. Lond. (B), 205:581–598.

Grant, V. 1957. The plant species in theory and practice, Pp. 39–80, in The species problem (E. Mayr, ed.). Amer. Assoc. Adv. Sci., Publ. 50, Washington, D. C.

Grant, V. 1964. The biological composition of a taxonomic species in Gilia. Adv. Genet., 12:281–328.

Grant, V. 1971. Plant speciation. First edition. Columbia Univ. Press, New York.

Grant, V. 1980. Gene flow and the homogeneity of species populations. Biol. Zbl., 99:157–169.

Grant, V. 1981. Plant speciation. Second edition. Columbia Univ. Press, New York.

Hennig, W. 1966. Phylogenetic systematics. Univ. Illinois Press, Urbana, Ill.

Hill, C. R., and P. R. Crane. 1982. Evolutionary cladistics and the origin of angiosperms. Pp. 269–361, *in* Problems of phylogenetic reconstruction (K. A. Joyse and A. E. Friday, eds.). Systematics Association Special Volume No. 21. Academic Press, London and New York.

Holmes, E. B. 1980. Reconsideration of some systematic concepts and terms. Evol. Theory, 5:35–87.

Hull, D. L. 1965. The effect of essentialism on taxonomy—two thousand years of stasis (II). British J. Phil. Sci., 16:1–18.

Hull, D. L. 1968. The operational imperative: sense and nonsense in operationism. Syst. Zool., 17:438–457.

Hull, D. L. 1970. Contemporary systematic philosophies. Ann. Rev. Ecol. Syst., 1:19–54.

Hull, D. L. 1976. Are species really individuals? Syst. Zool., 25:174–191.

Hull, D. L. 1978. A matter of individuality. Phil. Sci., 45:335–360.

Hull, D. L. 1980. Individuality and selection. Ann. Rev. Ecol. Syst., 11:311–332.

Jackson, J. F., and J. A. Pound. 1979. Comments on assessing the dedifferentiating effect of gene flow. Syst. Zool., 28:78–85.

Jain, S. K., and A. D. Bradshaw. 1966. Evolutionary divergence among adjacent plant populations. I. The evidence and its theoretical analysis. Heredity, 21:407–441.

Kiang, Y. T. 1982. Local differentiation of *Anthoxanthum odoratum* L. populations on roadsides. Amer. Midl. Nat., 107:340–350.

Kuhn, T. S. 1970. The structure of scientific revolutions. (Second enlarged edition) Univ. Chicago Press, Chicago.

Lande, R. 1980. Genetic variation and phenotypic evolution during allopatric speciation. Amer. Nat., 116:463–479.

Levin, D. A. 1978. The origin of isolating mechanisms in flowering plants. Evol. Biol., 11:185–317.

Levin, D. A. 1979. The nature of plant species. Science, 204:381–384.

Levin, D. A. 1981. Dispersal versus gene flow in plants. Ann. Missouri Bot. Gard., 68:233–253.

Levin, D. A., and H. W. Kerster. 1974. Gene flow in seed plants. Evol. Biol., 7:139–220.

Lewontin, R. C. 1974. The genetic basis of evolutionary change. Columbia Univ. Press, New York.

Mayr, E. 1942. Systematics and the origin of species: from the viewpoint of a zoologist. Columbia Univ. Press, New York.

Mayr, E. 1957. Species concepts and definitions. Pp. 1–22, *in* The species problem (E. Mayr, ed.). Amer. Assoc. Adv. Sci., Publ. 50, Washington, D. C.

Mayr, E. 1969. Principles of systematic zoology. McGraw-Hill Book Co., New York.

Mayr, E. 1970. Populations, species, and evolution. Harvard Univ. Press, Cambridge, Mass.

Mayr, E. 1982. The growth of biological thought. Harvard Univ. Press, Cambridge, Mass.

Mooney, H. A., and W. D. Billings. 1961. Comparative physiological ecology of arctic and alpine populations of *Oxyria digyna*. Ecol. Monogr., 31:1–29.

Nelson, G., and N. Platnick. 1981. Systematics and biogeography: cladistics and vicariance. Columbia Univ. Press, New York.

Ornduff, R. 1969. Reproductive biology in relation to systematics. Taxon, 18:121–133.

Raven, P. H. 1976. Systematics and plant population biology. Syst. Bot., 1:284–316.

Ricklefs, R. E. 1979. Ecology. Second edition. Chiron Press, New York.

Rosen, D. E. 1978. Vicariant patterns and historical expalanations in biogeography. Syst. Zool., 27:159–188.

Rosen, D. E. 1979. Fishes from the uplands and intermontane basins of Guatemala: revisionary studies and comparative geography. Bull. Amer. Mus. Nat. Hist., 162:267–376.

Simpson, G. G. 1961. Principles of animal taxonomy. Columbia Univ. Press, New York.

Small, E. 1971. The evolution of reproductive isolation in *Clarkia*, section *Myxocarpa*. Evolution, 25:330–346.

Sokal, R. R. 1973. The species problem reconsidered. Syst. Zool., 22:360–374.

Sokal, R. R., and T. J. Crovello. 1970. The biological species concept: a critical evaluation. Amer. Nat., 104:127–153.

Stace, C. A. 1978. Breeding systems, variation patterns and species delimitation. Pp. 57–78, *in* Essays in plant taxonomy (H. E. Street, ed.). Academic Press, New York.

Stanley, S. M. 1975. A theory of evolution above the species level. Proc. Nat. Acad. Sci. U.S.A., 72:646–650.

Stebbins, G. L. 1950. Variation and evolution in plants. Columbia Univ. Press, New York.

Stebbins, G. L. 1979. Fifty years of plant evolution. Pp. 18–41, *in* Topics in plant population biology (O. T. Solbrig, S. Jain, G. B. Johnson, and P. H. Raven, eds.). Columbia Univ. Press, New York.

Stevens, P. F. 1980a. A revision of the Old World species of *Calophyllum* L. (Guttiferae). J. Arnold Arb., 61:117–699.

Stevens, P. F. 1980b. Evolutionary polarity of character states. Ann. Rev. Ecol. Syst., 11:333–358.

Turesson, G. 1922a. The species and the variety as ecological units. Hereditas, 3:100–113.

Turreson, G. 1922b. The genotypical response of the plant species to the habitat. Hereditas, 3:211–350.

Van Valen, L. 1976. Ecological species, multispecies, and oaks. Taxon, 25:233–239.

Wake, D. B. 1980. A view of evolution [Review of Eldredge, N., and J. Cracraft. 1980. Phylogenetic patterns and the evolutionary process]. Science, 210:1239–1240.

White, M. J. D. 1978. Modes of speciation. W. H. Freeman and Co., San Francisco.

Wiley, E. O. 1978. The evolutionary species concept reconsidered. Syst. Zool., 27:17–26.

Wiley, E. O. 1980. Is the evolutionary species fiction?—A consideration of classes, individuals, and historical entities. Syst. Zool., 29:76–80.

Wiley, E. O. 1981. Phylogenetics: the theory and practice of phylogenetic systematics. John Wiley, New York.

Wiley, E. O., and D. R. Brooks. 1982. Victims of history—a nonequilibrium approach to evolution. Syst. Zool., 31:1–24.

Chapter 8

The Recognition Concept of Species

H. E. H. Paterson

When we trade in ideas in population biology, species constitute our currency. Their peculiar significance and universality was long ago appreciated by Darwin's mentor, Sir Charles Lyell: "The ordinary naturalist is not sufficiently aware that, when dogmatizing on what species are, he is grappling with the whole question of the organic world and its connection with a time past and with man; that it involves the question of man and his relation to the brutes, of instinct, intelligence and reason, of Creation, transmutation and progressive improvement or development. Each set of geological questions and of ethological and zoological and botanical are parts of the great problem which is always assuming a new aspect." (Wilson 1970, 164).

Any view of species must be cast in genetical terms if it is to be useful in understanding the process of evolution, and it must be comprehensive enough to cover most eukaryotes including man. However, aiming to provide a concept that effectively encompasses the sweep of living forms from unicellular algae, through the fungi, plants and animals to man is indeed an ambitious enterprise. It is, therefore, not really surprising that an entirely satisfactory outcome has not yet been achieved. Like Mayr (1963, 426) I believe it is possible that it can be achieved, provided one is able to identify correctly the genetical species' fundamental basis.

In this chapter I first consider the broad specifications necessary for any genetical concept of species, then examine the current paradigm and note its shortcomings and inconsistencies. Finally, I offer an alternative view in more detail than previously. This alternative is free from the difficulties that attend the prevailing biological species concept and generates distinct testable predictions, with pervasive implications for all branches of population biology.

With space strictly limited, I here do no more than deal with the main ideas of the two alternative views of genetical species. This is not the place for the detailed documentation of the new recognition concept; this will require book-length treatment, as did the isolation concept in its day (Dobzhansky 1937, Mayr 1942). I have been obliged to restrict my consideration of the isolation concept (biological species concept) to the views of the two grand masters, Dobzhansky and Mayr, and have neglected to use the views of other leaders such as Carson and his associates, White, Stebbins, Ayala, and others, despite their significance. Similarly I have been unable to do more than touch on species and speciation in kingdoms other than Animalia. In particular, special attention will have to be devoted to what happens in plants in a future work. Their relative neglect here should not be taken as implying that I believe them to warrant no closer attention.

The Heart of the Genetical Species

The very heart of any genetical species concept, however it is conceived, is vividly revealed by Carson's (1957) apt phrase: "The species as a field for gene recombination." Dobzhansky seems to have had essentially the same idea in his mind when he spoke (1951) of the species as "the most inclusive Mendelian population." Both authors restricted the term to biparental sexual eukaryotes, but otherwise their view seems entirely noncontroversial. Controversy, however, does arise over the way the following two questions should be answered.

1. What sets the limits to the field for gene recombination?
2. How do these limits arise *ab initio*?

Various genetical species concepts are distinguished by the way they answer these two questions. The concepts to be outlined and examined here are the currently orthodox biological species concept (= isolation concept), and the newer recognition concept of species (Paterson 1973, 1978). My aim is to demonstrate the inconsistencies involved in the former, and the advantages of the latter concept.

The Isolation Concept of Species

It was not until Dobzhansky coined the term "isolating mechanisms" and devoted an entire chapter to them in his classic *Genetics and the Origin of Species* (1937) that the full significance of these adaptations was recognized by evolutionists. (Mayr 1976, 129)

I refer to the prevailing concept of species as the isolation concept because this name explicitly specifies the way the field for gene recombination is supposed to be achieved, namely through the development of the ad hoc characters that were referred to by Dobzhansky (1935, 1937), and almost all later authors, as isolating mechanisms.

Thus, for Dobzhansky (1970, 357) "Species are ... systems of populations; the gene exchange between these systems is limited or prevented by a reproductive isolating mechanism or perhaps by a combination of several such mechanisms." It will be noticed that in accordance with this view, a species is defined in terms of its relationship to other species, i.e., it is a *relational* concept, as has long been emphasized by Mayr (1942, 1963, 1970).

Mayr and Provine (1980, 34) expressed a similar view: "The major intrinsic attribute characterizing a species is its set of isolating mechanisms that keeps it distinct from other species." These quotations make it evident that both Dobzhansky and Mayr would have answered the first question raised above with: "isolating mechanisms" (Mayr 1976, 520).

If the isolating mechanisms do indeed set the limits of a field for gene recombination, the question arises as to how these characters are acquired by all members of the species. Two obvious circumstances could lead to the fixation of the alleles involved: chance in small isolated populations, and natural selection.

Alleles or chromosomal rearrangements can become fixed by chance even if they are somewhat disadvantageous as heterozygotes. This is clear because pairs of closely related species are known which differ from each other by the fixation of alternative chromosomal arrangements, such as paracentric or pericentric inversions, or by some form of translocation, all of which are more or less disadvantageous in the heterozygous state in most species.

The well-established, and now reasonably understood, phenomenon of pleiotropy is also important in understanding the spread of alleles under selection. In general an allele has more than one phenotypic effect. Some of these may be advantageous, some disadvantageous, and some almost neutral. For an allele to spread by selection, there must be a net selective advantage to it in the heterozygous state. To understand the fixation of an allele under selection, it is essential to understand the nature of its advantage. One would fail to understand how an allele became fixed if, for example, one was aware of only a disadvantageous phenotypic side-effect. This type of misjudgment is all too easy to make, since the most conspicuous phenotypic effect may not be the advantageous one, which might well be physiological in character, and therefore cryptic. Williams (1966) looked at pleiotropy from an evolutionary viewpoint, and restricted the word *function* to apply to the principal advantageous phenotypic effect of an allele. All the remaining consequences, whether advantageous, disadvantageous, or somewhat less advantageous, he named *effects*. Thus, in seeking to elucidate the evolution of a species-specific character, we need first to decide whether it was fixed stochastically or by natural selection. If the latter, we need to identify the function it serves. This may be far from obvious, and our judgment may well be coloured by our point of view. For example, if we find two sympatric, congeneric species which breed at quite distinct times of the year, an evolutionist might seek a function in terms of *reproductive isolation*, and call the character an isolating mechanism. On the other hand, an ecologist might point out that each species breeds when its food is most abundant and might not even notice that it has any influence on the possibility of the members of the two populations hybridizing. Is reproductive isolation the character's *function* or merely an *effect*? I find it doubtful, to put it very mildly, that any "premating isolating mechanism" was ever evolved to serve the function of reproductively isolating the members of one species from those of another. To me, the isolating role seems always to be better accounted for if it is viewed as an effect. Quite certainly the "postmating isolating mechanisms" isolate only incidentally, as was made abundantly clear by Darwin (1859, 245 ff.), though a remarkable number of modern population geneticists have failed to see his point. With this argument in mind we can attend to the second question.

Accepting that the field of gene recombination is delimited by the isolating mechanisms imposes restrictions on the answering of the second question: "How do these limits [isolating mechanisms] arise *ab initio*?" These constraints demand that characters evolved to function as isolating mechanisms must arise in sympatry or parapatry. But this conflicts with the empirical observation that the only Class I (i.e., empirically supported) mode of speciation is speciation in allopatry (Paterson 1981). The difficulties arising from this conflict will be illustrated with quotations from the literature.

The two seminal advocates of the isolation concept, Dobzhansky and Mayr, have both been surprisingly inconsistent in their writings on isolating mechanisms, which makes it difficult to be certain what their concepts actually are, in part this was due to the conflation of the different species concepts (taxonomic, isolation and recognition) (e.g., Mayr 1963, 89, 95) but other conceptual problems are also involved. Even in his very first theoretical paper on species, Dobzhansky had difficulties. In discussing isolating mechanisms he wrote (1935, 349), "Although the mechanisms preventing free and unlimited interbreeding of related forms are as yet little understood, it is already clear enough that a large number of very different mechanisms of this kind are functioning in nature. This diversity of the isolating mechanisms is in itself remarkable and difficult to explain. It is unclear how such mechanisms can be created at all by natural selection, that is what use the organism derives directly from their development. We are almost forced to conjecture that the isolating mechanisms are merely by-products of some other differences between the organisms in question, these latter differences having some adaptive value and consequently being subject to natural selection." It will be noticed how the acceptance of speciation in allopatry compels authors to invoke pleiotropy as a basis for changing the limits of the field for gene recombination. But of course, isolating mechanisms can then no longer be called *mechanisms*, or be regarded as ad hoc, nor can speciation be regarded as adaptive per se. This is the price authors have been reluctant to pay.

The following passage shows that in 1970 Dobzhansky still had fundamental difficulties with this problem (p. 376): "The question naturally presents itself, what causes bring about the development of reproductive isolating mechanisms? Two hypothetical answers have been proposed. First, reproductive isolation is a by-product of the accumulation of genetic differences between the diverging races ... Second, the isolation is built up by natural selection, when and if the gene exchange between the diverging populations generates recombination products of low fitness ... These two hypotheses are not mutually exclusive. Needless disputes have arisen because they were mistakenly treated as alternative."

In practice the problem cannot so readily be disposed of. The assertion that these two hypotheses are not alternatives seems to me to be impossible to sustain; the first does not invoke any direct selection for "reproductive isolation," while the second does. This is a very fundamental difference between them, as each has very different consequences for evolutionary theory.

In 1950 Dobzhansky wrote (see also Dobzhansky 1976, 104), "The integration of individuals into Mendelian populations, into sexual supraorganisms if you will, is an evolutionary adaptation. The further integration of elementary Mendelian populations into populations of higher orders, such as races and species, is likewise adaptive. It can be shown that formation of races and species has become necessary owing to the great diversity of environments found on our planet." This statement provides us with an insight on how Dobzhansky conceived the role of species: why he required species to be the direct products of natural selection (cf. Mayr 1949, 284 for a comparable statement). In the following passage (Dobzhansky 1940), his bias in favor of the selection hypothesis clearly shows through: "Another difficulty is with species isolated on occanic islands or in similar situations. If the geographical barriers between races are secure enough, the precondition for the development of physiological [= reproductive] isolation is absent. Precisely how serious is this difficulty is not clear." In the third edition of his book (Dobzhansky 1951, 208) we find, "Isolating mechanisms encountered in nature appear to be *ad hoc* contrivances which prevent the exchange of genes between nascent species, rather than incongruities originating in accidental changes in the gene functions." A clear reluctance to rely on pleiotropy in isolation is evident.

Inevitably, Mayr (1963, 548, see also p. 109) was plagued by the same problem: "They are *ad hoc* mechanisms. It is therefore somewhat difficult to comprehend how isolating mechanisms can evolve in isolated populations." Mayr's problem was particularly acute since he is an ardent advocate of geographical or allopatric speciation. I have recently (1981, 113) emphasized that there is much observational evidence for the origin of new species in total isolation (Mayr 1942, 1963), and that there is no such support for any other model of speciation. Dobzhansky's favored model of speciation through the reinforcement of isolating mechanisms under natural selection is one among many for which there is no convincing evidence. Even after some 40 years of active research, the support for speciation by reinforcement today is still both meager and equivocal (Loftus-Hills 1975; Paterson 1978, 1981, 1982a).

These few difficulties alone seem sufficient to falsify the isolation concept of species, and yet they constitute but some of its problems.

The isolation concept was supported by Wallace (1889) but not by Darwin. Later it was further elaborated by Gulick (1905), in remarkably modern terms, who appears to have anticipated Dobzhansky to a considerable extent. Both Robson (1928) and Fisher (1930) supported the isolation concept. Doubtless, however, the concept's wide support stems from Dobzhansky's effective advocacy (1937, 1940, 1970).

As already stated, Dobzhansky was aware of problems and inconsistencies with the concept in 1935, and yet he adhered to it consistently throughout his life. It is important to ask why he should have done so. In a wider context, the very general, unquestioning support the isolation concept has received is suspicious. To me it suggests that this favor might stem from deep-seated biases inherent in our Western cultural background (cf. Masters et al. 1984, Paterson 1982b). One obvious source of bias is the creation stories in the Book of Genesis. That this has been, and indeed is, an important source of prejudice was made clear by Darwin at the beginning of his chapter on hybridism (Darwin 1859, 245): "The view generally entertained by naturalists is that species ... have been specially endowed with the quality of sterility in order to prevent the confusion of all organic forms."

Support for this contention can be gleaned from Ellegard (1958), who records the opinions of nineteenth-century general readers and scientists alike: "God forbids hybrids to breed," "the sterility of true hybrids affords another evidence of the jealousy with which the Creator regards all attempts to introduce confusion into His perfect plan," etc. From this widely held viewpoint, a species is seen as a group of organisms descended from the same original created pair.

Another, even older, source of bias in favor of the isolation concept stems from prehistoric attitudes to "purity of stock" and "purity of line," engendered by the practices of ancient plant and animal breeders. The introduction of managed breeding programs undoubtedly revolutionized man's whole way of life, and, one would think, influenced his language by enriching its vocabulary and imagery. In English, notice how approbative are words such as pure, purebred, thoroughbred, and how pejorative are those like mongrel, bastard, halfbreed, and hybrid. Such cultural biases, which act subtly, almost subliminally, through the vocabulary and imagery of languages, might well predispose the unwary to favor ideas like that of "isolating mechanisms" with the role of "protecting the integrity of species." When Dobzhansky introduced the isolation concept in 1937, it was accepted almost without resistance. This acceptance is in sharp contrast to the usual opposition that greets new ideas (cf. Kuhn 1970), and could well have been due to these cultural predisposing factors.

Thus, problems of function, logic, and consistency beset the isolation concept.

The Recognition Concept of Species

> It is no use for a species to have individuals of two sexes, supplied with reproductive apparatus mutually adapted for their propagation, if the individuals are not endowed with suitable genetically determined impulses. The potential parents must also have instincts, prompting them to desire one another and to provide for the resulting young such care as they need for their survival. (Darlington 1964, 335).

It is rather obvious that the complex act of fertilization, which is an essential part of sex, will not occur fortuitously, as is recognized by Darlington in the quotation above. The physiologist J. Z. Young (1975) provided an independent view of the same situation: "To ensure that reproduction occurs at times of the year when young are likely to survive, the slowly operating chemical signalling of the endocrine system is used . . . Control through the nervous system is important, however, for the performance of reproductive actions in relation to other members of the species, and in all mammals there are communication signs by which individuals recognize others of the same or opposite sex and elicit appropriate mating reactions from them . . . Further, there are *secondary sexual characters* providing signals ensuring that the sexes meet and pair."

Among evolutionists, recognition of the existence of a fertilization system in all biparental eukaryotes is general, though its full significance is seldom emphasized. Thus, both Dobzhansky (1951, 184) and Mayr (1963, 95) were aware of its existence. What has not been recognized and emphasized is that the form of the fertilization system accounts for the delineation of "fields for gene recombination" in a simple, rational, and yet comprehensively adequate way. Mayr (1963, 20) in fact rejects this approach explicitly in favor of a relational concept: "Species are more unequivocally defined by their relation to non-conspecific populations ("isolation") than by the rela-

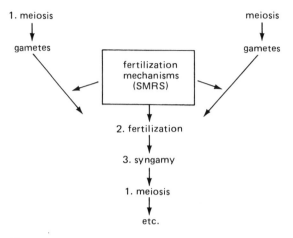

Figure 8.1
Sexual cycle in a biparental eukaryote.

tion of conspecific individuals to each other. The decisive criterion is not the fertility of individuals but the reproductive isolation of populations."

True sex is found only in biparental, eukaryotic organisms. Despite considerable variation in detail, sexual cycles always involve the two complex processes of meiosis and fertilization (Lewis and John 1964). Successful fertilization in even the simplest of unicellular eukaryotes requires the assistance of a series of adaptations which constitute what might be called the fertilization system of the organism (fig 8.1).

Each fertilization system comprises a number of components, each adapted to fulfill a subsidiary proximate function, which contributes to the ultimate function of bringing about fertilization while the organism occupies its normal habitat.

Fertilization systems are also adapted to the circumstances imposed by the organism's "way-of-life" (i.e., whether sessile, motile, nocturnal, diurnal, etc.). Thus, motile organisms have a special requirement for a subset of characters of the fertilization system that serve the function of bringing motile mating partners together as a necessary preliminary to the ultimate achievement of fertilization and syngamy.

This subset of adaptations, which are involved in signalling between mating partners or their cells, constitutes the Specific-Mate Recognition System or SMRS (fig 8.2) (Paterson 1978, 1980). I have chosen to use "specific-mate" instead of simply "mate" because it is important to distinguish between the process with which I am concerned and the quite

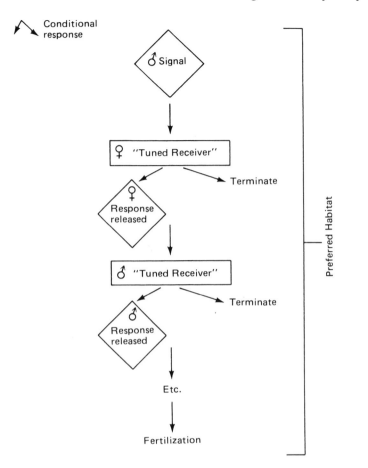

Figure 8.2
Simplified diagram illustrating the form of the Specific-Mate Recognition System (SMRS) as a coadapted signal-response reaction chain. A more realistic representation was given by Morris (1970, 338).

different kind of mate recognition, "individual mate recognition." I also avoid the common term "species recognition" because the process with which I am concerned most certainly does not involve species recognition, a strictly philosophical process, but the recognition of an appropriate mating partner. ("Appropriate" here implies no more than an individual of opposite sex drawn from the same "field for gene recombination.")

The response of one mating partner to a signal from the other is here regarded as an act of *recognition* (Paterson 1982a). Recognition is thus a specific response by one partner to a specific signal from the other. This process might be compared to the recognition of a specific antigen by its specific antibody, and hybridization involves a process having something in common with a cross-reaction. I strongly emphasize that I imply no act of judgment, and no act of choice on the part of the responding partner (Paterson 1982a).

As a working hypothesis I have assumed that all steps in a fertilization system have evolved to serve a particular role. In other words, I assume that all components are adaptations, or, at least, were adaptations, in the strict sense of Williams (1966). It is possible to sustain such a view if one examines the well-analyzed "courtships" of the three-spined and ten-spined sticklebacks (Tinbergen 1951, Morris 1970), though, admittedly, the case is less diagrammatically clear in species which have not yet been as closely analyzed (e.g., the ducks).

In sessile organisms the SMRS assumes a much less prominent role; positive assortative mating is determined in these organisms by other adaptations of the fertilization system. The sex cells of sessile biparental eukaryotes are transported by various agencies including wind, water, insects, birds and mammals (e.g., bats). In sessile organisms, as in motile, the fertilization system is closely adapted to the conditions of the organism's way-of-life and normal habitat. This becomes strikingly evident when one compares, for example, the fertilization systems of two very distantly related organisms from the intertidal zone of a rocky shore. The fertilizations system of an oyster (or a mussel) and of a species of brown alga are much more similar than are the systems of the oyster and its motile predatory fellow mollusc, *Sepia officinalis* (Tinbergen 1939). The fertilization system of the squid, in turn, resembles much more closely the systems of some fish (Packard 1972, Ghiselin 1974).

Among angiosperms the SMRS is limited to interactions such as between the pollen and the stigma (Clarke and Knox 1978), and in sessile animals it may be restricted to the recognition of the sperm by the ovum. Among orchids, several species, even of different genera, may share a common SMRS. This is evident from the observation that fertile experimental crosses can be made between them. In these species the "fields for gene recombination" are determined by the fertilization mechanisms other than those of the SMRS. In orchids they usually involve the attraction and exploitation of a particular insect species as a vector of pollen (e.g., the Western Australian slipper orchid, *Cryptostylus ovata*, Erickson 1951). Darwin, in the introductory sentences of his book (1862) on the pollination of orchids by insects, expresses a view in perfect agreement with the recognition concept: "The object of the following work is to show that the contrivances by which the orchids are fertilized are varied and almost as perfect as any of the most beautiful adaptations in the animal kingdom; and, secondly, to show that these contrivances have for their main object the fertilization of the flowers with pollen brought by insects from a distant plant."

Taking such facts as these into account, it is clear that the limits to a "field for gene recombination" can be set by the shared fertilization system of members of a population of organisms alone. It is the fertilization system which leads to the positive assortative mating that delimits the field.

We can, therefore, regard as a species that most inclusive population of individual biparental organisms which share a common fertilization system.

I now turn to the second question: How does a new fertilization system, and hence a new species, arise *ab initio*?

In terms of fitness, a mate is a crucial resource. Mate acquisition is, thus, as important an adaptive process as is avoidance of predators, the ability to find a refuge, or the acquisition of food. As with these other adaptive characters, the characters of the fertilization system are adapted to the circumstances impinging on the organism in its normal habitat. While members of a species are occupying their normal habitat the characters of the fertilization system, as well as their other adaptive characters, are all maintained under stabilizing selection. This means that while biparental eukaryotes remain in their normal habitats, their adaptive characters remain largely buffered from directional change.

From this insight, it is evident that for speciation to occur the buffering of adaptive characters must be overcome, so that a new constellation of adaptive character-states can evolve. This is most likely to happen if a small population (Paterson and Macnamara 1984, 315) of conspecific individuals becomes displaced into, and restricted to, a new habitat. The isolation envisaged here is allopatric isolation induced by extrinsic circumstances, such as a flock of birds being blown out to sea onto an island on which their normal habitat is not to be found. Many other scenarios might be invoked according to particular circumstances. Any adaptive characters, including those of the fertilization system, which are now less well adapted, will become subject to directional selection. Eventually, when the character-states of the population members have shifted under selection, etc., to become appropriate and effective under the new conditions, they will return once more to the control of stabilizing selection. At this point we say that the individual organisms of the population are adapted to the new habitat. Speciation will also have occurred if the new fertilization system has become sufficiently different from that of the members of the parent population, for then the new fertilization system will delimit a new field for gene recombination. At present the time needed for such speciation to occur is essentially unknown, but it may be relatively short (Greenwood 1965).

The adaptation of all the adaptive characters to the conditions of the new habitat also determines a new "niche" for the daughter species, and the stabilizing selection within the normal habitat stabilizes these ecological characteristics as well. It is clear that speciation and the acquisition of a new niche are part of the same process of adaptation to a new habitat. There is no special process of cladogenesis; speciation is an incidental *effect* resulting from the adaptation of the characters of the fertilization system, among others, to a new habitat, or way-of-life.

Although this view of speciation must be classified with Mayr's model of geographical speciation (Mayr 1963) it should be appreciated that they are not identical. Because Mayr conceives species in terms of reproductive isolation, he is obliged to invoke the pleiotropic modification of "isolating mechanisms" in allopatry to account for geographic speciation. No such problem faces the advocates of the new species concept. Since the characters of the fertilization system are clearly adaptive in relation to the species' normal habitat, speciation results from their adaptation to the conditions in the new habitat (see below).

Despite a major role being assigned to natural selection in the model of speciation discussed above, I do not count myself in the ranks of Kimura's "naive panselectionists." I do accept an important role for stochastic processess. This view can scarcely be avoided if one notices that closely related species may differ in possessing fixed alternative chromosomal arrangements (see above).

The correlation of fixed chromosome rearrangements with speciation cannot be regarded as evidence for a causal connection between the two events as White (1978) has argued (cf. Carson et al. 1967, Paterson 1981).

A small population isolated in a new habitat will more often than not become extinct. However, should it survive over a number of generations it is likely to remain small because its members are ill-adapted and are under directional selection. The population is likely to increase only after its members have adapted to the new conditions.

It is unlikely that the characters of the SMRS can adapt quickly to new conditions. This is because the coadaptation that exists between the mating partners with respect to signals and receivers constitutes an effective buffer to change (Paterson 1978). The signal and receiver can only change in small steps, with coadaptation being reestablished after each step. The details of this process deserve a more comprehensive treatment than can be offered here.

Discussion

In reviewing the consequences of the recognition concept, the first thing to consider is the proposition that the isolation and recognition concepts of species are merely "the two sides of the same coin."

According to the proponents of the isolation concept, species are determined by the functioning of the isolating mechanisms; that is, species are defined relationally in terms of reproductive isolation. Leading workers have regarded species explicitly, though inconsistently, as "adaptive devices."

In terms of the recognition concept, on the other hand, species are determined by the functioning of fertilization mechanism; species are not defined relationally but independently, since of necessity, all sexual organisms must possess an effective fertilization system. Species are seen as incidental consequences of adaptive evolution.

Applying the two concepts in turn to a newly arisen autotetraploid (see also Paterson 1981) in a population of an outbreeding diploid angiosperm will serve to show that they are in fact quite distinct, and lead to quite different expectations. The situation described is generally accepted as a case of "instantaneous speciation" by advocates of the isolation concept (e.g., by Mayr 1963, 439, 448), because the tetraploid individuals are "reproductively isolated" from the parental diploid population. In genetical terms, however, the gene pool of the tetraploids is merely a subset of the gene pool of the diploids. Accordingly, "mating" is likely to occur at random. If this is considered in the light of population genetic theory, it will be seen that we are here dealing with an example of heterozygote disadvantage. The deterministic algebra makes it abundantly clear that, under the conditions outlined above, the tetraploid population would be rapidly eliminated. Inability to coexist is scarcely a criterion for a species in population genetics.

On the other hand, if the recognition concept is applied to this situation, the conclusion is inevitably reached that the two populations are conspecific because they share a common fertilization system. Natural selection, as shown above, thus eliminates the cause of the heterozygote disadvantage within the single species.

Besides revealing the distinctness of the two concepts, this scenario underlines a point which is not generally appreciated by evolutionists. This is that two populations that share a common SMRS cannot coexist if they are technically "reproductively isolated" by "sterility" alone (Paterson 1968). In such a case, with complete interpopulation sterility ($s = 1$), the less common population will rapidly disappear (Paterson 1978); but if the heterozygote disadvantage is less complete (i.e., if the coefficient of selection, s, is less than 1 but greater than 0), natural selection will act to eliminate the allele or chromosome rearrangement that is causing the hybrid disadvantage. Under these conditions, the "interpopulation sterility" is thus an intraspecific phenomenon, comparable to the phenomenon of "self-incompatibility" in plants (Clarke and Knox 1978).

An example from animals is the well-known *Drosophila paulistorum* (Dobzhansky 1970). Subpopulations are often semi-intersterile, despite sharing a common SMRS (in some cases they mate at random). The infertility is due to the interaction of the host genome with that of symbiotic mycoplasms in the gonads. In accordance with the recognition concept these subpopulations are conspecific, but Dobzhansky interpreted them as "semi-species *Culex molestus* Forskal of the *Culex pipiens* complex. The symbionts in this case are rickettsias (Irving-Bell 1983, Miles 1977). Some of these cases, at least, are laboratory artifacts arising from "bottlenecks" in the colonies. Studies with fresh material from the field should be done in both complexes. Theoretical models of "sympatric speciation" which depend on one or other form of "sterility" (heterozygote disadvantage) are fairly widely accepted by evolutionists. But, again, in many cases they do not even constitute speciation according to the recognition concept because both populations in these models share a common fertilization system. Summarizing this point: under the recognition concept, all phenomena covered by the category "postmating isolating mechanisms" (Mayr 1963) are incidental to delineating species, since they have nothing to do with bringing about fertilization.

It has been shown that the recognition concept is not simply the "obverse side of the same coin" as the isolation concept, and some of the logical and interpretive difficulties of the isolation concept have been enumerated. How well does the recognition concept accommodate currently debated ideas in population biology?

Reporting on the recent Chicago Macroevolution Conference, Maynard Smith (1981) made the following comment on the pattern of evolutionary change known as the punctuated equilibria model (Eldredge and Gould 1972): "As a geneticist I was left with the impression that the 'sudden' appearance of a new species called for no new explanations, but that stasis may do." In fact the recognition concept, and the mode of allopatric speciation it specifies, account for all aspects of the punctuated equilibria model very satisfactorily. The equilibrium is well explained by the stabilizing selection due to the coadaptation of the SMRS between the mating partners in their normal habitat, as has been explained. The "sudden appearance" of new species fits a speciation model in which small isolated populations develop into new species, and grow in population numbers only after stabilizing selection is again in effect on the new species. The best illustration of these events that I know of from the fossil record is Coope's (1979) documentation of Cenozoic beetles moving with their habitat. The isolation concept does not lead one to expect equilibrium following a speciation event, as Maynard Smith's comment implies.

A point of special interest is that the recognition concept leads one to expect that in those species where some of the SMRS signals are preserved (e.g., horns or antlers), the fossil record is likely to illustrate punctuated equilibria with least ambiguity (Paterson 1982a, Vrba 1984).

The stability of adaptive characters expected under the recognition concept is relevant to the assessment of Van Valen's (1973) red queen hypothesis (see Paterson 1982a). The recognition concept and Coope's observations on fossil beetle populations suggest that Van Valen's expectation that natural selection acts mainly "to enable the organisms to maintain their state of adaptation rather than to improve it" is not generally valid and may only apply under special circumstances. If Van Valen's hypothesis was, in fact, realistically conceived, the punctuated equilibria pattern would not be expected as an outcome.

It is not always appreciated that the nature of species and the way speciation occurs have a fundamental role in any attempt at understanding the structure of communities and ecosystems. This is because most ecologists and population biologists attribute the fundamental causal role of patterns in nature to interspecific competition. However, in recent years a number of workers have come to question the critical role attributed to interspecific competition (e.g., Andrewartha and Birch 1954, Wiens 1977, Connell 1980, Walter, Hulley and Craig 1984). The field is too large to review in detail here, but it should be noticed that no emphasis was placed on interspecific competition as an environmental factor when considering how speciation occurs. Generally speaking, I agree that interspecific competition lacks the credentials of a "motor" for evolutionary change. After much study there are still no really compelling examples of character displacement (Grine 1981). While adaptation to a habitat and the co-adaptation of the male and female parts of the SMRS are constraints, interspecific competition exerts only intermittent selective pressure on members of a species. Therefore, the evident stability of form in many species in space and time (see discussion above) with respect to adaptive characters does not favor interspecific competition as a selective force to account for niche characteristics.

If speciation occurs as postulated under the recognition concept, then we obtain a radically different picture of how the structures of communities and ecosystems emerge. The normal habitat of a species is likely to approximate closely to that in which it arose. Similarly, the adaptive characters that were fixed in the original small isolate were subsequently stabilized in a number of ways, including stabilizing selection within the normal habitat of the species (cf. Coope 1979). The increase in numbers of the original small population which speciated also constitutes a buffer to change. Accordingly, members of sympatric species do not come to "partition resources" in an ad hoc manner. Character displacement is not expected according to this model, and it is not surprising that clear-cut cases are virtually nonexistent. Species characteristics (fertilization system, niche characteristics, etc.) are expected to be largely stabilized throughout the range of the species. These expectations contrast strongly with those generated by interspecific competition theory, as Walter, Hulley, and Craig (1984) have emphasized.

Although many important consequences could be added to the few examined in this discussion, only one other will be emphasized: the bearing the recognition concept has on how we look at man.

The isolation concept has a very definite teleological flavour to it (Paterson 1982b). Species are seen as "adaptive devices," and speciation is considered a process of adaptation by the leaders in the field. Isolating mechanisms are said to be ad hoc devices evolved to protect the integrity of species. Such statements are teleological, or imply the involvement of group selection, or both.

In contrast, the recognition concept is free of teleological commitment and invokes only individual selection, as with Darwin's view (1859). Darwin conceived species in terms of structure, just as taxonomists did. He saw no essential difference between species and varieties. He believed that both arose in the same way, under natural selection. Inadequate though his view of species was, Darwin's view of speciation was detailed enough for us to see that he accepted that species arise as incidental consequences of adaptation. This was perhaps the most revolutionary conclusion in a revolutionary text, yet it is seldom stressed or even appreciated except by philosophers. Here it is emphasized by Hull (1973, 55): "Galileo and Newton replaced one physical theory with another, but they left the teleological world-picture intact. The findings of the paleontologists and geologists had necessitated a reinterpretation of Genesis. But it was Darwin who finally forced scientists to realize just how trivial teleology had become in their hands. The change in scientific thought marked by the appearance of the *Origin of Species* was so fundamental that it certainly deserves the title conceptual revolution." In the same vein, Thomas Kuhn (1970, 172) said: "For many men the abolition of that teleological kind of evolution was the most significant and least palatable of Darwin's suggestions. The *Origin of Species* recognized no goal set either by God or nature."

Thus, in sharp contrast to the isolation concept, the recognition concept is in complete accord with the revolutionary view of Darwin as far as it went. Moreover, the recognition concept emphasizes the incidental nature of speciation and expresses it in genetical terms, besides providing a genetical concept of species. Applied to man the concept is equally appropriate.

It was pointed out above that any comprehensive view of species must be able to deal satisfactorily with the question: What sets the limits to the field of gene recombination in man? In applying the isolation concept to man, a number of problems arise. Authors never seem to identify the isolating mechanisms that are supposed to delimit the field. Perhaps there are none, in accordance with this statement by Mayr (1963, 109): "Where no other closely related species occur, all courtship signals (= "ethological isolating mechanisms") can 'afford' to be general, nonspecific, and variable". However, I find Mayr's assertion to be poorly supported empirically (Paterson 1978). I believe that Mayr wrote these words with a case such as the mallard and pintail ducks and some of their insular congeners in mind (Lack 1974). It is hypothesized that the mallard and pintail are markedly sexually dimorphic in the Holarctic Region to isolate them reproductively from their many close congeners with which they are sympatric. On a number of islands such as Hawaii, Kerguellan, South Georgia, and the Falkland Islands monomorphic relatives exist which are allopatric from all close congeneric species. It is presumed that they can here "afford" to relax their "isolating mechanisms." In 1978 I pointed out that in Africa, Australia, and North America, a number of monomorphic relatives of the mallard and pintail coexist without requiring the striking sexual dimorphism of their close relatives of the Holarctic, which weakens the case considerably (see also Weller 1980, 68). It is further weakened when one notices that species with no close relatives on earth (e.g., the ostrich, the hamerkop (Scopus umbretta), the Madagascan partridge (Margaroperdis madagascariensis), etc.) nevertheless possess complex courtships. Thus, I believe the case for applying Mayr's statement to man is not convincing.

No such problem occurs in applying the recognition concept to Homo sapiens. This is not the place to analyze the SMRS of man in detail, and so I shall merely provide an independent and appealing lay statement of its existence by the psychologist Abraham Maslow (1970, 195): "It is not the welfare of the species, or the task of reproduction, or the future development of mankind that attracts people to each other ... it is basically an enjoyment and a delight, which is another thing altogether."

The isolation concept in its complete form was presented for testing in 1940. Today it is still logically unsatisfactory, and in virtually all accounts it is intricately conflated with either or both the recognition concept and a morphological concept of species. Identifying the recognition concept as fundamentally different from the isolation concept enables us to design stringent tests in attempts at refuting the one or the other. This is definite scientific progress. My earnest hope is that it will reduce the prevailing fog and induce new life into that very significant biological discipline once called by Ernst Mayr the science of species.

Acknowledgments

This paper is dedicated to Ernst Mayr, my first guide, for his 80th year. It is a contribution from the Animal Communications Research Group, which is funded by the Council Research Committee of the University of the Witwatersrand.

For critical comments and guidance, my deep gratitude is due to Michael Anderson, Neil Caithness, Marc Centner, Anthony Gordon, Pat Hulley, Shane McEvey, Judith Masters, Andy Potts, Rob Toms, and Elisabeth Vrba, and a referee. I also thank Adele Katz for her efficient secretarial assistance.

References

Andrewartha, H. G. and Birch, L. C., 1954. *The distribution and abundance of animals.* University of Chicago Press, Chicago.

Carson, L. H., 1957. The species as a field for gene recombination. *In:* Mayr, E., ed., *The species problem*, pp. 23–38. American Association for the Advancement of Science, Publication No. 50, Washington.

Carson, L. H., Clayton, F. E. and Stalker, H. D., 1967. Karyotypic stability and speciation in Hawaiian *Drosophila. Proceedings of the National Academy of Science of Washington* 57:1280–1285.

Clarke, A. E. and Knox, R. B., 1978. Cell recognition in flowering plants. *Quarterly Review of Biology* 53:3–28.

Connell, J. H., 1980. Diversity and the coevolution of competitors, or the ghost of competition past. *Oikos* 35:131–138.

Coope, G. R., 1979. Late Cenozoic fossil Coleoptera: evolution, biogeography, and ecology. *Annual Review of Ecology and Systematics* 10:247–267.

Darlington, C. D., 1964. *Genetics and man.* George Allen and Unwin, London.

Darwin, C., 1859. *The origin of species by means of natural selection.* John Murray, London.

Darwin, C., 1862. *The various contrivances by which orchids are fertilized by insects.* John Murray, London.

Dobzhansky, T., 1935. A critique of the species concept in Biology. *Philosophy of Science* 2:344–355.

Dobzhansky, T., 1937. *Genetics and the origin of species.* Columbia University Press, New York.

Dobzhansky, T., 1940. Speciaton as a stage in evolutionary divergence. *American Naturalist* 74:312–321.

Dobzhansky, T., 1950. Mendelian populations and their evolution. *American Naturalist* 84:401–418.

Dobzhansky, T., 1951. *Genetics and the origin of species*, 3rd edn. Columbia University Press, New York.

Dobzhansky, T., 1962. *Mankind evolving.* Yale University Press, New Haven.

Dobzhansky, T., 1970. *Genetics of the evolutionary process.* Columbia University Press, New York.

Dobzhansky, T., 1976. Organismic and molecular aspects of species formation. *In:* Ayala, F. J., ed., *Molecular evolution*, pp. 95–105. Sinauer Associates, Sunderland, Mass.

Eldredge, N. and Gould, S. J., 1972. Punctuated equilibria, an alternative to phyletic gradualism. *In:* Schopf, T. J. M., ed., *Models in paleobiology.* Freeman, Cooper and Company, San Francisco.

Ellegard, A., 1958. *Darwin and the general reader*. Gothenburg Studies in English, VIII, Goteborg.

Erickson, R., 1951. *Orchids of the west*. Paterson Brokensha, Perth, Western Australia.

Fisher, R. A., 1930. *The genetical theory of natural selection*. Oxford University Press, Oxford.

Futuyma, D. J., 1979. *Evolutionary biology*. Sinauer Associates, Sunderland, Mass.

Ghiselin, M. T., 1974. *The economy of nature and the evolution of sex*. University of California Press, Berkeley.

Greenwood, P. H., 1965. The cichlid fishes of Lake Nabugabo, Uganda. *Bulletin of the British Museum (Natural History) (Zoology)* 12:315–357.

Grine, F. E., 1981. Trophic differences between 'Gracile' and 'Robust' Australopithecines: A scanning electron microscope analysis of occlusal events. *South African Journal of Science* 77:203–320.

Gulick, J. T., 1905. *Evolution, racial and habitual*. Carnegie Institute of Washington Publication No. 25.

Hull, D., 1973. *Darwin and his critics*. Harvard University Press, Cambridge, Mass.

Irving-Bell, R. J., 1983. Cytoplasmic incompatibility within and between *Culex molestus* and *Cx. quinquifasciatus* (Diptera: Culicidae). *Journal of Medical Entomology* 20:44–48.

Kuhn, T., 1970. *The structure of scientific revolutions*, 2nd edn. University of Chicago Press, Chicago.

Lack, D., 1974. *Evolution illustrated by waterfowl*. Blackwell Scientific Publications, Oxford.

Lewis, K. R. and John, B., 1964. *The matter of Mendelian heredity*. J. & A. Churchill, London.

Loftus-Hills, J. J., 1975. The evidence for reproductive character displacement between the toads *Bufo americanus* and *B. woodhouseii fowleri*. *Evolution* 29:368–369.

Maslow, A., 1970. *Motivation and personality*. Harper and Row, New York.

Masters, J., Lambert, D. and Paterson, H., 1984. *Perspectives in biology and medicine.*, 28:107–116.

Maynard Smith, J., 1981. Macroevolution. *Nature, London* 289:13–14.

Mayr, E., 1942. *Systematics and the origin of species*. Columbia University Press, New York.

Mayr, E., 1949. Speciation and systematics. *In*: Jepsen, G. L., Mayr, E. and Simpson, G. G., eds, *Genetics, paleontology, and evolution*, pp. 281–298. Princeton University Press, Princeton.

Mayr, E., 1963. *Animal species and evolution*. Harvard University Press. Cambridge, Mass.

Mayr, E., 1970. *Populations, species, and evolution*. Harvard University Press, Cambridge, Mass.

Mayr, E., 1976. *Evolution and the diversity of life*. Harvard University Press, Cambridge, Mass.

Mayr, E., 1982. *The growth of biological thought*. Harvard University Press, Cambridge, Mass.

Mayr, E. and Provine, W. B., 1980. *The evolutionary synthesis*. Harvard University Press, Cambridge, Mass.

Miles, S. J., 1977. Laboratory evidence for mate recognition behaviour in a member of the *Culex pipiens* complex (Diptera: Culicidae). *Australian Journal of Zoology* 25:491–498.

Moore, J. A., 1957. An embryologist's view of the species concept. In: Mayr, E., ed., *The species problem*, pp. 325–338. American Association for the Advancement of Science Publication No. 50, Washington.

Morris, D., 1970. *Patterns of reproductive behaviour*. Jonathan Cape. Lond.

Packard, A., 1972. Cephalopods and fish: the limits of convergence. *Biological Reviews* 47:241–307.

Paterson. H. E., 1968. Evolutionary and population genetical studies of certain Diptera. Ph. D. thesis, University of the Witwatersrand, Johannesburg.

Paterson, H. E., 1973. Animal species studies. *Journal of the Royal Society of Western Australia* 56:31–36.

Paterson, H. E. H., 1978. More evidence against speciation by reinforcement. *South African Journal of Science* 74:369–371.

Paterson, H. E. H., 1980. A comment on 'mate recognition systems.' *Evolution* 34:330–331.

Paterson, H. E. H., 1981. The continuing search for the unknown and unknowable: a critique of contemporary ideas on speciation. *South African Journal of Science* 77:113–119.

Paterson, H. E. H., 1982a. Perspective on speciation by reinforcement. *South African Journal of Science* 78:53–57.

Paterson, H. E. H., 1982b. Darwin and the origin of species. *South African Journal of Science* 78:272–275.

Paterson, H. E. H. and Macnamara, M. 1984. The recognition concept of species. *South African Journal of Science* 80:312–318.

Robson, G. C., 1928. *The species problem.* Oliver and Boyd. Edinburgh.

Tinbergen, L., 1939. Zur Fortpflanzungsethologie von *Sepia officinalis* L. *Archives Neerlandaises de Zoologie* 3:323–364.

Tinbergen, N., 1951. *The study of instinct.* Oxford University Press, Oxford.

Van Valen, L., 1973. A new evolutionary law. *Evolutionary Theory* 1:1–30.

Vrba, E., 1984. Evolutionary pattern and process in the sister-group Alcelaphini-Aepycerotini (Mammalia: Bovidae). *In*: Eldredge. N. and Stanley, S. M., eds, *Living fossils*, pp. 62–79. Springer-Verlag, New York.

Wallage, A. R., 1989. *Darwinism.* Macmillan, London.

Walter, G. H., Hulley, P. E. and Graig, A. J. F. K., 1984. Speciation, adaptation and interspecific competition. *Oikos* 43:246–248.

White, M. J. D., 1978. *Modes of speciation.* W. H. Freeman, San Francisco.

Wiens, J. A., 1977. On competition and variable environments. *American Scientist* 65:590–597.

Williams, G. C., 1966. *Adaptation and natural selection.* Princeton University Press, Princeton.

Wilson, L. G., 1970. *Sir Charles Lyell's scientific journals on the species question.* Yale University Press, New Haven.

Young, J. Z., 1975. *The life of mammals.* Oxford University Press. Oxford.

Chapter 9

The Meaning of Species and Speciation:
A Genetic Perspective

Alan R. Templeton

What is a species? This fundamental question must be answered before the process of species formation can be investigated. As any survey of the evolutionary literature will quickly reveal, there are many definitions of species already in existence. These different definitions reflect the diverse types of evolutionary questions and/or organisms with which their authors were primarily concerned. Consequently, a species concept can be evaluated only in terms of a particular goal or purpose. My goal is to understand speciation as an evolutionary genetic process. A fundamental assumption behind this goal is that speciation, regardless of the precise definition of species, is best approached mechanistically by examining the evolutionary forces operating on individuals within populations or suhpopulations and tracing their effects upward until they ultimately cause all of the members of that population or subpopulation to acquire phenotypic attributes conferring species status on the group.

This emphasis on the evolutionary genetic mechanisms operating within populations of individuals places speciation fully within the province of population genetics. Accordingly, what is needed is a concept of species that can be directly related to the mechanistic framework of population genetics. To achieve this goal, I will first review three species concepts that have strong supporters in the current literature: the evolutionary species concept, the biological species concept, and the recognition species concept. All of these species concepts treat species as real biological entities and attempt to define species in terms of some fundamental biological property. In this regard, all of these definitions are biological species concepts, although one of them is often referred to as *"the* biological species concept." Since "the biological species concept" defines species in terms of isolating mechanisms, it is more accurately known as the isolation concept (Paterson 1985). Paterson's terminology will be used in the remainder of this chapter.

After reviewing the strengths and weaknesses of these three concepts, I will propose a fourth biological species concept, the cohesion concept, which attempts to utilize the strengths of the other three while avoiding their weakness with respect to the goal of defining species in a way that is compatible with a mechanistic population genetic framework. In this manner, a definition of species can be achieved that illuminates, rather than obscures or misleads, the mechanisms of speciation and their genetic consequences.

Three Biological Species Concepts

The Evolutionary Species Concept

Under this definition, a species consists of a population or group of populations that shares a common evolutionary fate through time. This definition has the advantage of being applicable to both living and extinct groups and to sexual and asexual organisms. Moreover, it emphasizes the fact that a species unit can be held together not only through gene flow but also through development, genetic, and ecological constraints. Finally, this concept is useful because it is close to the operational species definition used by most practicing taxonomists and paleontologists. Decisions as to species status are usually made on the basis of patterns of phenotypic cohesion within a group of organisms versus phenotypic discontinuity between groups. However, when a variety of phenotypes is studied, it is often discovered that the patterns of cohesion/discontinuity vary as a function of the phenotype being measured. One fault of the evolutionary species concept is that it provides little or no guidance as to which traits are the more important ones in defining species.

There are two other principal difficulties with this concept. First, there is the problem of judging what constitutes a "common" evolutionary fate. Obviously, polymorphisms can exist even within local populations, and many species are polytypic. Therefore, "common" does not mean "identical" evolutionary fates, so some judgment must be made as to just how much diversity is allowed within a "common" evolutionary fate. Finally, and most importantly with regard to the goal of this chapter, the evolutionary species concept is not a mechanistic definition. It deals only with the manifestation of cohesion rather than the evolutionary mechanisms responsible for cohesion. Hence it does not provide an adequate framework for integrating population genetic factors into the species concept.

The Isolation Species Concept

The species concept that is dominant in much of the evolutionary literature is popularly known as the biological species concept. Mayr (1963) defined the isolation species concept as "groups of actually or potentially interbreeding natural populations which are reproductively isolated from other such groups." Similarly, Dobzhansky (1970) states that "Species are systems of populations: the gene exchange between these systems is limited or prevented by a reproductive isolating mechanism or perhaps by a

combination of several such mechanisms." As White (1978) has emphasized, the isolation concept species "is at the same time a reproductive
community, a gene pool, and a genetic system." It is these later two
attributes that make this concept of species particularly useful for integrating population genetic considerations into the problem of the origin of
species. Population genetics is concerned with the evolutionary forces
operating on gene pools and with the types of genetic systems that arise
from the operation of these forces. The isolation species concept is therefore potentially useful in analyzing speciation from a population genetic
perspective, but it unfortunately has some serious difficulties that must be
rectified before this potential can be realized.

The difficulties stem from the fact that this species concept is defined in
terms of isolating mechanisms. Table 9.1 presents a brief classification of
the types of isolating barriers, and similar tables can be found in any of the
books on speciation by Mayr or Dobzhansky. Under the isolation species
concept, these isolating barriers define the boundaries of the reproductive
community and gene pool and preserve the integrity of the genetic system
of the species.

Paterson (1985) has pointed out that a fundamental difficulty with the
isolation concept of species is that it is misleading when thinking about the
process of speciation. For example, under the classic allopatric model of
speciation, speciation occurs when populations are totally separated from

Table 9.1
Classification of isolating mechanisms

I. Premating mechanisms that prevent interpopulational crosses
   A. Ecological or habitat isolation: the populations mate in different habitats in the
      same general region, or use different pollinators, etc.
   B. Temporal isolation: the populations mate at different times of the year
   C. Ethological isolation: potential interpopulational mates meet but do not mate

II. Postmating but prezygotic isolation
   A. Mechanical isolation: interpopulational matings occur but no transfer of sperm
      takes place
   B. Gametic mortality or incompatibility: sperm transfer occurs but the egg is not
      fertilized

III. Postzygotic isolation
   A. F_1 inviability: hybrid zygotes have a reduced viability
   B. F_1 sterility: hybrid adults have a reduced fertility
   C. Hybrid breakdown: the F_2 or backcross hybrids have reduced viability or
      fertility
   D. Coevolutionary or cytoplasmic interactions: individuals from a population
      infected by an endoparasite or with a particular cytoplasmic element are fertile
      with each other, but fertility and/or viability break down when matings occur
      between infected and uninfected individuals

each other by geographical barriers. The intrinsic isolating mechanisms given in table 9.1 are obvioulsy irrelevant as isolating barriers during speciation because they cannot function as isolating mechanisms in allopatry. Hence, the evolutionary forces responsible for this allopatric speciation process have nothing to do with "isolation." This is true for other speciation mechanisms as well (Templeton 1981). This is not to say that isolation is not a product of the speciation process in some cases, but the product (i.e., isolation) should not be confused with the process (i.e., speciation). The isolation concept has been detrimental to studies of speciation precisely because it has fostered that confusion (Paterson 1985).

The Recognition Species Concept
Paterson (1985) has argued strongly that this confusion can be avoided by looking at the so-called isolating mechanisms from a different perspective. For example, consider the premating isolation mechanisms listed in table 9.1. It is commonplace in the evolutionary literature to find statements that complex courtship rituals, mating signals, etc. function as premating isolating barriers that exist to prevent hybridization with other species. The works of Dobzhansky (1970) indicate how dominant this idea was in the thinking of one of the principal architects and proponents of the biological species concept. Yet, as Tinbergen (1953) has pointed out, such premating mechanisms have several functions in addition to isolation: the suppression of escape or aggressive behavior in a courted animal, the synchronization of mating activities, the persuasion of a potential mate to continue courtship, the coordination in time and space of the pattern of mating, the orientation of the potential mates for copulation, and, finally, fertilization itself. The importance of these other functions of premating behavior is illustrated by the work of Crews (1983) on pseudomale courtship and copulatory behavior in the all-female parthenogenetic lizard, *Cnemidophorus uniparens*. In these lizards, insemination and premating isolation are totally irrelevant since reproduction is strictly parthenogenetic. Yet females show elaborate courting behaviors that mimic male courtship in closely related species. These behaviors serve as a neuroendocrine primer that coordinates reproductive events. Obviously, mating behavior in these lizards facilitates reproduction, but isolation is irrelevant.

The critical question then becomes, which of these many functions (or which combination) is important in the process of speciation? Paterson (1985) has argued that isolation is an irrelevant function in the process of speciation. Consequently, to examine the reason why a premating "isolating" barrier arose, it is necessary to focus attention on the other functions of these premating mechanisms and to examine the evolutionary forces operating on these functions (Paterson 1985). In this regard, all the other functions of these premating behaviors can be thought of as facilitating reproduction, not hindering it as in the isolation function. The isolation function can indeed arise as a by-product of the evolution of the other functions, but in general it is not an active part of the process of speciation.

Consequently, isolating mechanisms are a misleading way of thinking about the process of speciation. Although all of the mechanisms listed in table 9.1 are defined in terms of preventing reproduction between populations, they can also be thought of in an intraspecific fashion as facilitating reproduction within populations. In general, it is this positive inverse of the functions given in table 9.1 that plays the major role in speciation. Paterson (1985) has focused upon the positive function of these mechanisms in facilitating reproduction among members of a certain population. Accordingly, Paterson accepts the premise, shared by the isolation concept, that a species is a field for gene recombination. Unlike the isolation concept, which defines the limits of this field in a negative sense through isolating mechanisms, Paterson defines the limits of this field in a positive sense through fertilization mechanisms, that is, adaptations that assist the processes of meiosis and fertilization. Species are defined as the most inclusive population of individual biparental organisms which share a common fertilization system.

In a sense, the isolation and recognition concepts of species are two sides of the same coin. Flipping the coin is worthwhile because the recognition concept yields a clearer vision of evolutionary process versus pattern, whereas the isolation concept is actively misleading. Hence, given the goal of defining species in such a manner that it facilitates the study of speciation as an evolutionary process, the recognition concept is clearly superior to the isolation concept.

Paterson (1985) has burdened the recognition concept with several restrictions that do not necessarily follow from his primary definition. The most serious of these is his exclusive use of fertilization mechanisms to define a species. Obviously, a field of genetic recombination requires more than fertilization; it requires a complete life cycle in which the products of fertilization are viable and fertile. Moreover, the so-called fertilization mechanisms of Paterson have other evolutionary functions that he ignores, as is well illustrated by the courtship behavior of the parthenogenetic lizards previously discussed. Hence, just as Paterson criticized isolation mechanisms because they may evolve for reasons other than isolation, his fertilization mechanisms may likewise evolve for reasons other than fertilization.

Other minor criticisms of Paterson's concept can be made (Templeton 1987), but I want to concentrate on two serious and fundamental difficulties that are shared by the both the isolation and recognition concepts. As with many other problems in the biological world, these problems are caused by sex—either too little or too much.

Sexual Hangups of the Isolation and Recognition Concepts

Too Little Sex

Both the isolation and recognition concepts of species are applicable only to sexually reproducing organisms (Vrba 1985). Accordingly, large portions of the organic world are outside the logical domain of these species definitions. This is a serious difficulty to people who work with parthenogenetic or asexual organisms.

One particular troublesome aspect of excluding nonsexual species is that most parthenogenetic "species" display the same patterns of phenotypic cohesion within and discontinuity between as do sexual species. For example, Holman (1987) examined the recognizability of sexual and asexual species of rotifers. Contrary to the predictions made by the isolation concept, he discovered that species in the asexual taxa are actually more consistently recognized than those from the sexual taxa. Thus, he concluded that for asexual rotifers "species are real and can be maintained by nonreproductive factors." As this example illustrates, the asexual world is for the most part just as well (or even better) subdivided into easily defined biological taxa as is the sexual world. This biological reality should not be ignored.

Ignoring nonsexual taxa is a major failure of the isolation and recognition concepts, but this failure is actually more extensive than many people realize. For example, the evolutionary genetics of self-mating populations is simply a special case of automictic parthenogenetic populations (e.g., Templeton 1974a). Hence, self-mating sexual species are also outside the logical domain of the isolation and recognition concepts. But the problem does not stop with self-mating sexual species. For example, many species of wasps have mandatory sib mating (Karlin and Lessard 1986). Such a system of mating, as well as any other closed system of mating, will display evolutionary dynamics that can be regarded as a special case of automixis, just as self-mating can. Hence, all sexual taxa with a closed system of mating are outside the logical domain of the isolation and recognition concepts.

The problem does not stop here, however. Models for analyzing multilocus selection in automictic and self-mating populations were very successfully applied to a barley population that was 99.43% self-mating (Templeton 1974b). The reason for this success is straightforward: with this much selfing, the evolutionary dynamics of the population closely approximate that of a 100% selfing population. When outbreeding is at such a low level, its primary role is to introduce genetic variability into the population. Once introduced, the evolutionary fate of that variation is more like that of a selfing population than that of an outcrossing population. Moreover, the genetic impact of the occasional outbreeding is further reduced by isolation by distance, which causes most outbreeding to be between nearly genetically identical individuals. Consequently, from a population genetic perspective, this barley population could not be regarded in any meaningful way as a "field for genetic recombination," and accordingly it lies outside the logical domain of both the isolation and recognition concepts.

The problem of isolation by distance previously mentioned creates a further restriction on the logical domain of the isolation and recognition concepts. An outcrossing population characterized by very limited gene flow and small local effective sizes has much the same genetic consequences and evolutionary dynamics as a predominantly selfing population. Ehrlich and Raven (1969) were among the first to point out in strong terms that many animal and plant species cannot be regarded as fields of genetic recombination in any meaningful sense with respect to basic evolutionary mechanisms, and therefore are also outside the logical domain of the isolation and recognition concepts.

The barley example leads to an interesting question. If a 99.47% selfing population is outside the logical domain of the isolation and recognition concepts, what about a 99% selfing population or a 95% selfing population? Ehrlich and Raven's (1969) work leads to a similar set of questions. At what point is isolation by distance and population subdivision sufficiently weak to bring a taxa into the logical domain of the isolation and recognition concepts? Although this is not an easy question to answer, the problem of genetically closed taxa is usually dismissed in a sentence or two, with sexual and genetically closed taxa being treated as distinct categorical types (e.g., Mayr 1970, Vrba 1985). However, from the viewpoint of evolutionary mechanisms (and, hence, from the viewpoint of speciation as an evolutionary process), there is a continuum from panmictic evolutionary dynamics to genetically closed evolutionary dynamics. Consequently, the logical domain of the isolation and recognition concepts is not at all clear or well defined. The only thing that is certain is that this domain is much more restrictive and limited than is generally perceived.

Too Much Sex

As discussed, genetically closed reproductive systems cause serious difficulties for the isolation and recognition concepts, but so do genetically open systems. For example, Grant (1957), one of the stronger proponents among botanists of the isolation concept, concluded that less than 50% of the outcrossing species in 11 genera of Californian plants were well delimited by isolation from other species. Again and again in plants, taxonomists have defined species that exist in larger units known as syngameons that are characterized by natural hybridization and limited gene exchange. Grant (1981) defines the syngameon as "the most inclusive unit of interbreeding in a hybridizing species group." The frequent occurrence of syngameons in plants creates serious difficulties for both the isolation and recognition concepts because the field of genetic recombination is obviously broader than the taxonomic species and the groups that are behaving as evolutionarily independent entities. One solution is simply to deny the species status of the members of the syngameon. For example, Grant (1981) refers to the members of a syngameon as "semispecies." Under the recognition concept, the syngameon itself would be the species, since Grant's definition of syngameon is virtually identical to Paterson's (1985) definition of species. However, botanists have not made these taxonomic decisions arbitrarily. The species within a syngameon are often real units in terms of morphology, ecology, genetics, and evolution. For example, the fossil record indicates that balsam poplars and cottonwoods (both from the genus *Populus*) have been distinct for at least 12 million years and have generated hybrids throughout this period (Eckenwalder 1984). Even though the hybrids are widespread, fertile, and ancient, these tree species have and are maintaining genetic, phenotypic, and ecological cohesion within and distinction between and have maintained themselves as distinct evolutionary lineages for at least 12 million years (Eckenwalder 1984). Hence, cottonwoods and poplars are real biological units that should not be ignored.

It is commonplace for zoologists to acknowledge that the isolation concept runs into serious difficulties when it is applied to outbreeding, higher plants, but then to argue that the isolation concept works reasonably well for sexually reproducing, multicellular animals. However, this view is no longer tenable with the increased resolution that recombinant DNA techniques provide. For example, in mammals, studies are being carried out in my laboratory on baboons, wild cattle, canids, and gophers and cotton rats, examples, respectively, of primates, ungulates, carnivores, and rodents—the four major mammalian groups. In every case, there is evidence for naturally occurring interspecific hybridization (Baker et al. 1989, Davis et al. 1988, unpublished data). In spite of hybridization, many of the taxonomic units within these groups represent real biological units in a morphological, ecological, genetic, and evolutionary sense. For example, wolves and coyotes can and do hybridize. Yet, they are morphologically quite distinct from each other, have extremely different behaviors in terms of social structure and hunting, and represent distinct evolutionary lineages with diagnostic genetic differences (figure 9.1). Moreover, the fossil record indicates that they have evolved as distinct and continuous lineages for at least 0.5 million years (Hall 1978) and perhaps for as much as 2 million years (Nowak 1978). Although these taxa do not satisfy the criterion of the isolation species concept, Hall (1978) argues that these are biologically real groups and that species status is clearly appropriate.

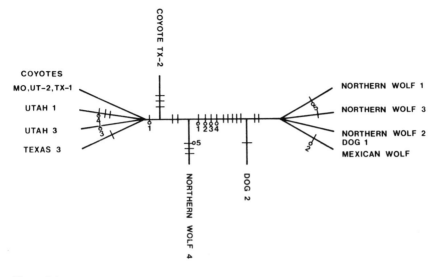

Figure 9.1
Unrooted cladogram of North American coyotes, wolves, and dogs as constructed by maximum parsimony. The cladogram is based upon restriction endonuclease site mapping of mitochondrial DNA. Each line that crosses a segment of the cladogram indicates a single evolutionary change in the map within that evolutionary segment. Five sites were inferred to have changed twice, and their two inferred positions within the cladogram are indicated by the numbered crosslines.

Animal syngameons are by no means limited to mammals. *Drosophila heteroneura* and *D. silvestris* are two Hawaiian *Drosophila* species on which we have worked. Although they are phylogenetically very close and broadly sympatric on the Island of Hawaii (Carson 1978), they are morphologically extremely distinct, with the most dramatic difference being that *silvestris* has a round head and *heteroneura* a hammer-shaped head (Val 1977). They can be hybridized in the laboratory, and the hybrids and subsequent F_2 and backcrosses are completely fertile and viable (Val 1977, Templeton 1977, Ahearn and Templeton 1989). Because the morphology of hybrids is known from these laboratory studies, Kaneshiro and Val (1977) were able to discover that interspecific hybridization occurs in nature. Our molecular studies (DeSalle and Templeton 1987) confirm that hybrids are indeed formed in nature, and, moreover, that these hybrids can and do backcross to such an extent that a *heteroneura* mitochondrial haplotype can occasionally be overlaid on a normal-looking *silvestris* morphology. In spite of this natural hybridization, the species can and do maintain their very distinct, genetically based morphologies (Templeton 1977, Val 1977) and have distinct nuclear DNA phylogenies (Hunt and Carson 1983,

Hunt et al. 1984) in spite of the limited introgression observed with mitochondrial DNA (DeSalle et al. 1986). Hence, both morphology and molecules define these taxa as real, evolutionarily distinct lineages.

As these and other studies illustrate, animal taxa frequently display natural hybridization that yields fertile and viable hybrids. These taxa have often been recognized as species because of their distinct morphologies and ecologies and because modern molecular studies have revealed that they are behaving as independent evolutionary lineages, at least with respect to their nuclear genomes. In other words, many animal species are members of syngameons, just as plants are. Hence, the problem of syngameons is a widespread one for the isolation and recognition concepts.

The Cohesion Species Concept

Another biological definition of species is now possible, which I call the cohesion concept of species. The cohesion concept species is the most inclusive population of individuals having the potential for phenotypic cohesion through intrinsic cohesion mechanisms (table 9.2). I will now elaborate on the meaning of this species concept, showing how it borrows

Table 9.2
Classification of cohesion mechanisms

I.   Genetic exchangeability: the factors that define the limits of spread of new genetic variants through *gene flow*
    A.   Mechanisms promoting genetic identity through *gene flow*
        1.   Fertilization system: the organisms are capable of exchanging gametes leading to successful fertilization
        2.   Developmental system: the products of fertilization are capable of giving rise to viable and fertile adults
    B.   Isolating mechanisms: genetic identity is preserved by the lack of *gene flow* with other groups

II. Demographic exchangeability: the factors that define the fundamental niche and the limits of spread of new genetic variants through *genetic drift* and *natural selection*
    A.   Replaceability: *genetic drift* (descent from a common ancestor) promotes genetic identity
    B.   Displaceability
        1.   Selective fixation: *natural selection* promotes genetic identity by favoring the fixation of a genetic variant
        2.   Adaptive transitions: *natural selection* favors adaptations that directly alter demographic exchangeability. The transition is constrained by:
            a.   Mutational constraints on the origin of heritable phenotypic variation
            b.   Constraints on the fate of heritable variation
                i.   Ecological constraints
                ii. Developmental constraints
                iii. Historical constraints
                iv. Population genetic constraints

parts of the evolutionary, isolation, and recognition concepts, while it avoids their serious defects.

As with the evolutionary species concept, the cohesion species concept defines species in terms of genetic and phenotypic cohesion. As a consequence, the cohesion concept shares with the evolutionary concept the strengths of being applicable to taxa reproducing asexually (or by some other closed or nearly closed breeding system) and to taxa belonging in syngameons. Unlike the evolutionary species concept, the cohesion concept defines species in terms of the mechanisms yielding cohesion rather than the manifestation of cohesion over evolutionary time. This is a mechanistic focus similar to that taken by the isolation concept, although in this case the focus is on cohesion mechanisms rather than isolation mechanisms. By defining a species in terms of cohesion mechanisms, the cohesion concept can easily be related to a mechanistic population genetic framework and can provide guidance in understanding speciation as an evolutionary process. In particular, speciation is now regarded as the evolution of cohesion mechanisms (as opposed to isolation mechanisms). This also means that the cohesion concept focuses primarily on living taxa rather than fossil taxa.

As pointed out by Paterson (1985), it is useful to define the mechanisms underlying species status in such a way that the definitions reflect the most likely evolutionary function of the mechanisms during the process of speciation. Accordingly, cohesion mechanisms will be defined to reflect their most likely evolutionary function. The basic task is to identify those cohesion mechanisms that help maintain a group as an evolutionary lineage. The very essence of an evolutionary lineage from a population genetic perspective is that new genetic variants can arise in it, spread, and replace old variants. These events occur through standard microevolutionary forces such as gene flow, genetic drift, and/or natural selection. The fact that the genetic variants present in an evolutionary lineage can be traced back to a common ancestor also means that the individuals that comprise this lineage must show a high degree of genetic relatedness. The cohesion mechanisms that define species status are therefore those that promote genetic relatedness and that determine the populational boundaries for the actions of microevolutionary forces.

The isolation and recognition concepts are exclusively concerned with genetic relatedness promoted through the exchange of genes via sexual reproduction. These definitions have elevated a single microevolutionary force—gene flow—into the conclusive and exclusive criterion for species status. There is no doubt that gene flow is a major microevolutionary force, and hence the factors that define the limits of spread of new genetic variants through gene flow are valid criteria for species status. Accordingly, genetic exchangeability is included in table 9.2 as a major class of cohesion mechanisms. Genetic exchangeability simply refers to the ability to exchange genes via sexual reproduction. This implies a shared fertilization system in the sense of Paterson (1985). Effective exchange of genes also demands that the products of fertilization be both potentially viable and fertile (Templeton 1987). As shown in table 9.2, the role of gene flow in determining species status can be defined in either a positive (I.A. in table 9.2) or a negative (I.B. in table 9.2) sense. As stated earlier, the positive sense generally provides a more accurate view of the evolutionary processes involved in speciation.

Gene flow is not the only microevolutionary force that defines the boundaries of an evolutionary lineage. Indeed, genetic drift and natural selection play a far more potent and universal role because these two classes of microevolutionary forces are applicable to all organisms, not just outcrossing sexual species. An important question is, therefore, what factors define the limits of spread of new genetic variants through genetic drift and natural selection? Since these forces can operate in asexual populations, it is obvious that the factors that limit the field of actions of drift and selection are not necessarily the same as those limiting the actions of gene flow. As seen, gene flow requires genetic exchangeability, that is, the ability to exchange genes during sexual reproduction. For genetic drift and natural selection to operate, another type of exchangeability is required: demographic exchangeability (table 9.2).

From an ecological perspective, members of a demographically exchangeable population share the same fundamental niche (Hutchinson 1965), although they need not be identical in their abilities to exploit that niche. The fundamental niche is defined by the intrinsic (i.e., genetic) tolerances of the individuals to various environmental factors that determine the range of environments in which the individuals are potentially capable of surviving and reproducing. The realized niche (Hutchinson 1965) refers to that subset of the fundamental niche that is actually occupied by a species. The realized niche is usually a proper subset of the fundamental niche because of the lack of opportunity to occupy certain portions of the fundamental niche (e.g., the environmental ranges might be within the tolerance limits in some locality, but geographical barriers prevent the colonization of that locality) or because of interactions with other species that prevent the exploitation of the entire range of ecological tolerance. Hence, the realized niche is influenced by many extrinsic factors, but demographic exchangeability depends only on the intrinsic ecological tolerances.

To the extent that individuals share the same fundamental niche, they are interchangeable with one another with respect to the factors that control and regulate population growth and other demographic attributes. It is demographic exchangeability that is used to define populations in most models of population and community ecology. Indeed, most models from these ecological disciplines do not even specify the mode of reproduction, so genetic exchangeability is not used to define a population.

From a genetic perspective, the chances of a neutral or selectively favorable mutation going to fixation in a demographically exchangeable population are nonzero regardless of the particular individual in which the mutation occurred. In other words, every individual in a demographically exchangeable population is a potential common ancestor to the entire population at some point in the future. Ancestor-descendant relationships can be defined just as readily in asexual populations as in sexual populations. Hence, demographic exchangeability does not require genetic exchangeability and is a distinct biological attribute at the population level.

Just as genetic exchangeability can vary in strength, so can demographic exchangeability. From an ecological perspective, complete demographic exchangeability occurs when all individuals in a population display exactly the same ranges and abilities of tolerance to all relevant ecological variables. Demographic exchangeability is weakened as individuals begin to differ in their tolerance ranges or abilities. From a genetic perspective, a population is completely demographically exchangeable if the probability of a neutral or selectively favorable mutation going to fixation is exactly the same regardless of the individual in which it occurs. A weakly demographically exchangeable population would consist of members who display very different (but still nonzero) fixation probabilities.

Demographic exchangeability allows us to readily incorporate microevolutionary forces other than gene flow as being important in defining an evolutionary lineage. One such microevolutionary force is genetic drift, which promotes genetic cohesion through ancestor-descendant relationships (i.e., the concept of identity-by-descent in population genetics). For the special case of neutral alleles (alleles that have no selective importance), the rate at which genetic drift promotes identity-by-descent depends only on the neutral mutation rate and is therefore equally important in both large and small populations. Interestingly, this prediction about the neutral rate of evolution and the other basic predictions of the standard neutral theory do not depend upon the assumption of sexual reproduction—these predictions are equally applicable to asexual organisms. Although the neutral theory does not require genetic exchangeability, demographic exchangeability is a critical and necessary assumption (e.g., Rothman and Templeton 1980). Making *only* the assumption of demographic exchangeability, it is inevitable that at some point in the future all the alleles will be descended from one allele that presently exists. It makes no difference for the operation of genetic drift whether alleles or the individuals carrying the alleles are exchangeable. Hence, demographic exchangeability must be regarded as a major cohesion mechanism because it defines the populational limits for the action of genetic drift. This aspect of demographic exchangeability is called replaceability in table 9.2.

Natural selection is another powerful force that can help define an evolutionary lineage. The concept of natural selection does not require genetic exchangeability because selection models are as easily formulated for genetically closed populations as for genetically open ones (e.g., Templeton 1974a, 1974b). As pointed out by Darwin, natural selection requires two demographic conditions: (1) that organisms can produce more offspring than are needed for strict replacement, and (2) that unlimited population growth cannot be sustained indefinitely. When these demographic conditions are coupled with heritable variation in traits influencing survival and reproduction, the logical consequence is that the offspring of some individuals will displace those of others within the population. This aspect of demographic exchangeability is called displaceability in table 9.2.

Natural selection promotes cohesion both through favoring genetic relatedness and through affecting the limits of demographic exchangeability itself. Whenever natural selection causes a new, favorable mutation to go to fixation, genetic relatedness at that locus is obviously a direct consequence. Moreover, as this mutation goes to fixation, that subset of the species' genetic variation that remains linked to the new mutation likewise goes to fixation. This is known as the hitchhiking effect, and it is important to note that as genetic exchangeability declines in importance, hitchhiking effects increase in importance, for the simple reason that genetic recombination is less effective in breaking down the initial linkage states that were created at the moment of mutation. Hence, selective fixation of one allele by another is an extremely powerful cohesion mechanism in populations with genetically closed systems of reproduction (Levin 1981). As an example, figure 9.2 shows the results of selection in a parthenogenetic strain of *D. mercatorum* (Annest and Templeton 1978). As can be seen from that figure, the population rapidly converged to a single genotype for all the marker loci being examined. The dynamics of this convergence indicated that very strong selective forces were operating (Annest and Templeton 1978). Other replicates of this same population, all subject to genetic recombination during the first parthenogenetic generation, selectively converged to other genotypic states at the marker loci, thereby indicating that the marker loci were not being selected directly. Thus, selection at perhaps a few loci promoted genetic identity at all loci in these parthenogenetic populations.

The extent of demographic exchangeability is intimately intertwined with the ecological niche requirements of the organisms and the habitats that are available for satisfying those requirements. It is these very same ecological requirements and available habitats that provide many of the selective forces that drive the process of adaptation. Hence, the process of

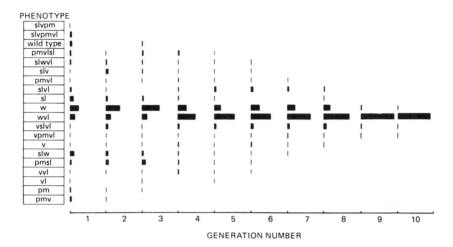

Figure 9.2
Clonal selection in a parthenogenetic population of *Drosophila mercatorum*. The initial generation was heterozygous for several visible markers on all the major chromosomes (sl, w, v, pm, and vl). Parthenogenetic reproduction during this initial generation creates a large number of genotypes since meiotic recombination and assortment occur in these automictic strains. After the first generation genetic recombination is irrelevant since virtually all flies are totally homozygous. From Annest and Templeton (1978).

adaptation by natural selection can directly alter the traits that determine the extent of demographic exchangeability. Adaptive transitions therefore play a direct role in defining demographically exchangeable groups of organisms.

The importance of adaptive transitions in defining demographic exchangeability opens up a whole new set of cohesion mechanisms that constrain the possible courses of adaptive transitions, as shown in table 9.2 (II.B.2). The first is mutational constraints that limit the types of phenotypic variants that are likely to be produced. Such constraints make it difficult to alter some aspects of the existing genetic/developmental system, but facilitate evolutionary change along other lines. For example, the genus *Drosophila* consists of some flies that have pigmented spots, clouds, or patterns on their wings, such as the Hawaiian "picture-wings," and others that have clear wings, such as *D. melanogaster*. Yet, as Basden (1984) points out, no picture-winged *Drosophila* has ever produced a clear-winged mutant, nor has a clear-winged species produced a picture-winged mutant. This negative result is of biological significance for *D. melanogaster*, for probably no other higher eukaryote has been examined more thoroughly for visible mutations. Thus, Basden concluded that at the species level there is a block to certain types of mutations. This is simply another way of stating that constraints exist that make certain types of mutations impossible or highly improbable.

Given that phenotypic variation has been produced by the mutational process, there are constraints that influence the selective fate of that variation (table 9.2, II.B.2.b). First, there are ecological constraints that select against certain phenotypes and that restrict the range of environmental variability experienced by the species. Moreover, for an adaptive transition to persist, a niche must be available for the organisms with the new adaptation. Ecological constraints are undoubtedly one of the more important cohesion mechanisms maintaining species within syngameons, as is demonstrated by what happens within syngameons when the constraints are altered. For example, under most environmental conditions, red and black oaks live together in the same woods and cross-pollinate. Nevertheless, they remain two distinct, cohesive populations because the F_1 hybrid acorns do not germinate well under the dark, cool conditions of a mature forest. When a forest is partially cleared and thinned (mostly by humans), the black oak and red oak acorns germinate poorly, whereas the hybrid acorns do very well. As a result, many current woods consist of a continuous intergradation between black and red oaks. Hence, the normal cohesion of red and black oak populations is lost when the ecological constraints are altered.

Ecological constraints are also important in asexual taxa because these constraints often determine the populational limits of selective fixation, which, as previously mentioned, is a major cohesion mechanism in taxa with closed systems of reproduction. Moreover, the work of Roughgarden (1972) predicts that asexual populations can evolve more sharply delimited niche widths than can otherwise equivalent sexual populations. This property may help explain the greater recognizability of asexual species over sexual species (Holman 1987).

Developmental constraints constitute the second class of cohesion mechanisms related to the fate of heritable variation in adaptive transitions. When there is strong selection on one trait, pleiotropy (a form of developmental constraint) ensures that other traits will evolve as well. Hence, pleiotropy can facilitate evolutionary changes that would otherwise not occur. Although many people have emphasized the nonadaptive, even maladaptive nature of these pleiotropic-induced changes, Wagner (1988) has shown that pleiotropy is essential for the evolution of complex adaptive traits. He examined a model in which fitness depends on the simultaneous states of several traits and then contrasted models of adaptive evolution in which all traits are genetically independent (no pleiotropy or developmental constraints) with a model in which development constraints were imposed. He found that, when there are no development constraints, the rate of adaptive evolution decreases dramatically as the number of characters involved in functional integration increases. Hence, developmental constraints and pleiotropy seem to be necessary for the evolution of functionally integrated phenotypes.

Further adaptive evolution can be facilitated even when the primary adaptation induces pleiotropic effects that are maladaptive. This phenomenon can be illustrated by malarial adaptations in humans (Templeton 1982). The primary malarial adaptations (such as sickle cell) often induce highly deleterious pleiotropic effects (such as anemia), which, in turn, generate secondary adaptive processes on modifiers to diminsh or eliminate the deleterious effects (such as persistence of fetal hemoglobin to suppress anemia). In this manner a single adaptive transition can trigger a cascade of secondary transitions, which cumulatively can have a large impact on demographic exchangeability.

Another cohesion mechanism that constrains the selective fate of phenotypic variability is historical constraint. Evolution is a historical process, and, consequently, the evolutionary potential of a lineage is shaped by its past adaptive transitions. For example, a prerequisite for the evolution of aposematic coloration in insects with gregarious larvae is the evolution of unpalatability. Without the prior existence of distastefulness, there is no selective force for warning coloration within the broods (Templeton 1979). Hence, the adaptation of distastefulness is a historical constraint on the evolution of aposematic coloration and gregarious larvae. This prediction was recently tested by Sillen-Tullberg (1988), who showed through a phylogenetic analysis that in every case in which resolution was possible, distastefulness evolved prior to the evolution of gregarious, aposematic larvae. As shown by this example, one adaptation can make a second one more likely, thus reinforcing the cohesion of the lineage that shares these adaptive transitions.

Population genetic constraints also limit the selective fate of new phenotypic variability. These constraints arise from the interaction of population structure (system of mating, population size, population subdivison) with the genetic architecture underlying selected traits (the genotype-phenotype relationship, number of loci, linkage relationships, etc.). For example, in 1924 Haldane showed that selectively favorable dominant genes are much more likely to be fixed than selectively favorable recessive genes in randomly mating populations. However, this constraint disappears if the system of mating is changed from random mating to inbreeding (Templeton 1982). Thus, an alteration of system of mating can alter the phenotypic and genetic cohesion of a population by making whole new classes of genetic variability responsive to natural selection.

Advantages of the Cohesion Concept of Species

The cohesion concept of species defines a species as an evolutionary lineage through the mechanisms that limit the populational boundaries for the action of such basic microevolutionary forces as gene flow, natural selection, and genetic drift. The genetic essence of an evolutionary lineage is that a new mutation can go to fixation within it; and genetic drift and natural selection as well as gene flow are powerful forces that can cause such fixations. Hence, there is no good rationale for why gene flow should be the only microevolutionary mechanism that is used to define an evolutionary lineage; yet this is precisely what the isolation and recognition concepts do.

Under the cohesion concept, many genetically based cohesion mechanisms (table 9.2) can play role in defining a species. Not all species will be maintained by the same cohesion mechanism or mixture of cohesion mechanisms, just as proponents of the isolation concept acknowledge that not all isolating mechanisms are equally important in every case. By adjusting the mixture of cohesion mechanisms, it is possible to take into account under a single species concept asexual taxa, the taxa that fall within the domain of the isolation and recognition concepts, and the members of syngameons.

Figure 9.3 gives a simplified graphic portrayal of the relative importance of genetic versus demographic exchangeability in defining species over the entire reproductive continuum. For asexual taxa, genetic exchangeability has no relevance, and species status is determined exclusively by demographic exchangeability. As the reproductive system becomes more open, not only does genetic exchangeability become a factor, but demographic exchangeability is diminished in importance because selective replacement becomes increasingly less effective in promoting genetic relatedness. In the middle range, genetic exchangeability dominates because the factors determining the limits of gene flow also limit the actions of drift and selection in outbreeding Mendelian populations. In this domain, the recognition and isolation concepts are valid, and hence, both are special cases of the more general cohesion concept of species. Finally, in moving toward the syngameon end of the continuum, genetic exchangeability decreases in importance relative to the ecological constraints that define demographic exchangeability.

This continuity of applicability of the cohesion concept is consistent with the biological reality that there is a continuum in the degree of genetic openness of reproductive systems found in the organic world. This is a tremendous advantage over the recognition or isolation concepts that are applicable only to the middle range of this reproductive continuum and that deal with the remainder of the range either by denying the existence

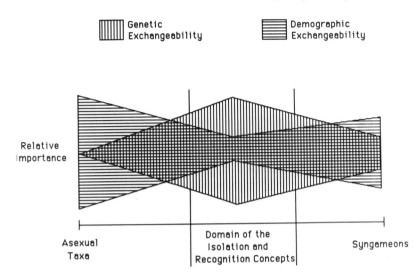

Figure 9.3
The relative importance of demographic and genetic exchangeability over the reproductive continuum. The areas marked by vertical lines indicate the importance of genetic exchangeability, with the width of that area at any particular point in the reproductive continuum indicating its importance in defining species. Similarly, the areas marked by horizontal lines are used to indicate the importance of demographic exchangeability. The diagram gives only the general trend in relative importance. Because the strength of both genetic and demographic exchangeability can vary continuously, the relative importance can be altered from that shown in the diagram at virtually any point in the reproductive continuum, except for asexual taxa.

of species outside this range (e.g., Vrba 1985) or by using qualitatively different species concepts (e.g., Mayr 1970) to impose an artificial discreteness on the reproductive continuum.

Another strength of the cohesion concept is that it clarifies what is meant by a "good species" and the nature of the difficulties that can occur with the isolation and recognition concepts. "Good species" are generally regarded as geographically cohesive taxa that can coexist for long periods of time without any breakdown in genetic integrity. The fact that there is no breakdown in genetic integrity in spite of sympatry implies the lack of genetic exchangeability between the taxa. However, the condition of prolonged coexistence also implies that they have distinct ecological niches (Mayr 1970). Hence, "good species" are those that are well defined both by genetic and demographic exchangeability. (Similarly, members of a "good" higher taxa lack both genetic and demographic exchangeability.) Given this definition of a "good species," there are two principal ways to deviate from this ideal. One occurs when the population boundaries defined by genetic exchangeability are more narrow than those defined by demographic exchangeability. This is precisely the problem of asexual taxa previously discussed. The other mode of deviation occurs when the boundaries defined by genetic exchangeability are broader than those defined by demographic exchangeability—in other words, the problem posed by the syngameon. Hence, these two seemingly very disparate problems with the isolation and recognition concepts actually have a common underlying cause: the boundaries defined by demographic exchangeability are different than those defined by genetic exchangeability.

Speciation is generally a process, not an event (Templeton 1981). While the process is still occurring, the tendency is to have "bad" species. Although the taxa associated with these incomplete speciation processes are the bane of the taxonomist, they provide the most insight into speciation. By providing a precise definition of "bad species" (the conflict between genetic and demographic exchangeability), the cohesion concept is a useful tool for gaining insight into the process of speciation. "Bad species" need no longer be regarded as a diverse set of special cases; rather, the cohesion concept provides the means for seeing the patterns found in these troublesome taxa. For example, Levene (1953) long ago postulated a model in which different genotypes display different fitnesses in niches that are demographically independent. However, in this model, there is complete genetic exchangeability and there is still sufficient demographic exchangeability among all the genotypes within the various realized niches (through within-niche selective displacement) that this is clearly a model of intraspecific polymorphism. The situation modeled by Levene (1953) bears some resemblance to the syngameon examples discussed earlier in that a conflict arises between genetic and demographic exchangeability (through adaptation to different realized ecological niches that alter the intrinsic tolerances that define the fundamental niche). Hence, there can be a continuum in relative strength between these conflicting species boundary criteria. Interestingly, there has been an implicit acknowledgment of this tension in the speciation literature. Most models of sympatric speciation start with a Levene-type model, with the model of Wilson (1989) being an example (also see Maynard Smith 1966). Although these models differ greatly in detail, the cohesion concept clarifies the evolutionary significance of this entire class of speciation models: it is the evolution of demographic *non*exchangeability that triggers the speciation process in these cases, and speciation proceeds through shifts in the relative importance of demographic and genetic exchangeability within and between populations adapting to different realized niches. Thus, a seemingly diverse set of speciation models all have a common theme, and the cohesion concept allows that theme to be clearly discerned.

Note also that natural selection is the driving force of speciation in all of these sympatric speciation models, with the effects on gene flow being secondary. Because the cohesion concept explicitly incorporates a broad set of microevolutionary forces as being important in speciation, we can deal directly with natural selection as being the primary trigger of speciation in these models rather than having to constantly rephrase the evolutionary significance of natural selection in terms of its secondary effects on gene flow. The cohesion concept therefore facilitates the study of speciation as an evolutionary process by making explicit the role played by a broad array of evolutionary forces that includes, but is not limited to, gene flow.

As illustrated by the Levene-type speciation models, one of the evolutionary forces important in speciation is natural selection. Natural selection is important in defining a species under the cohesion concept in part because of the impact of adaptive transitions on demographic exchangeability. Interestingly, Mayr (1970) argues that most species have distinct ecological niches (that is, they are not demographically exchangeable), and that this ecological distinctiveness is the "keystone of evolution" because it serves as the basis of diversification of the organic world, adaptive radiation, and evolutionary progress. Although Mayr therefore concludes that the "evolutionary significance of species" lies in their ecological distinctiveness, he still argues that adaptive transitions and natural selection generally play no direct role in speciation and contribute to defining a species only through the "incidental by-product" of isolating mechanisms. Mayr does allow for selective pressures to reinforce isolating mechanisms and to accentuate ecological exclusion if sympatry has been established, but he emphasizes that this occurs only after the process of speciation has been basically completed. Hence, under the isolation concept, the factors responsible for the "evolutionary significance of species" play no direct role in defining species. Under the cohesion concept, the evolutionary significance of a species can arise directly out of its defining attributes.

Speciation

Now that species has been defined, what is speciation? *Speciation* is the process by which new genetic systems of cohesion mechanisms evolve within a population. This process can be thought of as being analogous to the process of genetic assimilation of individual phenotypes. Genetic assimilation is a process discussed by Waddington (1957) in light of his work with the fruit fly, *Drosophila melanogaster*. For example, he discovered that by subjecting strains of this fly to a heat shock, many of the flies would express the phenotype of lacking a certain vein on their wings. Initially, this "crossveinless" phenotype appeared to be purely environmental. By artificially selecting those flies expressing the phenotype, Waddington discovered he was selecting for the genetic predisposition to express this phenotype as well. Therefore, over several generations this "environmental" phenotype acquired a genetic basis to such an extent that the phenotype eventually came to be expressed even in the absence of the heat shock. Similarly, a purely environmental alteration in the manifestation of cohesion can lead to evolutionary conditions that favor the assimilation of the new pattern of cohesion into the gene pool. For example, consider the case of allopatric speciation in which an ancestral taxa that was continuously distributed in a region is now, by the erection of some geographical barrier, split in two totally isolated subpopulations. The erection of the geographical barrier potentially alters the manifestation of several cohesion mechanisms. For sexual taxa, genetic relatedness through gene flow has been altered, and for both sexual and asexual taxa, the potential for genetic relatedness through genetic drift and natural selection is altered as soon as the populations become demographically independent due to geographical separation. Moreover, if the geographical barrier is associated with altered environments and/or altered breeding systems, alterations in the constraints on adaptive transitions could be directly induced and a new realized niche may be occupied. However, none of this constitutes speciation until these alterations in the manifestion of genetic and demographic exchangeability are genetically assimilated into the gene pool as new cohesion mechanisms. Thus, speciation is the genetic assimilation of altered patterns of genetic and demographic exchangeability into intrinsic cohesion mechanisms.

This is a simple definition of speciation, but because of the breadth of the cohesion species concept, this definition can be used to study a wide variety of evolutionary processes that contribute to the formation of a new species within a single mechanistic framework. This is an exciting prospect, and one that I hope will result in a deeper application of evolutionary genetics to the problem of the origin of species.

Summary

The "biological species concept" defines species as reproductive communities that are separated from other similar communities by intrinsic isolating barriers. However, there are other "biological" concepts of species, so the classic biological species concept is more accurately described as the "isolation" species concept. The purpose of this chapter was to provide a biological definition of species that follows directly from the evolutionary mechanisms responsible for speciation and their genetic consequences.

The strengths and weaknesses of the evolutionary, isolation, and recognition concepts were reviewed and all three were judged to be inadequate for this purpose. As an alternative, I proposed the cohesion concept that defines a species as the most inclusive group of organisms having the potential for genetic and/or demographic exchangeability. This concept borrows from all three biological species concepts. Unlike the isolation and recognition concepts, it is applicable to the entire continuum of reproductive systems observed in the organic world. Unlike the evolutionary concept, it identifies specific mechanisms that drive the evolutionary process of speciation. The cohesion concept both facilitates the study of speciation as an evolutionary process and is compatible with the genetic consequence of that process.

Acknowledgments

The ideas in this chapter were greatly influenced by my discussion with the other participants at the symposium and with the people working in my laboratory, and I thank them all for the challenging intellectual stimulation that they have provided. Special thanks go to Allan Larson and John Endler for their helpful comments on an earlier version of this manuscript. This work was supported by NIH Grant R01 GM31571.

References

Ahearn, J. N., and A. R. Templeton. 1989. Interspecific hybrids of *Drosophila heteroneura* and *D. silvestris*. I. Courtship success. Evolution 43:347–361.

Annest, L., and A. R. Templeton. 1978. Genetic recombination and clonal selection in *Drosophila mercatorum*. Genetics 89:193–210.

Baker, R. J., S. K. Davis, R. D. Bradley, M. J. Hamilton, and R. A. Van Den Bussche. 1989. Ribosomal DNA, mitochondrial DNA, chromosomal and electrophoretic studies on a contact zone in the pocket gopher, *Geomys*. Evolution 43:63–75.

Basden, E. B. 1984. The species as a block to mutations. Drosophila Inform. Serv. 60:57.

Carson, H. L. 1978. Speciation and sexual selection in Hawaiian *Drosophila*. Pp. 93–107 in: P. F. Brussard (ed.), *Ecological Genetics: The Interface*. Springer-Verlag, New York.

Crews, D. 1983. Alternative reproductive tactics in reptiles. BioScience 33:562–566.

Davis, S. K., B. Read, and J. Balke. 1988. Protein electrophoresis as a management tool: Detection of hybridization between Banteng (*Bos javanicus* d'Alton) and domestic cattle. Zoo Biol. 7:155–164.

DeSalle, R., L. V. Giddings, and A. R. Templeton, 1986. Mitochondrial DNA variability in natural populations of Hawaiian *Drosophila*. I. Methods and levels of variability in *D. silvestris* and *D. heteroneura* populations. Heredity 56:75–85.

DeSalle, R., and A. R. Templeton. 1987. Comments on "The Significance of Asymmetrical Sexual Isolation." Evolution. Biol. 21:21–27.

Dobzhansky, Th. 1970. *Genetics of the Evolutionary Process*. Columbia University Press, New York.

Eckenwalder, J. E. 1984. Natural intersectional hybridization between North American Species of *Populus* (Salicaceae) in sections *Aigeiros* and *Tacamahaca*. III. Paleobotany and evolution. Can. J. Bot. 62:336–342.

Ehrlich, P., and P. Raven. 1969. Differentiation of populations. Science 165:1228–1232.

Grant, V. 1957. The plant species in theory and practice. Pp. 39–80 in: E. Mayr (ed.), *The Species Problem*. American Association for the Advancement of Science, Publication No. 50, Washington, D. C.

Grant, V. 1981. *Plant Speciation*, 2nd ed. Columbia University Press, New York.

Haldane, J. B. S. 1924. A mathematical theory of natural and artificial selection. Part 1. Trans. Cambridge Philos. Soc. 23:19–41.

Hall, R. L. 1978. Variability and speciation in canids and hominids. Pp. 153–177 in: R. L. Hall and H. S. Sharp (eds.), *Wolf and Man: Evolution in Parallel*. Academic Press, New York.

Holman, E. W. 1987. Recognizability of sexual and asexual species of rotifers. System. Zool. 36:381–386.

Hunt, J. A., J. G. Bishop III, and H. L. Carson. 1984. Chromosomal mapping of a middle-repetitive DNA sequence in a cluster of five species of Hawaiian *Drosophila*. Proc. Natl. Acad. Sci. U.S.A. 81:7146–7150.

Hunt, J. A., and H. L. Carson. 1983. Evolutionary relationships of four species of Hawaiian *Drosophila* as measured by DNA reassociation. Genetics 104:353–364.

Hutchinson, G. E. 1965. The niche: An abstractly inhabited hypervolume. Pp. 26–78 in: *The Ecological Theatre and the Evolutionary Play*. Yale University Press, New Haven.

Kaneshiro, K., and F. C. Val. 1977. Natural hybridization between a sympatric pair of Hawaiian *Drosophila*. Am. Natur. 111:897–902.

Karlin, S., and S. Lessard. 1986. *Theoretical Studies on Sex Ratio Evolution*. Princeton University Press, Princeton, N. J.

Levene, H. 1953. Genetic equilibrium when more than one ecological niche is available. Am. Natur. 87:311–313.

Levin, B. R. 1981. Periodic selection, infectious gene exchange and the genetic structure of *E. coli* populations. Genetics 99:1–23.

Maynard Smith, J. 1966. Sympatric speciation. Am. Natur. 100:637–650.

Mayr, E. 1963. *Animal Species and Evolution*. Harvard University Press, Cambridge, MA.

Mayr, E. 1970. *Populations, Species, and Evolution*. Belknap Press, Cambridge, MA.

Nowak, R. M. 1978. Evolution and taxonomy of coyotes and related *Canis*. Pp. 3–16 in: M. Bekoff (ed.), *Coyotes: Biology, Behavior, and Management*. Academic Press, New York.

Paterson, H. E. H. 1985. The recognition concept of species. Pp. 21–29 in: E. S. Vrba (ed.), *Species and Speciation*. Transvaal Museum Monograph No. 4, Pretoria.

Rothman, E. D., and A. R. Templeton. 1980. A class of models of selectively neutral alleles. Theor. Pop. Biol. 18:135–150.

Roughgarden, J. 1972. Evolution of niche width. Am. Natur. 106:683–718.

Sillen-Tullberg, B. 1988. Evolution of gregariousness in aposematic butterfly larvae: A phylogenetic analysis. Evolution 42:293–305.

Templeton, A. R. 1974a. Density dependent selection in parthenogenetic and self-mating populations. Theor. Pop. Biol. 5:229–250.

Templeton, A. R. 1974b. Analysis of selection in populations observed over a sequence of consecutive generations. I. Some one locus models with a single, constant fitness component per genotype. Theor. Appl. Genet. 45:179–191.

Templeton, A. R. 1977. Analysis of head shape differences between two interfertile species of Hawaiian *Drosophila*. Evolution 31:630–642.

Templeton, A. R. 1979. A frequency-dependent model of brood selection. Am. Natur. 114:515–524.

Templeton, A. R. 1981. Mechanisms of speciation—a population genetic approach. Annu. Rev. Ecol. System. 12:23–48.

Templeton, A. R. 1982. Adaptation and the integration of evolutionary forces. Pp. 15–31 in: R. Milkman (ed.), *Perspectives on Evolution*. Sinauer, Sunderland, MA.

Templeton, A. R. 1987. Species and speciation. Evolution 41:233–235.

Tinbergen, N. 1953. *Social Behaviour in Animals*. Methuen, London.

Val, F. C. 1977. Genetic analysis of the morphological differences between two interfertile species of Hawaiian *Drosophila*. Evolution 31:611–629.

Vrba, E. S. 1985. Introductory comments on species and speciation. Pp. ix—xviii in: E. S. Vrba (ed.), *Species and Speciation*. Transvaal Museum Monograph No. 4, Pretoria.

Waddington, C. H. 1957. *The Strategy of the Genes*. Allen & Unwin, London.

Wagner, G. 1988. The influence of variation and of developmental constraints on the rate of multivariate phenotypic evolution. J. Evol. Biol. 1:45—66.

White, M. J. D. 1978. *Modes of Speciation*. Freeman, San Francisco.

Wilson, D. 1989. The Diversification of Single Gene Pools by Density- and Freqency-Dependent Selection Pp. 366—385 in: Otte and Endler (eds.), *Speciation and its Consequences*. Sinauer, Sunderland, MA.

Part II
Philosophical Issues

Introduction to Part II: Philosophical Issues

Species are the basal taxonomic units in the standard Linnaean hierarchy of the organic world. Consequently, determining the nature of the species category is essential for providing a taxonomy of the organic world. The essays in part I contain different proposals for the definition of the species category. The nature of species has implications beyond taxonomic concerns. Species are the basal units considered by evolutionary theory. Therefore a number of authors maintain that the status of species affects the nature of evolutionary theory. Indeed, many authors believe that the nature of species affects our general view of scientific theories. The philosophical implications of the nature of species are surveyed in part II. There are pressing philosophical questions concerning the nature of species as well. Are species taxa real entities or is our assignment of organisms to species merely a useful fiction for organizing biological phenomena? Is there a single type of species taxa in the biological world or is there a plurality of incompatible types of species taxa?

Prior to this century, the common philosophical stance towards species was essentialism. Linneaus, John Ray, Maupertuis, Bonnet, Lamarck, and Lyell all adopted an essentialist (or typological) view toward systematics (see Mayr 1982, 256ff.; Hull chapter 10; Sober chapter 12). On this view, classification systems highlight natural kinds—groups whose members share kind-specific essences. Consider the taxonomy of chemical elements provided by Mendeleev's periodic table. The members of each element are distinguished by their kind-specific essential property, namely, the atomic structure found in all and only the members of an element. Those essential properties play a crucial role in explaining the behavior associated with the members of an element. For example, all gold objects are good electrical conductors, dissolve in mixtures of hydrochloric and nitric acids, and melt when heated beyond a certain temperature. The atomic structure of all and only gold objects is responsible for these characteristics. Thus the periodic table provides a taxonomy of chemical elements based on the essential properties responsible for the characteristic behaviors of each element.

Unless otherwise noted, all references are to chapters within this volume.

According to those biologists who adopted an essentialist view of species, species should have the same role in biological taxonomy as the chemical elements have on the periodic table. All and only the members of a species taxon should have a common essential property. In addition, that property should be crucial for explaining the common traits found among the members of that species taxon. But biologists have been hard-pressed to find properties that occur in all and only the members of a particular species taxon (Hull chapter 10). The introduction of evolutionary theory in the nineteenth century provided a diagnosis of the problem. Species, and all taxa, are evolving entities—lineages of organisms whose traits vary across generations. As Hull illustrates, the evolution within and among species is responsible for the lack of species-specific essences.

Consider the possibility of a biological property occurring in all and only the members of a particular species. Such properties, whether genetic or phenotypic, have not been forthcoming, but suppose one was found in all and only the members of a species. Mutation, random drift, or recombination could cause that property to disappear in some members of subsequent generations. All it takes is the disappearance of a trait in a single member of a species to establish that it is not essential for membership in that species. One may counter that there are many properties that each member of a species must have, for example, all *Homo sapiens* must have brain cells. This may be true, but the essential property of a species taxon is one found in all and *only* the members of that taxon. Yet parallel traits commonly occur among the members of different species. Different species have common ancestors that provide common stores of genetic and phenotypic traits. Furthermore, different species frequently live in similar habitats, developing similar traits and life-styles.

Hull suggests that species essentialism is also defeated by the evolutionary nature of speciation events. As discussed in the introduction to part I, the most commonly recognized form of speciation is geographic speciation. Such speciation events are multigenerational. Instantaneous speciation events, those occurring in one generation, do occur when chromosome numbers are multiplied—a process called "polyploidy." But most speciation events last many generations. They are gradual "on the human time scale" (Mayr 1982, 617–618; Mayr 1970, 256). (The notion of gradual here should not be confused with "gradualism" in the debate concerning whether the pattern of evolution is one of gradualism or punctuated equilibria (Eldredge and Gould 1972). Besides, on either view, speciation usually takes a number of generations.) According to Hull, "if species evolved so gradually, they cannot be delimited by means of a single property or set of properties" (chapter 10). The boundaries of species are vague in the same sense that the boundaries between rich and poor, bald and not bald, are vague. There is no precise number of dollars that marks the boundary between rich and poor. Similarly, there is no genetic or phenotypic trait that marks the boundary from one species to the next. Therefore no trait is essential for membership within a species. (For a response to this argument, see Sober chapter 12.)

These arguments against species essentialism do not entail that there are no properties typically found among the members of a species. For example, the budworm species *pinus* and *fumiferana* of the genus *Choristoneura* generally differ in their size, coloration, wing expanse, and wing pattern (Mayr 1970, 27). Still, such differences are a far cry from the differences required by species essentialism. They are differences typically but not always found among the organisms of those species. Thus they violate the essentialist requirement that such traits occur in all and only the members of particular species. Besides, evolutionary forces can easily render those traits atypical among the future members of a species.

Such preevolutionists as Aristotle, John Ray, Maupertuis, and Bonnet proposed a way of preserving species essentialism despite the observed variation within species. For example, Aristotle argued that the members of a species have a common natural state. But he suggested that interfering forces commonly prevent zygotes from achieving their natural state, giving rise to the variation found within species (Sober chapter 12). Aristotle, and other preevolutionists, attempted to preserve species essentialism by asserting the such essences are dispositional traits—traits that organisms would have if there was no interference. This is not an unusual move; many accepted scientific theories define systems by the natural states that few systems ever achieve. For example, in Newtonian mechanics, a body's natural state is one of rest or uniform motion, provided no forces interfere. In population genetics, the frequencies of genotypes in a panmictic population are described by the Hardy-Weinberg law, provided no evolutionary forces are at work.

Nevertheless, Sober argues that the natural state model for species has no basis in contemporary evolutionary theory. In modern terms, the model asserts that the members of a species have similar genotypes that would result in similar natural phenotypes provided no forces interfere. "But when one looks to genetic theory for a conception of the relation between genotype and phenotype, one finds no distinction between natural states and states which are the results of interference" (Sober chapter 12). Instead, one finds the *norm of reaction* that graphs the different phenotypic results a genotype may have in varying environments. No environment is considered the natural one, with the rest containing unnatural interfering forces. The different phenotypes that result from a genotype are just the upshot of that genotype occurring in different environments. Each phenotype is a natural result of its genotype and environment; no particular phenotype is *the* natural one. Perhaps the natural state model would be better off positing a particular genotype as the natural state. But similar considerations apply to the genotypes found in a species. Each genotype is the natural upshot of its parents' genetic contributions. No genotype is enshrined as the natural one for a species. Indeed, the forces of mutation and recombination render genetic change the norm rather than the exception in species of sexually reproducing organisms.

With the acceptance of evolutionary theory, the occurrence of forces causing variation in species came to be seen as the norm rather than the exception. Natural state models were no longer accepted, and species essentialism was cast into doubt. Nevertheless, such early evolutionists as Darwin, Lamarck, and Lyell believed that real taxonomic units must be designated by essential properties (Hull chapter 10). The failure of species essentialism posed a dilemma for these early evolutionists. They believed that species taxa are real only if their members contain species-specific essences, yet they held that the evolutionary nature of species prevents the existence of such essences. This dilemma led Darwin, Lamarck, and Lyell to doubt the existence of species taxa. Consider Darwin's remarks. "In short, we shall have to treat species in the same manner as those naturalists treat genera, who admit that genera are merely artificial combinations made for convenience. This may not be a cheering prospect; but we shall at least be freed from the vain search for the undiscovered and undiscoverable essence of the term species" (1859, 485, also 53).

The apparent lack of species-specific essences is seen to have further philosophical ramifications. It has caused some philosophers to doubt the scientific status of evolutionary theory and still others to doubt the traditional philosophical approach to scientific theories. On the traditional or "received" view held by philosophers for much of this century, scientific theories are sets of deductively related laws (see Suppe 1977 for a summary of this view and criticisms of it). Such laws are universal statements whose predicates refer to natural kinds and to the properties universally associated with the members of those kinds. Examples of such universal statements are "All water boils at 100°C" and "All gold conducts electricity." According to proponents of the received view, such laws are required for scientific predictions and explanations. We can predict that a cup of water will boil at 100°C only if we know that all water boils at that temperature. Furthermore, knowing that the cup contains water and that all water boils at 100°C explains why the liquid in the cup boiled.

According to Smart (1963, 54; 1968, 93ff), there are no such laws in evolutionary theory. As Smart sees it, the problem stems from the absence of universal statements of the form "All the members of species X have biological trait Y." Species evolve and exceptions to such statements constantly occur. Consequently, no predictions or explanations can be given concerning the members of a particular species. For Smart, this implies that evolutionary theory falls outside the domain of genuine scientific theories. Some authors (for example, Beatty 1981 and Lloyd 1988), however, have countered that the problem is not with evolutionary theory. They argue that evolutionary theory is clearly scientific, thus the problem lies in the received view's requirement that theories contain universal laws.

Hull and Ghiselin suggest that the charge that evolutionary theory lacks universal laws stems from a misunderstanding of the ontological status of species taxa. Species taxa are not natural kinds (what Hull calls "classes") but individuals or particulars; they are "spatiotemporally localized cohesive and continuous entities (historical entities)" (Hull chapter 14). Species are analogous to particular organisms. Organisms contain parts, not members. And, the parts of a particular organism are parts of that organism due to the spatiotemporal and causal relations they have to one another. Contrast this with the type of property required for membership in a kind. All chunks of gold must have a certain atomic property. Being a member of the kind gold does not depend on any particular spatiotemporal or casual relation to other chunks of gold. Having a common atomic structure is a *qualitative* property shared by all gold objects.

Hull argues that species are spatiotemporally continuous entities because species are units of evolution—entities that can evolve by natural selection. Three criteria must be met for a population (or a species) to evolve by natural selection: the organisms vary in their traits, that variation causes those organisms to have different fitness values, and those traits are heritable. The third criterion is of importance here. A trait is heritable when it is transmitted faithfully through reproduction. Reproduction is a spatiotemporally localized process—parents and offspring must have some spatiotemporal continuity. So traits are passed through the generations of a species (i.e., are heritable) only if those generations contain organisms spatiotemporally connected by reproduction relations. Hence species evolve via natural selection only if they form spatiotemporally continuous entities.

According to Hull, if species are individuals, then evolutionary theory should not be charged for lacking universal laws. Consider an analogous situation in chemistry and geology. Chemical and geological laws range over the members of kinds, not over the parts of particular individuals. For example, there are no laws in those theories concerning all and only the parts of a particular meteor or a particular rock. Yet no one charges that those theories are missing universal laws. The laws of those theories lie at different ontological levels; they concern meteors in general, kinds of rocks (for example, granite rocks), and kinds of elements that comprise those rocks (for example, gold and iron). Similar considerations apply to evolutionary theory and species. There may be no biological laws concerning all and only the members of a particular species, but that does not imply that evolutionary theory is void of universal laws. Species are individuals, not kinds, in that theory; so if there are laws in evolutionary theory, they will exist at other ontological levels. Hull (chapter 14) suggests that there may be laws about kinds of species. For example, population ecologists talk of k-selected and r-selected species—species that live in stable and unstable environments (Wilson and Bossert 1971, 110). Biologists also generalize over kinds of populations. Mayr's notion of geographic speciation specifies when isolated populations become new species. The Hardy-Weinberg law predicts the gene frequencies found in certain kinds of panmictic, interbreeding populations.

The individuality of species also dispels the nominalistic stance towards species taken by some early evolutionists (Hull chapter 14 and Ghiselin chapters 13 and 17). Darwin, Lyell, Lamarck, and other early evolutionists required that species taxa have essential properties—qualitative properties found in all and only the members of each species taxon. If species are individuals and not kinds, then species need not have such essential properties to be real entities. Of course some sort of identity conditions must govern the existence of species taxa. But as evidenced by the essays in part I, biologists widely disagree on those conditions. Nevertheless, none of the proposed species definitions require that all and only the members of a species taxon share a common qualitative property.

Hull and Ghiselin's thesis that species are individuals is widely accepted. But some objections have been launched against it. Kitcher and Ruse, for example, suggest that species can consist of spatiotemporally disconnected organisms. Both authors present hypothetical cases to illustrate this point. Consider Kitcher's example (chapter 15): suppose successful lizard hybrids are produced from the same parental species, but in separate hybridization events. Furthermore, suppose the hybrids give rise to fertile lineages whose members fall within the same genetic, morphological, ecological, and behavioral ranges. These lineages are spatiotemporally disconnected—they arose in separate hybridization events. Yet Kitcher argues that no "biological purpose would be served by distinguishing" these lineages as two species; indeed, to do so would "obfuscate all the biological similarities that matter." Kitcher concludes that species may consist of spatiotemporally disconnected organisms and may form natural kinds. (See Sober 1984 for a response to Kitcher's argument; see Kitcher 1984 for a rejoinder to Sober's response.)

Other charges have been launched against the individuality thesis. Mishler and Donoghue and Ereshefsky regard species as spatiotemporally continuous entities, yet they argue that many species are not individuals. Their objection turns on the claim that many species consist of populations not connected by gene flow—species consisting of geographically isolated populations or asexual organisms. The members of such species are

spatiotemporally connected to a common ancestor. But with the absence of
gene flow, the members and populations of such species fail to interact
casually. Mishler and Donoghue, Ereshefsky, and Ruse argue that there is
more to the individuality of an entity than its parts being spatiotemporally
connected to a common origin. The parts of an individual must also
interact causally. These authors suggest that because many species fail to
be integrated by gene flow, many species fail to be individuals. Mishler and
Donoghue and Ereshefsky conclude that such species are historical entities:
spatiotemporally continuous entities whose members are not causally connected.

Ghiselin responds to such counters to the individuality thesis by asserting that "if anything is to evolve, or do anything else, it has to be an
individual. ... Species are those individuals that have to evolve independently of each other. For this to happen, it is a necessary condition that
they form separate reproductive units"—groups of populations integrated
by sexual reproduction (Ghiselin chapter 17). For Ghiselin, only causally
cohesive wholes form entities. And if an entity consisting of organisms is
to evolve as a unit, its organisms must be integrated by gene flow. Although biologists commonly recognize groups of organisms not integrated
by gene flow as species, Ghiselin responds that such groups cannot evolve
as units. Thus they are not species and fail as counterexamples to the thesis
that all species are individuals.

Ghiselin's defense of the individuality thesis turns on adopting a particular approach to species, namely, that only groups of organisms integrated
by sexual reproduction form species. Kitcher, however, argues that although reproductively based species concepts "bring out an important
pattern in the diversity of nature ... this is not the only important pattern
of organismic diversity" (chapter 15). Paleontologists, for example, often
recognize long extinct species without knowing whether their organisms
were integrated by sexual reproduction. And, many biologists consider
some groups of asexual organisms as distinct species. Kitcher argues that
no single species concept captures all the diversity of the organic world. As
a result, he advocates a pluralistic stance towards the species category: a
number of legitimate species concepts define species taxa. In particular, the
species category consists of two types of species concepts: historical and
structural. Historical concepts assume that species taxa are lineages—
spatiotemporally continuous entities—distinguished from other lineages
by various factors. Such concepts include Van Valen's ecological concept
and Wiley's evolutionary concept. Structural concepts demarcate species
taxa by their members having similar genetic structures or similar developmental programs.

Kitcher's pluralistic stance allows that species taxa are defined by different biological criteria. In addition, it allows the existence of incompatible

but equally legitimate taxonomies of the organic world. For example, one taxonomy may be based on the biological species concept, another on the evolutionary species concept. These two taxonomies may not coincide because only the latter allows the existence of species consisting of asexual organisms. Given the heterogeneous nature of the species category on Kitcher's pluralism, and the incompatible taxonomies it allows, one might wonder if Kitcher's suggestion is the null hypothesis that systematists ought to avoid. For instance, Ghiselin (1969) writes, "the necessity of classification systems has long been recognized ... for the very communication of general ideas" (p. 79). "Whatever standard one does take for ranking taxonomic groups, it should be clear that systematists work at cross-purposes when they do not agree on any such criteria" (p. 85).

Kitcher responds that to allow species pluralism does not "unlock the doors of Babel." Different species concepts pick out different species taxa and taxonomies of the biological world. To guard against confusion, biologists need only be explicit about what concept is being used when referring to a set of species taxa. In a particular biological situation, there may be five species present according to the biological species concept, but only three according to the phenetic concept. Still, the biologists applying these concepts can communicate over the species present by explicitly mentioning the species concepts being used. Kitcher argues that a similar situation faces the term "gene." There is no single natural way to segment DNA into functional units called "genes." But when confusion arises over the size of DNA segment referred to by "gene," biologists explicitly state the principle of segmentation being used. "The case of the many genes shows how the multiplicity of overlapping natural kinds can be acknowledged without either arbitrary choice or inevitable confusion. Similar resources are available for us with respect to the species category" (Kitcher chapter 15).

Ghiselin (chapter 17) counters that Kitcher's analogy between gene and the species category is incorrect. The word "gene" refers to different functional units of DNA, but it always refers to segments of DNA—spatiotemporally continuous entities. The same is not true of Kitcher's use of the term "species." Historical species concepts refer to groups of organisms that form spatiotemporally continuous entities. Structural concepts refer to groups of similar organisms that may not be spatiotemporally connected. Ghiselin charges that Kitcher's use of species refers to an ontological mixed bag, whereas the molecular geneticist's use of the word "gene," though pluralistic, refers to entities of a single ontological type.

There are other brands of species pluralism besides the one proposed by Kitcher. Mishler and Donoghue contend that all taxa are monophyletic and hence spatiotemporally continuous entities (see also Mishler and Brandon 1987). But they contend that there is no single ranking criterion that determines which taxa form species. "Because different factors may be "most important" in the evolution of different groups, a *universal* criterion for delimiting fundamental, cohesive evolutionary units does not exist" (Mishler and Donoghue chapter 7). Some species taxa owe their distinctiveness to reproductive factors, other species taxa owe their existence to ecological forces or homeostatic inertia. Mishler and Donoghue's phylogenetic species concept is monistic in that all species taxa are spatiotemporally continuous entities. But it is pluralistic in allowing that different evolutionary processes cause lineages to form species taxa. So Mishler and Donoghue's pluralism differs from Kitcher's in two ways. For Kitcher, the species category consists of both spatiotemporally continuous lineages and classes of spatiotemporally disconnected organisms. For Mishler and Donoghue, the species category consists only of spatiotemporally continuous lineages. Second, Kitcher's pluralism allows a number of incompatible taxonomies of the organic world. For Mishler and Donoghue, there is only one taxonomy of that world, even though the species of that taxonomy are maintained by different processes.

The authors of the essays in part II address another controversy concerning the nature of species. Species are commonly distinguished from higher taxa as the units of evolution. That distinction often is based on the view that species but not higher taxa form groups of interbreeding populations (Ghiselin chapter 17; Eldredge and Cracraft 1980, 89–90, 249, 327; Mayr 1970, 373–374). Supporters of this conception of the species/higher taxa distinction argue that species evolve as distinct units because of the gene flow among the populations of a species (see Mayr, Paterson, and Ghiselin). Higher taxa consist of species whose members do not successfully interbreed across species' boundaries, therefore the parts of a higher taxon do not evolve as a unit. Ereshefsky considers this argument for the species/higher taxa distinction. He cites a number of biologists who maintain that many species do not form groups of interbreeding populations (see Ehrlich and Raven, Van Valen, and Mishler and Donoghue). If these biologists are correct, then many species are not evolutionary units on the interbreeding criterion. Consequently, the distinction between species and higher taxa based on this criterion fails.

Supporters of reproductively based species concepts draw a different conclusion. They contend that we are wrong to think that species can consist of populations that do not form reproductive units—groups of interbreeding populations (Ghiselin chapter 17, Eldredge 1985). Ghiselin, for example, writes, "species do very few things ... they speciate, they evolve, they provide their component organisms with genetical resources, and they become extinct. Above the level of the species, genera and higher taxa never do anything. Clusters of related clones in this respect are the same as genera. They don't do anything either." In other words, lineages consisting of asexual organisms are like higher taxa: they fail to form reproductive units, thus their members do not evolve as a unit. Consequently, groups of asexual organisms do not form species. The same applies to alleged species that consist of populations that have been geographically isolated for extensive periods of time. If such groups exist, as Ehrlich and Raven and others contend, then such groups do not form species. The species/higher taxa distinction based on which groups form reproductive units remains. But many taxa thought to be species taxa are not species.

Mishler and Donoghue suggest a different approach. Instead of asserting that only reproductive units form evolutionary units and aligning the species category with those reproductive units, they suggest that a continuum of evolutionary units exists. "There are *many* evolutionary, genealogical units within a given lineage.... Thus, in the search to find *the* evolutionary unit, one is on a very slippery slope .... These units do require some sort of designation in order to be studied, but a formal hierarchical Linnaean name is not necessary." Thus, according to Mishler and Donoghue, as the evolutionary unit distinction falls, so falls the strict species/higher taxa distinction, and a formal definition of the species category!

"The suggestion that natural history could really get by without definitions of the categories of classification—especially a definition of "species" —is admittedly hard to swallow" (Beatty chapter 11). Mishler and Donoghue seem to suggest this. And Beatty argues that Darwin also made this suggestion. Darwin observed a vagueness between the taxonomic categories "species" and "variety" and between the categories "species" and "genus" (Beatty chapter 11; Ghiselin 1969, 92ff.). For Darwin, taxa called "varieties" gradually transmute into lineages called "species." And those taxa referred to as "species" gradually evolve into lineages called "genera." Writes Darwin, "It ceases to be surprising ... that there should exist the finest gradation in the differences between organic beings, from individual differences to quite distinct species;—that there should be often the gravest difficulty in knowing what to call species and what varieties" (Stauffer 1975, 167). As Darwin points out, determining whether a particular taxon is a species is like determining "whether a certain number of houses should be called a village, a town, or a city" (1871, 175). For some practical purpose, a definition for "town" may be given, for example, in a census count. But the decision for drawing the line between how many houses are in a town and how many are in a village is arbitrary. Compare this to what Darwin says of species. "I look at the term species as one arbitrarily given for the sake of convenience to a set of individuals closely resembling each other, and that it does not essentially differ from the term variety" (1859, 52).

According to Beatty, Darwin did believe that there are taxa—evolving lineages—that biologists commonly refer to as "species." Beatty's point, however, is that "Darwin's references to the arbitrariness and unreality of species pertained only to the species *category*." This leaves unresolved the question of how "natural history could really get by without definitions of the categories of classification." Beatty suggests that natural history was only temporarily without a definition of the species category. Darwin was attempting to liberate evolutionary biology from the nonevolutionary thinking built into pre-Darwinian definitions of species. That is why he rejected the species category. Yet according to Beatty, once the Darwinian revolution took hold, evolutionary definitions of the species were proposed that filled the void. Such definitions include Mayr's biological species concept and Simpson's (1961) evolutionary species concept. Still, whether these definitions or any definition of the species category preserve the species/higher taxa distinction is a controversial issue.

References

Beatty, J. (1981), "What's Wrong with the Received View of Evolutionary Theory?" In P. Asquith and R. Giere (eds.), *PSA 1980*, Vol. 2. East Lansing: Philosophy of Science Association.

Darwin, C. [1859] (1964), *On the Origin of Species: A Facsimile of the First Edition*. Cambridge, Mass.: Harvard University Press.

Darwin, C. (1889), *The Descent of Man, and Selection in Relation to Sex*, second edition. New York: D. Appleton.

Eldredge, N. (1985), *Unfinished Synthesis*. New York: Oxford University Press.

Eldredge, N., and Cracraft, J. (1980), *Phylogenetic Patterns and the Evolutionary Process*. New York: Columbia University Press.

Eldredge, N., and Gould, S. (1972), "Punctuated Equilibria: An Alternative to Phyletic Gradualism," in T. Schopf (ed.) *Models in Paleobiology*. San Fransico: Freeman, Cooper and Company, pp. 82–115.

Ghiselin, M. (1969), *The Triumph of the Darwinian Method*. Chicago: University of Chicago Press.

Kitcher, P. (1984), "Against Monism of the Moment: A Reply to Elliott Sober," *Philosophy of Science* 51:308–35.

Lloyd, E. (1988), *The Structure and Confirmation of Evolutionary Theory*. New York: Greenwood Press.

Mayr, E. (1970), *Populations, Species, and Evolution*. Cambridge, Mass.: Harvard University Press.

Mayr, E. (1982), *The Growth of Biological Thought*. Cambridge, Mass.: Harvard University Press.

Mishler, B., and Brandon, R. (1987), "Individuality, Pluralism, and the Phylogenetic Species Concept," *Biology and Philosophy* 2:397–414.

Simpson, G. (1961), *The Principles of Animal Taxonomy*. New York: Columbia University Press.

Smart, J. J. C. (1963), *Philosophy and Scientific Realism*. London: Routledge and Kegan Paul.

Smart, J. J. C. (1968), *Between Philosophy and Science*. London: Routledge and Kegan Paul.

Sober, E. (1984), "Sets, Species, and Evolution: Comments on Philip Kitcher's 'Species'," *Philosophy of Science* 51:334–41.

Stauffer, R. C. ed. (1975), *Charles Darwin's Natural Selection; being the second part of his big species book written from 1856 to 1858*. London: Cambridge University Press.

Suppe, F. (1977), *The Structure of Scientific Theories*, second edition. Urbana: University of Illinois Press.

Wilson, E. and Bossert, W. (1971), *A Primer of Population Biology*. Sunderland, Mass.: Sinauer Associates.

Chapter 10

The Effect of Essentialism on Taxonomy: Two Thousand Years of Stasis

David L. Hull

A convenient year to designate as the beginning of the scientific revolution is 1543. In that year Nicholas Copernicus published *De Revolutionibus Orbium Coelestium* and Andreas Vesalius published *De Humani Corporis Fabrica*. In a little more than a hundred years classical physics reached its fruition in Newton's *Principia*. At first biology promised a similar development with the work of Leewenhoek, Schwammerdam, and Malpighi, but no theoretical achievements even vaguely comparable to those in physics were forthcoming. It wasn't until the nineteenth century with the work of Darwin and Lamarck on evolution, of Mendel on genetics, of Pasteur on microorganisms, and of Schleiden and others on cell theory that biology came of age. In taxonomy the scientific revolution has been even slower in making itself felt. Although John Ray and Carolus Linnaeus made some advances in the methodology of taxonomy and in organizing their taxa, they made no significant contributions to taxonomic theory as devised by Aristotle. As biology lagged behind physics in divesting itself of scholastic influence, taxonomy lagged far behind the other biological sciences. In fact, contrary to popular opinion, the process is still far from complete. And taxonomy only now is reaching a stage of maturity comparable to that of physics three hundred years ago or to that of other biological sciences of fifty or a hundred years ago. Why is this?

Karl R. Popper's answer is that "the development of thought since Aristotle could, I think, be summed up by saying that every discipline as long as it used the Aristotelian method of definition has remained arrested in a state of empty verbiage and barren scholasticism, and that the degree to which the various sciences have been able to make any progress depended on the degree to which they have been able to get rid of this essentialist method."[1] In no other science is this statement as true as it is in taxonomy, for in no other science is definition as important as it is in taxonomy. Correspondingly, in no other science has there been as much empty verbiage about the meaning of a word as there has been in taxonomy about the meaning of "species." But Darwin supposedly put a stop all that. He himself said in commenting on such endless disputes, "When the views advanced by me in this volume ... are generally admitted, we can dimly foresee that there will be a considerable revolution in natural history. Systematists will be able to pursue their labours as at present; but they will not be incessantly haunted by the shadowy doubt whether this or that form be a true species. This, I feel sure and I speak after experience, will be of no slight relief."[2]

Darwin's views on the evolution of species *have* been generally admitted; there *has* been a considerable revolution in natural history (phylogenetic taxonomy), but a specter of essentialism continues to haunt the taxonomist. Ernst Mayr says, for example, "It is a curious paradox that so many taxonomists still adhere to a strictly static species concept, even though they admit freely the existence of evolution."[3] And again, "It is a curious paradox in the history of biology that the rediscovery of Mendelian laws resulted in an even more unrealistic species concept among the experimentalists than had existed previously."[4] With the discovery of biology's two most important theories, one would think that something as basic as the unit of classification would have come into clearer perspective instead of becoming more blurred. In the first instance taxonomists admit that species evolve but find it impossible to define species names accordingly.[5] In the second they admit that there is a genetic continuity among the members of a species but deny species any reality. Both have combined to contribute to the continuation of the species problem.

As A. J. Cain has pointed out,[6] the solution to Mayr's paradoxes can be found in a remnant of essentialism which has not been fully eliminated from taxonomy. It is responsible for taxonomists retaining what is loosely called a static species concept, which in turn is responsible for species being divested of reality. Of couse, there are other reasons for taxonomists wanting to retain the trappings of Aristotelian definition, most probably the same reasons which led Aristotle to devise his system in the first place. Presented with the welter of diverse forms to be classified, a taxonomist can greatly simplify his task if he pretends that certain properties are "essential" for definition. But he would have to do just that—pretend— since the names of taxa cannot be defined in terms of essential characters without falsification on a scale which should have been evident even to the most uncritical investigator with only a limited knowledge of the organisms being classified.

The conflict between reality and theory was largely ignored by early taxonomists both because they did not understand the logic of Aristotelian definition very clearly and because even scientists have a way of not noticing what conflicts with their philosophical presuppositions. At any rate, the thesis of this paper is not that Aristotelian definition was responsible for taxonomists being unable to define taxa names appropriately (although this is certainly true). The thesis of this paper is that Aristotelain definition is responsible for taxonomists being unable to define "species" adequately. The actual distribution of properties among organisms has finally forced taxonomists to abandon Aristotelian definitions of taxa names. There is no comparable conflict to force taxonomists to abandon their attempts to define "species" in the Aristotelian manner. Nevertheless, it will be argued that Aristotelian definition is just as inappropriate for "species" as it is for the names of taxa.[7]

Essentialism

Karl Popper characterises essentialism as follows:

> I use the name *methodological essentialism* to characterize the view, held by Plato and many of his followers, that it is the task of pure knowledge or "science" to discover and to describe the true nature of things; i.e. their hidden reality or essence. It was Plato's peculiar belief that the essence of sensible things can be found in other and more real things—in their primogenitors or Forms. Many of the later methodological essentialists, for instance Aristotle, did not altogether follow him in determining this; but they all agreed with him in determining the task of pure knowledge as the discovery of the hidden nature or Form or essence of things. All these methodological essentialists also agreed with Plato in holding that these essences may be discovered and discerned with the help of intellectual intuition; that every essence has a name proper to it, the name after which the sensible things are called; and that is may be described in words. And a description of the essence of a thing they called a "definition."[8]

In taxonomy this philosophical position became known as typology. The three essentialistic tenets of typology are (1) the ontological assertion that forms exist, (2) the methodological assertion that the task of taxonomy as a science is to discern the essences of species, and (3) the logical assertion concerning definition. These three separate tenets must be distinguished if we are to avoid making such statements as those that have been made accusing Darwin and Lamarck of being "typologists." They were typologists only in the sense that they retained part of the third element of essentialism—the logical of Aristotelian definition. "According to essentialism (especially Aristotle's version of it) a definition is a restatement of the inherent essence or nature of a thing. At the same time, it states the meaning of a word—of the name that designates the essence."[9] In Aristotle's view three things can be known about any entity—its essence, its definition, and its name. The name names the essence. The definition gives a complete and exhaustive description of the essence. Derivatively, the name is the name of the entity and the definition a description of it. "Aristotle considers the term to be defined as a name of the essence of the thing, and the defining formula as the description of the essence. And he insists that the defining formula must give an exhaustive description of the essence or the essential properties of the thing in question."[10]

Disregarding all the talk about essences, what Aristotle was advocating in modern terms is definition by properties connected conjunctively which are severally necessary and jointly sufficient.[11] For example, being a three-sided plane closed figure is necessary and sufficient for being a triangle. Such a mode of definition is eminently suited for defining eternal forms. It is not very well suited for defining the names of evolving species or for "species" itself, and yet it is exactly this mode of definition which has been assumed to be the only mode of definition permissible until recently. Evolutionary theory necessarily challenged the ontological assertion that species as forms existed. Quite obviously it also challenged the method-ological assertion. If there were no forms, then the task of taxonomy could not be to discern them. But evolutionary theory had a third consequence for taxonomy, and it was *this* consequence which Darwin and his followers *did not see*. Aristotelian definition had to be abandoned both for species names and for "species." Typologists could ignore the actual untidy distri-bution of properties among living organisms and the variety of methods of reproduction used to perpetuate species. Evolutionists could not.

Aristotelian Definition and Evolution

From the beginning taxonomists have sought two things—a definition of "species" which would result in real species and a unifying principle which would result in a natural classification. The fervor with which taxonomists searched for such a unifying principle is evident in the following quotation by Linnaeus. "For a long time I have laboured to find it; I have discovered many things, but I have not been able to find it. I shall continue to search for it as long as I live."[12] In evolutionary theory taxonomists at last had their unifying principle. A natural classification would be a classification which in some sense "represented" phylogeny.[13] From its very inception the enthusiasm with which some taxonomists welcomed the phylogenetic program was equalled only by the vehemence with which others rejected it. It is obvious why typologists opposed phylogenetic taxonomy, but phylogenetic taxonomy also met with resistance from taxonomists who accepted evolutionary theory but who denied it any relevance to taxono-my. This latter group has come to be known as the classificatonists. Their modern counterparts are the numerical or neo-Adansonian taxonomists. The explanation for the early classificationist stand can be found again in the third element of essentialism.[14] Although all early phylogeneticists and most classificationists abandoned the first two assertions of essentialism, neither abandoned Aristotelian definition.

Because of evolution taxonomists felt confronted by a dilemma. If they accepted evolutionary theory as the unifying principle of natural classification, they had to abandon any hope of ever having real species. If they wished to retain real species, they had to give up any hope of ever having a natural classification. The rationale behind this dilemma can be seen in the following quotations from Lamarck, Lyell, and Darwin. Lamarck said, for example, "The part of the work of naturalists which concerns the determination of what one calls 'species' beomes day by day more defective, that is to say, more entangled and more confused, because it is executed in the almost universally admitted supposition that the productions of nature constitute species constantly distinguished by invariable characters, and whose existence is as ancient as that of nature itself."[15] Lamarck's conclusion was then that since species couldn't be defined by an invarying list of characters, they couldn't be real. Lyell replied, "If species are not real, the obvious consequences are alarming: unlimited change becomes not only possible but even necessary. Species will no longer have well-defined limits, classification becomes a purely arbitrary exercise, and any species may easily be transformed into another."[16] Even Darwin said that once his or an analogous view was accepted, "systematists will have only to decide (not that this will be easy) whether any form be sufficiently constant and distinct from other forms to be capable of definition; and if definable, whether the difference be sufficiently important to deserve a specific name ... In short, we shall have to treat species in the same manner as those naturalists treat genera, who admit that genera are merely artificial combinations made for convenience. This may not be a cheering prospect; but we shall at least be free from the vain search for the undiscovered and undiscoverable essence of the term species."[17]

When the logic of the preceding argument is set out in full, it goes something like this. The only basis for a natural classification is evolutionary theory, but according to evolutionary theory, species developed gradually, changing one into another. If species evolved so gradually, they cannot be delimited by means of a single property or set of properties. If species can't be so delineated, then species names can't be defined in the classic manner. If species names can't be defined in the classic manner, then they can't be defined at all. If they can't be defined at all, then species can't be real. If species aren't real, then "species" has no reference and classification is completley arbitrary.

Elements of this same argument can be found in the writings of modern taxonomists. For example, A. J. Cain says the following things: "But when good series are available, forms that seem to be good species at any one time may become indefinable since they are successive stages in a single evolutionary line and intrograde smoothly with each other[18] ... with the passage of time, they change continuously and are gradually transformed into two modern species, without any sudden discontinuity which could be used as a specific boundary....[19] The limits of both subspecies and species within a genus are equally arbitrary, since there is no reason to make a break in a continuous series at any one point rather than at another."[20] Cain concludes that the problem is insoluble.[21] Ernst Mayr concurs, saying, "Even though the number of cases that cause real difficulties is very small, the fact remains that an objective delimitation of species in a multidimensional system is an impossibility."[22] And G. G. Simpson says, "Certainly the lineage must be chopped into segments for the purposes of classification, and this must be done arbitrarily ..., because there is no non-arbitrary way to subdivide a continuous line...."[23]

Even though "species" has all the faults mentioned, A. J. Cain says that species as single phyletic lines are "less artificial, subjective or arbitrary than any other rank."[24] Mayr says, "The species is an important unit in evolution, in ecology, in the behavioral sciences, and in applied biology.[25] ... it has a very distinct biological significance...."[26] And Simpson says, "The point will be discussed later, but even here it is advisable just to mention that such arbitrary subdivision does not necessarily produce taxa that are either 'unreal' or 'unnatural,' as has sometimes been stated. A simple but, at this point, sufficiently explanatory analogy is provided by a piece of string that shades cointinuously from, say, blue at one end to green at the other. Cutting the string into two is an arbitrary act, but the resulting pieces are perfectly real sections of the string the existed as natural parts of the whole before they were severed."[27]

Quite obviously taxonomists still believe there is a species problem and at the heart of it is the biologically uninteresting but the logically crucial notion of *definition*.

Taxa Names as Cluster Concepts

Mayr says that although there has been steady clarification of the issue, "there is still much uncertainty and widespread divergence of opinion on many aspects of the species problem. It is rather surprising that not more agreement has been reached during the past two hundred years in which these questions have been tossed back and forth. This certainly cannot be due to lack of trying, for an immense amount of time and thought has been devoted to the subject during this period. One has the feeling that there is a hidden reason for so much disagreement."[28] One of the reasons why more agreement has not been reached is that the classificationists and phylogeneticists disagree over the purposes of taxonomy. One wants the unit of classification to be the unit of identification. The other wants it to be the unit of evolution. But there is also a hidden reason for so much disgreement—the philosphical predisposition on the part of taxonomists of both schools for Aristotelian definition. An important clue that Aristotelian definition is at fault is the conclusion reached by Mayr and almost all other taxonomists who have attended to the species problem that "perhaps the disagreement is due to the fact that there is more than one kind of species and that we need a different definition for each of these species."[29]

The influence of Aristotelian definition on taxonomic thought can best be revealed by investigating the definition of a type of term for which taxonomists have already abandoned Aristotelian definition—the definition of taxa names. It is commonplace now to recognize what Adanson realized almost two hundred years ago that taxa names cannot be defined by sets of properties the members of which are severally necessary and jointly sufficient, for seldom is a property of any taxonomic value distributed both universally and exclusively among the members of a taxon. The properties which are used to define the names of taxa do not respect taxonomic boundaries. For example, depending on whether the hemichordates are included in the phylum Chordata or whether they are made a separate phylum, none of the properties used to define "Chordata" are both necessary and sufficient. If the hemichordates are included in Chordata, then a few of the properties are possessed exclusively by the chordates; e.g., notochord, dorsal hollow nerve cord, metameric musculature, internal skeleton of cartilage or bone, and a closed circulatory system. But then none of the properties are possessed universally. Possession of internal gill slits comes the closest to being universally distributed; however, some hemichordates do not have anything that faintly resembles gill slits. If on the other hand the hemichordates are not included in Chordata, then several defining properties become universally possessed by the chordates; e.g., notochord, dorsal hollow nerve cord, and gill slits. But then several of the properties which were exclusively chordate cease to be possessed exclusively by them; e.g., dorsal hollow nerve cord. The only property that is both universally and exclusively possessed by the chordates is the notochord, although some vertebrates and urochordates posses one only in the embryo or larva. Even if only contemporary forms are taken into consideration, Aristotelian definition simply won't do.

Traditionally a word is considered to be explicitly defined if and only if a set of properties can be given such that each property is severally necessary and the entire set of necessary properties is jointly sufficient. For example, a bachelor is a male adult human being who has never married and a sibling is one of at least two children of the same parents. If "A" is the word to be defined and a, b, c, and d are properties, then the logical structure of such a definition is "A ^{DF} a. b. c. d." Words can also be defined disjunctively without violating the spirit of Aristotelian definition. For example, a sibling is a brother or a sister and an uncle is the brother of one's father or the brother of one's mother or the husband of one of one's aunts.

The logical structure of such a definition is "A ^{DF} a V b V c V d." In such a disjunctive defintion each property is severally sufficient and the possession of at least one of the properties in necessary.[30]

However, neither of these types of definition is appropriate for defining the names of taxa and, hence, for delineating taxa. Whether from the viewpoint of phylogenetic or numerical taxonomy, taxa names can be defined only *by sets of statistically covarying properties arranged in indefinitely long disjunctive definitions.* The logical structure of such a definition is "A ^{DF} a. b. c. d V b. c. d. eV a. c. d. f and so on." Usually no one particular property or set of properties is necessary and any one of numerous sets is sufficient. An example from ordinary discourse of a word which can be defined only in such a manner is "lemon." A description of a lemon would contain such properties as coming from a particular type of tree, having a sour taste, an ovoid shape and so on. None of these properties is necessary since a fruit could lack any one of them and still be a lemon. Several different but overlapping sets of properties are accordingly each sufficient.[31]

In defining taxa names as cluster concepts, taxonomists have (whether they realize it or not) adopted a new and rather controversial philosophical position. They have abandoned the simple dichotomy beween analytic and synthetic connections in definition. The traditional view is that either a defining property is analytically connected to the word it defines or it is not. There is no middle ground. According to one version of the new position, "Any property that is connected with another in such a way that it does not make sense to deny its application will be said to be analytically connected with it, as, e.g. brotherhood is connected with siblinghood. A property that does not meet this requirement, but which would have to occur in a thorough explanation of the meaning of the term nonetheless, will be said to be normically connected with it. Other connections will be called synthetic."[32] With rare exception the properties that occur in the definitions of the names of taxa are normically connected. They are not analytically connected because an individual or a population could lack any one or few of the properties and still be a member of the taxon. Yet they are not merely synthetic because they are the *only* properties used in the definitions.

In terming certain properties "normic," laws are implied. In phylogenetic taxonomy these laws are those of evolutionary and gene theories. Which properties are normic and how important each is for defintion is determined by these theories. Advocates of traditional Aristotelian definition and the simple, clear-cut analytic-synthetic distinction on which it is based usually counter attempts to define words as cluster concepts by one of two moves. They claim that such words are "used in a fuzzy way by the casual users, but that (a) usually these users can be persuaded on reflection to accept certain necessary and sufficient conditions as analytic and to reject other connections as synthetic , or (b) the fuzzy concept should be replaced by a more precise one, which can be defined in a traditional way."[33]

Neither of these alternatives is viable in the case of taxa names. Taxonomists certainly do not use the names of taxa casually and could not accept certain necessary and sufficient conditions as analytic even if they wanted to, as the chordate example showed. Nor can they replace the taxa names they now have with more precise ones and still fulfil the purposes of phylogenetic taxonomy. For example, all and only the vertebrates, the cephalochordates and the urochordates possess a notochord at some time in their ontological development. No other property covaries with this property. Even so a taxon "Notochordata" could be formed by making the possession of a notochord both necessary and sufficient. On the other hand, the vertebrates, cephalochordates, urochordates, enteropneusts and some pterobranchs (both of the hemichordates), and an extinct echinoderm possess gill slits at some time in their ontological development. No other property covaries with it. If the possession of gill slits was made both necessary and sufficient, a taxon "Branchiata" could be defined traditionally. But the preceding definitions are *just* the type of defintion of taxa names which modern taxonomists have striven to avoid.[34] Whether a classification is to be merely useful (the position of numerical taxononomy) or both useful and phylogenetically significant (the phylogenetic position), taxa names can be defined only by sets of statistically covarying properties.

All the examples of cluster concepts given thus far have a second peculiarity. After several members of the disjunction have been given, the definition is terminated with a phrase like "and so on." In the case of most taxa names, the reason for not listing all of the disjuncts is not that the list is too long or too well known to bother writing down but that it *cannot be completed*. The property of cluster concepts which bothers traditionalists most is that often the entire disjunction cannot be stated. It is indefinitely long. Instead of being detrimental for the purposes of phylogenetic taxonomy, such indefiniteness is essential.

Morton Beckner says of defining the name of a taxon K that if we had an enumeration of the defining properties and if the number of properties sufficient for membership were determined once and for all, then "we have provided ourselves with the means of defining K as a monotypic class. We can form all the distinct classes that are the Boolean product of k members of G (the set of defining properties), and then say that X is a member of K if and only if it is a member of the class which is the Boolean sum of these Boolean products. In short, K would be the disjunction of all conjunctions of k members of G. This function lays down a single condition which is both necessary and sufficient for membership in K."[35] But in the case of phylogenetic taxonomy seldom can either of the two conditions which prefaced the quotation be realized until K and its neighboring taxa have ceased to evolve, for not until all the species which must be distinguished from each other have ceased to evolve can it be decided which and how many properties are sufficient to distinguish them *once and for all*.[36] For example, very few properties are needed to distinguish modern man from any other known species. However, if a species of ape were to begin to develop along the same lines as man, acquiring comparable properties, the definition of *Homo sapiens* would have to be expanded to exclude this new form if *Homo sapiens* is to be kept minimally monophyletic. Even if a taxonomist wanted to, he could not supply these distinguishing properties in advance. Besides, until such an unlikely event occurs, there is no reason to complicate the definition. Taxonomists cannot be prepared in advance for all contingencies. All that they need do is to accommodate the contingencies that do arise as they arise.

In the case of entirely extinct species, it is at least in principle possible to define the names of these species once and for all *if* a complete fossil record is present for the species concerned and its neighboring taxa. If the fossil record is not complete, the definition of the name of an extinct species must be changed as fossils of similar species are discovered. Thus, the definitions of taxa names as cluster concepts are peculiar in a second respect. Unlike traditional definitions, they cannot be forever insulated against empirical findings. As more evidence is accumulated, they will have to be altered to accommodate this evidence.

The Species Problem

Thus far all that has been shown is that with respect to taxa names taxonomists have rejected Aristotelian definition. It has yet to be shown that they have failed to eliminate completely their predisposition for Aristotelian definition and that this failure has been at least in part responsible for the persistence of the species problem. Species will be treated in this paper only from the point of view of phylogenetic taxonomy; that is, from the point of view that classification must have some systematic relationship to phylogeny and that the unit of classification must be the unit of evolution. In order for such a position on the status of "species" to be justified, not only must an adequate definition of "species" as an evolutionary unit be given but also the phylogenetic program itself must be shown to be feasible and significant. Only the former will be attempted in this paper.

G. G. Simpson defines an evolutionary species as "a lineage (an ancestral-descendant sequence of populations) evolving separately from others and with its own unitary evolutionary role and tendencies."[37] Unfortunately, Simpson's definition itself does not provide any explicitly formulated criteria for determining exactly how unitary an evolutionary role is unitary enough for species status. He defines roles in terms of niches and niches in terms of whole ways of life. Simpson's definition is important because it brings to the fore one of the basic principles of phylogenetic taxonomy (that the unit of classification must be the unit of evolution), but it does not contribute much toward determining what level of evolutionary unity is to be considered specific. In short it is not "operational." The purpose of the following sections will be to provide criteria to implement Simpson's definition.

Dobzhansky provided one such criterion in his biological definition. When a group of organisms which usually reproduce by interbreeding interbreeds consistently and produces reasonably fertile offspring, this group of organisms is as distinct an evolutionary unit as there is in phylogeny. The members of the group are *genetically* affecting each other's phylogenetic development. But the biological definition is not without its faults. Cain summarizes the major difficulties confronting the criterion of actual interbreeding as follows: "The biospecies is a definable concept only if time and allopatric populations are ignored and asexual forms are excluded from consideration."[38] These are not the *only* difficulties confronting a successful definition of "species," but they are certainly three of the major ones. If they can be surmounted, the others will be relatively easy to account for.

Before each of these major difficulties is treated, reference must be made to Dobzhansky's second criterion for species status. Dobzhansky was well aware that actual interbreeding applied to only a small percentage of organisms. (Our ability to observe such actual interbreeding directly applies to an even smaller percentage.) To accommodate all other cases (that is, to accommodate a majority of the cases) he introduced the criterion of potential interbreeding. In doing so he adopted a nontraditional form of definition, a disjunctive definition. He did not, however, depart very radically from traditional definition, since the two disjuncts were considered to be the only pertinent conditions. Each was sufficient, the fulfillment of at least one necessary. Dobzhansky's definition has much to recommend it. One of the criteria is at least the basis for a sufficient condition for delineating species as units of evolution. The form of the definition, although not completely adequate, is more appropriate than the form of all previous definitions. Unfortunately, Dobzhansky chose potential interbreeding as his second criterion.

If it had not other faults, the criterion of potential interbreeding would be undesirable on the grounds of vagueness alone. It is intended to cover too many too varied exceptions to the first criterion. In one sense a population of mice on one island is potentially interbreeding with a population of mice on another island. They would interbreed if they could get at each other. In a second sense a population of Drosophila living in 1942 is potentially interbreeding with a population of that species living in 1922 or 1962. If they had lived at the same time in the same area, they would have interbred. In still another sense, two interfertile sibling species which are both sympatric and synchronic are potentially interbreeding. They could interbreed if they were so inclined. In another sense all the breeds of domestic dogs are potentially interbreeding. They would (and do) inter-breed whenever their masters permit. The list could be extended indefin-itely. There is, however, a more fundamental philosophical reason for abandoning potential interbreeding as a criterion for species status. Ber-trand Russell says, for example:

> The concept of potentiality is convenient in some connections, pro-vided it is so used that we can translate our statements into a form in which the concept is absent. "A block of marble is a potential statue" means "from a block of marble, by suitable acts, a statue is produced." But when potentiality is used as a fundamental and irreducible con-cept it always conceals confusion of thought. Aristotle's use of it is one of the bad points in his system.[39]

Whether or not such a blanket indictment of the concept of potentiality is completely justified, there are reasons peculiar to evolutionary taxonomy for avoiding it. What is important in evolution is not which organisms could interbreed but which organisms do interbreed. The fact that two groups of organisms *cannot* interbreed (regardless of the isolating mecha-nism) is important only in the respect that it follows deductively that they are *not* interbreeding. On the other hand the fact that two groups of organisms can or could interbreed even though they are not so inter-breeding (regardless of how this is to be ascertained) is important in only two respects. First, it means that the two groups of organisms have not diverged appreciably from each other in interbreeding habits since they had a common ancestry which was actually interbreeding. Second, it means that if in the future the isolating mechanisms are removed, then the two groups would interbreed. But taxonomists are not obliged to predict the future course of evolution. Taxonomists are obliged to classify only those species that have evolved given the environment that did pertain, not to classify all possible species that might have evolved in some possible environment. Until potentially interbreeding organisms actually use this potentiality, it is of only "potential" interest in classification. In evolution-ary taxonomy *unrealized* potentialities don't count.

Allopatric Populations
Synchronic populations can be geographically separated in two ways. Either they can be separated but connected by intermediate populations or else they can be completely isolated from each other. Chains of contiguous or overlapping populations are termed geographic *Rassenkreise*. Such chains

may vary with respect to any property or type of property, but the two most important kinds of *Rassenkreise* are those that vary with respect to morphological similarity and those that vary with respect to interbreeding. Douglas Gasking defines a morphological species as all those forms that are serially very like each other[40] and a biological species as all those populations that are serially crossable with each other.[41] A serial relation is a relation such that the simple relation holds between any two consecutive terms in the series but need not hold between any two terms that are not consecutive.

For example in a morphological *Rassenkreise*, population A may be very like population B, which is very like population C, which is very like population D, and so on, but A and a distant population, say, G may not be very like each other at all. Such continuous variation among contemporary populations presents no problem for the biological definition because interbreeding status is the criterion for species status among contemporary populations, not morphological similarity. However, interbreeding *Rassenkreise* do present a minor difficulty. In some cases population A is interbreeding with population B, B with C, C with D and so on; but not only is it the case that A is not interbreeding with a distant member of the chain, but also it is sometimes the case that they are not even interfertile. Nevertheless, genes are exchanged via intermediate populations. All members of the interbreeding *Rassenkreise* belong to the same "gene pool" and are evolving with a sufficient degree of separateness and unity to be classed as species. They are genetically affecting each other's evolutionary development.

The second respect in which two synchronic populations can be separated geographically is by complete isolation. In such cases the populations are neither interbreeding nor serially interbreeding, and yet taxonomists class these isolated populations in the same species if they are morphologically similar to each other and distinct from other species; that is, if they possess a degree of morphological similarity and difference usually indicative of species status in organisms of that type. The degree of morphological similarity and difference usually indicative of species status is determined by the degree of morphological similarity and difference present among contemporary interbreeding species.

The question of greatest interest to the biologist is how good morphological similarity and difference is at indicating species status if species are to be units of evolution. Although this is primarily an empirical question and can be answered only after extensive empirical investigation, its solution has been hindered by logical and philosophical confusions. The phylogeneticists themselves have been responsible for some of the confusion by treating consistent interbreeding with the production of fertile offspring as both a necessary and a sufficient condition when it is obviously only sufficient. For example, true sibling species have been extremely troublesome to the phylogeneticists. From a practical standpoint, taxonomists would like to treat them as single species although they do not interbreed even when given every opportunity. On the other hand, from a theoretical point of view, classing them as a single species seems to run counter to the biological definition.[42] Classing two groups of organisms which are morphologically and ecologically quite similar as a single species although they never interbreed conflicts with the biological definition only if interbreeding is mistakenly considered to be a necessary condition. As Simpson has pointed out, a pair of sibling species which are distinguishable neither morphologically nor ecologically are evolving as an evolutionary unit—albeit without the aid of genetic interchange.[43] As will be seen shortly, the same can be said for species of asexual organisms.

A second confusion must be laid at the doorstep of the opponents of phylogenetic taxonomy. Although the point has been made often and well, it bears repeating: it does not follow from the fact that morphological similarity and difference are used as the evidence from which species status is inferred that the morphological definition of "species" has been substituted for the biological definition. Morphological similarity and difference is only the *evidence* being used to determine species status. How similar is similar enough is determined by the criterion of interbreeding and *this* is what is logically important.

Finally, A. J. Cain voices a common complaint against inferring species status from morphological similarity when he says, "We can determine by observation the specific or merely varietal status of partially or completely sympatric forms, but can only guess at the status of wholly allopatric ones."[44] Several factors contribute to this view, including such basic philosophical problems as the justification of induction and the role of deduction in science. The inferences taxonomists make from morphological similarity to species status are not readily put into a form which lends itself to easy manipulation within any of the various theories of probability which have presently been devised. This fact says more against the present development of probability theory than it does against such scientific inferences. Most of the inferences scientists make cannot be accounted for in probability theory. It might also be fruitfully mentioned that the most scathing critics of inferring that two populations belong to the same species from morphological similarity advocate a comparable inference that two different instances of a property are instances of the same property.

The importance of justifying the inference from morphological similarity to phylogenetic relationship should not be underestimated. If it is not justified in a good percentage of the cases, then the entire phylogenetic program becomes untenable since in most cases morphological properties are *all* the taxonomist has to go on. But before such a harsh judgment is passed, one should make sure that phylogenetic taxonomy is not being measured against an unrealistic standard. On the one hand, science is not as empirical as many scientists seem to think it is. Unobserved and even unobservable entities play an important part in it. Science is not just the making of observations: it is the making of inferences on the basis of observations within the framework of a theory. On the other hand, most of the inferences made by scientists are not deductions as many logicians and philosophers seem to think they are. All inferences made by scientists need not match the accuracy possible in certain restricted areas of physics to be justified.[46] Inductive inferences are not deductively certain.

If the inferences made by phylogeneticists are guessing, then so are those of meteorolgists, economists, historians, pollsters, and so on. According to the definition of "guessing" implied by Cain's comment, most of what is known as science, including all of the social sciences, becomes guessing. Pershaps the scepticism with which Cain and others view inference from morphological similarity to species status arises from the confusion wrought by the criterion of potential interbreeding. If the status which taxonomists are to determine for wholly allopatric forms is whether or not they are potentially interbreeding, then perhaps the critics are justified in terming such inference "guessing." If taxonomists are expected to predict the future development of the organisms being classified, then they are guessing in the strictest sense of the word, since both gene and evolutionary theory are not predictive but retrodictive theories. If on the other hand taxonomists are expected only to infer what has actually happened, what species have actually evolved, what groups were actually interbreeding, then these inferences are well outside the range of guessing.

In any case the purpose of this paper is to present a *type* of definition appropriate for evolutionary taxonomy. Even if the opponents of phylogenetic taxonomy can show that phylogenetic relationships cannot be inferred with reasonable accuracy from the type and extent of evidence that the phylogeneticists have at their disposal, this fact will have no bearing on the *logical* assertion which is the thesis of this paper that Aristotelian definition in terms of a set of necessary and sufficient conditons is inadequate for defining "species" if species are to be the units of evolution.

Allochronic Populations

Taxonomists are unanimous in their opinion that temporal isolation presents a more serious problem for the biological definition of "species" than geographic isolation presents. A. J. Cain says, for example:

> The palaeospecies is an expression of the attempted imposition of a hierarchy developed for classifying discrete groups, on to a continuous evolutionary series. Because of the imperfections of the fossil record many fossils do fall into morphologically discrete groups and

can readily be incorporated into the hierarchy. Nevertheless, the whole concept of the species as a morphologically (and by implication genetically) discrete group is based upon the observation of present-day animals, and holds only for short periods of time which on the evolutionary scale are mere instants.[47]

Evolving lineages form what might be called temporal *Rassenkreise* both with respect to morphological similarity and with respect to interbreeding. Each successive generation in a progressively evolving lineage changes only slightly. Each generation is serially very like all of its ancestral generations. Similarly, each generation of interbreeding forms is serially interbreeding with all of its ancestral generations. Thus, "species" cannot be defined in terms of a serial relation unless a temporal restriction is imposed on pain of classifying all organisms in a single species.

Morphological *Rassenkreise* among contemporary forms presented no problems for the biological definition because interbreeding status could be determined directly. In temporally separated populations, however, whether there is or is not a complete fossil record, interbreeding status cannot be determined directly. Yet phylogeneticists must find some way to divide progressively evolving lineages into evolutionary units. In the case of lineages broken by fossil gaps, the task is easy. In the case of lineages for which there is a reasonably complete fossil record, the task is not so easy. Even so, there is a solution to the problem of dividing progressively evolving lineages objectively and nonarbitrarily, and the key to the solution is again interbreeding.

The importance of interbreeding for determining species status has been emphasized time and again, but the extent of the criterion's significance has not been fully appreciated even by its strongest proponents. Mayr, using a suggestive metaphor, compares the biological definition to a "yardstick" for determining species status, and he rightly maintains that division by such a yardstick is both objective and nonarbitrary.[48] Further, he sees that what difficulties there are concerning the biological definition are not "with the yardstick but with its application."[49] A further development of Mayr's spatial analogy comparable to Simpson's analogy of a string gradually changing color proves quite enlightening in the determination of the roles of interbreeding and morphological similarity and difference and placing them in their proper perspective.

The paradigm case of objective measurement is the measurement of objects in space or of the distance between spatially separated objects. Space as such is an amorphous continuum with no intrinsic metric.[50] What this means is that there is nothing about space itself to indicate how long to make the unit of measurement or at what point to begin measuring once the unit of length has been chosen. With respect to objects in space, the choice of the unit of length is primarily a matter of convenience. Bacteria are measured in microns, rugs in feet (or yards or meters), roads in miles or kilometers, and interstellar distances in light years. One highly advantageous property for a system of measurement is to have the units commensurable. A mile can be divided evenly into yards, feet, or inches. At what point we begin to measure is a matter of convenience. We could begin to measure a rug by laying down our ruler anywhere on it, although it is most convenient to begin at one corner and measure one edge. Nothing about space itself dictates either the length of the unit of measurement or the point at which to begin measuring, but it does dictate what type of unit is appropriate—a spatial unit.

Comparable points can be made about what might be called "taxonomic space," but it must be emphasized that everything that is said in terms of taxonomic space is meant merely to be explanatory and suggestive. Talk of taxonomic space, like talk of gene pools, is strictly metaphorical. Before either metaphor can actually function in taxonomic theory, a rigorous development in exclusively taxonomic terms is required. Taxonomic space is constructed by plotting "morphological distance" on the horizontal axis and development in time on the other. "Morphological distance" means morphological similarity and difference. Taxonomic space, like physical space, is an amorphous continuum with no intrinsic metric; there is nothing about taxonomic space to indicate how long to make the unit of measurement or at what point to begin measuring once the unit is chosen.

With respect to the objects in taxonomic space, the choice of the unit of length is neither arbitrary nor a matter of choice for the phylogeneticists. (This is not the case for the classificationists and their numerical progeny.) The unit of taxonomic space is the morphological distance usually indicative of interbreeding status among contemporary organisms which usually reproduce by interbreeding. However, interbreeding is not the unit of taxonomic space; interbreeding merely determines the length of the unit of taxonomic space. In terms of Mayr's metaphor, the yardstick is morphological distance. Interbreeding determines how long a yard of morphological space is. Nor is the choice of the point at which to begin measuring lineages arbitrary or purely a matter of convenience. In the case of lineages which terminate in contemporary species, it is certainly most convenient to begin laying down our yardstick with them; but there are also theoretical reasons to begin with contemporary species, for only with them can we check the accuracy of our yardstick. The purpose of the yardstick is to delineate evolutionary units. The rationale for making the yardstick one length rather than another is that for the group of organisms in question a particular morphological distance is usually indicative of interbreeding status, which is indicative that the group is evolving as a unit and is, hence, righly called a spacies. The nature of taxonomic space as we constructed it determines what type of unit is appropriate for measuring lineages—morphological distance. In the case of lineages which are entirely extinct, measurement begins at the point of extinction or with the most recent fossil. These points may or may not coincide. In the case of lineages which are known only by isolated groups of fossils, the length of the object to be measured is usually less than the length of the yardstick so no division is necessary.

One rather disconcerting property of both physical and taxonomic space, which has been referred to only tangentially, is that fact that length of the unit of measurement varies. Just as spatially extended objects determine the contours of physical space, evolutionary lineages determine the topography of taxonomic space. To stretch the analogy to its breaking point, taxonomic space is "non-euclidean." The vertical temporal axis is divided evenly into segments, but the horizontal axis which indicates morphological distance is not. The units of morphological distance vary in length depending on what morphological distance is indicative of species status for the contemporary members of the general type of organism. Some organisms interbreed even if there is great morphological dissimilarity; others permit almost none. If the properties under consideration are weighted, still another dimension of complexity is added. The logic of the situation remains unchanged, however.

Taxonomists use the yardstick of morphological distance to indicate species status among contemporary allopatric populations. There is no reason why its use cannot be extended to allochronic or even to allochronic and allopatric forms.[51] Although Simpson feels that the resulting dvisions will be arbitrary, he condones chopping a progresssively evolving lineage into segments by use of morphological distance. He goes on to say, however, "In practice all that is needed is some criterion as to how large (and in what sense 'large') to make the segments.... Successive species should be so defined as to make the morphological differences between them at least as great as sequential differences among contemporaneous species of the same or closely allied group."[52] In progressively evolving lineages there is no sudden discontinuity which can be used as a specific boundary, just as there is none in a synchronic morphological *Rassenkreise*; but there *is* a reason in both cases to make a break in the continuous series at one point rather than at another.

Asexual Populations
Taxonomists universally agree (if universal agreement among taxonomists is possible) that organisms which never reproduce by interbreeding, whether contemporary or ancestral, present an insurmountable difficulty for the biological definition which no amount of modification could accommodate.[53] The following quotations are typical:

In summary, the existence of the species as an objective biological unit is not impaired by morpholgical indistinctness or by the continuity of the evolutionary process. The loss of sexuality, on the other hand, removes the very foundations on which the species exists as a type of breeding population. As a result biological species do not exist in asexual groups.[54]

The essence of the biological species concept is discontinuity due to reproductive isolation. Without sexuality this concept cannot be applied. Asexuality then is the most formidable and most fundamental obstacle of a biological species concept.[55]

The agamospecies represents an advance on the morphospecies, since the mode of reproduction is known. Unfortunately, it is a mode which allows no possibility of framing a definition of the species which is any less arbitrary than the morphospecies.[56]

In the case of asexual forms, taxonomists feel they have come to an impasse in applying the yardstick they have devised to determine species status, for it is logically impossible for a noninterbreeding species to be interbreeding (not to *become* interbreeding but to *be* interbreeding). What they have neglected is that the yardstick is not interbreeding status but the degree of morphological distance usually indicative of interbreeding status. When a taxonomist says that a certain asexual species possesses a degree of morphological similarity and difference comparable to that of contemporary interbreeding species, he is not saying something that is logically impossible, although it may be empirically false. Mayr says, "It it possible to use the same kind of inference to classify asexual organisms into species. Those asexual individuals are included in a single species that display no more morphological difference from each other than do conspecific individuals in related sexual species."[57]

Although T. M. Sonneborn wants to retain the word "species" to refer to the unit of identification and coins the word "syngen" to refer to the unit of evolution as determined by the biological definition, he says, "The question of whether asexual equivalents of syngens exist and can be recognized is more difficult, but not hopeless. The key to progress in this direction is to recognize in the syngen of sexual organisms a distinction between the means of ascertainment and that which is ascertained."[58] He goes on to say in more detail:

The preceding attempt to generalize the biological species or syngen runs counter to the view of proponents of the biological species concept ... that biological species do not exist among obligatory inbreeders or asexual organisms. This denial, as indicated above, is based on an operational definition of biological species. Since the operation, testing gene flow, is impossible in asexual organisms, they deny the existence in them of the thing this operation discovers in sexual organisms, i.e., the biological species or syngen. Their statement of the situation thus implies an abrupt change in the organization of nature and in the units of evolutionary divergence correlated with an abrupt change from outbreeding to obligatory inbreeding and asexual reproduction. By subordinating the method of ascertainment to the thing ascertained and by seeking methods of ascertainment in asexual reproduction, the concept of biological species or syngens was generalized. This implies the absence of an abrupt change in the organization of nature and in the units of evolutionary divergence with changes in breeding systems or method of reproduction.

No such abrupt change is in fact found in the present review of conditons in Protozoa.[59]

A Disjunctive Definition of "Species"

If the yardstick used to determine species status among allochronic and allopatric interbreeding species is accurate enough to indicate evolutionary units, and if it can be extended to apply to asexual species without any great loss in accuracy, then it would seem that the phylogeneticists at least are in a position to formulate a definition of "species" adequate for their purposes. "Species" could be defined *disjunctively* as populations that:

> 1. consistently interbreed producing a reasonably large proportion of reasonably fertile offspring, or
> 2. consistently serially interbreed with synchronic populations producing a reasonably large proportion of reasonably fertile offspring, or
> 3. do not fulfill either of the first two conditions but have not diverged appreciably from a common ancestry which did fulfill one of them, or
> 4. do not fulfill any of the first three conditions because they do not apply but are analogous to populations which do fulfill at least one of the first three conditions.

Conditions 1 and 2 are quite straightforward and require no application of the yardstick of morphological distance. In fact they are the basis for determining the length of the morphological yardstick. However, they apply only to contemporary sympatric populations of organisms which usually reproduce by interbreeding. Condition 3 applies only to populations which usually reproduce by interbreeding, but there are no temporal or spatial restrictions. How much divergence is "appreciable" is determined by the morphological yardstick. Condition 4 applies only to noninterbreeding populations with no temporal or spatial restrictions. How analogous the populations have to be is determined again by the morphological yardstick.

As in the case of all disjunctive definitions, the fulfilling of *any one* of the conditions is sufficient and the fulfilling of *at least one* is necessary. Like the disjunctive definitions of taxa names, it is not insulated against empirical considerations, both because the objects in taxonomic space determine the length of the morphological yardstick and because new methods of reproduction might arise or be discovered. For example, some asexual forms exhibit a phenomenon called "parasexuality," in which all or some of the genetic material of one individual is transferred to another. If it is found that these nonmeiotic mechanisms of gene flow are sufficient to ensure evolutionary unity and separateness, then either an additional conditon would have to be added to the disjunctive definition of "species" or else the meaning of "interbreeding" would have to be expanded to encompass parasexuality. The former is the more probable move.

However, instead of taxonomists concluding that "species" can be defined, albeit disjunctively, the have concluded just the opposite. "Species" cannot be defined because there are several *kinds* of species. Mayr says, for example, "Two facts emerge from these and other classifications. One is that there is more than one species concept and that it is futile to search for *the* species concept."[60] The reasons which taxonomists give for refusing to accept a disjunctive definition of "species" and the moves they make to avoid defining it disjunctively are exactly the reasons that the traditionalists give and the moves they make for avoiding disjunctive definition of *any* term. According to the advocates of traditional Aristotelian definition, whenever a word can be defined only disjunctively, either one or more conditions must be accepted as necessary and sufficient or else the fuzzy concept must be divided into terms that can be defined traditionally. The first alternative is not open to phylogeneticists given evolutionary development as it is. Sonneborn outlines the possibilities given the second alternative.

> 1. Apply the word "species" to all the various kinds of species, including species as the unit of identification and as the unit of evolution.
> 2. Retain the term to apply to the unit of evolution as determined by the biological definition.
> 3. Continue to use the term to apply to the unit of identification as determined by the morphological definition.[61]

Sonneborn rejects the first alternative "on the grounds that a technical term should have a single meaning, and the second alternative on the grounds of priority and generality."[62] Thus, "species" is to be reserved for the units of identification and groups of orgainsms which fulfill the requirements of the biological definition are to be termed "syngens." V. Grant opts for the second alternative and suggests the term "binom" for groups of organisms which do not fulfill the requirements of the biological definition.[63] Cain suggests adopting either 1 or 2. He says, "One can either restrict the name to one meaning (presumably the biological species) or use it with appropriate prefixes for all."[64] Regardless of how it may sound, these biologists are *not* arguing about words. "Species" has no magic power, and they are well aware of it. What they are arguing about is whether the unit of identification or the unit of evolution will be the unit of classification and, thus, will remain intact as higher taxa are constructed. In order for the purposes of phylogenetic taxonomy to be fulfilled, the unit of evolution must remain intact.[65]

As is usually the case with disjunctive definitions, taxonomists feel two opposing pulls. On the one hand, since several alternative conditions are each sufficient, they feel that several different terms are being defined. Thus, they conclude that there are several different kinds of species. On the other hand, these different kinds of species seem to function with amazing similarity in both evolutionary and gene theory. Almost everything that a biologist would want to say about one kind of species, he would want to say about the other, with the exception of statements directly pertaining to their defining criteria. Thus, G. G. Simpson says, "The evolution of uniparental and biparental populations is different in many important ways. That does not alter the fact that both form species and, by appropriate definition, the same kind of species."[66]

Such a situation is not unique to taxonomic terms. For example, since some grapefruit have yellow, sour flesh and others have pink, sweet flesh, the fuzzy concept "grapefruit" could be replaced by two precise concepts ... "Florida grapefruit" and "Texas grapefruit." But in most contexts in which the word "grapefruit" is used, everything that is said about one kind of grapefruit is true of the other. In other contexts the distinction between the two slightly different fruits might be important and the distinction could be made. However, "grapefruit" cannot be defined traditionally so that it is impossible to make a true statement about grapefruit in general which is false with respect to some individual grapefruit.

An example which is more like "species" is the word "dishonesty." There are at least three different criteria for dishonesty—lying, cheating, and stealing. The fulfillment of any one of these criteria is sufficient for proper application of the predicate "dishonest." If someone lies, he is being dishonest. If someone cheats, he is being dishonest. If someone steals, he is being dishonest. But it does not follow that if someone performs a dishonest act, he has stolen. He may have lied or cheated or both. Thus, a traditionalist would say that there are three kinds of dishonesty and want to abandon the word "dishonesty" for three more precise words. In a sense there are three kinds of dishonesty, but it is not a sense in which the term "dishonest" is fuzzy, meaningless, or indefinable. M. J. Scriven says of this example:

> There are cases of special interest here where we are led to apply the same term even when no natural cluster exists; the classic example is that of dishonesty, where we may discover that lying, cheating and stealing, the three main criteria, are not correlated with each other. This does not destroy the social utility of the term, though it may impair its value for personality-theory.[67]

There are several criteria for determining species as evolutionary units. Several criteria are required because evolutionary development is extended in time and space, because numerous factors affect this development, and because there are various ways in which species reproduce themselves. This does not destroy the general utility of the term "species" in biology, though it may impair its value in particular areas.

To some the "solution" to the species problem presented in this paper may seem no solution at all (which means it's not the kind of solution they had in mind). Instead it might seem merely philosophical sleight of hand. All that is necessary to solve any problem in definition is to trot out a disjunctive definition. Two examples in which this procedure cannot be used may help to dispel this illusion of fakery. In the early days of genetics, genes were held to be the units of heredity. For each gross trait such as eye color there was supposedly a discrete particle which controlled it. When a radical change occurred in a trait, a gene mutation was postualted as the cause. As genetics developed "gene" was also defined operationally as the smallest unit of recombination. It was assumed that the smallest units of heredity, mutation, action, and crossing over were discrete units and one and the same unit. However, as larger and larger numbers were taken into consideration as more conveniently studied organisms were investigated, the limits of what had been envisaged as a gene were passed right through. The progression stopped only at the molecular level with the nucleotide pair (in the case of DNA), and no one wanted to call a pair of nucleotides a "gene" in its original sense.

In place of the classic gene several new units have been introduced. The smallest unit of mutation is termed the muton and consists of one nucleotide pair. The smallest unit of recombination is termed the recon and is also one nucleotide pair long. The unit of information, the codon, is most probably three nucleotides long. What comes closest to the classic gene is the cistron, the unit of function, which averages about five hundred nucleotide pairs in length. But the product of one cistron is not one trait but one protein. And the whole situation is complicated further by the possible existence of operators which control one or more cistrons, providing a larger natural unit, the operon. In any case nothing approximates the classic gene. This fact presents no serious barrier to the definition of "gene." Scientific words often acquire additional or even radically different meaning as science progresses, but in the case of the word "gene" all but two of the meanings happen to conflict. Almost nothing a geneticist would want to say about a muton or recon would he want to say about a codon, a cistron or an operon, and almost nothing he would want to say about any of the new units would he want to say about the classic gene. The fate of the word "gene" in modern genetics is that except in general discourse or in the first few chapters of an introductory text (and its use here is debatable), its function has entirely evaporated. Using such a truly ambiguous term like "gene" in intermediate or advanced discourse can lead to nothing but confusion.

"Protoplasm" is an earlier example. It has already passed out of scientific discourse. Not too many years ago protoplasm was thought to be the stuff of life. If only its complex structure could be analyzed, the secret of life would be revealed. As it turned out, it was primarily the nucleic acid constituents (a relatively simple molecule) that were of importance in heredity. Perhaps "protoplasm" could be defined now that there is so much knowledge of the molecular makeup of the cell, but it is doubtful whether any scientist would take the time to try since the concept of protoplasm is no longer of any use in biology. Its original function has been entirely usurped by other concepts.

The fate of "gene" and "protoplasm" has not befallen "species." An appropriate definition of it is not ambiguous, and it is still an important concept in biology. Thus, the defining of it disjunctively is both possible and justified. The definition of "species" presented in this paper may prove inadequate for the purposes of evolutionary taxonomy, but its formulation will have shown at least in what respects a definition of its kind is superior to the typical Aristotelian definitions of "species" thus far offered in the literature.

Conclusion

It is commonly held that Darwin shattered the essentialist or static concept of species. Darwin shattered something all right, but it was only the first two tenets of essentialism, the ontological and methodological assertions. Darwin did not alter taxonomists' predisposition for Aristotelian definitions, either for species names or for "species." Contemporary taxonomists have finally abandoned attempts to define taxa names traditionally, but they still refuse to accept any but an Aristotelian definition of "species." To be sure, there are many objections to abandoning the clear-cut analytic-synthetic distinction which the adoption of cluster concept analysis implies, not the least of these being that it has broad philosophical ramifications; but taxonomists have already committed themselves to the necessity of defining taxa names as cluster concepts. No new logical or philosophical obstacles stand in the way of their extending this practice to include "species."

Notes and References

1. Karl R. Popper, *The Open Society and Its Enemies*, Princeton, 1950, p. 206.
2. Charles Darwin, *The Origin of Species*, New York, 1859, p. 447.
3. Ernst Mayr, *Systematics and the Origin of Species*, New York, 1942, p. 103.
4. Ernst Mayr, "Species concepts and definition," *The Species Problem*, Washington, 1957, p. 5.
5. Throughout this paper "species names" and "taxa names" will be used. These phrases are not presently used in taxonomy, but some terminological device must be made to mark the logically crucial distinction between defining the names of categories such as species, genus, and phylum and defining the names of taxa classed at these category levels such as *Bos bos*, Homo and Protozoa. A second distinction is also important—the distinction between defining a word and defining (or delineating) a group. The name of a particular taxon is defined in terms of certain properties. The membership of that taxon is thus delineated.
6. A. J. Cain, "Logic and memory in Linnaeus's system of taxonomy," *Proceedings of the Linnaean Society London*, 1958, 169, 149. In this article Cain makes the point that Aristotelian definition of species names had given rise to difficulties in the species concept. He does not go on to extend his analysis to "species" itself which is the purpose of this paper.

    Also in this article Cain criticizes the use of "diagnostic" properties by present day phylogeneticists, which he identifies with the practice of weighting some properties more heavily than others because of their varying phylogenetic significance. Thus, it is charged that the variable weighting of properties according to their phylogenetic significance is a development from Aristotelian logic. Cain, op. cit., pp. 150, 161–162. R. R. Sokal and P. H. A. Sneath reiterate the charge in their recent book. R. R. Sokal and P. H. A. Sneath, *Principles of Numerical Taxonomy*, San Francisco, 1963, pp. 8, 16, 34. Unfortunately for this thesis the variable weighting of different characters according to their presumed phylogenetic importance is in direct opposition to the Aristotelian theory of essences. According to Aristotle either a character is essential or it is not. One character cannot be more essential than another. If the variable weighting of properties as now practised by the phylogeneticists is a development from Aristotle, it is an illogical development. Perhaps this is what Cain intended. This is not what Sokal and Sneath interpreted him to mean.
7. It is not being claimed here that the typical practising taxonomist is consciously aware of the logic of Aristotelian definition and has opted for it rather than for some other type of definition.
8. Popper, 1950, p. 34.
9. Karl R. Popper, *Conjectures and Refutations*, New York, 1962, 19.
10. Popper, 1950, p. 208.
11. The important distinction for this paper, however, is not between definite conjunctive and definite disjunctive definitions but between definite definitions of either kind and indefinitely long disjunctive definitions.

12. Tindell Hopwood, "Animal classification from the Greeks to Linnaeus," *Lectures on the Development of Taxonomy*, London, 1950, p. 26.

13. David L. Hull, "Consistency and Monophyly," *Systematic Zoology*, 1960, 13, 1–11.

14. Adanson was unique in several respects, two of which are that he abandoned all the tenets of essentialism before evolutionary theory and that evolution had no relevance for taxonomy but for the very simple reason that it hadn't been discovered yet.

15. J.-B. Lamarck, *Discours D'Ouverture*, Paris, 1097, p. 110.

16. William Coleman, "Lyell and the 'reality' of species," *Isis*, 1962, 53, 326.

17. Darwin, 1859, p. 447.

18. A. J. Cain, *Animal Species and Their Evolution*, London, 1954, p. 107.

19. Cain, 1954, p. 111.

20. Cain, 1954, p. 113.

21. Cain, 1954, p. 114.

22. Ernst Mayr, 'Difficulties and importance of the biological species', *The Species Problem*, Washington, 1957, p. 376.

23. G. G. Simpson, *Principles of Animal Taxonomy*, New York, 1961, p. 165.

24. Cain, 1954, p. 183.

25. Mayr, 1957, p. 385.

26. Mayr, 1957, p. 384.

27. Simpson, 1961, pp. 60–61.

28. Mayr, 1957, p. 10.

29. Mayr, 1957, p. 10.

30. Each disjunct may also be a conjunction of two or more properties without altering the logic of a definite disjunctive definition as long as each conjunction has a certain set of members.

31. Michael J. Scriven, "The Logic of Criteria," *The Journal of Philosophy*, 1959, 56, p. 860.

32. Scriven, 1959, p. 861.

33. Scriven, 1959, p. 859.

34. Cain, 1954, p. 18.

35. Morton Beckner, *The Biological Way of Thought*, New York, 1959, p. 24. Ludwig Wittgenstein was an early proponent of cluster concepts of "family resemblances," as he termed them. He also foresaw the possibility of Beckner's move and commented on it appropriately. Ludwig Wittgenstein, *Philosophical Investigation*, New York, 1945 sect. 67.

36. The species are "neighbouring" in the sense of being near each other in taxonomic space.

37. Simpson, 1961, p. 153.

38. Cain, 1954, p. 24.

39. Bertrand Russell, *A History of Western Philosophy*, New York, 1945, p. 167.

40. Douglas Gasking, "Clusters," *Australasian Review of Psychology*, 1960, 38, 13, 18.

41. Gasking, 1960, p. 38.

42. Mayr (1957), p. 376; note Mayr, 1942, p. 200, for his treating interbreeding as if it were a necessary condition at least with respect to sibling species.

43. Simpson, 1961, p. 160.

44. Cain, 1954, p. 73.

45. For example, Sockal and Sneath, 1963. Either both types of inference are justified or else neither is.

46. Michael J. Scriven, "The Key Property of Physical Laws—Inaccuracy," H. Feigl and G. Maxwell (eds.), *Current Issues in the Philosophy of Science*, New York, 1961.

47. Cain, 1954, p. 123.

48. Mayr, 1957, pp. 15, 16, 18, 19.

49. Mayr, 1959, p. 375.
50. Adolf Grünbaum, *Philosophical Problems of Space and Time*, New York, 1963.
51. Mayr, 1957, p. 120, and Cain, 1954, p. 111.
52. Simpson, 1961, p. 165.
53. Mayr disapproves of calling groups of asexual organisms "populations." Simpson has no reservations concerning the term. For example, see his evolutionary definition of "species" as quoted in this paper.
54. Verne Grant, "The plant species in theory and practice," *The Species Problem*, Washington, 1957, p. 61.
55. Mayr, 1957, p. 379.
56. Cain, 1954, p. 123.
57. Mayr, 1957, p. 381. Happily organisms which reproduce sexually are scattered throughout the animal kingdom from Protozoa to Chordata enabling taxonomists to establish the morphological yardstick without making unreasonable inductive leaps.
58. T. M. Sonneborn, "Breeding Systems, reproductive methods, and species problems in Protozoa," *The Species Problem*, Washington, 1957, p. 290.
59. T. M. Sonneborn, 1957, p. 296.
60. Mayr, 1957, p. 10.
61. Sonneborn, 1957, p. 201.
62. Ibid., p. 201.
63. Grant, 1957, pp. 46, 61.
64. Cain, 1954, p. 106.
65. Hull, 1964, pp. 1–11.
66. Simpson, 1961, p. 163.
67. Scriven, 1959, p. 867.

Chapter 11

Speaking of Species: Darwin's Strategy

John Beatty

I am often in despair in making the generality of naturalists even comprehend me. Intelligent men who are not naturalists and have not a bigoted idea of the term species, show more clearness of mind.
Darwin to Ansted, 27 October 1860 ML 1

There is a wealth of secondary literature on Darwin's species concept, covering many different perspectives of the topic.[1] Of the various accounts available, I have always been particularly intrigued by Frank Sulloway's suggestion that Darwin's choice of species concept was guided by "tactical" considerations. Among those tactical considerations was the decision to employ his fellow naturalists' species concept, in order to speak to them "in their own language" (Sulloway 1979, 37). Implicit in the suggestion is that Darwin was a member of a fairly clear-cut community of naturalists. In order to communicate with them about natural history, either to agree or disagree, he had to conform to some extent to their language rules, including their rules for using the term "species."

The suggestion is more perplexing when we consider the respects in which "species" definitions of the time were at odds with evolutionary theory. Darwin apparently faced a dilemma: to communicate his theory of the evolution of species to the community of naturalists, he had to conform to their rules for using the term "species," but his theory undermined their definitions.

We can pursue Sulloway's suggestion down another avenue, however. Perhaps it was possible for Darwin to conform to the language rules of his community without accepting its definitions. Perhaps, in particular, it was possible for Darwin to use the term "species" in a way that agreed with the use of the term by his contemporaries, but not in a way that agreed with his contemporaries' definitions of the term. Another way of asking this question is to consider whether historians might not sometimes more fruitfully approach scientific concepts—like Darwin's species concept—in ways other than via the definitions of the terms associated with those concepts. An alternative is to try to distinguish "what in the world" scientific terms are used to refer to in practice, from what beliefs about those things serve to define the terms. Agreement of the former sort among members of a scientific community might be conformity enough for purposes of intercommunication.

I shall argue that Darwin indeed perceived the difficulty posed by definitional language rules that undermined the theory he wished to communicate. He tried to get around this difficulty by distinguishing between what his fellow naturalists *called* "species" and the nonevolutionary beliefs in terms of which they *defined* "species." Regardless of their definitions, he argued, what they *called* "species" evolved. His species concept was therefore interestingly minimal: species were, for Darwin, just what expert naturalists *called* "species." By trying to talk about the same things that his contemporaries were talking about, he hoped that his language would conform satisfactorily enough for him to communicate his position to them.

Perhaps it is worth emphasizing from the outset that the so-called community of "naturalists," of which Darwin considered himself a member and to which he addressed his theory, is no mere philosophical construct. It is not my concern to delimit either the members or the membership requirements of the group, but just to show that the group was a real and distinct one *in Darwin's mind*. For now, it suffices to consider Darwin's many references to "naturalists" in the *Origin*. Darwin considered himself a naturalist: for example, "When on board the H.M.S. 'Beagle,' as naturalist, . . ." (*Origin*, p. 1). He acknowledged the assistance he received through communication with other "naturalists" (p. 2). He cited majority and minority opinions and cases of dissent among "naturalists": for example, "the view which most naturalists entertain" (p. 6), "the very general opinion of naturalists" (p. 149), "in the eyes of most naturalists" (p. 449), "the protest lately made by some naturalists" (p. 199), and "Let it be observed how naturalists differ . . ." (p. 469).

Moreover, Darwin made clear that it was to "naturalists" that the *Origin* was addressed. For example, he lamented, "I by no means expect to convince experienced naturalists whose minds are stocked with a multitude of facts all viewed, during a long course of years, from a point of view directly opposite to mine" (p. 481). But he hoped that "a few naturalists, endowed with much flexibility of mind, and who have already begun to doubt on the immutability of species, may be influenced by this volume; but I look with confidence to the future, to young and rising naturalists, who will be able to view both sides of the question with impartiality" (p. 482). In short, Darwin recognized a group whose members had common interests, and whose members communicated to each other agreements and disagreements concerning those interests. It was a group to which he also belonged, and the group to which he most wanted to communicate his theory of the evolution of species. But communication was a problem.

Definitions, Referents, Examples of Practice, and Theory Change

There are some constraints on theory change that make it a wonder that theory change occurs at all. Theory-laden definition is such a constraint. Consider, for instance, the many pre-Darwinian definitions of "species" in terms of immutability. Those definitions not only reflected nonevolutionary theories of natural history, but also served those theories well, making it difficult to communicate alternative theories in the same terms. How, for example, was one to argue for the mutability of species given Buffon's definition, according to which "we should regard two animals as belonging to the same species if, by means of copulation, they can perpetuate themselves and preserve the likeness of the species; and we should regard them as belonging to different species if they are incapable of producing progeny by the same means" (Buffon 1749, 10; quoted in Lovejoy 1959c, 93) On such a definition, one-and-the-same species cannot possibly change with regard to its "likeness," and that represents a significant constraint on the communication of a theory of the evolution of species.[2]

Other definitions of "species" were at odds with evolutionary theory in yet other respects. Some were compatible with the mutability of species, but at odds with the transmutation, or lineal descent, of species. Consider, in this regard, Cuvier's definition of "species": "a species comprehends all the individuals which descend from each other, or from a common parentage, and those which resemble them as much as they do each other" (Cuvier 1813, 120). Cuvier's definition does not rule out, a priori, unlimited change in a species, but it does rule out the possibility that one species should be descended from another. Thus definitions of "species" in the late eighteenth and early nineteenth centuries were at odds with both the mutability and transmutability of species.

Where scientific terminology is so loaded in behalf of received theory, the proponent of a new, contrary theory apparently faces a dilemma. In order to communicate his alternative in the same terms, he must use those terms differently—he cannot use them in the way they are defined without contradicting himself. But to use the terms differently—to use them contrary to the ways they are defined—is to invite the objection that the difference at issue is purely verbal, a dispute about words rather than about the world. How, in other words, can one respect the language rules to which the other members of one's community are subject *and still* communicate to them an alternative view of the world? How, on the other hand, can one communicate to them an alternative view of the world *without* respecting their language rules? Is it possible, perhaps, to communicate an alternative view of the world by respecting *enough* of the language rules of one's community (or by paying them *enough* respect)?

The answer to the last question is yes—a substantive difference can be communicated even though one respects the previous language rules of one's community only in part. The substance of such differences becomes apparent only when we distinguish between "what in the world" scientific terms are used to refer to in practice, and what beliefs about those things serve to define the terms.

Consider a scientist in the position of questioning a nonevolutionary theory about species, where the definition of "species" is loaded in behalf of the very nonevolutionary theory in question. How, according to that scientist, could his rivals possibly be wrong in any substantive sense? The dissenting scientist has at least two options, depending on what *kinds* of language rules he chooses to respect. First, he might respect his community's *definition* of "species," in the sense that he accepts that the term is to be used only to refer to things that satisfy the nonevolutionary definition of the term. He might, however, still object that there is nothing in the world that actually satisfies the definition of the term. So the theory about species may not be altogether incorrect, in the sense that it is true of whatever satisfies the nonevolutionary definition of "species"; but it is still substantially lacking in the sense that it is not about anything whatever in the world.

The scientist might also choose *not* to respect his community's non-evolutionary definition of "species," in the sense that he *rejects* that the term is to be used only to refer to things that satisfy the nonevolutionary definition. His grounds for not respecting this language rule, however, may be his respect for another of his community's language practices—namely, *examples* of his fellow community members' use of the term "species." By some sort of mistake, he argues, the other members of his community have used the term "species" to refer to things that do not satisfy their non-evolutionary definitions of the term. So, again, the old theory about species may not be altogether incorrect in the sense that it is true of whatever satisfes the nonevolutionary definition of "species." But the old theory about species, and the theory-laden definition of the term, are substantial mischaracterizations of things that the community members have actually *called* "species."

In both cases, the dissenting scientist can communicate substantial dis-agreement to the other members of his community by satisfying, at least in part, their language rules. In the first case, he accepts their *definitions* as rules governing how their terms are used to refer. He disagrees with their belief that there is anything that satisfies the definitions of their terms—he disagrees, that is, with their belief that their terms refer to anything real. In the second case, he accepts *examples* of the way his community uses its terms as rules governing further such use. He disagrees with their belief that the definitions of their terms correctly characterize what they refer to when they use those terms.

Darwin's ploy was more the latter than the former. Rather than use the term "species" in a way that agreed with his fellow naturalists' definitions of the term, he chose to use it in a way that agreed with his fellow naturalists' actual referential uses of the term. This point is obscured by a couple of factors. First, Darwin did not propose an evolutionary redefinition of the term. This decision not to amend the definitional language rules of his community might be perceived as evidence of his acceptance of those rules. Second, that interpretation is reinforced by his many references to the unreality of species, which suggest that he took nonevolutionary "species" definitions seriously, but denied that anything existed that satisfied those definitions.

As for the first "obscuring" factor, Darwin may not have proposed a redefinition of "species," but he also did not recognize any one definition with which all naturalists, including himself, agreed. And as for the second factor, Darwin did not altogether deny the reality of species. He acknowledged the reality of referents of the term "species," but he also did not recognize any one definition with which all naturalists, including himself, agreed. And as for the second factor, Darwin did not altogether deny the reality of species. He acknowledged the reality of referents of the term "species," as the term was actually used, but simply denied that there was any one definition that all those referents satisfied.

Definitions of "species" are part of the story of Darwin's species concept, inasmuch as nonevolutionary definitions placed constrains on the communication of his evolutionary alternative. But Darwin's own species concept is not to be found in any definition. Once we appreciate the extent to which Darwin tried to get beyond definitions to referents, we can better understand his conceptions of the reality and unreality of species, and we can better understand the substance of the dispute at the heart of the Darwinian revolution.[3]

Darwin's Strategy

Given a nonevolutionary definition of "species," and the assumption that definition *determines* reference, the reality of species goes hand in hand with their immutability and nontransmutability. For, given those assumptions, no single real species can change with respect to its likeness, and there can be no real daughter species separate from their parent species. Thus, defenders of nonevolutionary conceptions of species often presented the evolution issue as a choice between the reality or unreality of species. Charles Lyell is a case in point. Consider first the nonevolutionary definition of "species" that prefaced his discussion of the transformation issue in his *Principles of Geology*:

> The name of species, observes Lamarck, has been usually applied to "every collection of similar individuals produced by other individuals like themselves." This definition, he admits, is correct; because every living individual bears a very close resemblane to those from which it springs. But this is not all which is usually implied by the term species; for the majority of naturalists agree with Linnaeus in supposing that all the individuals propagated from one stock have certain distinguishing characters in common, which will never vary, and which have remained the same since the creation of each species. (Lyell 1835, 2:407)

Assuming this definition determines the reference of "species," a real species cannot be modified with regard to its essential characteristics. Lyell himself made explicit the connection between the reality of species and their immutability. The choice of the matter, as he put it, was "whether species have a real and permanent existence in nature? or whether they are capable, as some naturalists pretend, of being indefinitely modified in the course of a long series of generations?" (Lyell 1835, 2:405; see also Coleman 1962).[4]

Basically the same choice was offered by other nonevolutionists of the time. As William Hopkins put it, in creationist, nontransmutationist terms, "Every natural species must by definition have had a separate and independent origin, so that all theories—like those of Lamarck and Mr. Darwin—which assert the derivation of all classes of animals from one origin, do, in fact, deny the existence of natural species at all" (Hopkins 1860, 747).

Apparently in keeping with this choice, Darwin not only defended the mutation and transmutation of species, but also often seemed to deny the reality of species. In the context of Darwin's evolutionism, and in the context of the sort of choice offered by Lyell and Hopkins, that seems a reasonable interpretation of passages like the following: "In short, we shall have to treat species in the same manner as those naturalists treat genera, who admit that genera are merely artificial combinations made for the sake of convenience" (*Origin*, 485).

Louis Agassiz also interpreted Darwin—as a "transmutationist"—to be denying the reality of species, and noted a peculiar consequence of Darwin's having done so: "It seems to me that there is much confusion of ideas in the general statement, of the variability of species, so often repeated of late. If species do not exist at all, as the suporters of the transmutation theory maintain, how can they vary?" (1860, 89–90, no. 1). In other words,

Agassiz objected, who cares if species evolve by natural selection or any other means if there are no such things as species?

Darwin's purported confusion, and the denial of the reality of species that apparently occasioned it, make sense in light of the assumption that Darwin accepted the nonevolutionary "species" definitions entertained by his fellow naturalists. And the latter assumption makes sense in light of the assumption that Darwin had to respect the definitions of the community of naturalists in order to communicate with them. But as I suggested earlier, Darwin chose another channel of communication with his fellow naturalists. It is still possible to make sense of his apparent denials of the reality of species, given this alternative manner of communication, though the sense is somewhat different.

Darwin's actual strategy of communication is perhaps more apparent in his never-completed manuscript *Natural Selection* than in the *Origin*. *Natural Selection*—Darwin's detailed account of evolution by natural selection, begun in 1856—was interrupted by Wallace's independent discovery of the same, and Darwin's scurry to get a complete, if necessarily less detailed version of his theory into print. The version he published was the *Origin*. But for more detailed analysis of problems raised in the *Origin*, it is sometimes helpful to consult *Natural Selection*.

In chapter 4 of *Natural Selection*, "Variation Under Nature," Darwin dealt more comprehensively than anywhere else with the nature of species and his fellow naturalists' conceptions of species. He made significant use of the work of the British botanist Hewett Cottrell Watson, in whose publications Darwin would have found explicit references to the problems of theory-laden language. For instant, in a two-part review of Robert Chamber's *Vestiges of Creation*—which Darwin made much of—Watson twice pointed out the incompatibility between accepted definitions of "species" and the theory of the transmutation of species. First, he warned: "as to the metamorphosis of one species into another, it must be remembered, that the very definition of 'species' comes in the form of a *petitio principii*; since the widest change ever seen, in the descendants of any plant or animal, would only entitle them to the name of 'variety,' according to recognized usage of these terms" (Watson 1845a, 111). And in concluding the review, Watson reminded his readers that the transition of one species into another would be "a difficult subject to treat, because the very definition of the term species,' as usually given, involves an assumption of non-transition; so that any cause of real transition—supposing such a case to be adduced—would be set down simply as evidence to disprove the duality of the species" (p. 147). Thus, Darwin might have been made aware of the constraints of theory-laden language on theory change by Watson (or by some other similarly concerned naturalist), if he was not aware of it already.

Watson might not only have brought the problem of theory-ladenness to Darwin's attention, he might also have suggested to Darwin a means of dealing with that difficulty. At any rate, Watson's treatment of the evolution issue is similar in very important respects to Darwin's. In an earlier article, Watson had drawn a distinction similar to the distinction previously discussed between definitions and referential use in practice. It was important to recognize, he pointed out,

> the necessity of distinguishing two kinds of species; namely, those forms which nature appears to have made permanentaly distinct, and those which are described in books under a supposition that they are so. The former I shall beg here to designate *natural species*; applying to the latter the epithet of *book species*. A book species and a natural species may be strictly identical, or one natural species may be improperly divided into two or more species. (1843, pp. 617–618)

By saying that "natural species" were "permanently distinct," Watson meant that natural species were what actually satisfied the accepted nonevolutionary definition of "species." "Book species," on the other hand, were those entities to which naturalists referred (in books) as "species," on the *supposition* that those entities were permanentaly distinct. Of course, the entities to which naturalists referred (in books) as "species" might nevertheless turn out *not* to satisfy the accepted definition of "species"— i.e., *not* permanently distinct. This point was made increasingly clear in Watson's later works (1845a; 1845b; and especially 1859, pp. 27–64).

Watson's distinction allows a naturalist to communicate a theory of the evolution of species to his fellow naturalists, even when the latter employ a nonevolutionary definition of the term "species." That is, the dissenting naturalist must certainly acknowledge that whatever satisfies a nonevolutionary definition of "species" does not evolve and is not a product of evolution. But he can also maintain that what nonevolutionists *call* "species" are not only mutable, but also related by descent. In short, he can communicate the point that, while "natural species" do not evolve, "book species" do. Indeed, by way of introducing the distinction, Watson referred to the suggestion that the "alleged" species *Primula veris* (cowslips) and *Primula vulgaris* (primroses) were actually related by descent (Watson 1843, p. 617). In other words, what were *called* species in books were sometimes not natural species according to the nonevolutionary definition of "species."

The genealogical relationship of cowslips to primrose was taken up later in the report of an "experiment" that purportedly showed just that. From seeds of a recognized variety of primrose, namely oxlips (*Primula vulgaris intermedia*), Watson claimed to have grown cowslips as well as true primroses, neither of which, he further claimed, could have cross-fertilized the original oxlips (1845b). What is most important about the report is the manner in which Watson communicated the results of his experiment. First, he pointed out that his materials were *recognized* varieties and species—"book" varieties and species. The publicaion he invoked for this purpose was the *London Catalogue*. And in reporting his conclusion, he made explicit the reputation of his materials: "The conclusion appears unavoidable to me, that a variety of primrose gave origin at the same time to cowslips, to primroses, and to many varieties of these two *reputed* species" (Watson 1845b, p. 218; my italics).

Watson further argued that his results supported the abandonment of the *definition* of "species" (whatever "the" definition was) as a mischaracterization of what are *called* "species": "If we allow the cowslip and primrose to be two species, and yet allow that one can pass into the other, either directly or through the intermediate oxlip, we abandon the definition of species, as usually given, and fall into the transition-of-species theory, advocated in 'Vestiges'" (1845, 219).

Of the two kinds of rules for using the term "species," Watson thus considered the possibility that examples of referential use in practice might prevail over definitions. He actually made that choice in his review of *Vestiges*, where he proposed "to write of 'species' as commonly understood by botanists, without attempting any rigorous definition of the term, which may hereafter be found to represent only a fiction of the human mind" (1845a, 142). He intended, in other words, to discuss the transmutability of what botanists *called* "species," rather than to concern himself with whatever satisfied their *definitions* of "species," which might amount to nothing at all. This strategy was remarkably similar to the one Darwin employed.

Watson and Lyell both prefaced their discussions of the evolution of species with discussions of a preliminary semantic issue, namely their use of the term "species." They differed in their means of settling that issue. Lyell conditioned his use of the term on a definition—a nonevolutionary one at that—while Watson conditioned his use on examples of the use of the term by his fellow naturalists. Darwin also prefaced his discussion of the evolution of species with a discussion of his use of the term—a semantic issue he settled like Watson and unlike Lyell. As he explained in *Natural Selection*, "In the following pages I mean by species, those collections of individuals, which have commonly been so designated by naturalists" (p. 98).

Elsewhere, Darwin explicitly objected to nontransmutationist definitions as rules for using the term "species," in favor of examples of established usage. One such objection was raised, interestingly enough, in the context of the primrose-cowslip issue. Reflecting upon Watson's and others investigations of primroses, cowslips, and oxlips, and upon the consequences of using the nontransmutationist definition in light of those investigations, Darwin reasoned,

> An able Botanist has remarked that if the primrose and cowslip are proved to be specifically identical, "we may question 20,000 other presumed species." If common descent is to enter into the definition of species, as is almost universally admitted, then I think it is almost impossible to doubt that the primrose and cowslip are one species. But if, in accordance with the views we are examining in this work, all the species of the same genus have a common descent; this case differs from ordinary cases, only in as much as the intermediate forms still exist in a state of nature, and that we are enabled to prove experimentally the common descent. ⟨Hence common practice and common language is right in giving to the primrose and cowslip distinct names.⟩ (*Natural Selection*, 133)

In other words, proof of genealogical ties between forms that were commonly *called* "species" would be an *argument ad absurdum* against the use of the nontransmutationist definition. Thus "common practice" was given priority over traditional definition as a guide for using the term "species."

The evolution issue was accordingly, for Darwin, an issue concerning the evolution of *species so designated by naturalists*. As he formulated the transmutation issue in particular, "we have to discuss in this work whether *forms called by all naturalists distinct species* are not lineal descendants of other forms" (*Natural Selection*, 97; my italics). This is clearly a different issue from "whether forms that satisfy the definition of 'species' are not lineal descendants of other forms." The former version leaves open the question in a way that the latter does not—and in a way that Darwin clearly wanted that question left open.

But Darwin's decision to talk about what naturalists called "species," rather than to talk about what satisfied their definitions of "species," served more of a purpose than just leaving open the question of whether species evolve. It also allowed Darwin to communicate the position that the term "species" was undefinable. In other words, Darwin not only rejected nonevolutionary definitions of "species," he also rejected the idea that the term could be defined at all. As it turns out, his position concerning the undefinability of "species" was part and parcel of his argument for the evolution of species. It is worth considering, briefly, the connection between Darwin's concern about what his fellow naturalists called "species," his position on the *undefinability* of the term "species," and his position on the *evolution* of species.

The discussion so far has aimed at explaining why Darwin dissociated his use of the term "species" from his fellow naturalists' predominantly nonevolutionary definitions of the term. But Darwin went further in rejecting his fellow naturalists' definitions, denying even that there was one definition upon which they all agreed:

> In this Chapter we have to discuss the variability of species in a state of nature. The first and obvious thing to do would be to give a clear and simple definition of what is meant by a species; but this has been found hopelessly difficult by naturalists, if we may judge by scarcely two having given the same. (*Natural Selection*, 95)

There was good reason, Darwin believed, for lack of agreement on a definition of "species." The term was simply "indefinable." As he expressed his scepticism about the term's definability to Joseph Hooker:

> It is really laughable to see what different ideas are prominent in various naturalists' minds, when they speak of "species"; in some, resemblance is everything and descent of little weight—in some, resemblance seems to go for nothing, and Creation the reigning idea—in some, descent is the key,—in some, sterility an unfailing test, with others it is not worth a farthing. It all comes, I believe, from trying to define the indefinable. (Darwin to Hooker, 24 December 1856. *LL* 2:88)

Similarly, in the final pages of the *Origin* Darwin urged that, upon adoption of his views, naturalists would "at least be freed from the vain search for the undiscovered and undiscoverable essence of the term species" (*Origin*, 485).

To hold such a position, and still to want to talk about the nature of species, one would have to base one's use of the term "species" on something besides a definition of the term. And as we have seen, Darwin did. But why did he ever defend the undefinability of "species" in the first place?

This question has been taken up already by Michael Ghiselin (1969, 89–102) and Frank Sulloway (1979, 36–39), and I shall rely in part on their analyses. In order to understand the point of maintaining the undefinability of "species," Ghiselin argues, we must first take a closer look at what was being maintained. According to Ghiselin, the crucial issue was that there was no way of defining "species" that distinguished species from varieties—no way of defining the difference. Indeed, that was often the context in which the undefinability position was raised. For instance, in *Natural Selection*, Darwin elaborated upon his remarks to Hooker:

> how various are the ideas that enter into the minds of naturalists when speaking of species. With some, resemblance is the reigning idea and descent goes for little; with others descent is the infallible criterion; with others resemblance goes for almost nothing, and Creation is everything; with others sterility in crossed forms is an unfail-

ing test, whilst with others it is regarded of no value. At the end of this chapter, it will be seen that according to the views, which we have to discuss in this volume, it is no wonder that there should be difficulty in defining the difference between a species and a variety; —there being no essential, only an arbitrary difference. (p. 98)

Before discussing the point of this position, it is also worth taking a closer look at it in terms of the distinctions raised in this paper. Since the definability of "species" and "variety" is at issue here, a position with regard to that issue cannot take for granted any particular definitions of those terms. Communication concerning that issue must instead be based on some other sort of use of those terms—like examples of their use. And that is precisely how Darwin set up his position on the issue. The passage just quoted immediately preceded the announcement that he would use the term "species" to mean "those collections of individuals, which have commonly been so designated by naturalists." He used "variety" in the same manner. And that allowed him to argue essential differences between species and varieties on the grounds that what many naturalists *called* "species," many other naturalists *called* "vaireties." In other words, if we take as species and varieties what naturalists *call* "species" and "varieties," then we must admit that there is no definition of "species" that excludes all varieties, and no definition of "variety" that excludes all species. Apparently, Watson was of great service to Darwin in this regard, listing for him many of those forms ranked species by some naturalists and varieties by others (*Natural Selection*, 102–103, 159, 168–169; *Origin*, 48). From such considerations, Darwin concluded,

in determining whether a form should be ranked as a species or a variety, the opinion of naturalists having sound judgement and wide experience seems the only guide to follow. We must, however, in many cases, decide by a majority of naturalists, for few well-marked and well-known varieties can be named which have not been ranked as species by at least some competent judges. (*Origin*, 47)

The significance of this position, as Ghiselin and Sulloway point out, is that it is intelligible on the assumption of the evolution of species, or more correctly, on the assumption of divergent evolution. In turn it supports that assumption. According to Darwin's notion of divergent evolution, the varieties of a species are incipient species in their own right.[5] More specifically, *what are called "varieties"* of species are, in time, transmuted into *what would be called "species"* in their own right. As Darwin stated that notion, and qualified it at the same time, in those very terms:

Now comes the question, what is the value of the *varieties recorded in Botanical works*? Am I justified in hypothetically looking at them as incipient species? ... I may here repeat that I am far from supposing that all varieties become converted into *what are called species*; extinction may equally well annihilate varieties, as it has so infinitely many species. (*Natural Selection*, 159; my italics)

If what are called "varieties" are gradually being transmuted into what are called "species," then it is no wonder that there are intermediate stages that are called "varieties" by some naturalists and "species" by others. Divergent evolution thus accounts for the fact that there is no definition of "species" that excludes all of what are called "varieties", and no definition of "variety" that excludes all of what are called "species." As Darwin concluded,

> According to these views it is not surprising that naturalists should have found such extreme difficulty in defining to each other's satisfaction the term species ⟨as distinct from variety⟩. It ceases to be surprising, indeed it is what might have been expected, that there should exist the finest gradation in the differences between organic beings, from individual differences to quite distinct species;—that there should be often the gravest difficulty in knowing what to call species and what varieties ... (*Natural Selection*, p. 167)

Thus by formulating his position in terms of the evolution of *what naturalists call "species" and "varieties,"* Darwin was not only able to avoid contradicting himself with regard to predominantly nonevolutionary definitions of those terms, but was also able to communicate and defend a position concerning the undefinability of those terms. The latter position substantiated the evolutionary position. So Darwin's strategy was quite well chosen.

Before concluding, I would like to return briefly to Darwin's views on the reality of species. As I suggested earlier, his references to the "arbitrariness" and "convenience" of species groupings might be interpreted as denials of the reality of species. Such an interpretation make sense in light of the nonevolutionary "species" definitions that Darwin faced. Had those definitions determined his referential use of the term "species," he would certainly have denied that there was anything to which the term referred (see also Ghiselin 1969, 92). But that would have left his position on the evolution of species unclear. For if the nonevolutionary definitions of "species" had determined his referential use of the term, and if he had denied the reality of species accordingly, then his theory of the evolution of species would have amounted either to a contradiction in terms, or as Agassiz noted, to a theory about nothing whatsoever.

As we have seen, however, Darwin did not tailor his use of the term "species" to suit pre-Darwinian, nonevolutionary *definitions* of the term. Instead, he used the term in accordance with *examples* of its referential use by members of his naturalist community. But we still have to contend with all those references to the "arbitrariness" and "convenience" of species groupings, and hence with the possibility that Darwin denied the reality of species after all, on some other grounds. In fact, I have already discussed those other grounds. I just discussed the fact that Darwin not only rejected nonevolutionary definitions of "species" as determining the reference of the term, but also denied that *any* definition determined the reference of the term. And *that* is why he viewed the term "species" "as one arbitrarily given for the sake of convenience ..." (*Origin*, 52). So we are still left with that nagging worry whether Darwin's theory of the evolution of species was a theory of the evolution of anything whatsoever.

Ghiselin has also addressed this problem, and has offered a solution to the apparent confusion. His approach is, moreover, very much in accord with the approach taken in this paper. According to Ghiselin, Darwin's references to the arbitrariness and unreality of species pertained only to the species *category*, not to species *taxa*. In other words, Darwin denied the reality of a species category distinct from a genus category on the one hand, and from a variety category on the other hand. But he did not deny the reality of the various species taxa like the cabbage and the radish (Ghiselin 1969, 96; and see *Natural Selection*, 98). Darwin's theory of the evolution of species was, of course, about the evolution of species taxa rather than the evolution of the species category. So his denial of the reality of the species category did not render his theory domainless.[6]

Basically the same solution can be constructed in terms of the distinctions employed in this paper. That is, Darwin denied that there was a definition of "species" that excluded all of what were called "varieties," or a definition of "variety" that excluded all of what were called "species." But he affirmed the reality of what naturalists called "species" and of what they called "varieties"—of what were given species and variety names. In other words, Darwin affirmed the reality of recognized taxa. And, as we have seen, it was the evolution of these taxa—what were *called* "species" and "varieties"—that was at issue in Darwin's work.

What, then, *were* called "species" and "varieties" according to Darwin? To what in the world did he believe his fellow naturalists were referring when using their various species and variety names? They were referring, Darwin believed, to chunks with the genealogical nexus of life. They did not refer to *one kind* of chunk with their species names and to *another kind* of chunk with their variety names. That was why there was no definition of "species" that excluded all of what were called "varieties," and so on. Nevertheless, their names referred to real genealogical segments in each case.

This raises the question why Darwin did not at least define a joint "species-variety" category in genealogical terms? The reason might have been that he was concerned to avoid distinguishing them in that manner from the *higher* categories. That is precisely what some of the traditional transmutationist definitions had done, distinguishing the species category from higher categories as *the* category whose taxa were genealogical segments. But this placed constraints upon transmutationist theories of the genealogical relationships of species in a genus, genera in a family, and so on. Understandably, that was a constraint Darwin wanted to avoid:

> On the views here discussed, the idea of common descent of all the individuals of the same species ... comes into play; but it is not confined, as in the ordinary definition, to the individuals of the same species, but is extended to the species themselves belonging to the same genus and family, or to whatever high group our facts will lead us.(*Natural Selection*, 166)

So Darwin was more than just content to do without a definition of "species" that distinguished "species" from "variety" and "genus." He was more than just content to talk about the evolution of what naturalists *called* "species." This means of formulating his position provided him not only with common grounds for discourse with his fellow naturalists, but also common grounds for disagreement. Semantic issues thus settled, he sought to convince his fellow naturalists that the genealogical segments they called "species" evolved over time and were connected to each other genealogically:

> Although much remains obscure, and will long remain obscure, I can entertain no doubt, after the most deliberate study and dispassionate judgement of which I am capable, that the view which most naturalists entertain, and which I formerly entertained—namely, that each species has been independently created—is erroneous. I am fully convinced that species are not immutable; but that *those belonging to what are called the same genera* are lineal descendants of some other and generally extinct species, in the same manner as the *acknowledged* varieties of any one species are the descendants of that species. Furthermore, I am convinced that Natural Selection has been the main but not exclusive means of modification. (*Origin*, 6; my italics)

Conclusion

In order to communicate any more than a verbal disagreement with members of one's scientific community, it is necessary to respect their language rules, at least in part. But when the community's theory-laden definition undermine the rival position being proposed, then those particular language rules cannot be respected—some other language rules of the community must be adopted instead as common grounds for discourse. Those other rules may include actual examples of language use within the community.

For instance, Darwin's theory of the evolution of species was undermined by the nonmutationist and nontransmutationist definitions of "species" to which his fellow naturalists adhered. He clearly could not defend the evolution of species, in any of those senses of "species." He could and did defend, however, the evolution of what his fellow naturalists actually *called* "species"—on the supposition that what they called "species" did not satisfy their nonevolutionary definitions of "species." As Darwin explained his use of the term "species," "In the following pages I mean by species, those collections of individuals, which have been so designated by naturalists" (*Natural Selection*, 98). And as he formulated his transmutation position in particular, "we have to discuss in this work whether *forms called by all naturalists distinct species* are not lineal descendants of other forms" (*Natural Selection*, 97; my italics).

Darwin's decision to talk about what naturalists *called* "species," rather than about what satisfied naturalists' definitions of "species," served another important function as well. It allowed Darwin to make sense of the position that the term "species" was not definably distinct from the term "variety." What he argued, in effect, was that there was no definition of "species" that excluded all of what were called "varieties," and no definition of "variety" that excluded all of what were called "species." This position was part and parcel of Darwin's notion of divergent evolution, according to which varieties are incipient species.

The suggestion that natural history could really get by without definitions of the categories of classification—especially a definition of "species" —is admittedly hard to swallow. Of course, it should be acknowledged that natural history was only temporarily without a definition of "species." The nonevolutionary definitions rejected by Darwin have since been replaced. Definitions such as Ernst Mayr's "biological species concept" and George Gaylord Simpson's "evolutionary species concept" are already so well entrenched as to be considered traditional. Moreover, just as the old definitions reflected the nonevolutionary theories of natural history in which they were employed, the new definitions reflect the version of evolutionary theory generally accepted at the time they were composed (Beatty 1982).[7]

Following the Darwinian revolution, then, theory-laden definitions of "species" were replaced by theory-laden redefinitions. But the apparent inevitability of theory-laden definition should not be overemphasized—especially not to the point of overlooking possible rationales behind dispensing with definitions at particular periods in the history of science. Far from just "getting by" without a definition of "species," Darwin felt that natural history would be liberated by abandoning the search for one—liberated in particular from the constraints of nonevolutionary thinking built into pre-Darwinian definitions of the term.

Acknowledgments

This paper is dedicated to the long life of the Systematics and Biogeography Discussion Group at Harvard. I am also indebted to Michael Ghiselin, David Hull, David Kohn, Ernst Mayr, and Frank Sulloway for sharing their insights into the nature of species and the Darwinian revolution.

Notes

1. The list includes Ghiselin (1969, chap. 4), Hull (1967b, 1976, 1978a, 1980), Kottler (1978), Mayr (1957, 1964, 1972a, 1985), Sulloway (1979), Vorzimmer (1970, chap. 7), and Beatty (1982). I am greatly indebted to all these contributions except my own, which raised more problems than it solved. The present paper in some ways takes off from, and in some ways corrects Beatty (1982).
2. I do not mean to overemphasize the nonevolutionary, "likeness-preserving" aspect of Buffon's definition, especially to the point of overlooking other important features of the definition. Phillip Sloan (1979) has argued persuasively that Buffon's definition is part of a tradition of historical-genealogical definitions—a tradition inspired in part by epistemological considerations. However, Sloan seems to me to overemphasize the historical, "perpetuation-through-copulation" aspect of the definition to the point of overlooking the static, "likeness-preserving" aspect.
3. The problem of actually distinguishing between what a term is used to refer to in practice, and what satisfies the definition of the term, is a thorny problem indeed. In fact, it is one of the most central issues in philosophy of science today. A solution to the problem would considerably enlighten this paper. But what is most important for the purposes of this paper is that *Darwin* actually thought such a distinction could be drawn. That fact will, it is hoped, become clear in what follows. The distinction, clues to its solution, and suggestions as to its use in the history of science are discussed in a very clear and very thoughtful essay by Philip Kitcher (1979).
4. That the dichotomy between the reality and mutability of species actually constrained evolutionary thinking has been pointed out on numerous occasions by Ernst Mayr. In one place Mayr refers to this failure to distinguish reality from constancy as "one of the minor tragedies in the history of biology" (1957, 2), and in another place as a "violation of scientific logic" (1972a, 987). But these epithets obscure the intrinsic place of such language constraints in theory change.
5. The development of Darwin's theory of divergent evolution has been carefully analyzed by Ospovat (1981), Browne (1980), Kohn (1985), Schweber (1980), and Sulloway (1979).
6. The distinction between species taxa and the species category has received a good deal of attention lately, in the context of discussions of the notion of "species as individuals." According to this notion, the species category is a spatiotemporally unrestricted class whose member taxa are spatiotemporally restricted individuals. See Ghiselin (1966; 1969, chap. 4; and 1974), Hull (1976, 1978a, 1980), and Mayr (1976d).
7. The newer definitions reflect in particular the reproductive isolation theory of divergent evolution. According to this theory, breeding groups are the units of evolutionary change. Divergent evolution occurs *between* them, not *within* them. To speak of the evolutionary divergence of species is thus to imply that species are reproductively

isolated breeding groups. Mayr defined "species" as "groups of actually or potentially interbreeding natural populations, which are reproductively isolated from other such groups" (1942, 120). And Simpson defined "species" as "a phyletic lineage (ancestral-descent sequence of interbreeding populations) evolving independently of others, with its own separate and unitary evolutionary role" (1951, 289).

References

Short Titles

LL   Darwin, F., ed. 1887. *The Life and Letters of Charles Darwin, including an autobiographical chapter.* 2 vols. New York: Appleton.

ML   Darwin, F. and Seward, A., eds., 1903. *More letters of Charles Darwin; a record of his works in a series of hitherto unpublished letters.* 2 vols. London: John Murray.

Origin   Darwin, C. 1859. *On the origin of species by means of natural selection, or the preservation of favoured races in the struggle for life.* London: John Murray. Reprint 1975. Introduction by E. Mayr. Cambridge: Harvard University Press.

Natural Selection   Stauffer, R., ed. 1975. *Charles Darwin's Natural Selection; being the second part of this big species book written from 1856 to 1858.* London: Cambridge University Press.

Other Titles

Beatty, J. 1980. Optimal-design models and the strategy of model building in evolutionary biology. *Phil. sci.* 47:532–562.

Beatty, J. 1982. Clades and classes. *Syst. zoo.* 31:25–34.

Browne, E. 1980. Darwin's botanical arithmetic and the principle of divergence, 1854–1858. *J. hist. bio.* 13:53–89.

Coleman, W., 1962. Lyell and the reality of species. *Isis* 53:325–338.

Ghiselin, M. 1966. On psychologism in the logic of taxonomic principles. *Syst. zoo.* 15:207–215.

Ghiselin, M. 1969. *The triumph of the Darwinian method.* Berkeley: University of California Press.

Ghiselin, M. 1974. A radical solution to the species problem. *Syst. zoo.* 23:536–544.

Hopkins, W. 1860. Physical theories of the phenomena of life. *Fraser's mag.* 61:739–752.

Hull, D. 1967 The metaphysics of evolution. *Brit. j. hist. sci.* 3:309–337.

Hull, D. 1976. Are species really individuals? *Syst. zoo.* 25:174–191.

Hull, D. 1978. A matter of individuality. *Phil. sci.* 45:335–360.

Hull, D. 1980. Individuality and Selection. *Ann. rev. ecol. syst.* 11:311–332.

Kitcher, P. 1979. Theories, theorists, and theory change. *Phil. rev.* 87:519–547.

Kohn, D. 1985. Darwin's principle of divergence as internal dialogue. In D. Kohn (ed.), *The Darwinian Heritage.* Princeton: Princeton University Press. pp. 245–258.

Kottler, M. 1978. Charles Darwin's biological species concept and theory of geographic speciation: the transmutation notebooks. *Ann. sci.* 35:275–297.

Lovejoy, A. 1959. Buffon and the problem of species. In B. Glass, O. Temkin, and W. Straus, Jr. (eds.), *Forerunners of Darwin 1745–1859.* Baltimore: Johns Hopkins University Press. pp. 84–113.

Lyell, C. 1835. *Principles of geology.* 4th ed. 4 vols. London: John Murray.

Mayr, E. 1942. *Systematics and the origin of species from the viewpoint of a zoologist.* New York: Columbia University Press.

Mayr, E. 1957. Species concepts and definitions, the species problem. In E. Mayr (ed.), *The Species Problem*. Washington: American Association for the Advancement of Science. pp. 1–22.

Mayr, E. 1964. Introduction to C. Darwin *"On the Origin of Species" A facsimile of the first edition*. Cambridge: Harvard Unversity Press.

Mayr, E. 1972. The nature of the Darwinian revolution. *Nature*. 981–989.

Mayr, E. 1976. Is the species a class or an individual? *Syst. zoo*. 25:192.

Mayr, E. 1985. Darwin's five theories of evolution. In D. Kohn (ed.), *The Darwinian Heritage*. Princeton University Press. pp. 755–772.

Ospovat, D. 1981. *The development of Darwin's theory*. Cambridge: Cambridge University Press.

Schweber, S. 1980. Darwin and the political economists: divergence of character. *J. hist. biol* 13:195–289.

Simpson, G. 1951. The species concept. *Evolution* 5:285–298.

Sloan, P. 1979. Buffon, German biology, and the historical interpretation of species. *Brit. j. hist. scie.* 12:109–153.

Sulloway, F. 1979. Geographic isolation in Darwin's thinking. *Stud. hist. biol*. 3:23–65.

Vorzimmer, P. 1970. *Charles Darwin: the years of controversy*. Philadelphia: Temple University Press.

Watson, H. 1843. Remarks on the distinction of species in nature, and in books. *Lond. j. bot.* 2:613–622.

Watson, H. 1845. On the theory of "progressive development," applied in explanation of the origin and transmutation of species. *Phytologist* 2:217–219.

Watson, H. 1859. *Cybele Britannica, or, British plants and their geographical relations*. Vol. 4. London: Longman.

Chapter 12

Evolution, Population Thinking, and Essentialism

Elliott Sober

Philosophers have tended to discuss essentiatialism as if it were a *global* doctrine—a philosophy which, for some uniform reason, is to be adopted by all the sciences, or by none of them. Popper (1972) has taken a negative global view because he sees essentialism as a major obstacle to scientific rationality. And Quine (1953b, 1960), for a combination of semantical and epistemological reasons, likewise wishes to banish essentialism from the whole of scientific discourse. More recently, however, Putnam (1975) and Kripke (1972) have advocated essentialist doctrines and have claimed that it is the task of each science to investigate the essential properties of its constitutive natural kinds.

In contrast to these global viewpoints is a tradition which sees the theory of evolution as having some special relevance to essentialist doctrines within biology. Hull (1965) and Mayr (1959) are perhaps the two best known exponents of this attitude; they are *local* anti-essentialists. For Mayr, Darwin's hypothesis of evolution by natural selection was not simply a new theory, but a new *kind of theory*—one which discredited essentialist modes of thought within biology and replaced them with what Mayr has called "population thinking." Mayr describes essentialism as holding that

> ... [t]here are a limited number of fixed, unchangeable "ideas" underlying the observed variability [in nature], with the *eidos* (idea) being the only thing that is fixed and real, while the observed variability has no more reality than the shadows of an object on a cave wall ... [In contrast], the populationist stresses the uniqueness of everything in the organic world.... All organisms and organic phenomena are composed of unique features and can be described collectively only in statistical terms. Individuals, or any kind of organic entities, form populations of which we can determine the arithmetic mean and the statistics of variation. Averages are merely statistical abstractions, only the individuals of which the population are composed have reality. The ultimate conclusions of the population thinker and of the typoloist are precisely the opposite. For the typologist the type (*eidos*)

is real and the variation an illusion, while for the populationist, the type (average) is an abstraction and only the variation is real. No two ways of looking at nature could be more different. (Mayr 1959, 28–9).

A contemporary biologist reading this might well conclude that essentialists had no scientifically respectable way of understanding the existence of variation in nature. In the absence of this, typologists managed to ignore the fact of variability by inventing some altogether mysterious and unverifiable subject matter for themselves. The notion of *types* and the kind of anti-empiricism that seems to accompany it, appear to bear only the most distant connection with modern conceptions of evidence and argument. But this reaction raises a question about the precise relation of evolution to essentialism. How could the *specifics* of a particular scientific theory have mattered much here, since the main obstacle presented by essentialist thinking was just to get people to be scientific about nature by paying attention to the evidence? The problem was to bring people down to earth by rubbing their noses in the diversity of nature. Viewed in this way, Mayr's position does not look much like a form of *local* anti-essentialism.

Other perplexities arise when a contemporary biologist tries to understand Mayr's idea of population thinking as applying to his or her own activity. If "only the individuals of which the population are composed have reality," it would appear that much of population biology has its head in the clouds. The Lotke-Volterra equations, for example, describe the interactions of predator and prey populations. Presumably, population thinking, properly so called, must allow that there is something real over and above individual organisms. Population thinking countenances organisms and populations; typological thinking grants that both organisms and types exist. Neither embodies a resolute and ontologically austere focus on individual organisms alone. That way lies nominalism, which Mayr (1969) himself rejects.

Another issue that arises from Mayr's conception of typological and population thinking is that of how we are to understand his distinction between "reality" and "abstraction." One natural way of taking this distinction is simply to understand reality as meaning existence. But presumably no population thinker will deny that there are such things as averages. If there are groups of individuals, then there are numerous properties that those groups possess. The *average* fecundity within a population is no more a property which we invent by "mere abstraction" than is the fecundity of individual organisms. Individual and group properties are equally "out there" to be discovered. And similarly, it is unclear how one could suggest that typologists held that variability is unreal; surely the historical record shows that typologists realized that differences between individuals *exist*.

How, then, are we to understand the difference between essentialism and population thinking in terms of what each holds to be "real" about biological reality?

Answering these questions about the difference between essentialist and population modes of thought will be the main purpose of this paper. How did essentialists propose to account for variability in nature? How did evolutionary theory undermine the explanatory strategy that they pursued? In what way does post-Darwinian biology embody a novel conception of variability? How has population thinking transformed our conception of what is *real*? The form of local anti-essentialism which I will propound in what follows will be congenial to many of Mayr's views. In one sense, then, our task will be to explicate and explain Mayr's insight that the shift from essentialist to populationist modes of thinking constituted a shift in the concept of biological reality. However, I will try to show why essentialism was a manifestly *scientific* working hypothesis. Typologists did not close their eyes to variation but rather tried to explain it in a particular way. And the failure of their explanatory strategy depends on details of evolutionary theory in ways which have not been much recognized.[1]

The approach to these questions will be somewhat historical. Essentialism about species is today a dead issue, not because there is no conceivable way to defend it, but because the way in which it was defended by biologists was thoroughly discredited. At first glance, rejecting a metaphysics or a scientific research program because one of its formulations is mistaken may appear to be fallacious. But more careful attention vindicates this pattern of evaluation. It is pie-in-the-sky metaphysics and science to hold on to some guiding principle simply because *it is possible* that there might be some substantive formulation and development of it. Thus, Newtonianism, guided by the maxim that physical phenomena can be accounted for in terms of matter in motion, would have been rejected were it not for the success of particular Newtonian explanations. One evaluates regulative principles by the way in which they regulate the actual theories of scientists. At the same time, I will try in what follows to identify precisely what it is in essentialism and in evolutionary theory that makes the former a victim of the latter. It is an open question to what degree the source of this incompatibility struck working biologists as central. As I will argue at the end of this section, one diagnosis of the situation which seems to have been historically important is much less decisive than has been supposed.

The essentialist's method of explaining variability, I will argue, was coherently formulated in Aristotle, and was applied by Aristotle in both his biology and in his physics. Seventeenth and eighteenth century biologists, whether they argued for evolution or against it, made use of Aristotle's natural state model. And to this day, the model has not been refuted in mechanics. Within contemporary biology, however, the model met with less success. Twentieth-century population genetics shows that the model cannot be applied in the way that the essentialist requires. But the natural state model is not wholly without a home in contemporary biology; in fact, the way in which it finds an application there highlights some salient facts about what population thinking amounts to.

An essentialist view of a given species is committed to there being some property which all and only the members of that species possess. Since there are almost certainly only finitely many individuals in any given species, we are quite safe in assuming there is some finitely statable condition which all and only the members of the species satisfy.[2] This could trivially be a list of the spatiotemporal locations of the organisms involved. But the fact that such a condition exists is hardly enough to vindicate essentialism. The essentialist thinks that there is a diagnostic property which any *possible* organism must have if it is to be a member of the species. It cannot be the case that the property in question is possessed by all organisms belonging to *Homo sapiens*, even though there might exist a member of *Homo sapiens* who lacked the trait. It must be necessarily true, and not just accidental, that all and only the organisms in *Homo sapiens* have the characteristic.

However, even this requirement of essentialism is trivially satisfiable. Is it not necessarily true that to be a member of *Homo sapiens* an organism must be a member of *Homo sapiens*? This is guaranteed if logical truths are necessary. But essentialism about biology is hardly vindicated by the existence of logical truths. In a similar vein, if it is impossible for perpetual motion machines to exist, then it is necessarily true that something belongs to *Homo sapiens* if and only if it belongs to *Homo sapiens* or is a perpetual motion machine. This necessary truth is not a truth of logic; it is a result of the theory of thermodynamics. But it too fails to vindicate biological essentialism. What more, then, is required?

The key idea, I think, is that the membership condition must be *explanatory*. The essentialist hypothesizes that there exists some characteristic unique to and shared by all members of *Homo sapiens* which explains why they are the way they are. A species essence will be a causal mechanism which works on each member of the species, making it the kind of thing that it is.

The characterization of essentialism just presented is fairly vague. For one thing, a great deal will depend on how one understands the crucial idea of *explanation*. But since explanation is clearly to be a scientific notion, I hope that, on my sketch, essentialism has the appearance of a scientific thesis, although perhaps one that is not terribly precise. Although historically prey to obscurantism, essentialism has nothing essentially to do with mystery mongering, or with the irrational injunction that one should ignore empirical data. It is a perfectly respectable claim about the existence of hidden structures which unite diverse individuals into natural kinds.

Besides its stress on the giving of explanations, there is another feature of our characterization of essentialism which will be important in what follows. The essentialist requires that a *species* be defined in terms of the characteristics of the *organisms* which belong to it. We might call this kind of definition a *constituent definition*; wholes are to be defined in terms of their parts, sets are to be defined in terms of their members, and so on. Pre-Darwinian critics of the species concept, like Buffon and Bonnet, argued that species are unreal, because no such characteristics of organisms can be singled out (see Lovejoy 1936), and pre-Darwinian defenders of the species concept likewise agreed that the concept is legitimate only if constituent definitions could be provided. Constituent definitions are *reductionistic*, in that concepts at higher levels of organization (e.g., species) are legitimate only if they are definable in terms of concepts applying at lower levels of organization (e.g., organisms). It is quite clear that if there are finitely many levels of organization, one cannot demand constituent definitions for concepts at every level of organization (Kripke 1978). As we will see in what follows, evolutionary theory emancipated the species concept from the requirement that it be provided with a constituent definition. The scientific coherence of discourse at the population level of organization was to be assured in another way, one to which the label "population thinking" is especially appropriate.

Chemistry is prima facie a clear case in which essentialist thinking has been vindicated. The periodic table of elements is a taxonomy of chemical kinds. The essence of each kind is its atomic number. Not only is it the case that all actual samples of nitrogen happen to have atomic number 14; it is necessarily the case that a thing is made of nitrogen if and only if it is made of stuff having atomic number 14. Moreover, this characteristic atomic number plays a central role in explaining other chemical properties of nitrogen. Although things made of this substance differ from each other in numerous respects, underlying this diversity there is a common feature. It was hardly irrational for chemists to search for this feature, and the working assumption that such essences were out there to be found, far from stifling inquiry, was a principle contributor to that inquiry's bearing fruit.

Can an equally strong case be made for an essentialist view of biological species? One often hears it said that evolution undermined essentialism because the essentialist held that species are static, but from 1859 on we had conclusive evidence that species evolve. This comment makes a straw man of essentialism and is in any case historically untrue to the thinking of many essentialists. For one thing, notice that the discovery of the transmutation of elements has not in the slightest degree undermined the periodic table. The fact that nitrogen can be changed into oxygen does not in any way show that nitrogen and oxygen lack essences. To be nitrogen is to have one atomic number; to be oxygen is to have another. To change from nitrogen into oxygen, a thing must therefore shift from one atomic number to another. The mere fact of evolution does not show that species lack essences.

As a historical matter, some essentialists, like Agassiz (1859), did assert a connection between essentialism and stasis. But others considered the possibility that new species should have arisen on earth since the beginning (if they thought that there was a beginning). Thus, Linnaeus originally hypothesized that all species were created once and for all at the beginning, but later in his career he changed his mind because he thought that he had discovered a species, *Peloria*, which arose through cross-species hybridization (Rabel 1939, Ramsbottom 1938). And in *Generation of Animals* (II 746a30), Aristotle himself speculates about the possibility of new species arising as fertile hybrids. Countenancing such species need have no effect on binomial nomenclature or on deciding which characteristics of organisms to view as diagnostic. The question of when there started to be various kinds of things in the universe seems to be quite independent of what makes for differences between kinds.

Another, more plausible, suggestion, concerning how evolution undermined essentialism, is this: The fact that species evolve *gradually* entails that the boundaries of species are vague. The essentialist holds that there are characteristics which all and only the members of a given species possess. But this is no longer a tenable view; it is just as implausible as demanding that there should be a precise number of dollars which marks the boundary between rich and poor. This is the Sorites problem. Since ancient Greece, we have known that being a heap of stones, being bald, and being rich are concepts beset by line-drawing problems. But, the suggestion goes, it was only since 1859 that we have come to see that *Homo sapiens* is in the same boat. Thus, Hull (1965) has argued that essentialism was refuted because of its Aristotelian theory of *definition*; the requirement that species have non-trivial necessary and sufficient conditions runs afoul of the kind of continuity found in nature.

Unfortunately, this limpid solution to our problem becomes clouded a bit when we consider the historical fact that many essentialists conceded the existence of line-drawing problems. Thus, Aristotle in his *History of Animals*, (5888b4 ff.), remarks:

> ... nature proceeds little by little from inanimate things to living creatures, in such a way that we are unable, in the continuous sequence to determine the boundary line between them or to say which side an intermediate kind falls. Next, after inanimate things come the plants: and among the plants there are differences between one kind

and another in the extent to which they seem to share in life, and the whole genus of plants appears to be alive when compared with other objects, but seems lifeless when compared with animals. The transition from them to the animals is a continuous one, as remarked before. For with some kinds of things found in the sea one would be at a loss to tell whether they are animals or plants.

It is unclear exactly how one should interpret this remark. Does it indicate that there are in fact no boundaries in nature, or does it mean that the boundaries are difficult to discern? From the time of Aristotle up to the time of Darwin, the principle of continuity seems to have coexisted peacefully with strong essentialist convictions in the minds of many thinkers (Lovejoy 1936). Bonnet, Akenside, and Robinet are eighteenth-century biologists who exemplify this curious combination of doctrines. Does this coexistence imply that the two doctrines are in fact compatible, or rather, does it show that their conceptual dissonance was a long time in being appreciated? To answer this question, let us return to our analogy with the transmutation of elements.

In what sense are the boundaries between chemical kinds any more definite than those which we encounter in biology? At first glance, there appears to be all the difference in the world: in the periodic table, we have discrete jumps—between atomic number 36 and atomic number 37 there are no intermediate atomic numbers to blur distinctions. But let us reflect for a moment on the mechanism of transmutation. Consider, as an example, the experiment which settled the question of how nitrogen can be transmuted into oxygen (Ihde 1964, 509):

$$\,^4_2\text{He} + \,^{14}_7\text{N} \rightarrow \,^{17}_8\text{O} + \,^1_1\text{H}.$$

In this reaction, the α-particle is absorbed and a proton is expelled. Let us ask of this process a typical Sorites question: At what point does the bombarded nucleus cease to be a nitrogen nucleus and when does it start being a nucleus of oxygen?

There *may* be a precise and principled answer to this question which is given by the relevant physical theory. But then again there may not.[3] I would suggest that which of these outcomes prevails really does not matter to the question of whether essentialism is a correct doctrine concerning the chemical kinds. It may well be that having a particular atomic number is a vague concept. But this is quite consistent with that (vague) property's being the essence of a chemical kind. This really does not matter, as long as the vagueness of "nitrogen" and that of "atomic number 14" coincide. Essentialism is in principle consistent with *vague essences*.[4] In spite of this, one wonders what the history of chemistry, and its attendant metaphysics, would have looked like, if the transmutation of elements had been a frequent and familiar phenomenon during the second half of the nineteenth century. Just as the fact of evolution at times tempted Darwin to adopt a nominalist attitude towards species, so in chemistry the impressive taxonomy which we now have in the form of the periodic table might never have been arrived at, line-drawing problems having convinced chemists that chemical kinds are unreal.[5]

As a historical matter, Hull (1965) was right in arguing that essentialism was standardly associated with a theory of definition in which vagueness is proscribed. Given this association, nonsaltative evolution was a profound embarassment to the essentialist. But, if I am right, this theory of definition is inessential to essentialism. Our argument that the gradualness of evolution is not the decisive issue in undermining essentialism is further supported, I think, by the fact that contemporary evolutionary theory contains proposals in which evolutionary gradualism is rejected. Eldredge and Gould (1972) have argued that the standard view of speciation (as given, for example, in Ayala 1978 and Mayr 1963) is one in which phylogeny is to be seen as a series of "punctuated equilibria." Discontinuities in the fossil record are not to be chalked up to incompleteness, but rather to the fact that, in geological time, jumps are the norm. I would suggest that this theory of discontinuous speciation is cold comfort to the essentialist. Whether lines are easy or hard to draw is not the main issue, or so I shall argue.[6]

Another local anti-essentialist argument has been developed by Ghiselin (1966), (1969), and (1974) and Hull (1976) and (1978). They have argued that evolutionary theory makes it more plausible to view species as spatiotemporally extended individuals than as natural kinds. A genuine natural kind like gold may "go extinct" and then reappear; it is quite possible for there to be gold things at one time, for there to be no gold at some later time, and then, finally, for gold to exist at some still later time. But the conception of species given by evolutionary theory does not allow this sort of flip-flopping in and out of existence: once a biological taxon goes extinct, it must remain so. Hull (1978) argues that the difference between chemical natural kinds and biological species is that the latter, but not the former, are historical entities. Like organisms, biological species are individuated in part by historical criteria of spatiotemporal continuity. I am inclined to agree with this interpretation; its impact on pre-Darwinian conceptions of species could hardly be more profound. But what of its impact on essentialism? If essentialism is simply the view that species have essential properties (where a property need not be purely qualitative), then the doctrine remains untouched (as Hull himself realizes). Kripke (1972) has suggested that each individual human being has the essential property of being born of precisely the sperm and the egg of which he or she was born. If such individuals as organisms have essential properties, then it will presumably also be possible for individuals like *Drosophila melanogaster* to have essential properties as well. Of course, these essences will be a far cry from the "purely qualitative" characteristics which traditional essentialism thought it was in the business of discovering.

My analysis of the impact of evolutionary theory on essentialism is parallel, though additional. Whether species are natural kinds or spatio-temporally extended individuals, essentialist theories about them are un-tenable. Two kinds of arguments will be developed for this conclusion. First, I will describe the way in which essentialism seeks to explain the existence of variability, and will argue that this conception is rendered implausible by evolutionary theory. Secondly, I will show how evolution-ary theory has removed *the need* for providing species with constituent definitions; population thinking provides another way of making species scientifically intelligible. This consideration, coupled with the principle of parsimony, provides an additional reason for thinking that species do not have essences.

Aristotle's Natural State Model

One of the fundamental ideas in Aristotle's scientific thinking is what I will call his natural state model. This model provides a technique for explaining the great diversity found in natural objects. Within the domain of physics, there are heavy and light objects, ones that move violently and ones that do not move at all. How is one to find some order that unites and underlies all this variety? Aristotle's hypothesis was that there is a distinction be-tween the *natural state* of a kind of object and those states which are not natural. These latter are produced by subjecting the object to an *interfering force*. In the sublunar sphere, for a heavy object to be in its natural state is for it to be located where the center of the Earth is now (*On the Heavens*, ii, clr, 296b and 310b, 2–5). But, of course, many heavy objects fail to be there. The cause for this divergence from what is natural is that these objects are acted on by interfering forces which prevent them from achiev-ing their natural state by frustrating their natural tendency. Variability within nature is thus to be accounted for as a deviation from what is natural; were there no interfering forces, all heavy objects would be located in the same place (Lloyd 1968).

Newton made use of Aristotle's distinction, but disagreed with him about what the natural state of physical objects is. The first law of motion says that if a body is not acted upon by a force, then it will remain at rest or in uniform motion. And even in general relativity, the geometry of space-time specifies a set of geodesics along which an object will move as long as it is not subjected to a force. Although the terms "natural" and "unnatural" no longer survive in Newtonian and post-Newtonian physics, Aristotle's distinction can clearly be made within those theories. If there are no forces at all acting on an object, then, *a fortiori*, there are no interfering forces acting on it either. A natural state, within these theories, is a zero-force state.

The explanatory value of Aristotle's distinction is fairly familiar. If an object is not in its natural state, we know that the object must have been acted on by a force, and we set about finding it. We do this by consulting our catalog of known forces. If none of these is present, we might augment our catalog, or perhaps revise our conception of what the natural state of the system is. This pattern of analysis is used in population genetics under the rubric of the Hardy-Weinberg law. This law specifies an equilibrium state for the frequencies of genotypes in a panmictic population; this natural state is achieved when the evolutionary forces of mutation, migration, selection and drift are not at work.

In the biological world, Aristotle sets forth the same sort of explanatory model. Diversity was to be accounted for as the joint product of natural regularities and interfering forces. Aristotle invokes this model when he specifies the regularities governing how organisms reproduce themselves:

> ... [for] any living thing that has reached its normal development and which is unmutilated, and whose mode of generation is not spontaneous, the most natural act is the production of another like itself, an animal producing an animal, a plant a plant ... (*De Anima*, 415a26).

Like producing like, excepting the case of spontaneous generation, is the natural state, subject to a multitude of interferences, as we shall see.

In the case of spontaneous generation, the natural state of an organism is different. Although in the *Metaphysics* and the *Physics* "spontaneous" is used to mean unusual or random, in the later biological writings, *History of Animals* and *Generation of Animals*, Aristotle uses the term in a different way (Balme 1962, Hull 1967). Spontaneous generation obeys its own laws. For a whole range of organisms classified between the intermediate animals and the plants, like *never* naturally produces like. Rather, a bit of earth will spontaneously generate an earthworm, and the earthworm will then produce an eel. Similarly, the progression from slime to ascarid to gnat and that from cabbage leaf to grub to caterpillar to chrysallis to butterfly likewise counts as the natural reproductive pattern for this part of the living world (*History of Animals*, 570a5, 551b26, 551a13).

So much for the natural states. What counts as an interference for Aristotle? According to Aristotle's theory of sexual reproduction, the male semen provides a set of instructions which dictates how the female matter is to be shaped into an organism.[7] Interference may arise when the form fails to completely master the matter. This may happen, for example, when one or both parents are abnormal, or when the parents are from different species, or when there is trauma during foetal development. Such interferences are anything but rare, according to Aristotle. Mules—sterile hybrids —count as deviations from the natural state (*Generation of Animals*, ii, 8). In fact, the females of a species do too, even though they are necessary for the species to reproduce itself (*Generation of Animals*, ii, 732a; ii, 3, 737a27; iv, 3, 767b8; iv, 6, 775a15). In fact, reproduction that is completely free of interference would result in an offspring which exactly resembles the father.[8] So failure to exactly resemble the male parent counts as a departure from the natural state. Deviations from type, whether mild or extreme, Aristotle labels *"terata"*—monsters. They are the result of interfering forces (*biaion*) deflecting reproduction from its natural pattern.

Besides trying to account for variation within species by using the natural state model, Aristotle at times seems to suggest that there are entire species which count as monsters (Preuss 1975, 215–16; Hull 1968). Seals are deformed as a group because they resemble lower classes of animals, owing to their lack of ears. Snails, since they move like animals with their feet cut off, and lobsters, because they use their claws for locomotion, are likewise to be counted as monsters (*Generation of Animals*, 19, 714b, 18- 19; *Parts of Animals*, iv, 8, 684a35). These so-called "dualizing species" arise because they are the best possible organisms that can result from the matter out of which they are made. The scale of nature, it is suggested, arises in all its graduated diversity because the quality of the matter out of which organisms are made also varies—and nature persists in doing the best possible, given the ingredients at hand.

One cannot fault Aristotle for viewing so much of the biological domain as monstrous. Natural state models habitually have this characteristic; Newton's first law of motion is not impugned by the fact that no physical object is wholly unaffected by an outside force. Even so, Aristotle's partition of natural state and non-natural state in biology sounds to the modern ear like a reasonable distinction run wild. "Real terrata are one thing," one might say, "but to call entire species, and all females, and all males who don't exactly resemble their fathers monsters, seems absurd." Notice that our "modern" conceptions of health and disease and our notion of normality as something other than a statistical average enshrine Aristotle's model. We therefore are tempted to make only a conservative criticism of Aristotle's biology: we preserve the form of model he propounded, but criticize the applications he made of it. Whether this minimal critique of Aristotle is possible in the light of evolutionary theory, remains to be seen.

The natural state model constitutes a powerful tool for accounting for variation. Even when two species seem to blend into each other continuously, it may still be the case that all the members of one species have one natural tendency while the members of the other species have a quite different natural tendency. Interfering forces may, in varying degrees, deflect the individuals in both species from their natural states, thus yielding the surface impression that there are no boundaries between the species. This essentialist response to the fact of diversity has the virtue that it avoids the ad hoc maneuver of contracting the boundaries of species so as to preserve their internal homogeneity[9] This latter strategy was not unknown to the essentialist, but its methodological defects are too well known to be worth recounting here. Instead of insisting that species be defined in terms of some surface morphological feature, and thereby having each species shrink to a point, the essentialist can countenance unlimited variety in, and continuity between, species, as long as underlying this plenum one can expect to find discrete natural tendencies. The failure to discover such underlying mechanisms is no strong reason to think that none exist; but the development of a theory which implies that natural tendencies are not part of the natural order is another matter entirely.

Aristotle's model was a fixed point in the diverse conjectures to be found in pre-Darwinian biology. Preformationists and epigeneticists, advocates of evolution and proponents of stasis, all assumed that there is a real difference between natural states and states caused by interfering forces. The study of monstrosity—teratology—which in this period made the transition from unbridled speculation to encyclopedic catalogues of experimental oddities (Meyer 1939), is an especially revealing example of the power exerted by the natural state model. Consider, for example, the eighteenth-century disagreement between Maupertuis and Bonnet over the proper explanation of polydactyly. Both had at their fingertips a genealogy; it was clear to both that somehow or other the trait regularly reappeared through the generations. Maupertuis conjectured that defective hereditary material was passed along, having originally made its appearance in the family because of *an error in nature* (Glass 1959b, 62–7). Maupertuis, a convinced Newtonian, thought that traits, both normal and anomalous, resulted from the lawful combination of hereditary particles (Roger 1963). When such particles have normal quantities of attraction for each other, normal characteristics result. However, when particles depart from this natural state, either too many or too few of them combine, thus resulting in *monstres par exces* or *monstres par defaut*. Bonnet, a convinced ovist, offered a different hypothesis. For him, polydactyly is never encoded in the germ, but rather results from abnormal interuterine conditions or from male sperm interfering with normal development (Glass 1959a, 169). Thus whether polydactyly is "naturalized" by Maupertuis' appeal to heredity or by Bonnet's appeal to environment, the trait is never regarded as being completely natural. Variability in nature—in this case variability as to the number of digits—is a deviation from type.

In pre-Darwinian disputes over evolution, natural states loom equally large. Evolutionary claims during this period mainly assumed that living things were programmed to develop in a certain sequence, and that the emergence of biological novelty was therefore in conformity with some natural plan. Lovejoy (1936) discusses how the Great Chain of Being was "temporalized" during the eighteenth century; by this, he has in mind the tendency to think that the natural ordering of living things from those of higher type down to those of lower type also represented an historical progression. Such programmed, directed evolution—in which some types naturally give rise to others—is very much in the spirit of the natural state model. Whether species are subject to historical unfolding, or rather exist unchanged for all time, the concept of species was inevitably associated with that of type; on either view, variation is deviation caused by interfering forces.

It was generally presupposed that somewhere within the possible variations that a species is capable of, there is a privileged state—a state which has a special causal and explanatory role. The laws governing a species will specify this state, just as the laws which make sense of the diversity of kinematic states found in physics tell us what is the natural state of a physical object. The diversity of individual organisms is a veil which must be penetrated in the search for invariance. The transformation in thinking which we will trace in the next two sections consisted in the realization that this diversity itself constituted an invariance, obeying its own laws.

The Law of Errors and the Emergence of Population Thinking

So far, I have sketched several of the applications that have been made of Aristotle's model within biology. This strategy for explaining variation, I will argue in the next section, has been discredited by modern evolutionary theory. Our current theories of biological variation provide no more role for the idea of natural state than our current physical theories do for the notion of absolute simultaneity. Theories in population genetics enshrine a different model of variation, one which only became possible during the second half of the nineteenth century. Some brief account of the evolution within the field of statistics of our understanding of the law of errors will lay the groundwork for discussing the modern understanding of biological variation.

From its theoretical formulation and articulation in the eighteenth century, up until the middle of the nineteenth century, the law of errors was understood as a law about *errors*. Daniel Bernouilli, Lagrange, and Laplace each tried to develop mathematical techniques for determining how a set of discordant observations was to be interpreted (Todhunter 1865). The model for this problem was, of course, that there is a single true value for some observational variable, and a multiplicity of inconsistent readings that have been obtained. Here we have a straightforward instance of Aristotle's model: interfering forces cause variation in opinion; in nature there is but one true value. The problem for the theory of errors was to penetrate the veil of variability and to discover behind it the single value which was the constant cause of the multiplicity of different readings. Each observation was thus viewed as the causal upshot of two kinds of factors: part of what determines an observational outcome is the real value of the variable, but interfering forces which distort the communication of this information from nature to mind, also play a role. If these interfering forces are random—if they are as likely to take one value as any other—then the mean value of the readings is likely to represent the truth, when the number of observations is large. In this case, one reaches the truth by ascending to the summit of the bell curve. It is important to notice that this application of the natural state model is epistemological, not ontological. One seeks to account for variation in our observations of nature, not variation in nature itself. The decisive transition, from this epistemological to an ontological application, was made in the 1830s by the influential Belgian statistician Adolphe Quetelet .

Quetelet's insight was that the law of errors could be given an ontological interpretation by invoking a distinction which Laplace had earlier exploited in his work in Newtonian mechanics.[10] Laplace decomposed the forces at work in the solar system into two kinds. First, there are the *constant causes* by which the planets are affected by the sun's gravitation; second, there are the particular *disturbing causes* which arise from the mutual influences of the planets, their satellites, and the comets. Laplace's strategy was a familiar analytic one. He tried to decompose the factors at work in a phenomenon into components, and to analyze their separate contributions to the outcome. The character of this decomposition, however, is of special interest: one, central, causal agent is at work on the components of a system, but the effects of this force are complicated by the presence of numerous interferences which act in different directions.

In his book of 1835, *Sur l'homme et le développement de ses facultés, ou essai de physique social*, Quetelet put forward his conception of the *average man* which for him constituted the true subject of the discipline of social physics. By studying the average man, Quetelet hoped to filter out the mutifarious and idiosyncratic characteristics which make for diversity in a population, and to focus on the central facts which constitute the social body itself. Like Weber's later idea of an ideal type, Quetelet's conception of the average man was introduced as a "fiction" whose utility was to facilitate a clear view of social facts by allowing one to abstract from the vagaries of individual differences. But unlike Weber, Quetelet quickly came to view his construct as real—a subject matter in its own right. Quetelet was struck by the analogy between a society's average man and a physical system's center of gravity. Since the latter could play a causal role, so too could the former; neither was a mere abstraction. For Quetelet, variability within a population is *caused* by deviation from type. When the astronomer John Herschel reviewed Quetelet's *Lettres sur les probabilités* in 1850, he nicely captured Quetelet's idea that the average man is no mere artefact of reflection: .

> An average may exist of the most different objects, as the heights of houses in a town, or the sizes of books in a library. It may be convenient to convey a general notion of the things averaged; but it involves no conception of a natural and recognizable central magnitude, all differences from which ought to be regarded as deviations from a standard. The notion of a mean, on the other hand, does imply such a conception, standing distinguished from an average by this very feature, *viz.* the regular marching of the groups, increasing to a maximum and thence again diminishing. An average gives us no assurance that the future will be like the past. A mean may be reckoned on with the most implicit confidence (Hilts 1973, 217).

Quetelet found little theoretical significance in the fact of individual differences. Concepts of correlation and amount of variation were unknown to him. For Quetelet, the law of errors is still a law about errors, only for him the mistakes are made by nature, not by observers. Our belief that there is variation in a population is no mistake on our part. Rather, it is the result of interferences confounding the expression of a prototype. Were interfering forces not to occur, there would be no variation.

It may strike the modern reader as incredible that anyone could view a trait like girth on this mode. However, Quetelet, who was perhaps the most influential statistician of his time, did understand biological differences in this way. He was impressed, not to say awe struck, by the fact that the results of accurately measuring the waists of a thousand Scottish soldiers would assume the same bell-shaped distribution as the results of inaccurately measuring the girth of a single, average, soldier a thousand times. For Quetelet, the point of attending to variation was to *see through it*—to render it transparent. Averages were the very antitheses of artefacts; they alone were the true objects of inquiry.[11]

Frances Galton, who was Darwin's cousin, was responsible for fundamental innovations in the analysis of individual differences.[12] He discovered the standard deviation and the correlation coefficient. His work on heredity was later claimed by both Mendelians and biometricians as seminal, and thus can be viewed as a crucial step towards the synthetic theory of evolution (Provine 1971). But his interest to our story is more restricted. Galton, despite his frequently sympathetic comments about the concept of type, helped to displace the average man and the idea of deviation from type.[13] He did this, not by attacking these typological constructs directly, but by developing an alternative model for accounting for variability. This model is a nascent form of the kind of population thinking which evolutionary biologists today engage in.

One of Galton's main intellectual goals was to show that heredity is a central cause of individual differences. Although the arguments which Galton put forward for his hereditarian thesis were weak, the conception of variability he exploited in his book *Hereditary Genius* (1869) is of great significance. For Galton, variability is not to be explained away as the result of interference with a single prototype. Rather, variability within one generation is explained by appeal to variability in the previous generation and to facts about the transmission of variability. Galton used the law of errors, but no longer viewed it as a law *about* errors. As Hilts (1973, 223–24) remarks: "Because Galton was able to associate the error distribution with individual differences caused by heredity, the distinction between constant and accidental causes lost much of its meaning." At the end of his life, Galton judged that one of his most important ideas was that the science of heredity should be concerned with deviations measured in statistical units. Quetelet had earlier denied that such units exist. Galton's discovery of the standard deviation gave him the mathematical machinery to begin treating variability as obeying its own laws, as something other than an idiosyncratic artefact.

Eight years after the publication of *Hereditary Genius*, Galton was able to sketch a solution for the problem he had noted in that work: What fraction of the parental deviations from the norm are passed on to offspring? Galton described a model in which hereditary causes and nonhereditary causes are partitioned. Were only the former of these at work, he conjectured, each child would have traits that are intermediate between those of its parents. In this case, the amount of variation would decrease in each generation. But Galton suspected that the amount of variation is constant across generations. To account for this, he posited a second, counteracting force which causes variability within each family. Were this second force the only one at work, the amount of variation would increase. But in reality, the centrifugal and centripetal forces combine to yield a constant quantity of variability across the generations. An error distribution is thus accounted for by way of a hypothesis which characterizes it as the sum of two other error distributions.

In his *Natural Inheritance* of 1889, Galton went on to complete his investigations of the correlation coefficient, and introduced the name "normal law" as a more appropriate label for what had traditionally been called the law of errors.[14] Bell curves are normal; they are found everywhere, Galton thought. This change in nomenclature crystallized a significant transformation in thinking. Bell curves need not represent mistakes made by fallible observers or by sportive nature. Regardless of the underlying etiology, they *are real*; they enter into explanations because the variability they represent is lawful and causally efficacious.

The transition made possible by statistical thinking from typological to population thinking was not completed by Galton.[15] Although his innovations loosened the grip of essentialism, he himself was deeply committed to the idea of racial types and believed that evolutionary theory presupposes the reality of types. Both Galton and Darwin (1859, ch. 5; 1868, ch. 13) spoke sympathetically about the ideas of unity of type and of reversion to type, and sought to provide historical justifications of these ideas in terms of common descent. Unity of type was just similarity owing to common ancestry; reversion to type was the reappearance of latent ancestral traits. But the presence of these ideas in their writings should not obscure the way in which their theorizing began to undermine typological thinking.

Darwin and Galton focused on the population as a unit of organization. The population is an entity, subject to its own forces, and obeying its own laws. The details concerning the individuals who are parts of this whole are pretty much irrelevant. Describing a single individual is as theoretically peripheral to a populationist as describing the motion of a single molecule is to the kinetic theory of gases. In this important sense, population thinking involves *ignoring individuals*: it is holistic, not atomistic. This conclusion contradicts Mayr's (1959, 28) assertion that for the populationist, "the individual alone is real."

Typologists and populationists agree that averages exist; and both grant the existence of variation. They disagree about the explanator character of these. For Quetelet, and for typologists generally, variability does not explain anything. Rather it is something to be explained or explained away. Quetelet posited a process in which uniformity gives rise to diversity; a single prototype—the average man—is mapped onto a variable resulting population. Galton, on the other hand, explained diversity in terms of an earlier diversity and constructed the mathematical tools to make this kind of analysis possible.

Both typologists and populationists seek to transcend the blooming, buzzing confusion of individual variation. Like all scientists, they do this by trying to identify properties of systems which remain constant in spite of the system's changes. For the typologist, the search for invariances takes the form of a search for natural tendencies. The typologist formulates a causal hypothesis about the forces at work on each individual within a population. The invariance underlying this diversity is the possession of a particular natural tendency *by each individual organism*. The populationist, on the other hand, tries to identify invariances by ascending to a different level of organization. For Galton, the invariant property across generations within a lineage is the amount of variability, and this is a property *of populations*. Again we see a way in which the essentialist is more concerned with individual organisms than the populationist is. Far from ignoring individuals, the typologist, *via* his use of the natural state model, resolutely focuses on individual organisms as the entities which possess invariant properties. The populationist, on the other hand, sees that it is not just individual organisms which can be the bearers of unchanging characteristics. Rather than looking for a reality that *underlies* diversity, the populationist can postulate a reality *sustained* by diversity.

I have just argued that there is an important sense in which typologists are more concerned with individual organisms than populationists are. However, looked at in another way, Mayr's point that populationists assign a more central role to organisms than typologists do can be established. In models of natural selection in which organisms enjoy different rates of reproductive success because of differences in fitness, natural selection is a force that acts on individual (organismic) differences. This standard way of viewing evolution assigns a causal role to individual idiosyncracies. Individual differences are not *the effects* of interfering forces confounding the expression of a prototype; rather they are *the causes* of events that are absolutely central to the history of evolution. It is in this sense that Mayr is right in saying that evolutionary theory treats individuals as real in a way that typological thought does not (see also Lewontin 1974, 5–6). Putting my point and Mayr's point, thus interpreted, together, we might say that population thinking endows individual organisms with more reality *and* with less reality than typological thinking attributes to them.

To be real is to have causal efficacy; to be unreal is to be a mere artefact of some causal process. This characterization of what it is to be real, also used by Hacking (1975), is markedly different from the one used in traditional metaphysical disputes concerning realism, verificationism, and idealism (Sober 1980b). There, the problem is not how things are causally related, but rather it concerns what in fact *exists*, and whether what exists exists "independently" of us. The causal view of what it is to be real offers an explanation of a peculiar fact that is part of the more traditional metaphysical problem. Although two predicates may name real physical properties, natural kinds, theoretical magnitudes, or physical objects, simple operations on that pair of predicates may yield predicates which fail to name anything real. Thus, for example, "mass" and "charge" may name real physical magnitudes, even though "$mass^2/charge^3$" fails to name anything real. This is hard to explain, if reality is simply equated with existence (or with existence-that-is-independent-of-us). After all, if an object has a mass and if it has a charge, then there must be such a thing as what the square of its mass over the cube of its charge is. While this is quite true, it is *not* similarly correct to infer that because an object's mass causes some things and its charge causes other things, then there must be something which is caused by appeal to the square of its mass divided by the cube of its charge. Realism, in this case at least, is a thesis about what is cause and what is effect.

If we look forward in time, from the time of Galton and Darwin to the Modern Synthesis and beyond, we can see how population models have come to play a profoundly important role in evolutionary theorizing. In such models, properties of populations are identified and laws are formulated about their interrelations. Hypotheses in theoretical ecology and in island biogeography, for example, *generalize over populations* (see, for example, Wilson and Bossert 1971, chs. 3 and 4). The use of population concepts is not legitimized in those disciplines by defining them in terms of concepts applying at some lower level of organization. Rather, the use of one population concept is vindicated by showing how it stands in lawlike relations with other concepts *at the same level of organization*. It is in this way that we can see that there is an alternative to constituent definition. Here, then, is one way in which evolutionary theorizing undermined essentialism: Essentialism requires that species concepts be legitimized by constituent definition, but evolutionary theory, in its articulation of population models, makes such demands unnecessary. Explanations can proceed without this reductionistic requirement being met.

If this argument is correct, there is a standard assumption made in traditional metaphysical problems having to do with identity which needs to be reevaluated. There could hardly be a more central category in our metaphysics, both scientific and everyday, than that of an enduring physical object. The way philosophers have tried to understand this category is as follows: Imagine a collection of instantaneous objects—i.e., objects at a moment in time. How are these various instantaneous objects united into the temporally enduring objects of our ontology? What criteria do we use when we lump together some time slices, but not others? This approach to the problem is basically that of looking for a constituent definition: enduring objects are to be defined out of their constituent time-slices. But, if populations can be scientifically legitimized in ways other than by using constituent definitions, perhaps the same thing is true of the category of physical object itself. I take it that Quine's (1953a) slogan "no entity without identity" is basically a demand for constituent definitions; this demand, which has been so fruitful in mathematics, should not be generalized into a universal maxim (nor can it be, if there are finitely many levels of organization. See Kripke 1978).

If constituent definitions for population concepts are theoretically unnecessary, then we have one argument, via the principle of parsimony (Sober 1980a), for the view that species do not have essences. However, there are equally pressing problems which essentialism faces when the natural state model is evaluated in the light of our current understanding of the origins of variability. It is to these problems that we now turn.

The Disappearance of a Distinction

The fate of Aristotle's model at the hands of population biology bears a striking resemblance to what happened to the notion of absolute simultaneity with the advent of relativity theory. Within classical physics, there was a single, well-defined answer to the question "What is the temporal separation of two events x and y?" However, relativity theory revealed that answering this question at all depends on one's choice of a rest frame; given different rest frames, one gets different answers. We might represent the way the temporal separation of a pair of events may depend on a choice of frame as in the graph in figure 12.1. As is well known, the classical notions of temporal separation and spatial separation gave way in relativity theory to a magnitude that is not relative at all: this is the spatiotemporal separation of the two events. How large this quantity is does not depend on any choice of rest frame; it is frame invariant. Minkowski (1908) took this fact about relativity theory to indicate that space and time are not real physical properties at all, since they depend for their values on choices that are wholly arbitrary. For Minkowski, to be real is to be invariant, and space and time become mere shadows.

Special relativity fails to discriminate between the various temporal intervals represented in figure 12.1; they are all on a par. No one specifica-

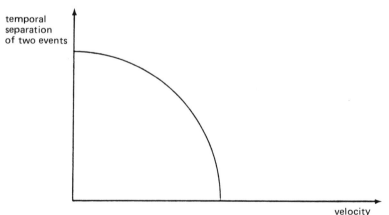

Figure 12.1
The temporal separation of a pair of events, relative to choices of rest frame.

tion of the temporal separation is any more correct than any other. It would be utterly implausible to interpret this fact as indicating that there is a physically real distinction which special relativity fails to make. The fact that our best theory fails to draw this distinction gives us a very good reason for suspecting that the distinction is unreal, and this is the standard view of the matter which was crystallized in the work of Minkowski.

According to the natural state model, there is one path of fetal development which counts as the realization of the organism's natural state, while other developmental results are consequences of unnatural interferences. Put slightly differently, for a given genotype, there is a single phenotype which it can have that is the natural one. Or, more modestly, the requirement might be that there is some restricted range of phenotypes which count as natural. But when one looks to genetic theory for a conception of the relation between genotype and phenotype, one finds no such distinction between natural state and states which are the results of interference. One finds, instead, the *norm of reaction*, which graphs the different phenotypic results that a genotype can have in different environments.[16] Thus the height of a single corn plant genotype might vary according to environmental differences in temperature, as is shown in figure 12.2. How would one answer the question: "Which of these phenotypes is the natural one for the corn plant to have?" One way to take this obscure question is

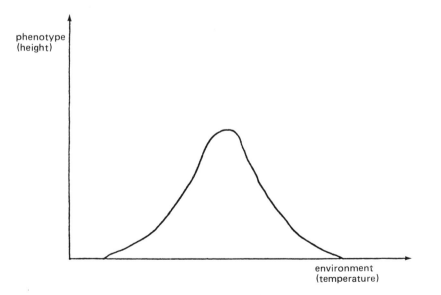

Figure 12.2
The norm of reaction of a given corn plant genotype, showing height as a function of temperature.

indicated by the following answer: Each of the heights indicated in the norm of reaction is as "natural" as any other, since each happens in nature. Choose an environment, and relative to that choice we know what the phenotypic upshot in that environment is. But, of course, if the question we are considering is understood in terms of the natural state model, this sort of answer will not do. The natural state model presupposes that there is some phenotype which is the natural one *which is independent of a choice of environment*. The natural state model presupposes that there is some environment which is the natural environment for the genotype to be in, which determines, in conjunction with the norm of reaction, what the natural phenotype for the genotype is. But these presuppositions find no expression in the norm of reaction: all environments are on a par, and all phenotypes are on a par. The required distinctions simply are not made.

When one turns from the various phenotypes that a single genotype might produce, to the various genotypes that a population might contain the same result obtains. Again, according to the natural state model, there is a single genotype or restricted class of genotypes, which count as the natural states of the population or species, all other genotypes being the result of interfering forces. But again, statistical profiles of genotypic variance within a population enshrine no such difference. Genotypes differ from each other in frequency; but unusual genotypes are not in any literal sense to be understood as deviations from type.

When a corn plant of a particular genotype withers and dies, owing to the absence of trace elements in the soil, the natural state model will view this as an outcome that is not natural. When it thrives and is reproductively successful, one wants to say that *this* environment might be the natural one. Given these ideas, one might try to vindicate the natural state model from a selectionist point of view by identifying the natural environment of a genotype with the environment in which it is fittest.[17]

This suggestion fails to coincide with important intuitions expressed in the natural state model. First of all, let us ask the question: What is the range of environments relative to which the fittest environment is to be understood? Shall we think of the natural state as that which obtains when the environment is the fittest *of all possible environments*? If so, the stud bull, injected with medications, its reproductive capacities boosted to phenomenal rates by an efficient artificial insemination program, has achieved its natural state. And in similar fashion, the kind of environment that biologists use to characterize the intrinsic rate of increase (r) of a population—one in which there is no disease, no predation, no limitations of space or food supplies—will likewise count as the natural environment. But these optimal environments are *not natural*, the natural state model tells us. They involve "artificially boosting" the fitness of resulting phenotypes by placing the genotypes in environments that are more advantageous than the natural environment.

Let us consider another, perhaps more plausible, way to understand the range of environments with respect to which the fittest environment is to be calculated. Instead of taking the best of all possible environments, why not, more modestly, consider the best of all environments that have been historically represented? This suggestion evades the second, but not the first, counterexample mentioned above. However, other problems present themselves. The natural state of a genotype is often understood to be one which has yet to occur. Perhaps every environment that a species has historically experienced is such that a given genotype in that environment results in a *diseased* phenotype, or one which is developmentally impaired in some way. The natural state of a genotype is often taken to be some sort of ideal state which may or may not be closely approximated in the history of the species.

I have just argued that the idea of a fittest environment does not allow one to impose on the norm of reaction the kind of distinction that the natural state model requires. Precisely the same reason, count against construing the idea of a genotype's being the natural state of a species in terms of maximal fitness. It is part of the natural state model that the natural genotype for a species can be less fit (in some range of environments) than the best of all possible genotypes. And the natural genotype can likewise fail to be historically represented.

Aristotle is typical of exponents of the natural state model in holding that variation is introduced into a population by virtue of interferences with normal sexual reproduction. Our current understanding of the mechanisms of reproduction shows that precisely the opposite is the case. Even if one dismisses mutations as "unnatural interferences," the fact of genetic recombination in meiosis looms large. Generally, the number of total genotypes that a gene pool can produce by recombination is the product of the number of diploid genotypes that can be constructed at each locus. For species like *Homo sapiens* and *Drosophila melanogaster*, the number of loci has been estimated to be about 10,000 or more. What this means is that the number of genotypes that can be generated by recombination is greater than the number of atoms in the visible universe (Wilson and Bossert 1971, 39). For species with this number of loci, even a single male and a single female can themselves reproduce a significant fraction of the variation found in a population from which they are drawn. All sorts of deleterious phenotypes may emerge from the recombination process initiated by a founder population.

A doctrinaire advocate of the natural state model may take these facts to show that recombination has the status of an interference with what is natural. But this desperate strategy conflicts with the received evolutionary view of the function of sexuality. The deploying of prodigious quantities of variability is not a dysfunction which sexual organisms are vulnerable to. Rather it is the principal advantage of sexuality; it is standardly construed to be *what sexuality is for* (but see Williams 1975 for a dissenting opinion). If the notion of a natural state is to make any sense at all, then variability must be viewed as the upshot of natural forces.

The natural state model is a *causal*, and thereby a *historical, hypothesis*. The essentialist attempts to understand variation within a species as arising through a process of deviation from type. By tracing back the origins of this variability we discover the natural state of a species. To do this is to uncover that natural tendency possessed by each member of the species. But the science which describes the laws governing the historical origins of variation within species—population genetics—makes no appeal to such "natural tendencies." Rather, this frame invariant "natural tendency"—this property that an organism is supposed to have regardless of what environment it might be in—has been replaced by a frame relative property—namely, the phenotype that a genotype will produce *in a given environment*. The historical concept of a natural state is discredited in much the same way that the kinematic concept of absolute simultaneity was.

Our current concepts of function and dysfunction, of disease and health, seem to be based on the kinds of distinctions recommended by the natural state model. And both of these distinctions resist characterization in terms of maximum fitness. For virtually any trait you please, there can be environments in which that trait is selected for, or selected against. Diseases can be rendered advantageous, and health can be made to represent a reproductive cost. And even if we restrict our attention to historically actual environments, we still encounter difficulties. A perfectly healthy phenotype may be historically nonexistent; the optimum actually attained might still be some diseased state.

The functional notions just mentioned make distinctions which are sanctioned by the natural state model. Given the inadequacy of this model, does this show that the difference between disease and health and the difference between function and dysfunction are mere illusions? I do not think that this follows. What we should conclude is that these functional notions of normality are not to be characterized in terms of a historical notion of fitness. Perhaps they can be understood in some other way; that remains to be seen.

In addition to the influence that the natural state model continues to exert in scientific thinking, perhaps even more pervasive is the way that notions of naturalness have had, and continue to have, an influence in politics and in popular culture. Political theorists of both the left and the right have appealed to something called "human nature" (Lewontin 1977,

Hull 1978)[18] Political optimists see human nature as essentially good; the evil that human beings have done is to be chalked up to interferences on the part of civilization, or of the state, or of particular economic institutions. Pessimists, on the other hand, see in human beings a natural tendency towards evil, which the restraints made possible by civilization can perhaps correct. The common presupposition here is that each human being has a particular dispositional property—a natural tendency—whose manifestation is contingent on whether environmental forces facilitate the expression of what is natural, or, on the other hand, go against nature by imposing unnatural interferences.

A more recent manifestation of the same habit of mind is to be found in debates about "environmental policy." Current environmental controversy, both on the part of those who want further industrialization to take its course and on the part of those who want to check or alter the way in which industry impinges on wildlife, tends to picture nature as something apart from us. The question before us, both sides imply, is how we should behave towards this separate sphere. We are not part of what is natural, and what we do has the character of an intervention from the outside into this natural domain. Our pollution of lakes, disruption of ecosystems, and extinction of species is just not natural. Natural, it would seem, is a good thing to be nowadays. Civilization is more often than not an interfering force, deflecting us from what is natural.

The Victorians, too, had their unnatural acts, thus hoping to find their ethics at least consistent with, and possibly vindicated by, the natural order. But they, at least, maintained some distance from the automatic equation of natural and good. Although some unnatural acts were wrong, others were decidedly right: here natural tendencies had to be checked if morally desirable qualities were to emerge. Perhaps it is a sign of our crumbling moral confidence that we no longer find it possible to separate questions of what is natural from what is good. By equating the two, we hope to read off our ethics directly from what happens in nature, and this gives us the illusion of needing to make no moral decisions for ourselves. This moral buck-passing is incoherent. What happens in nature is simply everything that happens. There is no other sense of "natural." Human society is not external to nature but a special part of it. It is no more a part of human nature to be healthy than to be diseased. Both kinds of phenotypes are to be found, and the norm of reaction makes no distinction between them. If we prefer one and wish to create environments in which it is encouraged, let us say so. But our reasons cannot be given in terms of allowing what is natural to occur unimpeded—by letting nature take its course, as if it has only one. Our activity, and inactivity, requires a more substantive justification than this.

Conclusion

Essentialism is as much entitled to appeal to the principle of tenacity as any other scientific hypothesis or guiding principle. It was hardly irrational for nineteenth-century research on the chemical elements to persist in its assumption that chemical kinds exist and have essential properties. The same holds true for those who hold that species are natural kinds and have essential properties; repeated failure to turn up the postulated items may be interpreted as simply showing that inquiry has not proceeded far enough. Matters change, however, when theoretical reasons start to emerge which cast doubt on the existence claim. For example, if the existence claim is shown to be theoretically superfluous, that counts as one reason for thinking that no such thing exists, or so the principle of parsimony would suggest (Sober 1980a). In another vein, if the causal mechanism associated with the postulated entity is cast in doubt, that too poses problems for the rationality of the existence claim. Our discussion of how population thinking emancipated biology from the need for constituent definitions of species is an argument of the first kind. Our examination of the theory of variation presupposed by essentialism is an argument of the second kind.

No phenotypic characteristic can be postulated as a species essence; the norm of reaction for each genotype shows that it is arbitrary to single out as privileged one phenotype as opposed to any other. Similar considerations show that no genotypic characteristic can be postulated as a species essence; the genetic variability found in sexual populations is prodigious and, again, there is no biologically plausible way to single out some genetic characteristics as natural while viewing others as the upshot of interfering forces. Even if a species were found in which some characteristic is shared by all and only the organisms that are in the species, this could not be counted as a species essence. Imagine, for example, that some novel form of life is created in the laboratory and subjected to some extreme form of stabilizing selection. If the number of organisms is kept small, it may turn out that the internal homogeneity of the species, as well as its distinctness from all other species, has been assured. However, the explanation of this phenomenon would be given in terms of the selection pressures acting on the population. If the universal property were a species essence, however, explaining why it is universal would be like explaining why all acids are proton donors, or why all bachelors are unmarried, or why all nitrogen has atomic number 14. These latter necessary truths, if they are explainable at all, are not explained by saying that some contingent causal force acted on acids, bachelors or samples of nitrogen, thereby endowing them with the property in question. Characteristics possessed by all and only the extant members of a species, if such were to exist, would not be species essences. It is for this reason that hypotheses of discontinuous evolution like that proposed by Eldredge and Gould (1972) in no way confirm the claims of essentialism.

The essentialist hoped to penetrate the veil of variability found within species by discovering some natural tendency which each individual in the species possesses. This natural tendency was to be a dispositional property which would be manifest, were interfering forces not at work. Heterogeneity is thus the result of a departure from the natural state. But, with the development of evolutionary theory, it turned out that no such property was available to the essentialist, and in fact our current model of variability radically differs from the essentialist's causal hypothesis about the origins of variability.

At the same time that evolutionary theory undermined the essentialist's model of variability, it also removed the need for discovering species essences. Characteristics of populations do not have to be defined in terms of characteristics of organisms for population concepts to be coherent and fruitful. Population biology attempts to formulate generalizations about kinds of populations. In spite of the fact that species cannot be precisely individuated in terms of their constituent organisms, species undergo evolutionary processes, and the character of such processes is what population biology attempts to describe. Laws generalizing over population will, of course, include the standard *ceteris paribus* rider: they will describe how various properties and magnitudes are related, as long as no other forces affect the system. At least one such law describes what happens when *no* evolutionary force is at work in a panmictic Mendelian population. This is the Hardy-Weinberg equilibrium law. This law describes an essential property—a property which is necessary for a population to be Mendelian. But, of course, such laws do not pick out *species'* essences. Perhaps essentialism can reemerge as a thesis, not about species, but about *kinds* of species. The natural state model arguably finds an application at that level of organization in that the Hardy-Weinberg zero-force state is distinguished from other possible population configurations.

The transposition of Aristotle's distinction is significant. The essentialist searched for a property *of individual organisms* which is invariant across the organisms in a species. The Hardy-Weinberg law and other more interesting population laws, on the other hand, identify properties of *populations* which are invariant across all populations of a certain kind. In this sense, essentialism pursued an individualistic (organismic) methodology, which population thinking supplants by specifying laws governing objects at a higher level of organization.[19] From the individualistic (organismic) perspective assumed by essentialism, species are real only if they can be delimited in terms of membership conditions applying to individual organisms. But the populationist point of view made possible by evolutionary theory made such reductionistic demands unnecessary. Since populations and their properties are subject to their own invariances and have their own causal efficacy, it is no more reasonable to demand a species definition in terms of the properties of constituent organisms than it is to require organismic biology to postpone its inquiries until a criterion for sameness of organism is formulated in terms of relations between constituent cells. Essentialism lost its grip when populations came to be thought of as real.[20] And the mark of this latter transformation in thought was the transposition of the search for invariances to a higher level of organization.[21]

Notes

Suggestions made by William Coleman, James Crow, Joan Kung, David Hull, Geoffrey Joseph, Steven Kimbrough, Richard Lewontin, Ernst Mayr, Terrence Penner, William Provine, Robert Stauffer, Dennis Stampe and Victor Hilts helped me considerably in writing this paper.

1. Mayr (1963) has argued additionally that essentialist errors continue to be made in population biology in the form of the distortions of "bean-bag genetics." The assumption that the fitness of single genes is independent of their genetic context is and has been known to be mistaken; but how this simplifying assumption is essentialist in character is obscure to me.

2. If species are *individuals*—spatiotemporally extended lineages—as Ghiselin (1966), (1969), (1974) and Hull (1976), (1978) have argued, then we have our assurance of finitude. If, on the other hand, species are kinds of things, which may in principle be found anywhere in the universe at any time, then a slightly different argument is needed for the claim that the same species is overwhelmingly unlikely to have evolved twice. Such an argument is provided by considering the way in which speciation depends on the coincidence of a huge number of initial conditions See Ayala (1978) for a summary of the received view of this matter.

3. I would suggest that quantum mechanical considerations show that the concept of being a nucleus with a particular atomic number is a vague one. Presumably, a collection of protons constitutes a nucleus when the strong force which causes them to attract each other overcomes their mutual electromagnetic repulsion. Whether this happens or not is a function of the distances between the protons. But *this* concept—that of "the" distance between particles—is indeterminate. Hence, the question of whether something is or is not a nucleus with a particular atomic number can only be answered probabilistically.

4. It is probably a mistake to talk about concepts being vague *simpliciter*. Rather, one should formulate matters in terms of concepts being vague relative to particular application. The issue of whether a concept is vague seems to reduce to the issue of whether there are cases in which it is indeterminate whether the concept applies or not. I would guess that practically every concept applying to physical objects is vague in this sense. Thus, even such concepts as "being two in number" are such that circumstances can be described in which it is indeterminate whether or not they apply to the objects in question. Degrees of vagueness can be partially defined as follows: If the set of circumstances in which concept P is indeterminate in its application is properly included in the set of circumstances in which concept Q is indeterminate, then Q is more vague than P.

5. Thus in his (1859), p. 52, Darwin says: "From these remarks it will be seen that I look at the term species, as one arbitrarily given for the sake of convenience to a set of individuals closely resembling each other, and that it does not essentially differ from the

term variety, which is given to less distinct and more fluctuating forms. The term variety, again, in comparson with mere individual differences, is also applied arbitrarily, and for mere convenience sake." Elsewhere in (1859) (e.g., pp. 432–33), Darwin espouses his perhaps more dominant populationist view that, in spite of line-drawing problems, species are real.

6. I am not arguing that Hull (1965) and others have misidentified the essence of essentialism and that their criticisms thereby fail to get to the heart of the matter. Essentialism, like most isms which evolve historically, probably does not even have an essence. Rather, I am trying to construe essentialism as a fairly flexible doctrine which, in at least some circumstances, can be seen to be quite consistent with the existence of insoluble line-drawing problems.

7. This characterization of Aristotle's view in terms of some information bearing entity is not completely anachronistic, as Delbrück (1971) points out when he (in jest) suggests that Aristotle should receive a Nobel Prize for having discovered DNA.

8. In this discussion of Aristotle's view of *terrata*, I have been much helped by Furth's (1975, section 11).

9. If one views Aristotle as excluding monstrous forms from membership in any species category, then one will have an extreme instance of this ad hoc strategy; *no* organism will belong to any species. Hull (1973, 39–40) sees Aristotle and scholastic science as hopelessly committed to this futile strategy. However, on the view I would attribute to Aristotle, most, if not all, monstrous forms are members of the species from which they arose. They, like Newtonian particles which fail to be at rest or in uniform motion, fail to achieve their natural states because of identifiable causal forces.

10. Hilts (1973, 209–210). My discussion of Quetelet and Galton in what follows leans heavily on Hilts (1973). It has a number of points in common with Hacking's (1975).

11. Boring (1929, 477) brings out the Aristotelian teleology contained in Quetelet's ideas quite well when he characterizes Quetelet as holding that "We might regard such human variation as if it occurred when nature aimed at an ideal and missed by varying amounts."

12. Although Galton found *The Origin of Species* an encouragement to pursue his own ideas, he indicates that his interest in variation and inheritance were of long standing. See Hilts (1973, 220).

13. In his *Hereditary Genius*, Galton compared the development of species with a many-faceted spheroid tumbling over from one facet or stable equilibrium to another. See Provine (1971, 14–15). This saltative process insured unity of type. In spite of Galton's adherence to the idea of discontinuous evolution and certain other essentialist predilections (Lewontin 1974, 4), his innovations in population thinking were antiessentialist in their consequences, or so I will argue.

14. Hilts (1973, 228). Walker (1929, 185) claims that the origin of the name "normal curve" is obscure. It occurs in Lexis and, she says, "it is not improbable that the term goes back to Quetelet." As natural and inevitable as Quetelet found his interpretation of the bell curve in terms of the Natural State Model, by the time Galton's *Natural Inheritance* appeared in 1889, there was growing sentiment that this interpretation was acceptable, if at all, only as a special case. Thus we find Galton, in that work (p. 58), saying that "the term Probable Error is absurd when applied to the subjects now in hand, such as Stature, Eye-colour, Artistic Faculty, or Disease." A year earlier, Venn, in his *The Logic of Chance* (p. 42), made a similar comment: "When we perform an operation ourselves with a clear consciousness of what we are aiming at, we may quite correctly speak of every deviation from this as being an error; but when Nature presents us with a group of objects of every kind, it is using a rather bold metaphor to speak in this case also of a law of error, as if she had been aiming at something all the time, and had like the rest

of us missed her mark more or less in every instance." Quotations are drawn from Walker (1929, 53).

15. It would be important to trace the development of statistical ideas from Galton through Pearson and his circle to R. A. Fisher, and to see whether Pearson's positivistic convictions had the effect of further proscribing the idea of types on the grounds that it is "unscientific." Cohen (1972) sees Galton as already adopting some positivistic attitudes in his idea that heredity was to be understood in terms of correlations, and not in terms of causal forces. Also, see Hacking's (1975) for a bold attempt to link Galton's innovations to other developments in nineteenth-century thought. I should point out that a fuller treatment of the emergence of population thinking would have to ascribe a central role to Mendel. He, much more than Galton, provided the central elements of our present conception of the relation of heredity and variation. I have stressed Galton, however, because of his interpretation of statistics and because of his view of the population as a unit of explanation.

16. The discussion of the norm of reaction in what follows depends heavily on some points made in Lewontin (1977).

17. This selectionist suggestion needs to be made more precise by specifying the notion of fitness used. I will not lay out these different conceptions here. Rather, I invite the reader to choose the one that he or she finds most plausible. The upshot of my argument does not seem to depend on which biologically plausible characterization is chosen.

18. Lewontin (1977, 11) has argued that the idea of a "natural phenotype" has been used in some hereditarian thinking in the IQ controversy. He quotes Herrnstein (1971, 54) as talking about "artificially boosting" an individual's IQ score. The presupposition seems to be that each human genotype has associated with it an IQ score (or range of such scores) which counts as its natural phenotype. As in Aristotle, the individual can be deflected from what is natural by environmental interference.

19. It is significant that biologists to this day tend to use "individual" and "organism" interchangeably. For arguments that populations, and even species, are to be construed as individuals, see Ghiselin (1966), (1969), (1974), and Hull (1976), (1978).

20. I borrow this way of putting matters from Hacking's (1975) in which he describes the series of transformations in thought which resulted in "chance becoming real."

21. The group selection controversy provides an interesting example of the question of whether, and in what respects, it is appropriate to view populations as objects. In some ways, this debate recapitulates elements of the dispute between methodological holism and methodological individualism in the social sciences. See Sober (1980c) for details.

References

Agassiz, L. (1859), *Essay on Classification*. Cambridge, Mass: Harvard University Press.

Ayala, F. (1978), "The Mechanisms of Evolution," *Scientific American 239*, 3 : 56–69.

Balme, D. (1962), "Development of Biology in Aristotle and Theophrastus: Theory of Spontaneous Generation," *Phronesis, 2*, 1 : 91–104.

Boring, E. (1929), *A History of Experimental Psychology*. New York: Appleton-Century-Crofts.

Buffon, L. (1749), *Histoire Naturelle*. Paris.

Cohen, R. (1972), "Francis Galton's Contribution to Genetics," *Journal of the History of Biology 5*, 2 : 389–412.

Darwin, C. (1859), *On the Origin of Species*. Cambridge, Mass.: Harvard University Press.

Darwin, C. (1868), *The Variation of Animals and Plants Under Domestication*. London: Murray.

Delbrück, M. (1971), "Aristotle-totle-totle," in Monod, J. and Borek, J. (eds), *Microbes and Life,*: 50–55. New York: Columbia University Press.

Eldredge, N. and Gould, S. (1972), "Punctuated Equilibria: an Alternative to Phyletic/ Gradualism," in T. Schopf (ed), *Models in Paleobiology*: 82–115. San Francisco: Freeman Cooper.

Furth, M. (1975), *Essence and Individual: Reconstruction of an Aristotelian Metaphysics*, chapter 11, duplicated for the meeting of the Society for Ancient Greek Philosophy, unpublished.

Ghiselin, M. (1966), "On Psychologism in the Logic of Taxonomic Controversies," *Systematic Zoology* 15 : 207–15.

Ghiselin, M. (1969), *The Triumph of the Darwinian Method*. Berkeley: University of California Press.

Ghiselin, M. (1974), "A Radical Solution to the Species Problem," *Systematic Zoology* 23 : 536–44.

Glass, B. (1959a), "Heredity and Variation in the Eighteenth Century Concept of the Species," in Glass, B., et al. (eds): *Forerunners of Darwin*: 144–72. Baltimore: The Johns Hopkins Press.

Glass, B. (1956b), "Maupertuis, Pioneer of Genetics and Evolution," in Glass, B., et al. (eds): *Forerunners of Darwin*: 51–83. Baltimore: The Johns Hopkins Press.

Hacking, I. (1975), "The Autonomy of Statistical Law," talk delivered to The American Philosophical Association, Pacific Division, unpublished.

Herrnstein, R. (1971), "IQ," *The Atlantic Monthly* 228 (3): 43–64.

Hilts, V. (1973), "Statistics and Social Science," in Giere, R. and Westfall, R. (eds.), *Foundations of Scientific Method in the Nineteenth Century*: 206–33. Bloomington: Indiana University Press.

Hull, D. (1965), "The Effect of Essentialism on Taxonomy: 2000 Years of Stasis," *British Journal for the Philosophy of Science* 15 : 314–16; 16 : 1–18.

Hull, D. (1967), "The Metaphysics of Evolution," *British Journal for the History of Science 3*, 12 : 309–37.

Hull, D. (1968), "The Conflict between Spontaneous Generation and Aristotle's Metaphysics." *Proceedings of the Seventh Inter-American Congress of Philosophy*, 2 (1968): 245–50. Quebec City: Les Presses de l'Université Laval.

Hull, D. (1973), *Darwin and his Critics*. Cambridge, Mass.: Harvard University Press.

Hull, D. (1976), "Are Species Really Individuals?" *Systematic Zoology* 25 : 174–91.

Hull, D. (1978), "A Matter of Individuality," *Philosophy of Science* 45 : 335–60.

Ihde, A. (1964), *The Development of Modern Chemistry*. New York: Harper & Row.

Kripke, S. (1972), "Naming and Necessity," in Davidson, D. and Harman, G. (eds.), *Semantics of Natural Languages*: 253–355; 763–9. Dordrecht: Reidel.

Kripke, S. (1978), "Time and Identity." Lectures given at Cornell University, unpublished.

Lewontin, R. (1974), *The Genetic Basis of Evolutionary Change*. New York: Columbia University Press.

Lewontin. R. (1977), "Biological Determinism as a Social Weapon" in the Ann Arbor Science for the People Editorial Collective: *Biology as a Social Weapon*: 6–20. Minneapolis Minnesota: Burgess.

Lloyd, G. (1968), *Aristotle: The Growth and Structure of His Thought*. Cambridge: Cambridge University Press.

Lovejoy, A. (1936), *The Great Chain of Being*. Cambridge, Mass. Harvard University Press.

Mayr, E. (1959), "Typological versus Population Thinking," in *Evolution and Anthropology: A Centennial Appraisal*: 409–12. Washington: The Anthropological Society of Washington; also in Mayr (1976): 26–9; page references to Mayr (1976).

Mayr, E. (1963), *Animal Species and Evolution*. Cambridge, Mass.: The Belknap Press of Harvard University Press.

Mayr, E. (1969), "The Biological Meaning of Species," *Biol. Journal of the Linnean Society* 1:311–20; also in Mayr (1976): 515–25; page references to Mayr (1976).

Mayr, E. (1976), *Evolution and the Diversity of Life*. Cambridge, Mass.: Harvard University Press.

Meyer, A. (1939), *The Rise of Embryology*. Stanford, Calif.: Stanford University Press.

Minkowski, H. (1908), "Space and Time" in Lorentz, H., Einstein, A., et al. *The Principle of Relativity*: 73–91. New York: Dover.

Popper, K. (1972), *Objective Knowledge*, Oxford: Oxford University Press.

Preuss, A. (1975), *Science and Philosophy in Aristotle's Biological Works*. New York: Georg Olms.

Provine, W. (1971), *The Origins of Theoretical Population Genetics*. Chicago: University of Chicago Press.

Putnam, H (1975), "The Meaning of 'Meaning'," *Mind, Language and Reality*: 215–71. Cambridge: Cambridge University Press.

Quetelet, A. (1842), *A Treatise on Man and the Development of his Faculties*, Edinburgh.

Quine (1953a), "Identity, Ostension, Hypostasis" in *From a Logical Point of View*: 65–79 New York: Harper Torchbooks.

Quine, W. (1953b), "Reference and Modality" in *From a Logical Point of View*: 139–59. New York: Harper Torchbooks

Quine, W. (1960), *Word and Object*. Cambridge, Mass: MIT Press.

Rabel, G. (1939), "Long Before Darwin: Linne's Views on the Origin of Species," *Discovery* N.S., 2:121–75.

Ramsbottom, J. (1938), "Linnaeus and the Species Concept." *Proceedings of the Linnean Society of London*: 192–219.

Roger, J. (1963), *Les Sciences de la Vie dans la Pensée Française du XVIII Siècle*. Paris: Armand Colin.

Sober, E. (1980a), "The Principle of Parsimony," *British Journal for Philosophy of Science*, forthcoming.

Sober, E. (1980b). "Realism and Independence," *Noûs*, forthcoming.

Sober, E. (1980c), "Significant Units and the Group Selection Controversy," *Proceedings of the Biennial Meeting of the Philosophy of Science Association*, forthcoming.

Todhunter, I. (1865), *History of the Theory of Probability to the Time of Laplace*. New York: Chelsea Publishing.

Walker, H. (1929), *Studies in the History of Statistical Method*. Baltimore: Williams & Wilkins.

Williams, G. C. (1975), *Sex and Evolution*. Princeton, New Jersey: Princeton University Press.

Wilson, E. and Bossert, W (1971), *A Primer of Population Biology*. Sunderland, Mass: Sinauer.

Chapter 13

A Radical Solution to the Species Problem

Michael T. Ghiselin

It would appear that the philosophy of taxonomy is about to undergo a major upheaval. Symptomatic is its Gordian knot, the species problem. Some years ago (Ghiselin 1966a) I attempted to cut it with the sword, casually remarking that, in the logical sense, species are individuals, not classes. So entrenched had the habit become of treating species as universals rather than as particular things, and their names as general rather than proper, that it took some time before this pronouncement was taken seriously. The position in question is hardly new. It goes back at least to Buffon, but I believe this was the first explicit use of it against what has been misleadingly called the nominalistic species concept. Even Ruse (1973), a philosopher who cites the foregoing work, passes the notion over in silence. On the other hand Hull (1974) has lately endorsed the idea that, from the point of view of evolutionary theory, biological species and monophyletic taxa are individuals. And Mayr (1969a), while not going so far, strongly emphasizes the point that species are more than just nominal classes. It would appear that the subject deserves further analysis and comment.

Philosophy

There are both advantages and disadvantages to treating species as individuals. This paper, however, only aims to show that such a position has attractive qualities from the point of view of logic and biology alike, and that it is perhaps not so radical as one might think. The basic point (Ghiselin 1969, 1974) is that multiplicity does not suffice to render an entity a mere class. In logic, "individual" is not a synonym for "organism." Rather, it means a particular thing. It can designate systems at various levels of integration. A human being is an individual in spite of being made up of atoms, molecules and cells. An individual, furthermore, need not be physically continuous. The United States of America is an individual in the class of national states, and this is true in spite of the interposition of Canadian territory and international waters between Alaska and the rest. (For a philosophical discussion of individuals see the book on that subject by Strawson 1959.)

It is characteristic of individuals that there cannot be instances of them. Thus, the class of national states has instances: the United States of America is a national state. We would not, however, say, "California is a United States of America." This is true in spite of the fact that we may treat any number of parts of the Union as a class, as when we say that these "states" are sovereign. California is a part of the United States of America.

Equally significant is that individuals do not have "intensions." That is to say, there are no properties necessary and sufficient to define their names. Of course, people, national states, and species do have properties, but these are not implied when we use the name. Much of the species problem has been the result of equivocal uses of species names as universal and proper. Thus, some biologists will never say "John Smith is a *Homo sapiens*," but insist that correct usage demands "John Smith is a specimen of *Homo sapiens*." In other words, some consider the taxonomic term to designate a class of people ("all men") others as a single thing ("humanity" or "the human race").

Some confusion, and indeed some continuing uncertainty upon the part of logicians, results from the fact that proper names can imply or suggest certain properties. It does not seem to me that this means that proper names really do have intensions, but perhaps some would disagree. A descriptive epithet facilitates communication and aids the memory. Consider, for example, *Phallus impudicus* Linnaeus, 1753. But let us not confound poetry with logic. Whether a name be apt or a misnomer is not the same question as what properties a thing must of logical necessity possess if the name is to be used.

As is well known, much confusion is avoided in dealing with such matters when one clearly distinguishes between categories and taxa. Taxonomic categories, in the sense of all taxa of a given rank, are like "national state": everybody agrees that these entities are classes. The point at issue is whether taxa are likewise classes, or whether, like California, they are individuals. It may be that some taxa (e.g., Mammalia) are classes, whereas particular species are individuals. In traditional analyses of the species problem, which presuppose that all taxa are classes, there has been some confusion over whether the names of categories should be defined so as to specify the defining properties of taxa. In the light of the present analysis, one would say that as particular species cannot have defining properties, the question is closed.

Biology

The most significant question for biologists is "Individual whats?" One answer is individual populations—in the sense of genetical populations (syngamea). These are breeding communities—composite wholes—not to be confused with classes of organisms sharing certain intrinsic genetical properties. Of course one has to add something, namely that they are reproductively isolated, to differentiate "species" from "subspecies" and other populational categories. This, the biological species definition, is adequate, but it is still affected by certain problems of interpretation and implication which suggest that a better way might be found to define this category. Some definitions, albeit technically sound, could use some improvement. "Gold," for example, could be unequivocally defined as the element with an atomic number of 79, but for most of us, this is not very informative.

One solution is to try to define the species and other categories in terms of the causes of evolution. This is one of the main reasons why the usual formulation of the biological species definition is so attractive. Gene flow and reproductive isolation obviously profoundly influence the properties of organisms. But might not something else be more important? One possibility is competition, including natural and sexual selection. Elsewhere (Ghiselin 1974) I have argued at some length, giving historical documentation, that biologists have misinterpreted the notion of competition and failed to appreciate its full significance. Ecological data have, to be sure, entered into the thinking of systematists, but nobody seems to have considered the possibility of defining categories in terms of modes of competition. Let us consider one possibility.

One can hardly deny that different kinds of competition occur between species and within them. Interspecifically we have the struggle for the means of existence only. Intraspecifically there occurs a competition with respect to genetical resources as well, and even the resources contended for by organisms irrespective of species in the final analysis are directed toward the intraspecific struggle for reproductive success. Species, then, are *the most extensive units in the natural economy such that reproductive competition occurs among their parts.* It would be circular, if perhaps not viciously so, to say that species and lower taxa are those entities within which intraspecific competition occurs. Some might object to the use of "reproductive" in the foregoing definition, but there seems to be no better alternative. By "reproductive competition" is meant a competition with respect to genetical resources as such, not just any competition involving reproduction.

Species are to evolutionary theory as firms are to economic theory. And organisms are productive units in both, competing in different ways within their larger units and with the parts of comparable units. Likewise some organisms exist autonomously—as asexual creatures and self-employed craftsmen. This analogy has its limitations, of course, not the least being that firms can reasonably be said to be adapted, while species cannot. Nonetheless the analogy can be shown to help resolve the paradoxes and conceptual difficulties that have so long plagued the subject.

Species are individuals, and they are real. They are as real as American Motors, Chrysler, Ford, and General Motors. If it be true that only individuals compete, then species as well as organisms can compete, just as corporations and craftsmen can. But clearly there exists a profound difference between two species competing, and competition between organisms belonging to different species.

Burma (1949) claimed that because species differ from moment to moment in geological history, they are, therefore, not the same, and hence that they are mere concepts without real existence in nature. This may be dismissed as merely a version of a paradox invented by Heraclitus (fragment LXXXI in the Loeb *Classical Library* edition): one cannot step in the same river twice. Who but a madman or a philosopher would maintain that he himself does not exist because he changes? Are we all figments of our own imaginations?

The rather forced dimensional-nondimensional dichotomy emphasized by Mayr (1963) is now seen to be irrelevant. Species need not be defined solely in relation to other species. "Species" is not a relational concept like "brother," but something comparable to "man." A firm is a firm because it forms a closed system of a given kind. It can compete with craftsmen and firms outside itself, and is characterized by a particular kind of internal organization. An only child cannot be a brother, but an economy might contain but a single firm.

The difficulties surrounding "potential interbreeding" become a dead issue too. If a species is an individual it hardly matters whether it is interbreeding at any given instant. All the "members" of a species are competing reproductively with all the others, irrespective of the distance between them or the existence of temporary spatial discontinuities between their component populations. Intraspecific competition is more perfect between organisms in close proximity, but the whole gene pool is nonetheless at issue. One should realize that all organisms, everywhere, like all the productive units in the world-wide political economy, are able to compete with one another to some degree. All can do that which diverts resources from the rest to themselves. They do so more or less intensely, or directly, or perfectly, and in diverse modes, but compete they do, and they can compete at a distance.

Some theorists have expressed the view that the existence of "different kinds" of species creates a problem for the biological species definition. Some have felt that there should be special categories (or kinds of categories) for designating these. The analogy with economics is particularly useful here. Differences in the range of divergence within species—as when some are monotypic, others polytypic—create no problem. After all, some corporations are like Mistsubishi, others like the local fish market, but both can be corporations. It has been most unfortunate in this context that niche theory has been so intimately bound up with the notion of species as classes, so that niches are conceived of as "abstractly inherited" attributes of sets of like organisms. Hence a typological conception of the niche could scarcely be avoided. It becomes easier to reason about such matters when one realizes that a craftsman or other organism makes his living in a sense distinct from that of operating within a sector or range of sectors of an economy. The economic activity of both can vary from time to time and place to place.

No paradox arises when a single factory constitutes the entirety of a firm. Likewise, some biologists wish to erect "agamospecies" for species-less organisms. It seems rather like creating imaginary firms for the self-employed. And no economist would ever erect "chronofirms" for the same firm at different times, although the name of a firm might be changed when it becomes reorganized.

Consider, too, the objection of Ehrlich and Raven (1969) to the biological species concept on the grounds that it overemphasizes integration and gene flow within species. Whether this be a valid criticism or not, it is circumvented by shifting the emphasis from integration and gene flow to the mode of competition. Firms are firms irrespectively of how tightly organized and closely integrated they may be, and they remain basic units of organization in spite of the fact that local productive units are important too. That limited exchange of genes may occur between species creates no more difficulty for the species concept than does the fact that someone might work for two firms creates difficulties for the notion of a firm. Gradual development of reproductive barriers creates intermediate conditions, but closed economic systems exist side by side with various stages in the formation and dissolution of trusts.

The morphological, genetical, and physiological species concepts suffer from a common fault. They treat composite wholes as if they were classes defined in terms of the intrinsic properties of their members. If one were to define "craftsman" in terms of the properties of cells in certain organisms, it might seem odd. Likewise, we are not interested in the properties of employees when we define "firm," but rather in the properties common to firms generally. The attributes of organisms are not defining of the names of social groups, in spite of the fact that social groups must have constituent organisms. That John Doe has a particular set of genes is about as relevant to his being a specimen of *Homo sapiens* L. as it is to his working for the manufacturers of Brand X. Hence I cannot agree with Mayr (1969a, 29) that the species "receives its reality from the historically evolved, shared information content of its gene pool." The species and the firm are "real" in the sense that they designate entities which exist: particular species and firms. And organisms are no more vessels for genes than they are vessels for industrial skills. Geneticists on the one hand, and employers on the other, may view them in such light; but the disadvantages to doing so should be obvious.

One problem with the "phenetic species concept" (see especially Sokal and Crovello 1970, Sneath and Sokal 1973) is that it treats species as classes defined in terms of the traits of organisms, rather than as individuals having the properties necessary and sufficient for membership in the species category. The pheneticists' position is that we should put things together according to their degree of resemblance. Yet, from the point of view of evolutionary theory, it is the causal nexus that matters. Of course, erecting classes on the basis of shared traits has its place, but this is not the issue. Some taxonomists may not care whether two organisms belong to different (cryptic) species, but it certainly matters to them. All banks are not the same when we are depositing money, no matter how much they look alike to us.

The realization that species are individuals helps us to understand some of the important daily activities of taxonomists. How, for example, do they define the names of species? If species were universals, then their names would have defining characters. The problem of there being much diversity within certain species has been solved in a rather makeshift fashion by considering them to be "disjunctively" or "polythetically" defined—to view them as "clusters" of similar objects, but without any one combination of properties being necessary and sufficient to qualify an entity for membership. But according to the view being examined here, species names are proper names—like American Motors. It is not only difficult, but logically impossible, to list the attributes necessary and sufficient to define their names. None such exist, and the only way to define these names is by an ostensive definition. That is to say, by "pointing" to the entity which bears the name. Much confusion about the role of nomenclatorial types has arisen because they are used in a peculiar kind of ostensive definition. Attention is drawn to only a part or aspect of the individual the name of which is being defined. This entity, the type specimen, is misinterpreted as an example of a class, which it is not. Likewise, the diagnosis, which in fact only "purports to differentiate the taxon," is often confused with a definition, which actually would differentiate it. It is as if one were to define "Mobil Oil Corporation" by pointing to a single service station.

The perplexing issues of the defining properties and ontological status of the categories lower than the species may be clarified in a similar vein. Subspecies are like local branches of a widespread industrial enterprise, but the degree of differentiation can hardly be so distinct as it is at the species level, for there can be all sorts and degrees of closure, and closure is not the same as differentiation. Nonetheless, subspecies may be expected to each have a characteristic local mode of competition, and what has been called their "reality" may be compared to that of any local productive unit. Yet as I have pointed out (Ghiselin 1966b) some lower categories do not refer to populations: the morph, the *forma sexualis*, the monstrosity, etc. These are strictly nominal classes, and for that reason are best left out of the hierarchy.

Are the taxa ranked at categorical levels higher than the species merely conceptual? The economic analogy here seems rather remote. Is the automobile industry real? One's answer depends upon his metaphysics, but at least industries have not the same ontological status as firms. Whatever answer is best, it may be worthwhile to explore the possibility of treating higher taxa as sectors of the natural economy. Inger (1958) suggests some thoughts along these lines for the genus, as have Gisin (1960) and Whittaker (1969) for the higher categories. On the other hand we should bear in mind the momentous difference between the natural and the political economy, in that a phylogenetic nexus is the inevitable consequence of the laws governing reproductive communities. Firms are established out of heterogeneous elements, ones not necessarily arising out of a common source. Be this as it may, the economy of nature is competitive from beginning to end, and assimilating so basic a process as competition into evolutionary classification might greatly strengthen the conceptual foundations of taxonomy.

History

One might wonder why all of this has not been self-evident for years on end. To give a full answer would require an extensive historical study, but the following suggestions may help.

Elsewhere (Ghiselin 1972) I have presented a theoretical scheme which attempts to explain scientific innovation. For the present discussion, three main features of this scheme need to be singled out. In the first place, dealing with a problem depends upon having an appropriate way of thinking about it. Method determines success. Second, an ability to invent or discover a new way of thinking largely is contingent upon some kind of input from without. This external input gives us the third point: discovery often involves interdisciplinary transfer. But this transfer of concepts and ways of thinking may be nonexistent, shallow, or profound, according to the habits and training of the scientists involved. For various reasons some fields of research and their practitioners are relatively open, others relatively closed, to the rest. It is partly a matter of personal situation, and partly a matter of innovative mentality that determines how a given scientist will behave in such respects.

The species problem has to do with biology, but it is fundamentally a philosophical problem—a matter for the "theory of universals." There are, so to speak, "different kinds of groups," and someone trained in logic should, one might think, long ago have stepped in and cleared up the confusion. Such is demonstrably not the case, for logicians ever since Aristotle, and even quite recently, have treated species as classes (e.g., Gregg 1950; Buck and Hull 1966; Lehman 1967; Ruse 1969, 1971). There may be quite a variety of reasons for this practice, but one significant point is that philosophers habitually seek only to erect internally consistent schemes. They have little to gain by attempting to discover how the living world really is organized, or how biologists in fact conceive of it. Hence although there has been much philosophizing *about* science, there has been little that truly deserves to be called the philosophy *of* science. The usual notions of logicians are adequate enough that these can be applied to scientific classification without breaking down. Something special was needed if logic were to cope with biology as it really is. This situation is unfortunate, for not only might philosophers have much to contribute, but they might learn something as well. Thus when Wittgenstein (1953, 32) wrote "'games' form a family," he should have realized that whatever it may be that they form, it is anything but a family. Poker does not copulate with Canasta or mourn for the passing of Whist. Of course, Wittgenstein wasn't talking about that; but this is just the point: he should have.

It seems curious that even Kant (1776, 1785), who made outstanding contributions to both science and philosophy, commented upon species and the views of Buffon, but contributed nothing of significance to the philosophy of taxonomy. Yet one must remember that neither Buffon nor Kant understood the competitive interactions that go on between species, between parts of different species, and within them. They, like all the pre-Darwinian biologists, had a teleological conception of the universe, featuring a harmonious and cooperative natural economy here on earth. Their world-view prevented biologists and philosophers alike from think-ing about species in terms other than "similarity and filiation" so that these groups almost had to be classes—analogous to defining "the Smith family" as that which resembles John Smith. No amount of study from this point of view would lead one to think in terms of natural selection, a process involving interactions between the organisms making up the group.

Only when Darwin, a geologist, transcended the limitations of the traditional way of thinking was the problem of specific transmutation possible. He reached beyond the limits of biology, to economics, and realized that evolution results from a reproductive competition between individual organisms. Hence the Darwinian revolution should be viewed as an ecological, and not as a taxonomic, revolution, in the sense that a new ecology implied a new systematics, not vice versa.

Yet Darwin's own outlook had significant limitations. He was so con-cerned with the transmutation of species that he gave insufficient emphasis to their origin. This led him to conceive of species more or less as open systems, rather than as closed systems. In his later years, he to some extent admitted this, and agreed that isolation, albeit not necessary for evolutionary change, is helpful in speciation (letters in F. Darwin, 1887: Vol. III, pp. 157–162). Confusion between these two processes continues to this day, especially in the writings of historians (see Ghiselin 1973). The problem becomes somewhat less difficult when one treats both species and organisms as individuals.

Biologists might have been able to understand the philosophical issues and hence to solve the species problem for themselves. However, the transfer of concepts across disciplinary boundaries from philosophy to biology proved shallow to say the least. In fact, the most elementary of philosophical notions became garbled. "Organism" was confounded with "particular" because, at least in part, "individual" had designated both. However, more may be involved than just an equivocation. When someone uses a notion borrowed from an unfamiliar field of experience, he tends to confuse it with a more familiar one which somewhat resembles it. An additional class of examples is available in what is sometimes called "psychologism in logic"—confusing logical concepts with psychological namesakes or analogues (Ghiselin 1966a).

The so-called "nominalistic species concept" is based on the idea that classes are not real, and if species are classes, it would follow that species are not real. One way of answering it is to deny the basic premise and affirm that classes are real. However, this is quite unnecessary, for species are individuals, and nominalists believe that individuals are real. The nominalistic species concept resulted from a garbled version of thirteenth-century philosophy. It is impressive to see how many biologists have supported it. To give a few examples: Bessey 1908; Britton 1908; Lotsy 1925; Burma 1949, 1954; Mason 1950; Thompson 1952; Davidson 1954; Cowan 1962. Rebuttals have taken various forms. One way of answering it has been to say that species are real in the sense that they are classes with members (Plate 1914, Turrill 1942, Gregg, 1950). A few have maintained a kind of idealism: to Agassiz (1857) species were thoughts of the Creator, which are real. Many biologists have conceived of species as individuals, but instead of putting it in these terms, they have merely said that they are not same kind of groups as classes are. Some have viewed them as phylogenetic units (e.g., Harper 1923; Hall 1926; Faegri 1937; Simpson 1951, 1961). Others have treated them as units of a genetical nature (e.g., Huxley 1940; Mayr 1940, 1957, 1963; Camp and Gilly 1943; Dobzhansky 1950; Carson 1957). Originally Dobzhansky (1935) treated them as classes of individuals, while Mayr treated them as classes of populations, but nonetheless the notion of a larger unit was there. Such genetical population concepts tended to grade into notions of species as classes of genetically similar individuals.

A more extreme variant of the biological species concept might be called the "organicist species concept." By this would be meant the notion that species are "superorganisms." It asserts that species have properties such as adaptation which do exist in organisms, but which have been attributed to the higher level systems mainly by false analogy. Organicism is an old notion, one closely associated with a vitalist doctrine called "holism" (for its history see Ghiselin 1974, 29–30), which treats the generality of classes as if they were composite wholes: as "aggregates" or individuals. This view carries strong teleological implications, for if species are presupposed to be cooperative units like organisms, then their component organisms would not compete, but would do things "for the good of the species." Holism strongly influenced Emerson (1938) and other systematists and ecologists of the Chicago school, and is particularly evident in the later writings of Du Rietz (1930). It is largely responsible for the group selectionist notions of many evolutionists (e.g., Darlington 1940). Indeed, one can find a strong trace of it in the writings of those who certainly would not endorse the organicist species concept were it formulated in explicit terms.

One good line of evidence suggesting that holism has been influential is the degree to which intraspecific competition has been deemphasized in favor of supposed advantages (often, but not always, to the species) of maintaining populational integrity and specific distinctness. In his well-known book on species Mayr (1963) strongly deemphasized sexual selection in favor of isolating mechanisms in explaining sexual dimorphism. Lately (Mayr 1972) he has changed the emphasis to a considerable extent, but some of us would feel that he has not gone far enough (Ghiselin 1974). Likewise, we find Mayr (1969b, 316) saying "The division of the total genetic variability of nature into discrete packages, the so-called species, which are separated from each other by reproductive barriers prevents the production of too great a number of disharmonious incompatible gene combinations." This could be interpreted as merely a by-product, rather than a function or reason for existence, of species. But one might wonder about the following (Mayr 1969b, 318) *"Species are the real units of evolution, they are the entities which specialize, which become adapted, or which shift their adaptation."* Species are units, and they have evolutionary importance, but the same may be said of organisms. Doubtless both organisms and species specialize. And probably organisms become adapted but species do not, except in so far as they consist of adapted organisms. Such ambiguities represent a transitional stage in our growing appreciation of what the two levels mean. We are experiencing a rapid and fundamental restructuring of our basic concepts.

Discussion

The species problem has thus involved difficulties in understanding the ontological status of fundamental biological units, and failure to interrelate levels of integration in the appropriate manner. The reason why the economic analogies have so much heuristical value is that we find it much easier to think of firms as individuals. For this very reason a host of biological problems are more readily soluble if one learns to think like an economist. In addition we should note that we often fail to solve our problems because we cannot even identify them. Under such circumstances, conceptual investigations do more than just help. They are the only way out.

Acknowledgments

For comments on drafts of the manuscript, I am grateful to Theodosius Dobzhansky, Patrick M. Gaffney, David L. Hull, Ernst Mayr, David Wake and Leigh Van Valen. Support was provided by N.S.F. Grant GS 33491.

References

Agassiz, L. 1857. Essay on classification. Reprint 1962, E. Lurie (Ed.). Cambridge: Harvard University Press.

Bessey, C. E. 1908. The taxonomic aspect of the species question. Amer. Nat. 42:218–224.

Britton, N. L. 1908. The taxonomic aspect of the species question. Amer. Nat. 42:224–242.

Buck, R. C., and D. L. Hull. 1966. The logical structure of the Linnaean hierarchy. Syst Zool. 15:97–111.

Burma, B. 1949. The species concept: a semantic review. Evolution 3:369–370.

Burma, B. H. 1954. Reality, existence, and classification: a discussion of the species problem. Madroño 127:193–209.

Camp, W. H., and C. L. Gilly. 1943. The structure and origin of species with a discussion of intraspecific variability and related nomenclatural problems. Brittonia 4:323–385.

Carson, H. L. 1957. The species as a field for gene recombination. *In*: E. Mayr (Ed.), The species problem. Washington: A.A.A.S. Pp. 23–38.

Cowan, S. T. 1962. The microbia species—a macromyth? Symp. Soc. Gen. Microbiol. 12:433–455.

Darlington, C. D. 1940. Taxonomic species and genetic systems. *In*: J. S. Huxley (Ed.), The new systematics. Oxford: University Press. Pp. 137–160.

Darwin, F. 1887. The life and letters of Charles Darwin, including an autobiographical chapter. Vol. III.

Davidson, J. F. 1954. A dephlogisticated species concept. Madroño 12:246–251.

Dobzhansky, Th. 1935. A critique of the species concept in biology. Phil. Sci. 2:344–355.

Dobzhansky, Th. 1950. Mendelian populations and their evolution. Amer. Nat. 84:401–418.

Du Rietz, G. E. 1930. The fundamental units of biological taxonomy. Svensk Bot. Tidskr. 24:333–428.

Ehrlich, P. R., and P. H. Raven. 1969. Differentiation of populations. Science 165:1228–1231.

Emerson, A. E. 1938. The origin of species. Ecology 19:152–154.

Faegri, K. 1937. Some fundamental problems of taxonomy and phylogenetics. Bot. Rev. 3:400–423.

Ghiselin, M. T. 1966a. On psychologism in the logic of taxonomic controversies. Syst. Zool. 26:207–215.

Ghiselin, M. T. 1966b. On some taxonomic categories which have been proposed for the classification of large gastropod genera. Veliger 9:141–144.

Ghiselin, M. T. 1969. The triumph of the Darwinian method. Berkeley: University of California Press.

Ghiselin, M. T. 1972. The individual in the Darwinian revolution. New Lit. Hist. 113–134.

Ghiselin, M. T. 1973. Mr. Darwin's Critics, old and new. J. Hist. Biol. 6:155–165.

Ghiselin, M. T. 1974. The economy of nature and the evolution of sex. Berkeley: University of California Press.

Gisin, H. 1966. Signification des modalités de l'évolution pour la théorie de la systématique. Z. Zool. Syst. Evol. 4:1–12.

Gregg, J. R. 1950. Taxonomy, language and reality. Amer. Nat. 84:419–435.

Hall, H. M. 1926. The taxonomic treatment of units smaller than species. Proc. Int. Congr. Plant Sci. Ithaca 2:1461–1468.

Harper, R. A. 1923. The species concept from the point of view of a morphologist. Amer. J. Bot. 10:229–233.

Hull, D. L. 1974. Philosophy of Biological Science. Englewood Cliffs: Prentice-Hall.

Huxley, J. S. 1940. Towards the new systematics. In: J. S. Huxley (Ed.), The new systematics. Oxford: University Press. Pp. 1–46.

Inger, R. F. 1958. Comments on the definition of genera. Evolution 12:370–384.

Kant, I. 1776. Von den verschiedenen Rassen der Menschen. Reprinted in K. Vorländer (Ed.), 1922, Immanuel Kant: vermischte Schriften. Leipzig: Felix Meiner. Pp. 79–98.

Kant, I. 1785. Bestimmung des Begriffs einer Menschenrasse. Reprinted in K. Vorländer (Ed.), 1922. Immanuel Kant: vermischte Schriften. Leipzig: Felix Meiner. Pp. 111–127.

Lehman, H. 1967. Are biological species real? Phil. Sci. 34:157–167.

Lotsy, J. P. 1925. Species or Linneon. Genetica 7:487–506.

Mason, H. L. 1950. Taxonomy, systematic botany and biosystematics. Madroño 10:193–208.

Mayr, E. 1940. Speciation phenomena in birds. Amer. Nat. 74:249–278.

Mayr, E. 1957. Difficulties and importance of the biological species concept. In: E. Mayr (Ed.), The species problem. Washington: A.A.A.S. Pp. 371–388.

Mayr, E. 1963. Animal species and evolution. Cambridge: Harvard University Press.

Mayr, E. 1969a. Principles of systematic zoology. New York: McGraw-Hill.

Mayr, E. 1969b. The biological meaning of species. Biol. J. Linn. Soc. 1:311–320.

Mayr, E. 1972. Sexual selection and natural selection. In: B. G. Campbell (Ed.), Sexual selection and The Descent of Man 1871–1971. Chicago: Aldine. Pp. 87–104.

Plate, L. 1914. Prinzipien der Systematik mit besonderer Berücksichtigung des Systems der Tiere. In: P. Hinneberg (Ed.), Die Kultur der Gegenwart, (3:4) 4:92–164.

Ruse, M. 1969. Definitions of species in biology. Brit. J. Phil. Sci. 20:97–119.

Ruse, M. 1971. The species problem: a reply to Hull. Brit. J. Phil. 22:369–371.

Ruse, M. 1973. The philosophy of biology. London: Hutchinson University Library.

Simpson, G. G. 1951. The species concept. Evolution 5:285–298.

Simpson, G. G. 1961. Principles of animal taxonomy. New York: Columbia University Press.

Sneath, P. H. A., and R. R. Sokal. 1973. Numerical taxonomy: the principles and practice of numerical classification. San Francisco: W. H. Freeman.

Sokal, R. R., and T. J. Crovello. 1970. The biological species concept: a critical evalution. Amer. Nat. 104:127–153.

Strawson, P. F. 1959. Individuals: an essay on descriptive metaphysics. London: Methuen.

Thompson, W. R. 1952. The philosophical foundations of systematics. Canad. Entomol. 84:1–16.

Turrill, W. B. 1942. Taxonomy and phylogeny. Bot. Rev. 8:247–270, 473–532, 655–707.

Whittaker, R. H. 1969. New concepts of kingdoms of organisms. Science 163:150–160.

Wittgenstein, L. 1958. Philosophical investigations. Second ed. New York: Macmillan.

Chapter 14
A Matter of Individuality
David L. Hull

The terms "gene," "organism," and "species" have been used in a wide variety of ways in a wide variety of contexts. Anyone who attempts merely to map this diversity is presented with a massive and probably pointless task. In this paper I consciously ignore "the ordinary uses" of these terms, whatever they might be, and concentrate on their biological uses. Even within biology, the variation and conflicts in meaning are sufficiently extensive to immobilize all but the most ambitious ordinary language philosopher. Thus, I have narrowed my focus even further to concentrate on the role which these terms play in evolutionary biology. In doing so, I do not mean to imply that this usage is primary or that all other biological uses which conflict with it are mistaken. Possibly evolutionary theory is *the* fundamental theory in biology, and all other biological theories must be brought into accord with it. Possibly all biological theories including evolutionary theory, eventually will be reduced to physics and chemistry. But regardless of the answers to these global questions, at the very least, various versions of evolutionary theory are sufficiently important in biology to warrant an investigation of the implications which they have for the biological entities which they concern.

Genes are the entities which are passed on in reproduction and which control the ontogenetic development of the organism. Organisms are the complex systems which anatomists, physiologists, embryologists, histologists, etc. analyze into their component parts. Species have been treated traditionally as the basic units of classification, the natural kinds of the living world, comparable to the physical elements. But these entities also function in the evolutionary process. Evolution consists in two processes (mutation and selection) which eventuate in a third (evolution). Genes provide the heritable variation required by the evolutionary process. Traditionally organisms have been viewed as the primary focus of selection, although considerable disagreement currently exists over the levels at which selection takes place. Some biologists maintain that selection occurs exclusively at the level of genes; others that supragenic, even supraorganismic units can also be selected. As one might gather from the title of Darwin's book, species are the things which are supposed to evolve.

Whether the relatively large units recognized by taxonomists as species evolve or whether much less extensive units such as populations are the effective units of evolution is an open question. In this paper when I use the term "species," I intend to refer to those supraorganismic entities which evolve regardless of how extensive they might turn out to be.

The purpose of this paper is to explore the implications which evolutionary theory has for the ontological status of genes, organisms and species. The only category distinction I discuss is between individuals and classes. By "individuals" I mean spatiotemporally localized cohesive and continuous entities (historical entities). By "classes" I intend spatiotemporal unrestricted classes, the sorts of things which can function in traditionally-defined laws of nature. The contrast is between Mars and planets, the Weald and geological strata, between Gargantua and organisms. The terms used to mark this distinction are not important, the distinction is. For example, one might distinguish two sorts of sets: those that are defined in terms of a spatiotemporal relation to a spatiotemporally localized focus and those that are not. On this view, historical entities such as Gargantua become sets. But they are sets of a very special kind—sets defined in terms of a spatiotemporal relation to a spatiotemporally localized focus. Gargantua, for instance, would be the set of all cells descended from the zygote which gave rise to Gargantua.

The reason for distinguishing between historical entities and genuine classes is the differing roles which each plays in science according to traditional analyses of scientific laws. Scientific laws are supposed to be spatiotemporally unrestricted generalizations. No uneliminable reference can be made in a genuine law of nature to a spatiotemporally individuated entity. To be sure, the distinction between accidentally true generalizations (such as all terrestrial organisms using the same genetic code) and genuine laws of nature (such as those enshrined in contemporary versions of celestial mechanics) is not easy to make. Nor are matters helped much by the tremendous emphasis placed on laws in traditional philosophies of science, as if they were the be-all and end-all of science. Nevertheless, I find the distinction between those generalizations that are spatiotemporally unrestricted and those that are not fundamental to our current understanding of science. Whether one calls the former "laws" and the latter something else, or whether one terms both sorts of statements "laws" is of little consequence. The point I wish to argue is that genes, organisms *and* species, as they function in the evolutionary process, are necessarily spatiotemporally localized individuals. They could not perform the functions which they perform if they were not.

The argument presented in this paper is metaphysical, not epistemological. Epistemologically red light may be fundamentally different from infrared light and mammals from amoebae. Most human beings can see with red light and not infrared light. Most people can see mammals; few if any can see amoebae with the naked eye. Metaphysically they are no different. Scientists know as much about one as the other. Given our relative size, period of duration, and perceptual acuity, organisms appear to be historical entities, species appear to be classes of some sort, and genes cannot be seen at all. However, after acquainting oneself with the various entities which biologists count as organisms and the roles which organisms and species play in the evolutionary process, one realizes exactly how problematic our commonsense notions actually are. The distinction between an organism and a colony is not sharp. If an organism is the "total product of the development of the impregnated embryo," then as far back as 1899, T. H. Huxley was forced to conclude that the medusa set free from a hydrozoan "are as much organs of the latter, as the multitudinous pinnules of a *Comatula*, with their genital glands, are organs of the Echinoderm. Morphologically, therefore, the equivalent of the individual Comatula is the Hydrozoic stock and all the Medusae which proceed from it" (24). More recently, Daniel Janzen (25) has remarked that the "study of dandelion ecology and evolution suffers from confusion of the layman's 'individual' with the 'individual' of evolutionary biology. The latter individual has 'reproductive fitness' and is the unit of selection in most evolutionary conceptualizations" (see also 2). According to evolutionists, units of selection, whether they be single genes, chromosomes, organisms, colonies, or kinship groups are individuals. In this paper I intend to extend this analysis to units of evolution.

If the ontological status of space-time in relativity theory is philosophically interesting in and of itself (and God knows enough philosophers have written on that topic), then the ontological status of species in evolutionary theory should also be sufficiently interesting philosophically to discuss without any additional justification. However, additional justification does exist. From Socrates and Plato to Kripke and Putnam, organisms have been paradigm examples of primary substances, particulars and/or individuals, while species have served as paradigm examples of secondary substances, universals, and/or classes. I do not think that this paper has any necessary implications for various solutions to the problem of universals, identity and the like. However, if the main contention of this paper is correct, if species are as much spatiotemporally localized individuals as organisms, then some of the confusion among philosophers over these issues is understandable. One of the commonest examples used in the philosophical literature is inappropriate. Regardless of whether one thinks that "Moses" is a proper name, a cluster concept or a rigid designator, "*Homo sapiens*" must be treated in the same way.

The Evolutionary Justification

Beginning with the highly original work of Michael Ghiselin (12, 13, 14), biologists in increasing numbers are beginning to argue that species as units of evolution are historical entities (15, 20, 21, 22, 23, 34, 38). The justification for such claims would be easier if there were one set of propositions (presented preferably in axiomatic form) which could be termed *the* theory of evolution. Unfortunately, there is not. Instead there are several, incomplete, partially incompatible versions of evolutionary theory currently extant. I do not take this state of affairs to be unusual, especially in periods of rapid theoretical change. In general the myth that some one set of propositions exists which can be designated unequivocally as Newtonian theory, relativity theory, etc. is an artifact introduced by lack of attention to historical development and unconcern with the primary literature of science. The only place one can find *the* version of a theory is in a textbook written long after the theory has ceased being of any theoretical interest to scientists.

In this section I set out what it is about the evolutionary process which results in species being historical entities, not spatiotemporally unrestricted classes. In doing so I have not attempted to paper over the disagreements which currently divide biologists working on evolutionary theory. For example, some disagreement exists over how abruptly evolution can occur. Some biologists have argued that evolution takes place saltatively, in relatively large steps. Extreme saltationists once claimed that in the space of a single generation new species can arise which are so different from all other species that they have to be placed in new genera, families, classes, etc. No contemporary biologist to my knowledge currently holds this view. Extreme gradualists, on the other side, argue that speciation *always* occurs very slowly, over periods of hundreds of generations, either by means of a single species changing into a new species (phyletic evolution) or else by splitting into two large subgroups which gradually diverge (speciation). No contemporary biologist holds this view either. Even the most enthusiastic gradualists admit that new species can arise in a single generation, e.g., by means of polyploidy. In addition, Eldredge and Gould (11), building on Mayr's founder principle (36), (37), have recently argued that speciation typically involves small, peripheral isolates which develop quite rapidly into new species. Speciation is a process of "punctuated equilibria."

However, the major dispute among contemporary evolutionary theorists is the level (or levels) at which selection operates. Does selection occur *only* and *literally* at the level of genes? Does selection take place *exclusively* at the level of organisms, the selection of genes being only a consequence of the selection of organisms? Can selection also take place at levels of organization more inclusive than the individual organism, e.g., at the level of kinship groups, populations and possibly even entire species? Biologists can be found opting for every single permutation of the answers to the preceding questions. I do not propose to go through all the arguments which are presented to support these various conclusions. For my purposes it is sufficient to show that the points of dispute are precisely those which one might expect if species are being interpreted as historical entities, rather than as spatiotemporally unrestricted classes. Richard Dawkins puts the crucial issue as follows:

> Natural selection in its most general form means the differential survival of entities. Some entities live and others die but, in order for this selective death to have any impact on the world, an additional condition must be met. Each entity must exist in the form of lots of copies, and at least some of the entities must be *potentially* capable of surviving—in the form of copies—for a significant period of evolutionary time. (8, p. 35)

The results of evolution by natural selection are *copies* of the entities being selected, not *sets*. Elements in a set must be characterized by one or more common characteristics. Even fuzzy sets must be characterized by at least a "cluster" of traits. Copies need not be.[1] A particular gene is a spatiotemporally localized individual which either may or may not replicate itself. In replication the DNA molecule splits down the middle producing two new molecules composed *physically* of half of the parent molecule while *largely* retaining its structure. In this way genes form lineages, ancestor-descendant copies of some original molecule. The relevant genetic units in evolution are not *sets* of genes defined in terms of structural similarity but lineages formed by the imperfect copying process of replication.[2] Genes can belong to the same lineage even though they are structurally different from other genes in that lineage. What is more, continued changes in structure can take place indefinitely. If evolution is to occur, not only can such indefinite structural variation take place within gene lineages but also it must. Single genes are historical entities, existing for short periods of time. The more important notion is that of a *gene lineage*. Gene lineages are also historical entities persisting while changing indefinitely through time. As Dawkins puts this point:

> Genes, like diamonds, are forever, but not quite in the same way as diamonds. It is an individual diamond crystal which lasts, as an unaltered pattern of atoms. DNA molecules don't have that kind of permanence. The life of any one physical DNA molecule is quite short—perhaps a matter of months, certainly not more than one lifetime. But a DNA molecule could theoretically live on in the form of *copies* of itself for a hundred million years. (8, p. 36)

Exactly the same observations can be made with respect to organisms. A particular organism is a spatiotemporally localized individual which either may or may not reproduce itself. In asexual reproduction, part of the parent organism buds off to produce new individuals. The division can be reasonably equitable as in binary fission or else extremely inequitable as in various forms of parthenogenesis. In sexual reproduction gametes are produced which unite to form new individuals. Like genes, organisms form lineages. The relevant organismal units in evolution are not sets of organisms defined in terms of structural similarity but lineages formed by the imperfect copying processes of reproduction. Organisms can belong to the same lineage even though they are structurally different from other organisms in that lineage. What is more, continued changes in structure can take place indefinitely. If evolution is to occur, not only can such indefinite structural variation take place within organism lineages but also it must. Single organisms are historical entities, existing for short periods of time. Organism lineages are also historical entities persisting while changing indefinitely through time.

Both replication and reproduction are spatiotemporally localized processes. There is no replication or reproduction at a distance. Spatiotemporal continuity through time is required. Which entities at which levels of organization are sufficiently cohesive to function as units of selection is more problematic. Dawkins presents one view:

> In sexually reproducing species, the individual [the organism] is too large and too temporary a genetic unit to qualify as a significant unit of natural selection. The group of individuals is an even larger unit. Genetically speaking, individuals and groups are like clouds in the sky or dust-storms in the desert. They are temporary aggregates of federations. They are not stable through evolutionary time. Populations may last a long while, but they are constantly blending with other populations and so losing their identity. They are subject to evolutionary change from within. A population is not a discrete enough entity to be a unit of natural selection, not stable and unitary enough to be 'selected' in preference to another population. (8, p. 37)

From a commonsense perspective, organisms are paradigms of tightly organized, hierarchically stratified systems. Kinship groups such as hives also seem to be internally cohesive entities. Populations and species are not. Dawkins argues that neither organisms (in sexually reproducing species) nor populations in any species are sufficiently permanent and cohesive to function as units in selection. In asexual species, organisms do not differ all that much from genes. They subdivide in much the same way that genes do, resulting in progeny which are identical (or nearly identical) with them. In sexual species, however, organisms must pool their genes to reproduce.

The resulting progeny contain a combined sample of parental genes. Populations lack even this much cohesion.

Other biologists are willing to countenance selection at levels more inclusive than the individual gene, possibly parts of chromosomes, whole chromosomes, entire organisms or even kinship groups (32). The issues, both empirical and conceptual are not simple. For example, G. C. Williams in his classic work (61) argues that selection occurs only at the level of individuals. By "individual" biologists usually mean "organism." However, when Williams is forced to admit that kinship groups can also function as units of selection, he promptly dubs them "individuals." One of the commonest objections to E. O. Wilson's (62) equally classic discussion of evolution is that he treats kin selection as a special case of group selection. According to the group selectionists, entities more inclusive than kinship groups can also function as units of selection (63).[3] Matters are not improved much by vagueness over what is meant by "units of selection." Gene frequencies are certainly altered from generation to generation, but so are genotype frequencies. Genes cannot be selected in isolation. They depend on the success of the organism which contains them for their survival. Most biologists admit that similar observations hold for certain kinship groups. Few are willing to extend this line of reasoning to include populations and entire species.

As inconclusive as the dispute over the level(s) at which selection takes place is, the points at issue are instructive. In arguing that neither organisms nor populations function as units of selection in the same sense that genes do, Dawkins does not complain that the cells in an organism or the organisms in a population are phenotypically quite diverse, though they frequently are. Rather he denigrates their cohesiveness and continuity through time, criteria which are relevant to individuating historical entities, not spatiotemporally unrestricted classes. Difficulties about the level(s) at which selection can operate to one side, the issue with which we are concerned is the ontological status of species. Even if entire species are not sufficiently well integrated to function as units of selection, they are the entities which evolve as a result of selection at lower levels. The requirements of selection at these lower levels place constraints on the manner in which species can be conceptualized. Species as the results of selection are necessarily lineages, not sets of similar organisms. In order for differences in gene frequencies to build up in populations, continuity through time must be maintained. To some extent genes in sexual species are reassorted each generation, but the organisms which make up populations cannot be. To put the point in the opposite way, if such shuffling of organisms were to take place, selection would be impossible.

The preceding characteristic of species as evolutionary lineages by itself is sufficient to preclude species being conceptualized as spatiotemporally unrestricted sets or classes. However, if Eldredge and Gould are right, the case for interpreting species as historical entities is even stronger. They ask why species are so coherent, why groups of relatively independent local populations continue to display fairly consistent, recognizable phenotypes, and why reproductive isolation does not arise in every local population if gene flow is the only means of preventing differentiation:

> The answer probably lies in a view of species and individuals [organisms] as homeostatic systems—as amazingly well-buffered to resist change and maintain stability in the face of disturbing influences ... In this view, the importance of peripheral isolates lies in their small size and the alien environment beyond the species border that they inhabit—for only here are selective pressures strong enough and the inertia of large numbers sufficiently reduced to produce the "genetic revolution" (Mayr 1963, p. 533) that overcomes homeostasis. The coherence of a species, therefore, is not maintained by interaction among its members (gene flow). It emerges, rather, as an historical consequence of the species' origin as a peripherally isolated population that acquired its own powerful homeostatic system. (11, p. 114)

Eldredge and Gould argue that, from a theoretical point of view, species appear so amorphous because of a combination of the gradualistic interpretation of speciation and the belief that gene exchange is the chief (or only) mechanism by which cohesion is maintained in natural populations. However, in the field, species of both sexual and asexual organisms seem amazingly coherent and unitary. If gene flow were the only mechanism for the maintenance of evolutionary unity, asexual species should be as diffuse as dust-storms in the desert. According to Eldredge and Gould, new species arise through the budding off of peripheral isolates which succeed in establishing new equilibria in novel environments. Thereafter they remain largely unchanged during the course of their existence and survive only as long as they maintain this equilibrium.

Another possibility is that evolutionary unity is maintained by both internal and external means. Gene flow and homeostasis within a species are internal mechanisms of evolutionary unity. Perhaps the external environment in the form of unitary selection pressures also contributes to the integrity of the entities which are evolving (10). For example, Jews have remained relatively distinct from the rest of humankind for centuries, in part by internal means (selective mating, social customs, etc.) but also in part by external means (discrimination, prejudice, laws, etc). An ecological niche is a relation between a particular species and key environmental variables. A different species in conjunction with the same environmental variables could define quite a different niche. In the past biologists have tended to play down the integrating effect of the environment, attributing whatever unity and coherence which exists in nature to the integrating effect of gene complexes. At the very least, if the coherence of asexual species is not illusory, mechanisms other than gene flow must be capable of bringing about evolutionary unity.

Individuating Organisms and Species

By and large, the criteria which biologists use to individuate organisms are the same as those suggested by philosophers—spatiotemporal continuity, unity and location. Differences between these two analyses have three sources: first, philosophers have been most interested in individuating persons, the hardest case of all, while biologists have been content to individuate organisms; second, when philosophers have discussed the individuation of organisms, they have usually limited themselves to adult mammals, while biologists have attempted to develop a notion of organism adequate to handle the wide variety of organisms which exist in nature; and finally, philosophers have felt free to resort to hypothetical, science fiction examples to test their conceptions, while biologists rely on actual cases. In each instance, I prefer the biologists' strategy. A clear notion of an individual organism seems an absolute prerequisite for any adequate notion of a person, and this notion should be applicable to all organisms, not just a minuscule fraction. But most importantly, real examples tend to be much more detailed and bizarre than those made up by philosophers. Too often the example is constructed for the sole purpose of supporting the preconceived intuitions of the philosophers and has no life of its own. It cannot force the philosopher to improve his analysis the way that real examples can. Biologists are in the fortunate position of being able to test their analyses against a large stock of extremely difficult, extensively documented actual cases.

Phenotypic similarity is irrelevant in the individuation of organisms. Identical twins do not become one organism simply because they are phenotypically indistinguishable. Conversely, an organism can undergo massive phenotypic change while remaining the same organism. The stages in the life cycles of various species of organisms frequently are so different that biologists have placed them in different species, genera, families and even classes—until the continuity of the organism was discovered. If a caterpillar develops into a butterfly, these apparently different organisms are stages in the life cycle of a single organism regardless of how dissimilar they might happen to be (see figure 14.1a). In ontogenetic development, a single lineage is never divided successively in time into separate organisms. Some sort of splitting is required. In certain cases, such as transverse fission in paramecia, a single organism splits equally into two new organisms (see figure 14.1b). In such cases, the parent organism no longer exists, and

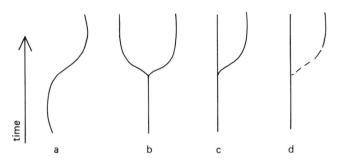

Figure 14.1
Diagrams which can be interpreted alternately as organisms undergoing ontogenetic change and the production of new organisms and as species undergoing phylogenetic change and speciation.

the daughter organisms are two new individuals. Sometimes a single individual will bud off other individuals which are roughly its own size but somewhat different in appearance, e.g., strobilization in certain forms of Scyphozoa (see figure 14.1c). At the other extreme, sometimes a small portion of the parent organism buds off to form a new individual, e.g., budding in Hydrozoa (see figure 14.1d). In the latter two cases, the parent organism continues to exist while budding off new individuals. The relevant consideration is how much of the parent organism is lost and its internal organization disrupted.

Fusion also takes place at the level of individual organisms. For example, when presented with a prey too large for a single individual to digest, two amoebae will fuse cytoplasmically in order to engulf and digest it. However, the nuclei remain distinct and the two organisms later separate, genetically unchanged. The commonest example of true fusion occurs when germ cells unite to form a zygote. In such cases, the germ cells as individuals cease to exist and are replaced by a new individual (see figure 14.2a). Sometimes one organism will invade another and become part of it. Initially, these organisms, even when they become obligate parasites, are conceived of as separate organisms, but sometimes they can become genuine parts of the host organism. For example, one theory of the origin of certain cell organelles is that they began as parasites. Blood transfusions are an unproblematic case of part of one organism becoming part of another; conjugation is another (see figure 14.2b). Sometimes parts of two different organisms can merge to form a third. Again, sexual reproduction is the commonest example of such an occurence (see figure 14.2c). In each of these cases, organisms are individuated on the basis of the amount of material involved and the effect of the change on the internal organization of the organisms. For example, after conjugation two paramecia are still

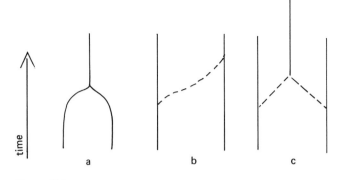

Figure 14.2
Diagrams which can be interpreted alternately as organisms merging totally or partially to give rise to new organisms and as species merging totally or partially to give rise to new species.

two organisms and the same two organisms even though they have exchanged some of their genetic material.

If species are historical entities, then the same sorts of considerations which apply in the individuation of organisms should also apply to them, and they do (35). The only apparent discrepancy results from the fact that not all biologists have been totally successful in throwing off the old preevolutionary view of species as classes of similar organisms and replacing it with a truly evolutionary view. However, even these discrepancies are extremely instructive. For example, G. G. Simpson (50) maintains that a single lineage which changes extensively through time without speciating (splitting) should be divided into separate species (see figure 14.1a). Willi Hennig (17) disagrees: new species should be recognized only upon splitting. This particular debate has been involved, touching upon both conceptual and empirical issues. For example, how can a gradually evolving lineage be divided into discrete species in an objective, nonarbitrary way? Are later organisms considered to belong to different species from their ancestors because they are sufficiently dissimilar or because they can no longer interbreed with them even if they coexisted? Can such extensive change take place in the absence of speciation?

I cannot attempt to answer fully all of these questions here. Instead, I must limit myself to the remark that, on Simpson's view, species and organisms are quite different sorts of things. An organism undergoes limited change, constrained by its largely unchanging genotype. A single species is capable of indefinite, open-ended development. Although the course of a species' development is constrained from generation to generation by its gene pool, this gene pool is indefinitely modifiable. However, if

Eldredge and Gould are right, species are more like organisms than anyone has previously supposed. Both are finite and can undergo only limited change before ceasing to exist. Significant evolutionary change can take place only through a series of successive species, not within the confines of a single species. Species lineages, not species, are the things which evolve. On this view, Hennig's refusal to divide a single lineage into two or more species is preferable to Simpson's alternative.

No disagreement exists between Simpson and Hennig over the situation depicted in figure 14.1b, a single species splitting equally into two. Both agree that the ancestor species is extinct, having given rise to two new daughter species. However, this figure is drawn as if divergence always takes place upon speciation. When this diagram was interpreted as depicting the splitting of one organism into two, divergence was not presupposed. Two euglenae resulting from binary fission are two organisms and not one even though they may be phenotypically and genotypically identical. The same is true of species. Sometimes speciation takes place with no (or at least extremely minimal) divergence; e.g., sibling species are no less two species simply because they look alike. The assumption is, however, that in reproductively isolated species some divergence, at least in the mechanisms of reproduction, must have taken place, even if we cannot detect it. The role of similarity becomes controversial once again when speciation takes place and one species remains unchanged, while the other diverges from the parental type (see figure 14.1c). According to Hennig (17), when speciation occurs, the ancestor species must be considered extinct regardless of how similar it might be to one of its daughter species. Simpson (50) disagrees.

The factor which is causing the confusion in the preceding discussion is the role of similarity in the individuation of species. If species are classes defined by sets (or clusters) of traits, then similarity should be relevant. At one extreme, the pheneticists (54) argue that all that matters is phenetic similarity and dissimilarity, regardless of descent, reproduction, evolutionary cohesiveness, etc. Highly polytypic species such as dogs must be considered to be numerous different "species" because of the existence of so many reasonably discrete clusters. Sibling species must be considered a single "species" because they form a single cluster. At the other extreme, the Hennigians (commonly termed "cladists") concentrate solely on the splitting of phylogenetic lineages regardless of phenetic similarity. Polytypic species are single species because they form a single clade; sibling species are separate species because they form more than one clade. The evolutionists, represented by Simpson and Mayr, argue that somehow the two considerations must be balanced against each other.

However, on the historical entity interpretation, similarity is a red herring. It is not the issue at all. What really matters is how many organisms are involved and how much the internal organization of the species involved is disrupted. If speciation takes place when a small, peripheral isolate succeeds in bringing about a genetic revolution (see figure 14.1d), then the parent species can still be said to persist unchanged. It has not lost significant numbers of organisms, nor has its internal organization been affected much. One Hennigian, at least, has come to this conclusion for precisely these reasons (60). If, however, the species is split into two or more relatively large subgroups then it is difficult to see how the ancestral species can still be said to exist, unless one of these subgroups succeeds in retaining the same organization and internal cohesion of the ancestral species. Incidentally, it would also be phenetically similar to the ancestral species, but that would be irrelevant.

Fusion can also take place at the level of species. The breaking down of reproductive isolation sufficient to permit two entire species to merge into one is extremely unlikely (see figure 14.2a). If it did occur, the consideration would be the same as those raised in connection with figure 14.1b. However, introgression and speciation by polyploidy are common (see figures 14.2b and 14.2c). In such cases, a few organisms belonging to separate species mate and produce fertile offspring. Contrary to popular opinion, the production of an occasional fertile hybrid is not enough for biologists to consider two species one. What matters is how extensive the introgression becomes—exactly the right consideration if species are historical entities. As Dobzhansky remarks, "What matters is not whether hybrids can be obtained but whether the Mendelian populations do or do not exchange genes, and if they do whether at a rate which destroys the adaptive equilibrium of the populations concerned" (9, p. 586).

One final parallel between organisms and species warrants mentioning. Organisms are unique. When an organism ceases to exist, numerically that same organism cannot come into existence again. For example, if a baby were born today who was identical in every respect to Adolf Hitler, including genetic makeup, he still would not be Adolf Hitler. He would be as distinct and separate a human being as ever existed because of his unique "insertion into history," to use Vendler's propitious phrase (58; see also 57). But the same observation can be made with respect to species. If a species evolved which was identical to a species of extinct pterodactyl save origin, it would still be a new, distinct species. Darwin himself notes, "When a species has once disappeared from the face of the earth, we have reason to believe that the same identical form never reappears" (7, p. 313). Darwin presents this point as if it were a contingent state of affairs, when actually it is conceptual. Species are segments of the phylogenetic tree. Once a segment is terminated, it cannot reappear somewhere else in the phylogenetic tree. As Griffiths observes, the "reference of an individual to a species is determined by its parentage, not by any morphological attribute" (15, p. 102).

If species were actually spatiotemporally unrestricted classes, this state of affairs would be strange. If all atoms with atomic number 79 ceased to exist, gold would cease to exist, although a slot would remain open in the periodic table. Later when atoms with the appropriate atomic number were generated, they would be atoms of gold regardless of their origins. But in the typical case, to *be* a horse one must be *born* of horse. Obviously, whether one is a gradualist or saltationist, there must have been instances in which non-horses (or borderline horses) gave rise to horses. The operative term is still "gave rise to." But what of the science fiction examples so beloved to philosophers? What if a scientist made a creature from scratch identical in every respect to a human being including consciousness, emotionality, a feeling of personhood, etc.? Wouldn't it be included in *Homo sapiens*? It all depends. If all the scientist did was to make such a creature and then destroy it, it was never part of our species. However, if it proceeded to mate with human beings born in the usual way and to produce offspring, introducing its genes into the human gene pool, then it would become part of our species. The criterion is precisely the same one used in cases of introgression. In the evolutionary world view, unlike the Aristotelian world view, an organism can change its species while remaining numerically the same individual (see 19).

One might complain that being born of human beings and/or mating with human beings are biological criteria, possibly good enough for individuating *Homo sapiens*, but inadequate for the humanistic notion of a human being. We are a social species. An entity which played the role of a human being in a society would *be* a "human being," even if it was not born of human beings or failed to mate with human beings. I'm not sure how one makes such decisions, but the conclusion is not totally incompatible with the position being presented in this paper. Species as they are commonly thought of are not the only things which evolve. Higher levels of organization also exist. Entities can belong to the same cultural system or ecosystem without belonging to the same biological species. As Eugene Odum has put it, "A human being, for example, is not only a hierarchical system composed of organs, cells, enzyme systems, and genes as subsystems, but is also a component of supraindividual hierarchical systems such as populations, cultural systems, and ecosystems" (44, p. 1289). If pets or computers function as human beings, then from certain perspectives they might well count as human beings even though they are not included in the biological species *Homo sapiens*.

Biological and Philosophical Consequences

Empirical evidence is usually too malleable to be very decisive in conceptual revolutions. The observation of stellar parallax, the evolution of new species right before our eyes, the red shift, etc. are the sorts of things which are pointed to as empirical reasons for accepting new scientific theories. However, all reasonable people had accepted the relevant theories in the absence of such observations. Initial acceptance of fundamentally new ideas leans more heavily on the increased coherence which the view brings to our general world picture. If the conceptual shift from species being classes to species being historical entities is to be successful, it must eliminate longstanding anomalies both within and about biology. In this section, I set out some of the implications of viewing species as historical entities, beginning with those that are most strictly biological and gradually working my way toward those that are more philosophical in nature.

The role of type specimens in biological systematics puzzles philosophers and biologists alike. As R. A. Crowson remarks, "The current Convention that a single specimen, the Holotype, is the only satisfactory basic criterion for a species would be difficult to justify logically on any theory but Special Creation" (5, p. 29). According to all three codes of biological nomenclature, a particular organism, part of an organism, or trace of an organism is selected as the type specimen for each species. In addition, each genus must have its type species, and so on. Whatever else one does with this type and for whatever reasons, the name goes with the type.[4] The puzzling aspect of the type method on the class interpretation is that the type need not be typical. In fact, it can be a monster. The following discussion by J. M. Schopf is representative:

> It has been emphasized repeatedly, for the benefit of plant taxonomists, at least, that the nomenclatural type (holotype) of a species is not to be confused or implicated in anyone's concept of what is "typical" for a taxon. A nomenclatural type is simply *the specimen*, or other element, with which a name is permanently associated. This element need not be "typical" in any sense; for organisms with a complicated life cycle, it is obvious that no single specimen could physically represent all the important characteristics, much less could it be taken to show many features near the mean of their range of variation (see also 6, 39, 50, 51), (49, p. 1043)

Species are polymorphic. Should the type specimen for *Homo sapiens*, for instance, be male or female? Species are also polytypic. What skin color, blood type, etc. should the type specimen for *Homo sapiens* have? Given the sort of variability characteristic of biological species, no one specimen could possibly be "typical" in even a statistical sense (37, p. 369). On the class interpretation, one would expect at the very least for a type specimen to have many or most of the more important traits characteristic of its species (16, p. 565–56), but on the historical entity interpretation, no such similarity is required. Just as a heart, kidneys, and lungs are included in the same organism because they are part of the same ontogenetic whole, parents and their progeny are included in the same species because they are part of the same genealogical nexus, no matter how much they might differ phenotypically. The part/whole relation does not require similarity.

A taxonomist in the field sees a specimen of what he takes to be a new species. It may be the only specimen available or else perhaps one of a small sample which he gathers. The taxonomist could not possibly select a typical specimen, even if the notion made any sense, because he has not begun to study the full range of the species' variation. He selects a specimen, any specimen, and names it. Thereafter, if he turns out to have been the first to name the species of which this specimen is part, that name will remain firmly attached to that species. A taxon has the name it has *in virtue of* the naming ceremony, not *in virtue of* any trait or traits it might have. If the way in which taxa are named sounds familiar, it should. It is the same way in which people are baptized.[5] They are named in the same way because they are the same sort of thing—historical entities (see Ghiselin 13, 14).

But what then is the role of all those traits which taxonomists include in their monographs? For example, Article 13 of the Zoological Code of Nomenclature states that any name introduced after 1930 must be accompanied by a statement that "purports to give characteristics differentiating the taxon." Taxonomists distinguish between descriptions and diagnoses. A description is a lengthy characterization of the taxon, including reference to characteristics which are easily recognizable and comparable, to known variability within a population and from population to population, to various morphs, and to traits which can help in distinguishing sibling species. A diagnosis is a much shorter and selective list of traits chosen primarily to help differentiate a taxon from its nearest neighbors of the same rank. As important as the traits listed in diagnoses and descriptions may be for a variety of purposes, they are not definitions. Organisms could possess these traits and not be included in the taxon; conversely, organisms could lack one or more of these traits and be clear cut instances of the taxon. They are, as the name implies, *descriptions*. As descriptions, they change through time as the entities which they describe change. Right now all specimens of *Cygnus olor* are white. No doubt the type specimen of this species of swan is also white. However, if a black variety were to arise, *Cygnus olor* would not on that account become a new species. Even if this variety were to become predominant, this species would remain the same species and the white type specimen would remain the type specimen. The species description would change but that is all. Organisms are not included in the same species *because* they are similar to the type specimen or to each other but *because* they are part of the same chunk of the genealogical nexus (Ghiselin 13, 14).

On the class interpretation, the role of particular organisms as type specimens is anomalous. The role of lower taxa as types for higher taxa is even more anomalous. On the class interpretation, organisms are members of their taxa, while lower taxa are included in higher taxa (3). How could entities of two such decidedly different logical types play the same role? But on the historical entity interpretation, both organisms and taxa are of the same logical type. Just as organisms are part of their species, lower taxa are part of higher taxa. Once again, parts do not have to be similar, let alone typical, to be part of the same whole.

A second consequence of treating species as historical entities concerns the nature of biological laws. If species are actually spatiotemporally unrestricted classes, then they are the sorts of things which can function in laws. "All swans are white," if true, might be a law of nature, and generations of philosophers have treated it as such. If statements of the form "species X has the property Y" were actually laws of nature, one might rightly expect biologists to be disturbed when they are proven false. To the contrary, biologists expect exceptions to exist. At any one time, a particular percentage of a species of crows will be nonblack. No one expects this percentage to be universal or to remain fixed. Species may be classes, but they are not very important classes because their names function in no scientific laws. Given the traditional analyses of scientific laws, statements which refer to particular species do not count as scientific laws, as they should not if species are spatiotemporally localized individuals (20, 21).

Hence, if biologists expect to find any evolutionary laws, they must look at levels of organization higher than particular taxa. Formulations of evolutionary theory will no more make explicit reference to *Bos bos* than celestial mechanics will refer to Mars. Predictions about these entities should be derivable from the appropriate theories but no uneliminable reference can be made to them. In point of fact, no purported evolutionary laws refer to particular species. One example of such a law is the claim that in diploid sexually-reproducing organisms, homozygotes are more specialized in their adaptive properties than heterozygotes (31, p. 397). Evolutionary theory deals with the rise of individual homeostasis as an evolutionary mode, the waxings and wanings of sexuality, the constancy or variability of extinction rates, and so on. People are dismayed to discover that evolutionists can make no specific predictions about the future of humankind *qua* humankind. Since that's all they are interested in, they conclude that evolutionary theory is not good for much. But dismissing evolutionary theory because it cannot be used to predict the percentage of people who will have blue eyes in the year 2000 is as misbegotten as dismissing celestial mechanics because it cannot be used to predict the physical makeup of Mars. Neither theory is designed to make such predictions.

The commonest objection raised by philosophers against evolutionary theory is that its subject matter—living creatures—are spatiotemporally localized (52, 53; see also 42). They exist here on earth and nowhere else. Even if the earth were the only place where life had arisen (and that is unlikely), this fact would not count in the least against the spatiotemporally unrestricted character of evolutionary theory. "Hitler" refers to a particular organism, a spatiotemporally localized individual. As such, Hitler is unique. But organisms are not. Things which biologists would recognize as organisms could develop (and probably have developed) elsewhere in the universe. "*Homo sapiens*" refers to a particular species, a spatiotemporally localized individual. As such, it is unique. But species are not. Things which biologists would recognize as species could develop (and probably have developed) elsewhere in the universe. Evolutionary theory refers explicitly to organisms and species, not to Hitler and *Homo sapiens* (see 43, 48).

One advantage to biologists of the historical entity interpretation of species is that it frees them of any necessity of looking for any lawlike regularities at the level of particular species. Both "Richard Nixon has hair" and "most swans are white" may be true, but they are hardly laws of nature. It forces them to look for evolutionary laws at higher levels of analysis, at the level of *kinds* of species. It also can explain certain prevalent anomalies in philosophy. From the beginning a completely satisfactory explication of the notion of a natural kind has eluded philosophers. One explanation for this failure is that the traditional examples of natural kinds were a mixed lot. The three commonest examples of natural kinds in the philosophical literature have been geometric figures, biological species and the physical elements. By now, it should be clear that all three are very different sorts of things. No wonder a general analysis, applicable equally to all of them, has eluded us.

Some of the implications of treating species as historical entities are more philosophical in nature. For example, one of Ludwig Wittgenstein's most famous (or infamous) contributions to philosophy is that of family resemblances, a notion which itself has a family resemblance to cluster concepts and multivariate analysis (64). Such notions have found their most fertile ground in ethics, aesthetics and the social sciences. Hence, critics have been able to claim that defining a word in terms of statistical covariation of traits merely results from ignorance and informality of context. If and when these areas become more rigorous, cluster concepts will give way to concepts defined in the traditional way. The names of biological species have been the chief counter-example to these objections. Not only are the methods of contemporary taxonomists rigorous, explicit, objective, etc., but also good reasons can be given for the claim that the names of species can never be defined in classical terms. They are inherently cluster concepts (18). On the analysis presented in this paper, advocates of cluster analysis lose their best example of a class term which is, nevertheless, a cluster concept. If *"Homo sapiens"* is or is not a cluster concept, it will be for the same reason that "Moses" is or (more likely) is not.

A second philosophical consequence of treating species as historical entities concerns the nature of scientific theories. Most contemporary philosophers view scientific theories as atemporal conceptual objects. A theory is a timeless set of axioms and that is that. Anyone who formulates a theory consisting of a particular set of axioms has formulated that theory period. Theories in this sense cannot change through time. Any change results in a new theory. Even if one decides to get reasonable and allow for some variation in axioms, one still must judge two versions of a theory to be versions of the "same" theory because of similarity of axioms. Actual causal connections are irrelevant. However, several philosophers have suggested that science might profitably be studied as an "evolutionary" phenomenon (4, 21, 27, 28, 29, 45, 46, 56). If one takes these claims seriously and accepts the analysis of biological species presented in this paper, then it follows that whatever conceptual entities are supposed to be analogous to species must also be historical entities. Theories seem to be the most likely analog to species. Because biological species cannot be characterized intelligibly in terms of timeless essences, it follows that theories can have no essences either. Like species, theories must be individuated in terms of some sort of descent and cohesiveness, not similarity.

The relative roles of similarity and descent in individuating scientific theories goes a long way in explaining the continuing battle between historians and philosophers of science. Philosophers individuate theories in terms of a set (or at least a cluster) of axioms. Historians tend to pay more attention to actual influence. For example, we all talk about contemporary Mendelian genetics. If theories are to be individuated in terms of a single set (or even cluster) of axioms, it is difficult to see the justification of such an appellation. Mendel's paper contained three statements which he took to be basic. Two of these statements were rapidly abandoned at the turn of the century when Mendel's so-called "laws" were rediscovered. The third has been modified since. If overlap in substantive claims is what makes two formulations versions of the "same" theory, then it is difficult to see the justification for interpreting all the various things which have gone under the title of "Mendelian genetics" versions of the same theory. Similar observations are appropriate for other theories as well, including Darwin's theory of evolution. The theory which was widely accepted in Darwin's day differed markedly from the one he originally set out. Modern theories of evolution differ from his just as markedly. Yet, some are "Darwinian" and others not.

When presented with comparable problems, biologists resort to the type specimen. One organism is selected as the type. Any organism related to it in the appropriate ways belongs to its species, regardless of how aberrant the type specimen might turn out to be or how dissimilar other organisms may be. Males and females belong to the same species even though they might not look anything like each other. A soldier termite belongs in the same species with its fertile congeners even though it cannot mate with them. One possible interpretation of Kuhn's notion of an exemplar (27) is that it is designed to function as a type specimen. Even though scientific change is extremely complicated and at times diffuse, one still might be able to designate particular theories by reference to "concrete problem-solutions," as long as one realizes that these exemplars have a temporal index and need not be in any sense typical.[6] Viewing theories as sets (or clusters) of axioms does considerable damage to our intuitions about scientific theories. On this interpretation, most examples of scientific theories degenerate into unrelated formulations. Viewing scientific theories as historical entities also results in significant departures from our usual modes of conception. Perhaps scientific theories really cannot be interpreted as historical entities. If so, then this is just one more way in which conceptual evolution differs from biological evolution. The more that these disanalogies accumulate the more doubtful the entire analogy becomes.

Finally, and most controversially, treating species as historical entities has certain implications for those sciences which are limited to the study of single species. For instance, if enough scientists were interested, one might devote an entire science to the study of *Orycteropus afer*, the African aardvark. Students of aardvarkology might discover all sorts of truths about aardvarks: that it is nocturnal, eats ants and termites, gives birth to its young alive, etc. Because aardvarks are highly monotypic, aardvarkologists might be able to discover sets of traits possessed by all and only extant aardvarks. But could they discover the essence of aardvarks, the traits which aardvarks must have necessarily to be aardvarks? Could there be scientific laws which govern aardvarks necessarily and exclusively? When these questions are asked of aardvarks or any other nonhuman species, they sound frivolous, but they are exactly the questions which students of human nature treat with utmost seriousness. What is human nature and its laws?

Early in the history of learning theory, Edward L. Thorndike (55) claimed that learning performance in fishes, chickens, cats, dogs and monkeys differed only quantitatively, not qualitatively. Recent work tends to contradict his claim (1). Regardless of who is right, why does it make a difference? Learning, like any other trait, has evolved. It may be universally distributed among all species of animals or limited to a few. It may be present in all organisms included in the same species or distributed less than universally. In either case, it may have evolved once or several times. If "learning" is defined in terms of its unique origin, if all instances of learning must be evolutionarily homologous, then "learning" is limited by definition to one segment of the phylogenetic tree. Any regularities which one discovers are necessarily descriptive. If, on the other hand, "learning" is defined so that it can apply to any organism (or machine) which behaves in appropriate ways, then it *may* be limited to one segment of the phylogenetic tree. It *need* not be. Any regularities which one discovers are at least candidates for laws of learning. What matters is whether the principles are generalizable. Learning may be species specific, but if learning theory is to be a genuine scientific theory, it cannot be limited *necessarily* to a single species the way that Freud's and Piaget's theories seem to be. As important as descriptions are in science, they are not theories.

If species are interpreted as historical entities, then particular organisms belong in a particular species because they are part of that genealogical nexus, not because they possess any essential traits. No species has an essence in this sense. Hence there is no such thing as human nature. There may be characteristics which all and only extant human beings possess, but this state of affairs is contingent, depending on the current evolutionary state of *Homo sapiens*. Just as not all crows are black (even potentially), it may well be the case that not all people are rational (even potentially). On the historical entity interpretation, retarded people are just as much instances of *Homo sapiens* as are their brighter congeners. The same can be said for women, blacks, homosexuals, and human fetuses. Some people may be incapable of speaking or understanding a genuine language; perhaps bees can. It makes no difference. Bees and people remain biologically distinct species. On other, nonbiological interpretations of the human species, problems arise (and have arisen) with all of the groups mentioned. Possibly women and blacks are human beings but do not "participate fully" in human nature. Homosexuals, retardates, and fetuses are somehow less than human. And if bees use language, then it seems we run the danger of considering them human. The biological interpretation has much to say in its favor, even from the humanistic point of view.

Notes

The research for this paper was supported by NSF grant Soc 75 03535. I am indebted to the following people for reading and criticizing early versions of this paper: Michael Ghiselin, Stephen Gould, G. C. D. Griffiths, John Koethe, Ernst Mayr, Bella Selan, W. J. van der Steen, Gareth Nelson, Michael Perloff, Mark Ridley, Michael Ruse, Thomas Schopf, Paul Teller, Leigh Van Valen, Linda Wessels, Mary Williams, and William Wimsatt. Their advice and criticisms are much appreciated.

1. Once again, I am excluding from the notion of class those "classes" defined by means of a spatiotemporal relation to a spatiotemporally localized individual. Needless to say, I am also excluding such constructions as "similar in origin" from the classes of similarities. I wish the need to state the obvious did not exist, but from past experience it does.

2. In population genetics the distinction between structurally similar genes forming a single lineage and those which do not is marked by the terms "identical" and "independent"; see (41) pp. 56–57.

3. Until recently even the most ardent group selectionists admitted that the circumstances under which selection can occur at the level of populations and/or entire species are so rare that group selection is unlikely to be a major force in the evolutionary process (30, 32, 33). Michael Wade (59), however, has presented a convincing argument to the effect that the apparent rarity of group selection may be the result of the assumptions commonly made in constructing mathematical models for group selection and not an accurate reflection of the actual state of nature. In his own research, the differential survival of entire populations has produced significant divergence.

4. The three major codes of biological nomenclature are the International Code of Botanical Nomenclature, 1966, International Bureau for Plant Taxonomy and Nomenclature, Utrecht; the International Code of Nomenclature of Bacteria, 1966, *International Journal of Systematic Bacteriology*, 16:459–490; and the *International Code of Zoological Nomenclature*, 1964, International Trust for Zoological Nomenclature, London. In special circumstances the priority rule is waived, usually because the earlier name is discovered only long after a later name has become firmly and widely established.

5. Although the position on the names of taxa argued in this paper might sound as if it supported S. Kripke's (26) analysis of general terms, it does not. Taxa names are very much like "rigid designators," as they should be if taxa are historical entities. However, Kripke's analysis is controversial because it applies to *general* terms. It is instructive to note that, during the extensive discussion of the applicability of Kripke's notion of a rigid designator to such terms as "tiger," no one saw fit to see how those scientists most intimately concerned actually designated tigers. According to Putnam's principle of the linguistic division of labor (47), they should have. If they had, they would have found rules explicitly formulated in the various codes of nomenclature which were in perfect accord with Kripke's analysis—but for the wrong reason. That no one bothered tells us something about the foundations of conceptual analysis.

6. Kuhn himself (28) discusses taxa names such as "*Cygnus olor*" and the biological type specimen. Unfortunately, he thinks swans are swans because of the distribution of such traits as the color of feathers.

References

1. Bitterman, M. E. "The Comparative Analysis of Learning." *Science*. 188(1975): 699–709.
2. Boyden, A. "The Significance of Asexual Reproduction." *Systematic Zoology*. 3(1954): 26–37.
3. Buck, R. C., and D. L. Hull. "The Logical Structure of the Linnaean Hierarchy." *Systematic Zoology*. 15(1966): 97–111.
4. Burian, R. M. "More than a Marriage of Convenience: On the Inextricability of History and Philosophy of Science." *Philosophy of Science*. 44(1977): 1–42.
5. Crowson, R. A. *Classification and Biology*. New York: Atherton Press, 1970.
6. Davis, P. H., and V. H. Heywood. *Principles of Angiosperm Taxonomy*. Princeton: Van Nostrand, 1963.
7. Darwin, C. *On the Origin of Species*. Cambridge, Mass.: Harvard University Press, 1966.
8. Dawkins, R. *The Selfish Gene*. New York and Oxford: Oxford University Press, 1976.
9. Dobzhansky, T. "Mendelian Populations and their Evolution." In L. C. Dunn (ed.) *Genetics in the 20th Century*. New York: Macmillan, 1951. pp. 573–589.
10. Ehrlich, P. R., and P. H. Raven. "Differentiation of Populations." *Science* 165(1969): 1228–1231.

11. Eldredge, N., and S. J. Gould. "Punctuated Equilibria: An Alternative to Phyletic Gradualism." In T. J. M. Schopf (ed.) *Models in Paleobiology*. San Francisco: Freeman, Cooper and Company. pp. 82–115.

12. Ghiselin, M. T. "On Psychologism in the Logic of Taxonomic Controversies." *Systematic Zoology*. 15(1966): 207–215.

13. Ghiselin, M. T. *The Triumph of the Darwinian Method*. Berkeley and London: University of California Press, 1969.

14. Ghiselin, M. T. "A Radical Solution to the Species Problem." *Systematic Zoology*. 23(1974): 536–544.

15. Griffiths, G. C. D. "On the Foundations of Biological Systematics." *Acta Biotheoretica*. 23(1974): 85–131.

16. Heise, H., and M. P. Starr. "Nomenifers: Are They Christened or Classified?" *Systematic Zoology*. 17(1968): 458–467.

17. Hennig, W. *Phylogenetic Systematics*. Urbana, Illinois: University of Illinois Press, 1966.

18. Hull, D. L. "The Effect of Essentialism on Taxonomy." *The British Joural for the Philosophy of Science*. 15(1965): 314–326; 16(1966): 1–18.

19. Hull, D. L. "The Conflict between Spontaneous Generation and Aristotle's Metaphysics." *Proceedings of the Seventh Inter-American Congress of Philosophy*. Québec City: Les Presses de l'Université Laval. 2(1968): 245–250.

20. Hull, D. L. *Philosophy of Biological Science*. Englewood Cliffs: Prentice-Hall, 1974.

21. Hull, D. L. "Central Subjects and Historical Narratives." *History and Theory*. 14(1975): 253–274.

22. Hull, D. L. "Are Species Really Individuals?" *Systematic Zoology*. 25(1976): 174–191.

23. Hull, D. L. "The Ontological Status of Biological Species." In R. Butts and J. Hintikka (eds.) *Boston Studies in the Philosophy of Science*, vol. 32. Dordrecht: D. Reidel, 1976. pp. 347–358.

24. Huxley, T. H. "Biology." *Encyclopedia Britannica* (1889).

25. Janzen, Daniel, "What Are Dandelions and Aphids?" *American Naturalist*. 111(1977): 586–589.

26. Kripke, S. S. "Naming and Necessity." In D. Davidson and H. Harman (eds.) *Semantics and Natural Language*. Dordrecht, Holland: D. Reidel, 1972. pp. 253–355.

27. Kuhn, T. S. *The Structure of Scientific Revolutions*. Chicago: The University of Chicago Press, 2nd ed., 1969.

28. Kuhn, T. S. "Second Thoughts on Paradigms." In F. Suppe (ed.) *The Structure of Scientific Theory*. Urbana, Illinois: University of Illinois Press, 1974.

29. Laudan, L. *Progress and Its Problems*. Berkeley and London: University of California Press, 1977.

30. Levins, R. *Evolution in Changing Environments*. Princeton: Princeton University Press, 1968.

31. Lewontin, R. C. "Evolution and the Theory of Games." *Journal of Theoretical Biology*. 1(1961): 382–403.

32. Lewontin, R. C. "The Units of Selection." *The Annual Review of Ecology and Systematics* 1(1970): 1–18.

33. Lewontin, R. C. *The Genetic Basis of Evolutionary Change*. New York: Columbia University Press, 1974.

34. Löther, R. *Die Beherrschung der Mannigfaltigkeit*. Jena: Gustav Fischer, 1972.

35. Mayr. E. (ed.) *The Species Problem*. Washington, D.C.: American Association for the Advancement of Science Publication Number 50, 1957.

36. Mayr, E. "Isolation as an Evolutionary Factor." *Proceedings of the American Philosophical Society*. 103(1959): 221–230.

37. Mayr, E. *Animal Species and Evolution*. Cambridge, Mass.: The Belknap Press of Harvard University Press, 1963.
38. Mayr, E. "Is the Species a Class or an Individual?" *Systematic Zoology*. 25(1976): 192.
39. Mayr, E., E. G. Linsley and R. L. Usinger. *Methods and Principles of Systematic Zoology*. New York: McGraw-Hill Book Company, 1953.
40. Meglitsch, P. A. "On the Nature of Species." *Systematic Zoology*. 3(1954): 49–65.
41. Mettler, L. E., and T. G. Gregg. *Population Genetics and Evolution*. Englewood Cliffs: Prentice-Hall, 1969.
42. Monod, J. L. "On the Molecular Theory of Evolution." In R. Harré (ed.) *Problems of Scientific Revolution*. Oxford: Clarendon Press, 1975. pp. 11–24.
43. Munson, R. "Is Biology a Provincial Science?" *Philosophy of Science*. 42(1975): 428–447.
44. Odum, E. P. "The Emergence of Ecology as a New Integrative Discipline." *Science*. 195(1977): 1289–1293.
45. Popper, K. R. *Objective Knowledge*. Oxford: Clarendon Press, 1972.
46. Popper, K. R. "The Rationality of Scientific Revolutions." In R. Harré (ed.) *Problems of Scientific Revolution*. Oxford: Clarendon Press, 1975. pp. 72–101.
47. Putnam, H. "The Meaning of 'Meaning.'" In K. Gunderson (ed.) *Minnesota Studies in the Philosophy of Science*, vii. Minneapolis: University of Minnesota Press, 1974. pp. 131–193.
48. Ruse, M. J. *The Philosophy of Biology*. London: Hutchinson University Library, 1973.
49. Schopf, J. M. "Emphasis on Holotype." *Science*. 131(1960): 1043.
50. Simpson, G. G. "The Principles of Classification and a Classification of Mammals." *Bulletin of the American Museum of Natural History*, Vol. 85, 1945. pp. 1–350.
51. Simpson, G. G. *Principles of Animal Taxonomy*. New York: Columbia University Press, 1961.
52. Smart, J. J. C. *Philosophy and Scientific Realism*. London: Routledge and Kegan Paul, 1963.
53. Smart, J. J. C. *Between Science and Philosophy*. New York: Random House, 1968.
54. Sneath, P. H. A. and R. R. Sokal. *Numerical Taxonomy*. San Francisco: W. H. Freeman and Company, 1973.
55. Thorndike, E. L. *Animal Intelligence*. New York: Macmillan, 1911.
56. Toulmin, S. *Human Understanding*. Princeton: Princeton University Press, 1972.
57. Van Fraassen, Bas. "Probabilities and the Problem of Individuation." In S. A. Luckenbach (ed.) *Probabilities, Problems and Paradoxes*. Encino, Cal.: Dickinson Publishing Co., 1972. pp. 121–138.
58. Vendler, Z. "On the Possibility of Possible Worlds." *Canadian Journal of Philosophy*. 5(1976): 57–72.
59. Wade, M. J. "A Critical Review of the Models of Group Selection." *Quarterly Review of Biology*. 1978, forthcoming.
60. Wiley, E. O. "The Evolutionary Species Concept Reconsidered." *Systematic Zoology*, forthcoming.
61. Williams, G. C. *Adaption and Natural Selection*. Princeton: Princeton University Press, 1966.
62. Wilson, E. O. *Sociobiology: The New Synthesis*. Cambridge, Mass.: The Belknap Press of Harvard University Press, 1975.
63. Wynne-Edwards, V. C. *Animal Dispersion in Relation to Social Behaviour*. Edinburgh & London: Oliver & Boyd, 1962.
64. Wittgenstein, L. *Philosophical Investigations*. New York: Macmillan, 1953.

Chapter 15

Species

Philip Kitcher

I Pluralistic Realism

The most accurate definition of "species" is the cynic's. Species are those groups of organisms which are recognized as species by competent taxonomists. Competent taxonomists, of course, are those who can recognize the true species. Cynicism is attractive for the weary systematist who despairs of doing better. But I think that philosophers and biologists need not despair. Despite the apparently endless squabbles about how species are to be characterized, it is possible to defend an account of the species category which will do justice to the insights of several divergent approaches.[1]

I shall try to explain a position about species that I shall call *pluralistic realism*, and to indicate in a general way why I think that this position is true. In particular, I want to defend four theses.

> 1. Species can be considered to be sets of organisms, so that the relation between organism and species can be construed as the familiar relation of set-membership.
> 2. Species are sets of organisms related to one another by complicated, biologically interesting relations. There are many such relations which could be used to delimit species taxa. However, there is no unique relation which is privileged in that the species taxa it generates will answer to the needs of all biologists and will be applicable to all groups of organisms. In short, the species category is heterogeneous.
> 3. The species category is heterogeneous because there are two main approaches to the demarcation of species taxa and within each of these approaches there are several legitimate variations. One approach is to group organisms by structural similarities. The taxa thus generated are useful in certain kinds of biological investigations and explanations. However, there are different levels at which structural similarities can be sought. The other approach is to group organisms by their phylogenetic relationships. Taxa resulting from this approach are appropriately used in answering different kinds of biological questions. But there are alternative ways to divide phylogeny into evolu-

tionary units. A pluralistic view of species taxa can be defended because the structural relations among organisms and the phylogenetic relations among organisms provide common ground on which the advocates of different taxonomic units can meet.

4. Pluralism about species taxa is not only compatible with realism about species. It also offers a way to disentangle various claims that can be made in maintaining that "... species are real entities existing in nature, whose origin, persistence, and extinction require explanation" (Eldredge and Cracraft 1980, 15).

I do not intend to provide a complete defense of all these claims. I shall concentrate primarily on the first three theses, saying little about the issue of realism about species, although I hope that my explanations of theses 1–3, together with the discussion in section V, will make it possible to see how to avoid the charge that species are merely fictions of the systematist's imagination.[2]

II Sets versus Individuals

My first thesis seems banal. After all, who would think of denying that species are sets of organisms? However, a number of philosophers and biologists—most prominently, David Hull and Michael Ghiselin—have recently campaigned aginst the notion that species are (what they call) "spatiotemporally unrestricted classes" and they have urged that species should be viewed as individuals.[3] Strange though this proposal may initially appear, it cannot be lightly dismissed. Hull and Ghiselin argue that their account of species is far more consonant with our current understanding of the evolutionary process than the view that they seek to replace.[4]

Let me begin by explaining what I take to be the commitments of the traditional idea that species are sets. First, there is no inconsistency in claiming that species are sets and denying that the members of these sets share a common property. Unless "property" is used in an attenuated sense, so that all sets are sets whose members share one trivial property —namely, the property of belonging to that set—then there are sets whose members are not distinguished by any common property. In particular, believing that species are sets does not entail believing that there is some homogeneous collection of morphological properties such that each species taxon is the set of organisms possessing one of the morphological properties in the collection. So we can accept 1 while endorsing Mayr's celebrated critique of the morphological concept of species (Mayr 1942, 1963, 1969, 1970, 1982).

Let me now turn to the main arguments that have been offered for thinking that the view of species as sets is at odds with our best biological theorizing. One of these arguments claims that construing species as sets is incompatible with the doctrine that species evolve.[5] Here is the starkest version: "Species evolve. Sets are atemporal entities. Hence sets cannot evolve. Therefore species are not sets."[6] Quite evidently, there is a fallacy here, the fallacy of incomplete translation. It would be futile to think that mathematicians need to revise their standard ontology because of the following argument: "Curves have tangents. Sets of triples of numbers are nonspatial entities. Hence sets of triples of real numbers cannot have tangents. Therefore curves are not sets of triples of real numbers." The correct response to the latter argument is to insist that, in the reduction of geometry to real arithmetic, the property of being a tangent is itself identified in arithmetical terms. Once the property has been so identified, it is possible to see how sets of triples of real numbers can have it. Only incomplete translation deludes us into thinking that sets of triples of real numbers cannot have tangents. An exactly parallel response is available in the case of species.

Assume, for the sake of the present argument, that a species is a set of organisms consisting of a founder population and some (but not necessarily all) of the descendants of that population. I make this assumption in order to show that there is a set-theoretic equivalent of the approach to species that Hull favors. For any given time, let the *stage* of the species at that time be the set of organisms belonging to the species which are alive at that time. To say that the species evolves is to say that the frequency distribution of properties (genetic or genetic plus phenotypic) changes from stage to stage.[7] To say that the species gives rise to a number of descendant species is to claim that the founding populations of those descendant species consist of organisms descending from the founding population of the original species. By proceeding in this way it is relatively easy to reconstruct the standard claims about the evolutionary behavior of species.

A second major theme in Hull's attack on the tradition is his suggestion that recognizing species as individuals will enable us to understand why there are no biological laws about particular species.

> If species are actually spatiotemporally unrestricted classes, then they are the sorts of things which can function in laws. "All swans are white," if true, might be a law of nature and generations of philosophers have treated it as such. If statements of the form "Species X has property Y" were actually laws of nature, one might rightly expect biologists to be disturbed when they are proven false. To the contrary, biologists expect exceptions to exist. At any one time, a particular percentage of a species of crows will be non-black. No one expects this percentage to be universal or to remain fixed. Species may be classes, but they are not very important classes because their

names function in no scientific laws. Given the traditional analyses of scientific laws, statements which refer to particular species do not count as scientific laws, as they should not if species are spatio-temporally localized individuals (Hull 1978, 353).

Ignoring all sorts of interesting issues, I shall concentrate on two central points. First, it seems to me that Hull is correct to dismiss statements like "All swans are white" as candidates for being laws of nature. But I think that he offers an incorrect explanation of why such statements are not laws. Second, I claim that he is far too quick to conclude that there are no laws about individual species. When we understand why "All swans are white" isn't a candidate for a law of nature—since it is neither lawlike nor true— we shall be able to recognize the possibility of laws about particular species.

Why isn't "All swans are white" a law? The answer is relatively obvious, given our understanding of the process of evolution: even if it had been true that all members of some swan species—*Cygnus olor*, for example— were white, then this would have been an evolutionary fluke. Organisms flouting the generalization could easily have been produced without any large-scale disruption of the course of nature. A small mutation or chromo-somal change could easily modify biosynthetic pathways, and thus result in differently colored plumage. Thus I suggest that "All swans are white" is what it appears to be, a generalization, but a generalization which fails to be lawlike. Biologists are unsurprised when generalizations like this prove to be false, because, given their understanding of the workings of evolu-tion, they would be flabbergasted if there were no exceptions.

In the light of this explanation, we can see what conditions would have to be met for a statement of form "All S are P," where S is a species and P a property, to count as a law. Mutations or chromosomal novelties produc-ing the absence of P in progeny of members of S would have to be so radical that they fell into one of two categories: (a) changes giving rise to inviable zygotes, (b) changes with effects large enough to count as events of instantaneous speciation. In other words, the property P would have to be so deeply connected with the genetic constitution of members of the species that alterations of the genome sufficient to lead to the absence of P would disrupt the genetic organization, leading to inviable offspring or to offspring of a new species.[8] So, *if* there are developmental systems whose modification in certain respects would generate either "hopeful" or "hope-less" monsters, then statements ascribing to members of a species appropri-ately chosen properties would be candidates for laws about the species. These laws, I suggest, would have the same status as low-level laws of chemistry, generalizations like "DNA molecules contain adenine and thymine molecules in (almost) equal numbers." While they are more particular than the grand equations of physics, these generalizations are scientifically significant, and are featured in numerous explanations.

So Hull is far too quick to foreclose the possibility of biological laws about particular species. Let me now consider the third main strand in his argument for the idea that species are individuals. What moves Hull is a sense of disanalogy between the set of atoms of an element and a typical biological species. Apparently, atoms of gold might occur anywhere in the universe, while members of *Rattus rattus* are bound to be much more localized. Now, despite the fact that Hull typically formulates the issue by claiming that species are spatiotemporally localized, the root of his observation is the connectedness of species rather than their boundedness in space-time.[9] The following passage contains the main idea:

> If a species evolved which was identical to a species of extinct pterodactyl save origin, it would still be a new distinct species. Darwin himself notes, "When a species has once disappeared from the face of the earth, we have reason to believe that the same identical form never reappears...." Darwin presents this point as if it were a contingent state of affairs, when actually it is conceptual. Species are segments of the phylogenetic tree. Once a segment is terminated, it cannot reappear somewhere else in the phylogenetic tree....
>
> If species were actually spatiotemporally unrestricted classes, this state of affairs would be strange. If all atoms with atomic number 79 ceased to exist, gold would cease to exist, although a slot would remain open in the periodic table. Later when atoms with the appropriate atomic number were generated, they would be atoms of gold regardless of their origins. But in the typical case, to *be* a horse one must be *born* of horse. (Hull 1978, 349)

Let us say that a set of organisms is *historically connected* just in case any organism belonging to the set is either a member of the initial population included in the set or else an immediate descendant of members of the set. Hull's argument can be reformulated as follows: if species were "spatiotemporally unrestricted classes" then species could be historically disconnected; since no species can be historically disconnected, species are not "spatiotemporally unrestricted classes."

One way to respond would be to concede that species are special kinds of sets (namely historically connected sets). To reply in this way would be to acquiesce in Hull's interpretation of biological practice, but to claim that a different ontological reconstruction of that practice is possible, a reconstruction whose chief merit is that it allows a perspicuous way of raising questions about the internal structure of species taxa. However, this reply grants too much. To be sure, one part of biological inquiry focuses on relations of descent in the phylogenetic nexus. But this is by no means the only type of inquiry with which biologists are concerned, nor should one develop one's approach to the ontology of species in such a way as to foreclose possibilities which are useful in some biological contexts.

More concretely, there are cases in which it would be proper to admit a historically disconnected set as a species. Let me offer an example which is based on an actual event of species formation through hybridization. In the lizard genus *Cnemidophorus*, several unisexual species have arisen through hybridization. In particular, the lizard *Cnemidophorus tesselatus* has resulted from a cross between *C. tigris* and *C. septemvittatus* (Parker and Selander 1976, Parker 1979). Although there are important differences between bisexual and unisexual species, the practice of naturalists and theoretical biologists has been to count *C. tesselatus* as a distinct species, whose status is not impugned by its unisexual character. In fact, *C. tesselatus* has served as a test case for comparing genetic diversity in bisexual and unisexual species.

C. tesselatus is probably not historically disconnected. But it might all too easily have been. The actual species probably originated when peripheral populations of the ancestral species came into contact. Clones could even have been established on many different occasions from parental individuals belonging to different breeding populations. A more radical type of discontinuity is also possible. Imagine that the entire initial population of *C. tesselatus* was wiped out and that the species was rederived after a second incident of hybridization between the two parental species. I claim that this would have been the correct description to give of a sequence of events in which first hybridization was followed by extinction and later by second hybridization. For, supposing that the clones founded in the first hybridization fall within the same range of genetic (morphological, behavioral, ecological) variation present in the population that has persisted to the present, what biological purpose would be served by distinguishing two species? To hypothesize "sibling species" in this case (and in like cases) seems to me not only to multiply species beyond necessity but also to obfuscate all the biological similarities that matter. Hence I conclude that Hull is wrong to chide Darwin for confusing a contingent state of affairs with a conceptual point. In most groups of organisms, historically disconnected species are unlikely—and conceding the logical possibility that *Homo sapiens* might reevolve after a holocaust does not offer us any genuine comfort. But it is not necessary, and it may not even be true, that all species are historically connected.[10]

III The Troubles of Monism

The traditional thesis that species are sets provides us with a framework within which we can investigate the species category and this framework is not at odds with insights drawn from evolutionary theory. But if species are sets, what kinds of sets are they?[11] The twentieth-century literature in biology is strewn with answers to this question. Most popular has been the so-called biological species concept, developed with great care by Ernst Mayr. According to Mayr's definition, species are "groups of interbreeding natural populations that are reproductively isolated from other such groups" (Mayr 1970, 12; 1969, 26). A somewhat different approach, developed in different ways by G. G. Simpson (1961), Willi Hennig (1966), E. O. Wiley (1981), and others, is to regard the notion of a speciation event as the basic notion and to take a species to be the set of organisms in a lineage (a sequence of ancestral-descendant populations) bounded by successive speciation events.[12] Speciation events themselves can be understood either as events in which a descendant population becomes reproductively isolated from its ancestors (Simpson) or as events in which an ancestral population gives rise to two descendant populations which are reproductively isolated from one another (Wiley and Hennig).[13] A more radical departure from traditional concepts of species is effected by viewing speciation as a process in which descendant populations are ecologically differentiated from their ancestors (Van Valen 1976). And there are still other approaches. In the early 1960s there arose an influential school of taxonomy which proclaimed the virtues of dividing organisms into species by constructing a measure of overall similarity and taking species to be sets of organisms which are clustered by this measure (Sokal and Sneath 1963, Sneath and Sokal 1973). Finally, in the last decade, another taxonomic school, the so-called "pattern cladists," have proposed that a species is a set of organisms distinguished by their common possession of a "minimal evolutionary novelty" (Nelson and Platnick 1981, 12; also Rosen 1979 and, perhaps, Eldredge and Cracraft 1980, 92).

I do not have space here to explain in detail what these various proposals are, much less to examine their merits. So I shall simply give a brief, dogmatic statement of my main claim and then offer a quick illustration of it. Most of the suggestions that I have mentioned can be motivated by their utility for pursuing a particular type of biological inquiry. But, in each case, the champions of the proposal contend that their species concept can serve the purposes of all biologists. In this I think that they err.

Consider Mayr's biological species concept. There is no doubting the importance of reproductive isolation as a criterion for demarcating certain groups of organisms. To cite a classic example, it was a major achievement to separate six sibling species within the *Anopheles* complex of mosquitoes, and thus to understand the distribution of malarial infection in Europe. (For a classic discussion, see Mayr 1963, 35–7, 1970, 24–5.) This example shows the biological species concept in its native habitat: reproductive isolation is important to recognize when we have organisms with overlapping ranges that are morphologically similar but which do not interbreed.

But it is all too familiar that there are difficult cases. Consider the plight of the paleontologist concerned to understand the rates of evolution in different lineages. Quite evidently, there is no way to evaluate directly some hypothesis about whether two forms, long extinct, were or were not reproductively isolated from one another. Thus conclusions about the succession of species in an evolving lineage must be based upon morphological data. Only the most enthusiastic operationalist would conclude directly from this that the paleontological species concept ought to be morphological. As has been repeatedly pointed out (Hull 1968, Simpson 1961), one can search for correlations between morphological changes and the changes which lead to reproductive isolation, using such correlations to reconstruct the division of the lineage into biological species. However, this response to the operationalist's recommendation misses one important feature of the continued insistence by some paleontologists that the biological species concept will not serve all their purposes. There is a perfectly legitimate paleontological question which focuses on the rates and patterns of morphological diversification within evolving lineages, and paleontologists pursue this question by dividing lineages into species according to morphological changes. To insist that they should always formulate their inquiries by using the biological species concept is to make them take a risky trip around Robin Hood's barn. (For further discussion of this point, see section V.)

But paleontology is not the only place in which there are shortcomings of the biological species concept. That concept also fails in application to organisms which do not reproduce themselves sexually. The typical response to that failure reveals a mistake that pervades much traditional thinking about the concept of species.

In an early explanation and defense of the biological species concept, Mayr acknowledged that there is a problem with asexual organisms, but this problem was not to be taken to be particularly threatening.

> There is, however, some question as to whether this species definition can also be applied to aberrant cases, such as the mating types of protozoa, the self-fertilizing hermaphrodites, animals with obligatory parthenogenesis, and certain groups of parasites and host specialists.... The known number of cases in which the above species definition may be inapplicable is very small, and there seems to be no reason at the present time for "watering" our species concept to include these exceptions. (Mayr 1942, 121–22)

Two interesting features of this passage set the tone for most subsequent defenses of the biological species concept. First, the problem is seen as one of *application*. How do we apply the criterion of reproductive isolation to organisms that do not mate? Second, Mayr attempts to minimize the scope of the problem. Only a few difficult cases are known, and it is suggested hopefully that these may disappear if we learn more about the organisms concerned. The joint effect of these two claims is to portray the biological species concept as a valuable *instrument*. It is recommended to us on the grounds that it will almost always pick out the right groups—as if it were a diagnostic machine that could reveal the patient's malady in 999 cases out of 1000.

This way of looking at the situation is curious. For it seemed originally that the biological species concept was intended as an *analysis* of previous discourse. For centuries, botanists, zoologists, field naturalists, and ordinary people have responded to the diversity of the living world by dividing organisms into species. The biological species concept appeared to offer a reconstruction of their remarks—we were to be given a description of what the species are which would parallel the chemist's account of what the elements are. But, in Mayr's response to the problem of asexuality, the goals of the enterprise seem to shift. The biological species concept is no longer seen as identifying the fundamental feature on which organismic diversity rests; it is viewed as a handy device for leading us to the right groups.

Theoretical systematics often seems to presuppose that there is a fundamental feature of organismic diversity, common to all groups of organisms, that taxonomists try to capture by making judgments of the form '*A* and *B* are distinct species.' Accounts of the species category propose explanations of what these judgments mean, by offering hypotheses about what the fundamental fact of organismic diversity is. The biological species concept claims that what constitutes the ground of diversity is the reproductive isolation of groups of populations. Asexual organisms teach us that this cannot be the ground of diversity in all groups of organisms. We can react to this lesson in one of a number of ways. One is to deny that there is any fundamental phenomenon of diversity among asexual organisms, abandoning judgments of form '*A* and *B* are distinct species,' in cases where *A* and *B* are sets of asexual organisms. But those who work with asexual organisms contend that there are theoretically significant distinctions among such organisms which defy any such radical revision of taxonomic practice. A second response, developed by Mayr, is to count morphological differences as indicators of species distinctness, treating sexual and asexual organisms alike. But this does not touch the real question which theoretical systematics seemed to address. For what we want to know is *what morphological difference is an indicator of*, what we are after when we attend to morphological distinctness.[14] If it is suggested that, in the case of asexual organisms there is nothing more fundamental than morphological difference, that here clustering in morphological space is not evidence of species distinctness but *constitutive* of species distinctness, then we should ask why we fail to attend to this patterning of organismic diversity in the case of sexual organisms as well. Why isn't morphological distinctness *always* constitutive of species distinctness?

It is here that the difficulties of the biological species concept expose an important moral. Although the biological species concept brings out an important pattern in the diversity of nature—the division of organisms into groups that are reproductively isolated from one another is theoretically significant—this is not the only important pattern of organismic diversity. Champions of the biological species concept—and defenders of alternative approaches to the species category—are too quick to assume that problematic groups of organisms can be dismissed as irritating exceptions, or that they can be handled by adding disjuncts to a definition of "species." By contrast, I suggest that the problem cases should be taken seriously, in that they point to distinctions among organisms which can be used to generate alternative legitimate conceptions of species. I shall now try to explain why it is to be expected that biology needs a number of different approaches to the division of organisms, a number of different sets of "species."

IV The Possibility of Pluralism

In the writings of great systematists, there are occasional passages in which the author recognizes the needs of different groups of biologists. Typically, these passages precede the moment at which monism takes over and the writer becomes an advocate for a single conception of species which is to answer to the interests of every one. An excellent example occurs at the beginning of Hennig's classic work on systematics (Hennig 1966, 5), where he emphasizes the multiplicity of admissible approaches to classification. Yet, within a few pages (1966, 9), Hennig reformulates the question in a way that makes it clear that some one of the systems is to be regarded as privileged, that biology must have a single general reference system.

I shall try to show why it is both desirable and possible to resist the Hennigian move. I begin with an important distinction due to Mayr. Pointing out that biology covers "two largely separate fields," Mayr claims that practitioners in one field ("functional biology") are primarily interested in questions of "proximate causation," while those in the other field ("evolutionary biology") are primarily concerned with issues of "ultimate causation" (1961; see 1976, 360). Mayr's choice of terms suggests his own predilections and threatens his own fundamental insight. There are indeed two kinds of biological investigation that can be carried out relatively independently of one another, neither of which has priority over the other.

These kinds of investigation demand different concepts of species. In fact, as I shall suggest, each main type of biological investigation subdivides further into inquiries that are best conducted by taking alternative views of the species category.

The main Mayrian division is easily explained by example. One interesting biological project is to explain the properties of organisms by means of underlying structures and mechanisms. A biologist may be concerned to understand how, in a particular group of bivalve molluscs, the hinge always comes to a particular form. The explanation that is sought will describe the developmental process of hinge formation, tracing the final morphology to a sequence of tissue or cellular interactions, perhaps even identifying the stages in ontogeny at which different genes are expressed. Explanations of this type abound in biology: think of the mechanical accounts of normal (and abnormal) meiosis, of respiration and digestion, of details of physiological functioning in all kinds of plants and animals. For obvious reasons, I shall call these explanations "structural explanations."[15] They contrast with *historical explanations*, accounts that seek to identify the evolutionary forces that have shaped the morphology, behavior, ecology, and distribution, of past and present organisms. So, for example, our imagined biologist—or, more likely, a colleague—may be concerned to understand why the bivalves evolved the form of hinge that they did. Here, what is sought is an evolutionary history that will disclose why the genes regulating the particular hinge morphology became fixed in the group of bivalves.

Neither mode of explanation is more fundamental than the other. If I want to relieve my ignorance about the structures and mechanisms underlying a morphological trait, then I cannot receive enlightenment from an account which tells me (for example) how natural selection favored the emergence of the trait. Equally, I can be well acquainted with the developmental details underlying the presence of a feature and still legitimately wonder why the structures and mechanisms concerned have come to be in place. This is not to deny that structural and historical investigations can prompt further historical and structural inquiries. As we understand more about the structures that underlie facets of morphology or pieces of behavior, new questions arise about the historical processes through which those structures emerged. In similar fashion, deeper understanding of evolutionary history raises new questions about the structures instantiated in the organisms who participated in the historical process. A study of a particular organism can easily give rise to a sequence of questions, some structural and some historical, with structural answers raising new historical questions and historical answers raising new structural questions. We should not confuse ourselves into thinking that one type of answer is appropriate to both types of questions or that one type of question is more "ultimate" than the other. The latter mistake is akin to thinking of even numbers as more "advanced" on the grounds that each odd number is followed by an even number.

I claim that these two main types of biological inquiry generate different schemes for classifying organisms. Consider the enterprise of structural explanation as it might be developed in microbiological investigations. Our study of viruses initially reveals certain patterns of morphological and physiological similarity and difference: we discover that there are different shapes and constitutions of the viral protein sheaths and that there are differences in the abilities of viruses to replicate on various hosts. These initial discoveries prompt us to ask certain questions: Why does this virus have a protein sheath of this shape? Why is it able to replicate on this host but not on that? Viral genetics proves some answers. We learn that the features that originally interested us depend upon certain properties of the viral genome. At this point our inquiries are transformed. We now regard viruses as grouped not by the superficial patterns that first caught our attention, but by similarities in those properties of the genome to which we appeal in giving our explanations. Our reclassification may prompt us to differentiate viruses that we would formerly have lumped together, or to regard as mere "variants" organisms previously viewed as of radically different types. But, irrespective of any reforms it may induce, the achievement of an explanatory framework goes hand in hand with a scheme for delineating the "real kinds" in nature.[16]

This example mixes science with science fiction. We at present know an enormous amount about the genetics of some viruses, enough to discern minute details of the process of sheath synthesis and even of viral replication. Fiction enters in my suggestion that knowledge of this sort is available across the board, so that we can actually reclassify viruses on the basis of genetic discontinuities. To the best of my knowledge, microbiologists are not currently in a position to apply explicit genetic criteria to demarcate structural species of viruses. Nevertheless, it is not hard to envisage the possibility that future science may operate with a species concept in which microorganisms are divided by particular differences in their genetic material, and in which these differences are regarded as "real" whether or not they correspond to morphological or pysiological distinctions, whether or not they coincide with the groupings produced by the evolutionary process.

Consider, by contrast, the enterprise of historical explanation. Again, our inquiries may begin with an unfocused question. We notice a pattern, of similarities and differences among certain animals, carnivorous mammals for example, and we ask how this diversity has arisen. Our project may initially be formulated in quite inadequate terms: we may begin by excluding giant pandas (because they are herbivores), hyenas may be classified with cats, marsupials like the Tasmanian "wolf" may be included, and so forth. As we proceed to reconstruct the phylogeny of the carnivores our groupings change, reflecting the recency of common ancestry. We learn to see the "important" similarities (like skull morphology), and to ignore "plastic" traits (like body size). In this way a new classification is produced, which may override similarities in gross morphology, in behavior, in ecology, even, in principle, in genetic structure.

So far I have outlined two main approaches to the classification of organisms, but within each of these more general schemes there are particular variations. Some patterns of organismic diversity may be explained by reference to structural similarities at different levels. When thinking about structural explanation, there is a strong temptation to adopt a reductionist perspective, to hold that the fundamental distinctions among organisms must be made in genetic terms. My example about the viruses exploits the hold that reductionism exerts on our thinking. Yet we should acknowledge that there may be phenomena whose structural explanation will ultimately be given by appealing to discontinuities in the architecture of chromosomes. (See, for example, White 1978.) Another possibility is that some biological phenomena—like those of phenotypic stability—may be explained by identifying developmental programs, conceived as flow charts that trace cell movements and tissue interactions. (See figure 15.1.) So we might arrive at a structural conception of species that identified a species as a set of organisms sharing a common program, without committing ourselves to the idea that there is any genetic similarity that covers exactly those

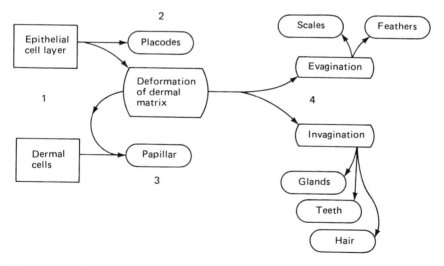

Figure 15.1
Diagrammatic summary of the skin developmental program (From Oster and Alberch 1982)

organisms instantiating the program. The situation I envisage is easily understood by taking seriously the metaphor of a *program*. Organisms may be divided into species according to their possession of a common "software," and this division might cut across the distinctions drawn by attending to genetic "hard wiring."

At present, we can only speculate about the possibilities for structural concepts of species. A far more detailed case can be made for pluralism about historical species concepts. Let me begin with an obvious point. The enterprise of phylogenetic reconstruction brings home to us the importance of the principle of grouping organisms according to recency of common ancestor. But that principle, by itself, does not legislate a division into kinds. It must be supplemented with a principle of *phylogenetic division*, something that tells us what the important steps in evolution are, what changes are sufficiently large to disrupt phylogenetic connections and to give rise to a new evolutionary unit.

There are three main views about the kinds of evolutionary change that break lineages: the production of reproductively isolated branches, the attainment of ecological distinctness, and the development of a new morphology.[17] Each of these principles of division identifies a relationship among organisms that is intrinsically of biological interest. Each can be used to yield an account of the species category in which the units of evolution are taken to correspond to the major types of discontinuity. Alternatively, each can be used in subordination to the principle of grouping organisms according to recency of common ancestor, and this approach generates another three different accounts of species.

Historical species concepts arise from applying two principles. The principle of continuity demands that a and b be more closely related than c and d if and only if a and b have a more recent common ancestor than c and d. The principle of division, of which there are three versions, takes the general form of specifying the conditions under which a and b are evolutionarily distinct. The candidate conditions are: (i) a and b belong to populations that are reproductively isolated from one another, (ii) a and b belong to different ecological (or adaptive) zones, (iii) a and b are morphologically distinct. Some currently popular approaches to species give precedence to the principle of continuity, using some favored version of the principle of division to segment lineages. Other conceptions are generated by focusing first on the criterion of division, using common ancestry only as a means of assigning borderline cases (for example, deviant organisms or evolutionary intermediates).[18]

This taxonomy of species concepts (figure 15.2) already helps us to see how different views of species may be produced by different biological priorities. There are three important types of division among organisms, and each of these three types of division can rightly be viewed as the

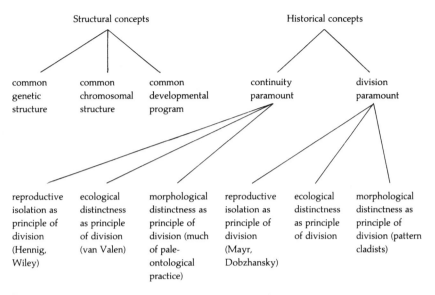

Figure 15.2
The taxonomy of species concepts.

criterion for disrupting phylogenetic continuity or as a phenomenon of interest in its own right. I have already remarked on the way in which the biological species concept illuminated the issue of the distribution of mosquitoes in the *Anopheles maculipennis* complex. Yet it should be evident that distinction according to reproductive isolation is not always the important criterion. For the ecologist concerned with the interactions of obligatorily asexual organisms on a coral reef, the important groupings may be those that trace the ways in which ecological requirements can be met in the marine environment and which bring out clearly the patterns of symbiosis and competition. Similarly, paleontologists reconstructing the phylogenies of major classes of organisms will want to attend primarily to considerations of phylogenetic continuity, breaking their lineages into species according to the considerations that seem most pertinent to the organisms under study: reproductive isolation of descendant branches, perhaps, in the case of well-understood vertebrates; ecological or morphological discontinuities, perhaps, in the cases of asexual plants or marine invertebrates. I suggest that when we come to see each of these common biological practices as resulting from a different view about what is important in dividing up the process of evolution we may see all of them as important and legitimate.

Although he did not articulate the point as I have done, Hennig appreciated the diversity of biological interests. Why then did he feel it necessary to demand for biology a single general reference system? Perhaps the most obvious worry about the pluralism that I recommend is that it will engender a return to Babel, a situation in which biological discourse is plunged into confusion. But I think that biology has already been forced to cope with a different case of the same general problem, and that it has done so successfully. One of the lessons of molecular biology is that there is no single natural way to segment DNA into functional units. Present uses of "gene" sometimes refer to segments whose functional activity affects the phenotype at the level of protein formation, sometimes to segments whose functional activity affects more gross aspects of the phenotype. Even if we pretend that all genes function to produce proteins, there is no privileged characterization of genes as functional units.[19] Yet geneticists (and other biologists) manage their investigations quite well, and the use of a plurality of gene concepts does not generate illusions of agreement and disagreement.

This happy state of affairs rests on the following features of the current practice of genetics. (1) For many general discussions about "genes," no particular principle of segmentation of DNA needs to be chosen. The questions that arise can be recast as questions about the *genetic material* without worrying about how that material divides up into natural units. For example, the issue of how genes replicate is reformulated as the question of the mode of replication of the genetic material. *Whatever* view one takes about the segments that constitute genes, the challenge is to understand how DNA makes copies of itself. (2) When general inquiries about genes do depend crucially on the segments of DNA identified as genes, it is important for investigators to note explicitly the principle of segmentation that is being used. So, for example, in introducing his thesis about genic selection Richard Dawkins takes pains to identify the units that he will count as genes (Dawkins 1976, 34; there is a much more refined discussion of the same point in Dawkins 1982).

The case of the many genes shows how the multiplicity of overlapping natural kinds can be acknowledged without either arbitrary choice or inevitable confusion. Similar resources are available with respect to the species category. Just as there are many ways to divide DNA into "natural functional units," so there are many ways to identify sets of "structurally similar" organisms or to pick out "units of phylogeny." In some discussions of species, what is important to the issue is not dependent on any particular criterion for dividing an evolving lineage into species. When ecologists discuss reproductive strategies, distinguishing between K-selected and r-selected species, for example, their remarks can be understood independently of any particular proposal for lineage division. Species are conceived as sets of organisms forming part of a lineage, and the distinction at hand is drawn by considering the characteristics of their stages. But in other cases the principle of segmentation is crucial. Paleontologists concerned with comparing species turnover in a group of lineages are likely to misunderstand one another unless they make clear their principle of lineage division.

As Hempel remarked long ago in his celebrated critique of operationalism, the risk of equivocation is ever present in scientific discourse (Hempel 1954; 1965, 126–27; 1966, 92–97). To guard against confusion it is futile to attempt to fashion some perfectly unambiguous language. Instead, responsible scientists should recognize where dangerous ambiguities are likely to occur and should be prepared to forestall misunderstandings. Biologists have already learned to be responsible in discussions of genes. The same responsibility can be attained in the case of species. To allow pluralism about species and to deny the need for a "general reference system" in biology is not to unlock the doors of Babel.[20]

V Three Consequences

I have tried to outline and to motivate a general approach to the category of species. I want to conclude by drawing three morals, one for an area of current biological dispute, one for a question in the philosophy of science, and one which overlaps biology and philosophy. I shall begin with the biological issue.

Paleontologists are currently divided on a number of important issues about the tempo and mode of evolution. In an important and much discussed contribution to these debates, Peter Williamson (1981) provides extensive documentation of the fossil record of several mollusc lineages from the Lake Turkana Basin. Williamson's data (see figure 15.3) reveal abrupt changes in phenotype punctuating periods of phenotypic stasis. Moreover, the episodes of phenotypic change are themselves associated with an increase in phenotypic variability. Williamson draws attention to this association, and goes on to make some speculations about the genetics of speciation (1981, 442–3).

There are two important ways in which Williamson's data may be interpreted. The first is to suppose that Williamson is employing Mayr's biological species concept, and that he intends to study transitions between biological species. When we choose this reading certain questions about the data become relevant. In particular, we have to ask if the species boundaries identified on the basis of phenotypic considerations coincide with the attainment of reproductive isolation.[21] Thus one contribution that the essay makes is towards advancing our understanding of speciation, *conceived as a process in which descendant populations achieve reproductive isolation from a persisting ancestral population.* If Williamson's findings are interpreted in this way, they bear on *one* issue of the tempo of evolutionary

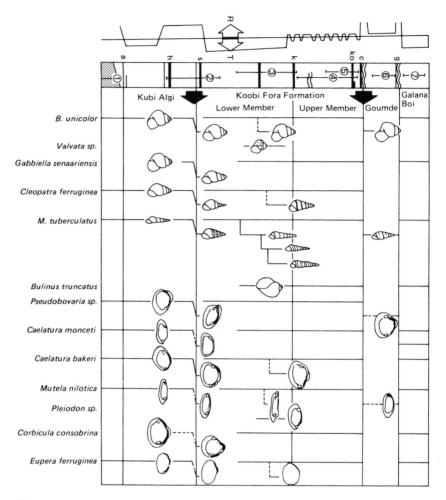

Figure 15.3
The pattern of morphological change in some molluscs from the Turkana basin (from Williamson 1981).

change and *one* issue of the genetics of speciation. Is the attainment of reproductive isolation a process that occurs rapidly, punctuating long periods of stasis? What mechanisms of population genetics underlie this process?

The second construal ignores any considerations about reproductive isolation. Williamson's data reveal a pattern of phenotypic change, and we can concentrate on this pattern without linking it to claims about reproductive isolation. If processes of speciation are simply identified with the rapid morphological transitions that Williamson describes, then we can inquire about the tempo of these processes and about their underlying genetic basis. Nor are these uninteresting questions. It is no less significant to ask after the tempo and mode of speciation, *conceived as a process of morphological discontinuity*, than it is to inquire about the attainment of reproductive isolation. Williamson's suggestions about genetic mechanisms can be construed as hypotheses about the genetic changes that underlie those episodes of phenotypic modification (with increased phenotypic variability) which are recorded in his data. We do not need to introduce the idea that these episodes lead to reproductive isolation.

Williamson has sometimes been criticized on the grounds that his morphological findings do not rule out the possibility of cryptic "speciation events" during periods of alleged stasis. (Schopf 1981 makes a similar point against claims of documentation of punctuated equilibrium.) Whether or not these criticisms succeed against the first interpretation, they are plainly irrelevant to the second. The pattern of phenotypic change, a pattern which the fossil record wears on its face, can itself serve as the basis for some important inquiries about the tempo and mode of evolution. By separating different conceptions of species and of speciation, we can disentangle different important issues that arise in biology, and recognize the significance of investigating a number of different patterns in the diversity of life.

At this point let me take up the question that is common to philosophy and biology, the question of the "reality" of species. It is important to understand that realism about species is quite independent of the view that species are individuals. Notice first that if realism about species is construed as the bare claim that species exist independently of human cognizance of them, then anyone who accepts a modest realism about sets can endorse realism about species. Organisms exist and so do sets of those organisms. The particular sets of organisms that are species exist independently of human cognition. So realism about species is trivially true.

To make realism come so cheap is obviously not to recognize what provokes biologists and philosophers to wave banners for the objectivity of systematics. (See Sober 1980 for a clear elaboration of this point.) What is at issue here is whether the division of organisms into species corresponds to something in the *objective structure* of nature. Articulating this realist claim is difficult. But I suggest that however it is developed, it will prove compatible with pluralism about species. *Pluralistic* realism rests on the idea that our objective interests may be diverse, that we may be objectively correct in pursuing biological inquiries which demand different forms of explanation, so that the patterning of nature generated in different areas of biology may cross-classify the constituents of nature. (There are suggestions about how to articulate this point in Boyd 1979 and in my own 1982.) Despite the fact that realist theses about the objectivity of classifications cry out for analysis, we can recognize the plausibility of those theses when we reflect on Williamson's molluscs. Williamson's lineages should remind us that there are a number of objective patterns of evolutionary change. The pluralistic realist is someone who is concerned to understand all of them.

Finally, let me turn to the moral for philosophy of science. In thinking about the general problem of conceptual change in science, we are inclined to consider two main possibilities. With the advantage of hindsight, we see that our predecessors were referring to natural groups of things, about which they may have had radically false beliefs. Or, perhaps, we view them as referring to sets that cut across the natural kinds in bizarre ways. The example of the concept of species—and, I would suggest, that of the concept of gene (1982)—reveals an intermediate situation. Here we find ourselves unable to provide some short description that will finally reveal the natural group that our predecessors struggled to characterize, but neither are we willing to dismiss them as simply producing an uninteresting heterogeneous collection. The set of species taxa is heterogeneous, but it is not wrongheaded in the way that some early attempts at chemical classification are.

If I am right, then there will be no simple description that will pick out exactly those sets of organisms which some biologists reasonably identify as species taxa. We shall not be able to reconstruct the language of biology and to trace its historical development in the way in which we have been able to cope with cases of conceptual change in chemistry. But this does not mean that we are swept into the cynic's view of species. For although it may be true that species are just those sets of organisms recognized as species by competent taxonomists, there is a way to understand why just those sets have been picked out. That way is not the familiar way of using current theory as an Archimedean point from which we can, at last, provide a single descriptive characterization of the groups to which our benighted predecessors have referred. Instead, we must recognize that there are many different contexts of investigation in which the concept of species is employed, and that the currently favored set of species taxa has emerged through a history in which different groups of organisms have been classified by biologists working on different biological problems. The species category can be partitioned into sets, each of which is a subset of some category of kinds. We can conceive of it as generated in the following way. A number of biologists, $B_1 \ldots, B_n$, each with a different focus of interest, investigate parts of the natural world. For each B_i there is a subset of the totality of organisms, O_i, which are investigated. B_i identifies a set of kinds, K_i, the kinds appropriate to her interest—that partition O_i. The set of species taxa bequeathed to us is the union of the K_i. In areas where the O_i overlap, of course, there may be fierce debate. My suggestion is that we recognize the legitimacy of all those natural partitions of the organic world of which at least one of the K_i is a part.

This schematic account of the set of species taxa we have inherited is intended to make clear the moral of my story. To appreciate the rationale for the species category we must reconstruct the history of our discourse about species, and there is no quick substitute for that reconstruction. The cynic's definition may be the beginning of wisdom about species. But it is only the beginning.

Notes

An earlier version of the present paper was given at the Eastern Division meeting of the American Philosophical Association in December 1982. I am very grateful to my commentator, Elliott Sober, for some helpful criticisms and suggestions, and to Alex Rosenberg, who chaired the session and later supplied me with valuable written comments. I would also like to thank David Hull for his detailed response to a much longer manuscript on this topic (*Species*, eventually to be published in revised and expanded form by Bradford Books). Finally, I want to acknowledge the enormous amount I have learned from correspondence and conversations with numerous biologists and philosophers, most notably: John Beatty, Jonathan Bennett, Bill Fink, Sara Fink, Steve Gould, Marjorie Grene, Kent Holsinger, Dick Lewontin, Gregory Mayer, Ernst Mayr, Brent Mishler, Michael Ruse, Husain Sarkar, Laurance Splitter, and Ernest Williams. Residual errors are probably my own.

1. Several—but not all those that have figured in the recent taxonomic literature. In particular, I hold no brief for phenetics.
2. The person who comes closest to advocating a realistic version of pluralism about species is John Dupré (1981), who defends what he calls (borrowing a name from John Perry) "promiscuous realism." Dupré's defense is brief (since the primary concern of his (1981) is to address some important issues in philosophy of language) and, to my mind, unconvincing. Pointing out that biological taxa cut across the divisions of organisms introduced by gastronomes hardly shows that there are alternative sets of kinds internal to biology. Nor does it help to note (1981, 83) that ecologists use the concept of population, for this does not indicate any commitment to alternative species taxa. Hence, although I find Dupré's short discussion of promiscuous realism provocative, I don't think he has made out a case for this view.
3. *Loci classici* are Ghiselin (1974), Hull (1976, 1978, 1980); Rosenberg (1981) provides a helpful summary. My discussion will be directed primarily at the arguments advanced by Hull. To the best of my knowledge, Ghiselin deserves credit for his original presentation of the thesis that species are individuals, but Hull's articles are more systematic and detailed in arguing for the thesis.

4. An exhaustive evaluation of this claim would require discussion of the merits and shortcomings of main features of phylogenetic systematics (cladism). This is undertaken in *Species*. For reasons of space, I have concentrated here on the main philosophical arguments.

5. Another general worry about construing species as sets was voiced by Elliott Sober. As Sober rightly points out, his own existence is not essential to the existence of *Homo sapiens*: there are worlds in which Sober does not exist but in which the species does exist. Hence, he contends, the species is not to be identified with the set of humans. I reply that this conclusion does not follow. In different worlds, *Homo sapiens* is a different set. Just as the extension of "car" varies from world to world, so does the referent of "*Homo sapiens*."

6. In fairness to Hull, I should note that he does not advocate any argument that is as stark as the one presented here. However, he sometimes comes very close: see, for example, his 1981, 146.

7. As Bill Fink pointed out to me, this allows for relatively trivial changes—such as chance fluctuations in frequency—to count as cases of evolution. Quite evidently, one can attempt to circumscribe the "genuine forces" of evolution, and use the resultant characterization to generate a more stringent conception of evolutionary change. Any such conception can easily be applied to the present context.

8. For those who are inclined to believe that the inviability of a zygote because of some genetic disruption does not signal a species boundary, let me suggest a slightly different criterion. One might propose that mutations or chromosomal novelties giving rise to the absence of P generate inviable gametes. In this way, the effect of the disruption of the genome is felt at the prezygotic stage. (I am grateful to Elliott Sober for bringing to my attention the possibility that an inviable *zygote* may not indicate a species boundary.)

9. The issue of the spatiotemporal localization of species is a tricky one. (For an illuminating discussion of localizability of the extensions of predicates and the character of natural laws, see John Earman's 1978.) Given contemporary cosmology, it appears that the extension of "atom of gold," no less than that of "organism belonging to *Rattus rattus*," is spatiotemporally localized (as noted in Kitts and Kitts 1979). Hull's most explicit discussion of this issue runs as follows: ". . . biological species are spatiotemporally localized in a way in which physical substances and elements are not. No spatiotemporal restrictions are built into the definitions of 'gold' and 'water'" (Hull 1981, 148–49). It seems to me that this response confuses semantical and ontological issues. A defender of the view that species are sets (an ontological view) is free to adopt a number of different theses about how the names of species are defined (or how their referents are fixed). I do not see that remarks about the semantical features of "gold," "*Homo spaiens*," and so forth, cut any ontological ice. We can use proper names (e.g., "2," "π") to refer to sets, and it's possible that our only way of referring to a person (a paradigm individual) should be via a description (e.g., "the first person to make fire"). Interestingly, Hull immediately proceeds from the passage I have cited to the point about the *connectedness* of species—the point that I regard as cental to his case. I see this as reflecting the fact that the official notion of a "spatiotemporally unrestricted class" is unworkable for Hull's purposes: in one sense, far too many classes are spatiotemporally restricted; in another, the distinction only holds with respect to class *names*.

10. Let me briefly respond to an obvious objection. It may be held that the set-theoretic reformulation of discourse about species—specifically the translation sketched in section II above—grants Hull everything he wants. At this stage, it ought to be clear that this is not so. At least two of the main consequences of the doctrine that species are individuals (the thesis that species are historically connected, and the explanation of the

nonexistence of laws about particular species) do not follow from my set-theoretic account. Indeed, I would contend that all of the apparently exciting results which Hull has wanted to establish are not honored by the set-theoretic version. (A more extensive defense of this claim is given in *Species*.)

11. There is a short answer: species are natural kinds. I accept this answer, but I don't adopt all the implications some may want to draw from it. In particular, I want to remain agnostic on the issue of whether any species taxon has a nontrivial essence. But what then distinguishes a natural kind? I suggest that natural kinds are the sets that one picks out in giving explanations. They are the sets corresponding to predicates that figure in our explanatory schemes. Are kinds then the extensions of predicates that occur in laws? Possibly—but not ncessarily. The account of explanation I favor (see my 1981) does not require that all explanation involve derivation from laws. One of the central features of that account is that the generality of a scientific explanation need not consist in its using some lawlike premise but in its instantiating a pattern exemplified in numerous other explanations. Hence, though I link natural kinds to the predicates that occur in scientific explanations, I do not require that there be laws about all kinds.

Subsequent discussion in the present paper will not rest on this all-too-brief elaboration of the idea that species are natural kinds. I am grateful to a number of people, most notably Alex Rosenberg, for helping me to see the relation between my own views and the traditional idea of species as natural kinds. A more elaborate account of this relation is undertaken in *Species*.

12. I should point out that this proposal for demarcating species taxa is the one most congenial to the Hull-Ghiselin thesis. The difficulties that arise for the Simpson-Hennig-Wiley approach provide more reasons to adopt the position defended in section II.

13. Wiley and Hennig diverge from Simpson in disallowing speciation through anagenesis. Wiley, unlike Hening, is prepared to grant that a species may persist through a speciation event.

14. There are some curious twists in recent versions of the biological species concept, including what appears to be a flirtation with essentialism. Consider the following recent statement by Ernst Mayr: "In spite of the variability caused by the genetic uniqueness of every individual, there is a species-specific unity to the genetic program (DNA) of nearly every species" (1982, 297). Similar suggestions have been voiced by others (Eldredge and Gould 1972, 114), and they reinforce the idea that morphological difference or reproductive isolation are indicators of a more fundamental cleavage among organisms.

15. In choosing this label, I don't intend to downplay the role of physiological (as opposed to anatomical) considerations. The contrast is between appeals to structure and present function, on the one hand, and appeals to history, on the other. (I am grateful to Marjorie Grene for suggesting to me that my label might mislead.)

16. Evidently, this scenario recapitulates the views of Putnam and Kripke about the conceptualization of natual kinds. See (Putnam 1975) and (Kripke 1980).

17. I should point out that the criterion of reproductive isolation can itself be applied in two different ways to divide lineages. One can count two stages of a lineage as parts of different species if they are reproductively isolated, or one can view speciation events as occurring only when one species gives rise to descendant populations that coexist and are reproductively isolated from one another. As I argue in *Species*, the first criterion is problematic unless certain theses about the geometry of evolution are true; the second represents the approach of Hennig, Wiley, and some other cladists.

18. This type of approach seems to be used by Nelson and Platnick (1981) and by Eldredge and Cracraft (1980). In *Species*, I argue that the use of the concept of a fuzzy set can help in avoiding some difficulties posed by transitional populations.

19. For amplification of these points, see my 1982. As Alex Rosenberg has pointed out to me, the increasing complexity of the systems revealed in molecular biology underscores the pluralism about genes defended in that paper.

20. Thus there is no univocal answer to the question of how to describe the type of hypothetical situation beloved of philosophers. Suppose we have a species S and discover the existence of a historically unrelated group of organisms that agree with the members of S in any respect we choose (reproductively compatible, genetically similar, and so forth). Does the group count as a subset of S? I claim that the answer must be relative to a *prior decision* on whether or not to employ a historical species concept. Use of such a concept is not forced on us, and it may prove helpful in seeing this to consider a range of organisms and a range of biological investigations. What we may be inclined to say when S is *Rattus rattus* may well be different from what we say when S is the bacteriophage T_4. (I am grateful to Jonathan Bennett for prodding me into making this point explicit.)

21. There are complications here. One of the lineages (*Melanoides tuberculata*) is asexual. Hence, Williamson's claim must be that the morphological discontinuities correspond to the lineage divisions marked out by reproductive isolation—*where demarcation by reproductive isolation is possible*. This example underscores the point made in section III.

References

Boyd, R. (1979), "Metaphor and Theory Change: What is 'Metaphor' a Metaphor for?," in A. Ortony (ed.), *Metaphor and Thought*. Cambridge: Cambridge University Press.

Dawkins, R. (1976), *The Selfish Gene*. Oxford: Oxford University Press.

Dawkins, R. (1982), *The Extended Phenotype*. San Francisco: Freeman.

Dupré, J. (1981), "Natural Kinds and Biological Taxa," *Philosophical Review* XC:66–90.

Earman, J. (1978), "The Universality of Laws," *Philosophy of Science* 45:173–81.

Eldredge, N. and Cracraft, J. (1980), *Phylogenetic Patterns and the Evolutionary Process*. New York: Columbia University Press.

Eldredge, N. and Gould, S. J. (1972), "Punctuated Equilibria: An Alternative to Phyletic Gradualism," in T. J. M. Schopf (ed.), *Models in Paleobiology*. San Francisco: Freeman.

Ghiselin, M. (1974), "A Radical Solution to the Species Problem," *Systematic Zoology* 23:536–44.

Hempel, C. G. (1954), "A Logical Appraisal of Operationism," in Hempel (1965).

Hempel, C. G. (1965), *Aspects of Scientific Explanation*. Glencoe: The Free Press.

Hempel, C. G. (1966), *Philosophy of Natural Science*. Englewood Cliffs: Prentice-Hall.

Hennig, W. (1966), *Phylogenetic Systematics*. Urbana: University of Illinois Press.

Hull, D. (1968), "The Operational Imperative—Sense and Nonsense in Operationism," *Systematic Zoology* 16:438–57.

Hull, D. (1976), "Are Species Really Individuals?," *Systematic Zoology* 25:174–91.

Hull, D. (1978), "A Matter of Individuality," *Philosophy of Science* 45:335–60.

Hull, D. (1980), "Individuality and Selection," *Annual Review of Ecology and Systematics* 11:311–332.

Hull, D. (1981), "Kitts and Kitts and Caplan on Species," *Philosophy of Science* 48:141–152.

Kitcher, P. S. (1981), "Explanatory Unification," *Philosophy of Science* 48:507–31.

Kitcher, P. S. (1982), "Genes," *British Journal for the Philosophy of Science* 33:337–59.

Kitts, D. B., and Kitts, D. J. (1979), "Biological Species as Natural Kinds," *Philosophy of Science* 46:613–22.

Kripke, S. (1980), *Naming and Necessity*. Cambridge: Harvard University Press.

Mayr, E. (1942), *Systematics and the Origin of Species*. New York: Columbia University Press.

Mayr, E. (1961), "Cause and Effect in Biology," in Mayr (1976).

Mayr, E. (1963), *Animal Species and Evolution*. Cambridge: Harvard University Press.

Mayr, E. (1969), *Principles of Systematic Zoology*. Cambridge: Harvard University Press.

Mayr, E. (1970), *Populations, Species, and Evolution*. Cambridge: Harvard University Press.

Mayr, E. (1976), *Evolution and the Diversity of Life*. Cambridge: Harvard University Press.

Mayr, E. (1982), *The Growth of Biological Thought*. Harvard University Press.

Nelson, G., and Platnick, N. (1981), *Systematics and Biogeography: Cladistics and Vicariance*. New York: Columbia University Press.

Oster, G., and Alberch, P. (1982), "Evolution and Bifurcation of Developmental Programs," *Evolution* 36:444–459.

Parker, E. D., and Selander, R. (1976), "The Organization of Genetic Diversity in the Parthenogenetic Lizard *Cnemidophorus Tesselatus*," *Genetics* 84:791–805.

Parker, E. D. (1979), "Phenotypic Consequences of Parthenogensis in *Cnemidophours* Lizards. I. Variability in Parthenogenetic and Sexual Populations," *Evolution* 33:1150–1166.

Putnam, H. (1975), *Philosophical Papers*, Volume 2. Cambridge: Cambridge University Press.

Rosen, D. (1979), "Fishes from the Upland Intermontane Basins of Guatemala: Revisionary Studies and Comparative Geography," *Bulletin of the American Museum of Natural History* 162:269–375.

Rosenberg, A. (1981), *Sociobiology and the Pre-Emption of Social Science*. Baltimore: Johns Hopkins University Press.

Schopf, T. J. M. (1981), "Punctuated Equilibrium and Evolutionary Stasis," *Paleobiology* 7:156–66.

Simpson, G. G. (1961), *Principles of Animal Taxonomy*. New York: Columbia University Press.

Sneath, P., and Sokal, R. (1973), *Numerical Taxonomy*. San Francisco: Freeman.

Sober, E. (1980), "Evolution, Population Thinking, and Essentialism," *Philosophy of Science* 47:350–83.

Sokal, R., and Sneath, P. (1961), *Principles of Numerical Taxonomy*. San Francisco: Freeman.

van Valen, L. (1976), "Ecological Species, Multispecies, and Oaks," *Taxon* 25:233–39.

White, M. J. D. (1978), *Modes of Speciation*. San Francisco: Freeman.

Wiley, E. O. (1981), *Phylogenetics*. New York: Wiley.

Williamson, P. (1981), "Paleontological Documentation of Speciation in Cenozoic Molluscs from Turkana Basin," *Nature* 293:437–43.

Chapter 16
Biological Species: Natural Kinds, Individuals, or What?

Michael Ruse

The status of biological species continues to attract attention and controversy. (See, for instance, Eldredge and Cracraft 1980; Gould 1979; Grant 1981a; Levin 1979; Mayr 1982; Wiley 1978, 1980; Splitter 1982; Mishler and Donoghue 1982; Holsinger 1984; Kitcher 1984; Eldredge 1985.) There is a strong feeling among biologists, at least there is a strong feeling among most zoologists and somewhat less of one among botanists (a difference to be discussed later), that species are somehow different from the other groupings of organisms we find (or make) in nature. Species, like *Drosophila melanogaster* or *Canis lupus*, are thought to be "natural," in some way objective or existing independently of the classifier. In this, species differ from the groups (taxa) found at other ranks, for instance that of the genus. The classifier's own thoughts and aims have a much greater role to play in the delimiting of members of these other groups.

But wherein lies the naturalness of species? With the coming of evolutionary theory, traditional answers seem less than adequate. Recently, in a brilliantly innovative move, the biologist Michael Ghiselin (1966, 1969, 1974a, b, 1981, 1987), supported by the philosopher David Hull (1975, 1976, 1978, 1979, 1981), has argued that evolution shows us to have misconstrued the nature of species. They are not groups or classes of organisms, like hockey players on a team. Rather, they are integrated *individuals*, with organisms having the relationship to their species of part to whole rather than member to class. And thus properly seen, argue Ghiselin and Hull, the specialness or naturalness of species is self-evident. Species are natural or real in the way any biological individual is natural or real.

In this essay, I argue that, stimulating though the species-as-individuals (s–a–i) thesis may be, it runs counter to much accepted biological thinking, as well as to logic. We must rely on more traditional conceptual tools to establish the naturalness of species. But, with some exceptions and qualifications, this can be done, and the very exceptions and qualifications themselves establish the correctness of the overall approach.

Biologists on Species

Let us start with what biologists have to say about species. The most interesting fact is that the category of species can be and is characterized in so many different ways, with corresponding ways of defining particular taxa names. Here, four major species concepts will suffice. (See Mayr 1982 and Grant 1981a for recent discussions of the multiplicity of species concepts.)

First, we have the most obvious and intuitive concept of all. We find the organic world broken up into groups of similar looking organisms, with gaps between the groups. The concept thus refers to some notion of overall similarity of appearance possessed by organisms within species taxa. In Charles Darwin's words, a species is "a set of individuals closely resembling each other" (Darwin 1859, 52).

Physical nature or *morphology* is the key to this species concept, and it is therefore invoked when one deals with particular species taxa. To be a member of *Homo sapiens* you must be relatively hairless, capable of walking upright, with a large brain, and so forth. In fact, today it is recognized that invariably there is diversity, even within such morphologically delimited groups, so biologists frequently use polytypic or polythetic definitions: lists of features, a combination of which is sufficient for species membership, but no one of which is necessary (Beckner 1959, Simpson 1961, Hull 1965).

Next, we have a concept which has, perhaps a little strongly, appropriated unto itself the title of *biological* species concept. This refers to breeding, or the lack of it. One well-known formulation, due to Ernst Mayr (1942), states that species are "groups of actually or potentially interbreeding natural populations which are reproductively isolated from other such groups." You do not normally find taxa name definitions using this concept, but I do not see in principle why not. Specify some individual, say Brigham Young, as your reference point, and then members of the same taxon are potential or actual interbreeders, with some obvious qualifications to take account of sex, and so forth. (See Mayr 1982 for his attempts to give a more refined version of the concept.)

Third, we have a concept which deliberately refers to *evolution*. In the words of the paleontologist G. G. Simpson (1961): "An evolutionary species is a lineage (an ancestral-descendant sequence of populations) evolving separately from others and with its own unitary evolutionary role and tendencies." A taxon name would get a related definition. If we suppose that humans first appeared about 1/2 million years ago, *Homo sapiens* is the name for the group which has descended from the original organisms. (This certainly seems to be the kind of definition that paleoanthropologists have in mind. See Johanson and Edey (1981), Johanson and White (1979).)

Fourth and finally, we have a concept which does for the world genes, what the first concept did for morphology. The category concept refers to overall *genetic* similarity clusterings, such clusterings, being separated from others by gaps. Mayr (1969) again: "When an evolutionary taxonomist speaks of the relationship of various taxa, he is quite right in thinking in terms of genetic similarity, rather than in terms of genealogy." A particular species name would be defined in terms of genes held in common (together perhaps with information about chromosomes, structure and so forth). For obvious reasons, you do not often see definitions of this ilk, but they do exist. With increasingly sophisticated methods of analysing genomes, their similarities and differences, we might expect to see more such definitions.

There are other concepts which could be and sometimes are invoked, for instance concepts based on ecology (Van Valen 1976). But, we have enough for our purposes. The question to be asked now is why a taxon which falls into a category characterised in one of the above ways should be thought natural or real in some sense. Since this is a question *about* science, rather than *within* it, we turn to philosophy for guidance.

Natural Kinds

Traditionally, philosophers have treated the status of species as being part and parcel of a larger question about the reality of "natural kinds." Why do we think the whole physical world to be divided into different sorts of things: gold, water, stars, as well as *Homo sapiens* and *Drosophila melanogaster*?

Roughly speaking, there have been two main answers to this question (Ayers 1981).[1] Credit for the first is given to *Aristotle*. He argued that the world—at least, the world of scientific inquiry—is made up of substances. Any particular substance, like a sample of gold or an individual man, results from the interaction between the substance's underlying matter and its form. This latter gives a substance its nature or essence. Objects of the same kind, like two men, are the same because they have the same form, which is embedded in different samples of matter. Substances have their form essentially, that is to say, one cannot be a substance of a particular kind without having the required form.

Crucial to the Aristotelian position is the distinction between a "real definition" and a "nominal definition." The former enables you to define a natural kind name, including the name of an organic species, in terms of attributes which stem necessarily from the very essence of a substance (Aristotle called these attributes "properties"). Thus, in the case of *Homo sapiens* the essence involves the notion of rationality. Unpacking, we get such properties as the power of speech. A real definition would consequently refer to this power. However, not all attributes of an individual stem from the essence. There are features which are possessed "accidentally." Although these features are nonessential, it might nevertheless be possible to distinguish a natural kind using only accidents. In the case of humans, both bipediality and featherlessness are accidents, and yet is so happens that the set of featherless bipeds is one and the same as the set of rational animals. Any characterization in terms of accidents yields a "nominal definition."

The great rival to Aristotle's analysis came in the seventeenth century, from the pen of John Locke. He argued that reality lies in the underlying particles which go to make up any particular substance. Locke himself was, in fact, doubtful that we could ever truly know these basic units. But, any real definition would have to make reference to these building blocks, specifically to their shape, structure, motion, composition, and so forth. Surface definitions are simply marks of the structure beneath. Consequently, any surface definition could never be more than nominal. For Locke, a definition of humans in terms of rationality has no more and no less status than a definition in terms of bipedality.

But what of the underlying real structure? Even here Locke wanted to deny the absoluteness of Aristotelian essences. Shapes and so forth can change, taking a substance from one kind to another. Not to mention borderline cases:

> There are Animals so near of kind both to Birds and Beasts, that they are in the Middle between both ... There are some Brutes, that seem to have as much Knowledge and Reason, as some that are called Men ... and so on till we come to the lowest and the most inorganical parts of Matter, we shall find everywhere, that the several Species are linked together, and differ but in almost insensible degrees (Locke 1975, III, vi, 12).

Hence, ultimately for Locke, even definition in terms of reality involves a conscious decision to divide. A Lockean definition is therefore never more than what an Aristotelian would label "nominal." Any difference between men and changelings "is only known to us, by their agreement, or disagreement with the complex *idea* that the name *Man* stands for" (Locke 1975, III, vi, 39).

In short, whereas for Aristotle natural kinds are ontological entities, for Locke they are at best epistemological concepts. You have the objective approach, *versus* the subjective approach. The approach which *finds* natural kinds, and the approach which *makes* them.

But Are Biological Species Really Natural Kinds?

Let us now try to put biology and philosophy together. Does either Aristotle or Locke capture the biologist's sense that species are real or natural?

The simple answer is that, as they stand, neither does. Take Aristotle. He would argue that species are real, because they are natural kinds. But, how then could one get a real definition? The morphological approach to taxa will not do, because if there is one thing that modern biology teaches, it is that evolution promotes morphological diversity. Species members are not all the same. Hence the need for polytypic definitions. But, for something to be an Aristotelian property (as opposed to an accident), it must be possessed by every member of the kind, and distinguishing the group from others. Polytypic definitions are not enough. Hence, morphology will not do. (Mayr 1963, Dobzhansky 1970, Dobzhansky et al. 1977, discuss variation within species.)

The same considerations apply to genetic features. Evolution promotes genetic diversity (Lewontin 1974). And, similarly, the features relied on by other approaches to species fail the Aristotelian. Is the sterile worker ant even a potential interbreeder, and would one really want to say that an entirely artificially produced fruit-fly could never really be in *Drosophila melanogaster*?

In any case, after Darwin, strict Aristotelianism simply will not work (Hull 1965; Mayr 1969, 1982). Evolution says that you can take virtually any property you like, and if you go back (or forwards) enough in time then ancestors (descendants) did not (will not) have it. But, this is just what Aristotle cannot handle. The whole point about a natural kind is that its properties exist in perpetuity, like mathematical objects. And clearly such properties have to be passed on by (to) ancestors (descendants). Evolution denies this.

What about Locke? Initially, things seem very much more promising. Morphological criteria give you nominal definitions of species names. Alternatively, if you favor phylogenies, you use relationships of descent—something which Locke himself, incidentally, was not that enamored with. ("[M]ust I go to the Indies to see the Sire and Dam of the one, and the Plant from which the seed was gather'd, that produced the other, to know whether this be a Tiger or that Tea," Locke 1975, III, vi, 23.) Then, genetic criteria give you the closest things you can get to real definitions. And, contrary to Locke's own doubts, we can know quite a bit about these. Nary an issue of *Science* or *Nature* appears without fresh details of the genetic structure of some organism.

One often finds versions of a neo-Lockean proposal in the literature (for instance, Mayr 1963, 1969). Unfortunately, you purchase your solution to the species problem at too high a price. You have to relinquish claims to the ultimate objectivity or reality of species. A Lockean natural kind is essentially subjective or arbitrary. And that is just what you do not want to concede, when it comes to species. In some sense, species are real!

We are caught in a dilemma. Evolution refutes Aristotelianism; but, Lockeanism is inadequate. According to Ghiselin and Hull, and an increasingly large number of supporters, we must go back to biology. When we do this, we see that Aristotle and Locke share a false premise. Reject this premise, and hope rises for a solution to the species problem. (Sympathisers with Ghiselin and Hull include Mayr 1976, Wiley 1978, Rosenberg 1980, Sober 1980, Beatty 1982, Splitter 1982, Eldredge and Cracraft 1980. Intimations of the Ghiselin/Hull approach are to be found in Theodosius Dobzhansky's classic, *Genetics and the Origin of Species*.)

Species as Individuals

Aristotle and Locke agree that species are natural kinds. The taxon *Homo sapiens* is a class, with individual humans like Michael Ruse and Charles Darwin as members. I qualify for membership in the class *Homo sapiens*, because I possess certain attributes, whatever they may be. So does Charles Darwin. My dog Spencer does not have these properties, and thus does not qualify. He has his own species, *Canis familiaris*.

Ghiselin and Hull argue that species are not natural kinds at all: they are not classes with members. Rather, species are *individuals*, just as particular organisms are individuals. Hence, just as the relationship between my arm and myself is one of part to whole, rather than member to class, so my relationship to the species *Homo sapiens* is one of part to whole. I, and Charles Darwin, are parts of the human species, just as Spencer is part of the species *Canis familiaris*.

The reformers argue that, once we see species in the true light, all of the problems about species start to fade. Of course, species are real. No one doubts the reality of Michael Ruse, or of Spencer. They are individuals. Real things. Part of the furniture of our world. So are species.

What kind of claim is the s—a—i thesis? It is not solely or even primarily an empirical claim. "Look! There's an individual!" Rather, it is more of a conceptual claim, whose plausibility must be argued for. Consider a chessboard. You can think of this as an individual, made up of 64 parts, or as a class of 64 squares. It depends on your perspective as to which makes more sense—are you making chessboards, or are you teaching someone the rules of chess. *The crux of the s—a—i thesis, therefore, is whether modern evolutionary biology inclines one to treat species more as individuals, or more as classes, as natural kinds.*

There is of course the initial question as to what precisely one means by an "individual." Ghiselin and Hull point to the fact that, whatever else an individual may or may not be, we recognize organisms as paradigm examples of individuals. Organisms are not just diffuse, artificially created entities. They are integrated beings. They have internal organization. Hence, if we can show that, in important respects, species are like organisms, we can reasonably say that species are individuals.

But, claim Ghiselin and Hull, from an evolutionary perspective species have the very marks of individuality that organisms have. Just like organisms, species come into being, exist for a period in space and time, and then go. And, they have at least some sense of organization. As the leading evolutionist Ernst Mayr said (before he himself was converted to the s–a–i thesis): *"Species are the real units of evolution, they are the entities which specialize, which become adapted, or which shift their adaptation"* (Hull 1976, 183, quoting Mayr 1969).

That evolutionary theory treats species as individuals becomes clear when we look at their uniqueness. Adolf Hitler was an individual—as such (unlike his diaries) he came uniquely and went uniquely. A copy of Adolf Hitler is not he. It cannot be. Similarly, we have this uniqueness for species. "If a species evolved which was identical to a species of extinct pterodactyl save origin, it would still be a new, distinct species" (Hull 1978, 349). If you are a species, you simply cannot be born again, any more than Adolf Hitler can be.

What about change? Organisms can undergo major change and still be the same organism. What counts is continuity. The limits of an organism are birth and death. The same is true of species. "There is no limit to the genetic change that can take place in a species or population before it becomes extinct or speciates" (Hull 1976, 182). In fact, just like an organism, so long as the continuity persists, we have the same species.

Finally, let us mention one revealing point. Biologists take one specimen from a species, using it as the marker. The species name (which, as with all individuals, is a proper name) is attached to this marker—the type specimen—by an act which is akin to baptism. This specimen does not have to be a "typical" member of the species, whatever that might mean. And, of course it does not. The type is part of the whole, not a member in the class.

> The fact that any specimen, no matter how atypical, can function as the typespecimen makes no sense on the class interpretation; it makes admirably good sense if species are interpreted as individuals (Hull 1976, 175).

All in all, whatever "common sense" may say, modern evolutionary biology demands that species be regarded as individuals. Hence, the naturalness of species.

Why Species Are Not Individuals: Biological Objections

Ingenious though it is, the Ghiselin/Hull attempt to slice through the Gordian knot constraining the species problem fails. There are several significant reasons why species cannot properly be considered as individuals.[2]

First, look at matters at the most basic biological level. We think organisms are individuals because the parts are all joined together. Charles Darwin's head was joined to Charles Darwin's trunk. But, in the case of species, this is not so. Charles Darwin was never linked up to Thomas Henry Huxley. Of course, you might object that although Darwin's head was never linked directly to his feet, they were linked indirectly through intermediate parts. Analogously, as evolutionists presumably we believe that Darwin and Huxley were linked by actual physical entities (namely, the succession of humans back to their shared ancestors). But, this objection fails, for the point is that these links have now been broken and lost. If (gruesome thought!) Darwin's head were physically severed from his feet, we would certainly have no biological individual.

Yet, with justice, Ghiselin and Hull will respond that these speculations are beside the point. The required condition for individuality is not mere spatiotemporal contiguity. It is rather some sort of internal integration or organization. Because of such internal organization, the United States is one country, even though Alaska and Hawaii do not touch any of the other states. The fifty states work together, in a way that (say) the forty-eight mainland states together with Ontario and Quebec do not. Analogously, Charles Darwin is an individual, not because of spatiotemporal contiguity, but because his parts are organized, working *together*. The same is true of other biological entities, even those which break into parts at some points in their life cycles, like slime molds. *And*, the same is true of species. They have an integrating organization, with the parts contributing to the whole.[3]

But, this will not do, at least not in the light of much modern thought about the working of evolution. First and foremost, thinking of a species as an integrated individual goes flatly in the face of the way in which the major evolutionary mechanism of natural selection is generally regarded today. Selection leads to adaptations, features which help organisms in life's struggles for survival and reproduction. But who precisely benefits from adaptations? Is it the possessors alone, or do others benefit? In short, at what level of biological organization does selection work? Is it between individuals, benefiting individuals, or is it between higher entities like species, benefiting species taken as a whole.

Until recently, most people casually assumed that selection could work at virtually every level of biological organization. In particular, one could have selection between groups of organisms, including between species. The units of selection, in vital respects, were species. As Mayr (1969) said: "Species are ... the entities ... which become adapted." However, majority opinion today is that selection just does not work in this way. As Charles Darwin himself argued, ardently, selection works chiefly if not exclusively at least at the level of the individual organism. "Group selection" at the level of the species does not work. A species is not adapted. An organism (or, at most, a limited number of organisms) is. Any species effects are just epiphenomena on individual effects, or at most, on population effects. (See Brandon and Burian 1984, for a review of this topic, and Ruse 1980 for Darwin's views on the subject.)

If this is all so, then there is something very odd indeed about speaking of a species as an individual. It is very far from being an integrated unit like an organism. The individual organisms of a species are all working for their own benefits, against those of others. Any species cooperation, any species integration, is secondary on the particular organism's self-interests. And, in any case, one is hardly likely to get species-wide secondary effects. Cooperation will, at most, be between relatives, or fellow population members. Generally, selection pits organisms against each other (although not necessarily in a crude "nature red in tooth and claw" fashion).[4]

Individual selection and the s−a−i thesis simply do not go together. What about obvious counters? Some biologists belive that group selection can work. This is true, but hardly makes the s−a−i-thesis again compelling. Group selection supporters think it works for populations, not species, and no one denies the importance of individual selection. (See Wilson 1975 and Wade 1978 for recent views on group selection.) Conversely, some biologists argue that the true "individual" in individual selection is the gene, not the whole organism (Dawkins 1976). Does not my argument prove too much, suggesting that organisms should not be considered true individuals —which is clearly absurd? But, while this point does show that for some biologists the level of individuality does not necessarily stop at the whole organism level, no one denies that organisms (thanks to selection) are sufficiently well organized to be considered individuals in their own right. Richard Dawkins (1982), for instance, speaks of organisms as "vehicles" which carry within them the units of selection, "replicators" or genes. An organism, to such a biologist, is no less an individual than a BMW is to a racing driver.

Continuing with biological counters to the above critique, what about Steven Stanley's (1979) notion of species selection, where it is suggested that trends are a function of the success or failure of species? Again there is little help for the s−a−i thesis. Even if one accepts species selection, and many would not, the key operation of natural selection is with the individual. Drawing attention to the trends that one often sees in the fossil record, Stanley suggests that there is nevertheless a randomness about the members of new species with respect to a trend. Although a trend may (say) be from smaller to bigger, a new species in the line of descent could well have smallbodied members. (No doubt, if one persisted, one could devise some form of species selection where the group as a whole was significant. But its realisation in nature is obviously another matter. See Arnold and Fristrup 1982.)

Perhaps the strongest biological case for the s—a—i thesis comes through the notion of a species as a number of organisms sharing a common "gene pool," with shared types of genes being passed on to common ancestors (i.e., a kind of hybrid notion formed from several of the species concepts, Dobzhansky 1970, Dobzhansky et al. 1977). Here you might think we have the kind of integration required for individuality. Certain genes flow between the organisms of a species, and between no others. But, this hardly denies the key importance of individual selection. Moreover, there are today strong questions about the biological importance, at the species level, of such genetic sharing. It was once thought that gene flow, between populations, is a key factor in keeping the organisms of a species alike. Now, it seems more likely that normalizing selection is the key causal factor. Species members sit on the top of the same "adaptive peak"—if they vary too much from the species norm, then selection wipes them out.

This downgrading of the significance of gene flow is a most important point, because (being itself one which comes from modern evolutionary theorising) it strikes right at the heart of the claim that the s—a—i thesis (however counterintuitive it may seem) must be accepted on the basis of modern biology. John Endler's (1977) already classic study brings both theoretical and empirical evidence to bear demonstrating the restricted effects of gene flow. Basically, gene flow would be expected due to migration ("the relatively long-distance movements made by large numbers of individuals in approximately the same direction at approximately the same direction at approximately the same time," 182) and dispersal ("the roughly random and nondirectional small-scale movements made by individuals rather than groups, continuously, rather than periodically, as a result of their daily activities," 181). One would expect that migration would be a most effective way of uniting a species, even if widely dispersed; but, as Endler points out, this is rarely so, since migration is usually accompanied by return migration and organisms give birth in the place where they were themselves born. Such "philopatry" has obvious adaptive virtues— birds may migrate to winter feeding grounds but they return to already-established and proven breeding grounds.

Dispersal is a priori a less promising way in which gene flow might be greatly effective, and there are a number of reasons why its importance should not be overestimated: ethological, ecological, and physiological inadequacy of hybrids between distant species members; random loss of new gene forms because they are rare; infrequency of long-distance travellers (as opposed to migrators); and more (pp. 28—9). All in all, therefore, one should not overemphasize the unity of the species because of the supposed circulation of shared genes. (Similar points are made by Grant

1981a, b; Levin 1981; and Mishler and Donoghue 1982. Although the point just made applies to both animals and plants, since the latter are spatially more fixed, expectedly the "genetic integration" argument has always seemed less plausible to botanists.)

So, once again we come back to the individual organism and to its response to the environment (including fellow species members). If you take Darwinian selection seriously, you simply must reject the s—a—i thesis. Note that I am certainly not denying that the members of a species are frequently "united" in having similar causal pressures, whether these be genetic or selective or whatever. Of course they do. That is what makes them part of the same species. The question is whether this "unification" is significantly more than similar causes. The s—a—i-supporter has to say that it is, even to the point of the kind of integration we find in individual organisms, and this is what I deny. (Caplan 1980 rightly emphasized that same causes lead to same effects, and this accounts for species members being similar.)

Why Species Are Not Individuals: Conceptual Objections

Let us move on to more conceptual-type objections to the s—a—i thesis. Crucial to the thesis is the claim that, logically, a species can appear only once. If it dies, that is it. In this, species are just like paradigm individual organisms. Adolf Hitler cannot be resurrected. Neither can extinct species of pterodactyl.

I will leave Christians to fight their own battles about human bodily resurrection. As far as species are concerned, time and technology have shown the s—a—i claim wrong. Today, through recombinant DNA techniques and the like, biologists are rushing to make new life forms. Significantly, for commercial reasons the scientists and their sponsors are busily applying for patents protecting the new creations. Were the origins of organisms things which uniquely separate and distinguish them, such protections would hardly be necessary. Old life form and new life form would necessarily be distinct. Since apparently they are not, this suggests that origins do not have the status claimed by the s—a—i boosters. (See Wade 1979, 1980a, b.)

Relatedly against the s—a—i thesis, in crucial respects it seems that it really does not treat species and their organisms all that very differently from the old way of treating of species as classes, with members included according to the possession of certain required properties. Take an organism. How do you know that my hand is part of the individual, Michael Ruse? Because it is joined on—that's why! But my dog Spencer certainly is not joined on, in the same way, to the species *Canis familiaris*. So why do we want to say that he is part of the species? Because he descended from the original ancestors, along with the rest of the group—that's why!

Descent is starting to look very much like an essential property. Spencer is part of the group *Canis familiaris*. Indeed, we even seem to have a real/nominal distinction at work here. In Spencer's case, if challenged about his status, I can in fact produce papers attesting to parentage. But in the case of the other four-legged being that lives in my house, I have no such documentary evidence about origins. And yet, I am as sure that Sesame is a cat, as that Spencer is a dog. Why? Because she looks and behaves like one. She miaows, purrs, keeps aloof, jumps from heights, stays up half the night, and is fastidiously clean. In short, she has all the identifying marks of catness (*Felis domestica*).

Clearly what I, and everyone else, am doing here is employing morphological and related criteria. Of course, Ghiselin and Hull recognize and appreciate the use of such criteria. They simply refuse to give such use any significant theoretical status (see Ghiselin 1981). What can this all mean, but that one is using nominal criteria, because real essence's descent relationships are unkown? Hence, for all the talk, the s−a−i thesis treats species as classes, with descent giving real essence and with morphology giving nominal definitions.

There are other objections you can raise against the s−a−i thesis. One is that it has controversial implications about the temporal limits of a species, and the possible evolutionary change that such a unit can encompass. So long as one gets no new group breaking off from an evolving lineage, one has one and only one species, whatever the change (just as one has one and only one organism, despite the change from caterpillar to butterfly). The cladistic school of taxonomy would accept this implication, but most biologists would not. They distinguish, for instance, between *Homo habilis, H. erectus,* and *H. sapiens,* despite the lack of branching. *Homo habilis* had a brain size of around 700 cc, much closer to that of a gorilla (*Gorilla gorilla*) at 500 cc, than to modern man at 1400 cc. Hence, species divisions are made—divisions which cladists and s−a−i supporters must ignore. (Cladism is discussed well in Eldredge and Cracraft 1980, and Wiley 1981.)

Indeed, the s−a−i thesis is more extreme than cladism. Cladists end a species as soon as there is any branching within the group. But, if just a small population broke from a parent species, leaving the parent unaffected, one would have a situation very similar to an asexual organism budding off a small part. The parent remains. Similarly, the s−a−i thesis would have to count an analogous parent species the same original individual. Carried to the extreme, classification could become very difficult indeed.[5]

And, finally, let me point to an implication which has rather drastic consequences for the social sciences. Laws of nature generally do not refer to specific spatiotemporally bounded objects. They are rather "timeless regularities in nature." But, if species are individuals, then any claims about the organism of species, restricted to the species, cannot be laws. In particular, any claims exclusively about human beings cannot possibly be laws. Hence, at one stroke, the social sciences, as they stand today, cease to be sciences in any worthwhile sense. To say the least, this is a somewhat drastic consequence.

The conclusion is clear. There is no absolute reason to treat species as individuals, and compelling reasons not to do so.

But What Then Are Species?

Either species must be groups, or they must be individuals. There is no third option. They are not individuals, hence they must be groups. But, we have seen that species cannot have the absoluteness of Aristotelian natural kinds. Evolution makes this impossible. The question which therefore remains is whether we can raise species above the rather subjective level of Lockean kinds? Are species more than just artificial collections of organisms?

They are indeed. Moreover, the reasons why we rightly think that species are more than artificial collections—why we think species are natural—are similar to reasons why we think there are natural groups encountered elsewhere in science, for instance in chemistry and geology.

The key reason why species are properly treated as natural kinds lies in that most distinctive fact noted earlier: the multiplicity of species concepts and of possible definitions of taxa names. To see the connection between naturalness and multiplicity, let us pull back for a moment and ask a general question about science. At what point is it in science that we feel we are onto something "real"? When is it we accept that we are not just dealing with hypothetical figments of a creative scientist's imagination? The strong consensus is that the breakthrough comes when we put *together* two or more *different* areas of theory into one unified whole. If you have two different subjects, and they are joined, so that the one complements the other, and vice-versa, then you are inclined to think that there's more than mere chance at work. Somehow, the unified theory tells you about the real. Such a coming togther, could not be mere coincidence—especially, if you can spell out the unification in terms of some overall theory (Leplin 1984).

This unification, known philosophically as a "consilience of inductions," was the one thing that Darwin always mentioned, when his theory was challenged. "I must freely confess, the difficulties and objections are terrific; but I cannot believe that a false theory would explain, as it seems to me it does explain, so many classes of facts" (Darwin 1887, 1, 455). And, it remains important today. For instance, in the recent geological revolution, people accepted plate tectonics when they saw that different areas of geology are unified in the one theory (Ruse 1981).

What about classification? Is there a possibility of some sort of consilience here, separating the natural or real from the merely arbitrary? William Whewell, who had the distinction of being both a professor of mineralogy and of moral philosophy, thought there was. A natural classification is one where different methods yield the same results. Particularly, if you have reasons for the coincidence, you feel sure that the classification cannot be just chance.

> The Maxim by which all Systems professing to be natural must be tested is this:—that the *arrangement obtained from one set of characters coincides with the arrangement obtained from another set*. (Whewell 1840, 1, 521, his italics. For more details on how Whewell used his ideas in mineralogy, see Ruse 1976.)

And, modern philosophers agree with Whewell. Thus Hempel:

> The rational core of the distinction between natural and artifical classifications is suggested by the consideration that in so-called natural classifications the determining characteristics are associated, universally or in a high percentage of all cases, with other characteristics, of which they are logically independent. (Hempel 1952, 53. See also Schlesinger 1963 for more references to this criterion.)

Coming back to organic species, we see that we have a paradigm for a natural classification. There are different ways of breaking organisms into groups, and they *coincide*! The genetic species is the morphological species is the reproductively isolated species is the group with common ancestors. Moreover, there are reasons for the coincidence. As the zoologist Mayr points out, bringing several of the definitions together:

> The reproductive isolation of a biological species, the protection of its collective gene-pool against pollution by genes from other species, results in a discontinuity not only of the genotype of the species, but also of its morphology and other aspects of the phenotype produced by this genotype. This is the fact on which taxonomic practice is based (Mayr 1969, 28).

Note, moreover, that the coincidence between variously delimited species is not unexplained. Certain genes do lead to certain morphological effects, and so forth. The consilience fits within overall biological thinking.

This consilience then is the reason why it is reasonable to think of species as natural kinds. Like the natural kinds of other sciences, they demand our attention, not because they represent some ultimate essentialist ontological carving up of the real world, but because they unite different criteria of division. They may not be Aristotelian kinds. But they are more than Lockean kinds. (See also Ruse 1973.)

Consequences

A number of questions arise. What about the real/nominal definition distinction? It vanishes—which is a good thing, because it is an outmoded Aristotelian holdover anyway. You might argue that genetic differences are more crucial than anything else. (Caplan 1980, 1981; and Kitts and Kitts 1980 argue just this.) But, from an evolutionary perspective, the genes do not have this kind of privileged status. If organisms do not have the right morphology, they will fail, no matter how superior their genotype. And in any case, a consilience is like a quarrel or a tango. You must have at least two parties. Hence, it really does not make much biological or philosophical sense to say that genes are more essential than morphology. Or that any other single feature is the "true" essence of a species.

Do we still have laws about species members? I do not see why not. The solution I am offering affirms the existence of natural kinds, albeit not Aristotelian kinds. This means that it is still open to everyone to make universal claims about the members of particular species. And, these claims can rise above the merely contingent or happenstance. This does not mean that every claim that has been made about human beings embodies genuine laws. I am not, for instance, defending the validity of every part of Freudian psychoanalytic theory. On the other hand, such theory is not being ruled out as a genuine science, on a priori grounds, before we even start.

Finally, let me make brief reference to some of the ongoing concerns that biologists have about species. I must emphasize that I am not trying to offer a quick and easy solution to every biological species query. Species which were difficult to evaluate before this essay, will be as difficult to evalute after this essay. I am trying to show why biologists, generally speaking, think that species are natural. But, the obverse side of the coin is that when difficulties arise and biologists no longer feel anything like as convinced of the naturalness of certain groups, the analysis offered above should show why. In particular, doubts about the reality of species should arise when the various ways of defining species names come apart and fail to coincide.

This is indeed the case. As mentioned earlier, botanists often find themselves less than convinced of the reality of many plant species. Why? Simply because so often plant groups which morphologically and ecologically and in other ways seem to be good species, fail the test of reproductive isolation or some like thing. One just does not have the consilience required for naturalness. Conversely, when there is isolation, there are sometimes few other differences. In such cases, and in analogous cases in the animal world, species—however drawn—are not considered that natural. It is interesting to note how, in the case of so-called "sibling species," where members of different reproductively isolated groups are morphologically similar, morphological differences are eagerly sought. Much relief is felt when such differences are found. (Grant 1981a has an excellent discussion on the difficulties plants raise for species concepts. Mayr 1963, Dobzhansky 1970, and Dobzhansky et al. 1977, discuss in full detail difficulties arising in the animal world.)

Also, the analysis I have offered shows just why it is that biologists are far less convinced of the reality of taxa of higher levels, than they are of species taxa. There simply is not the required consilience. Reproductive barriers are irrelevant, and there are no measures of morphological difference to coincide with genetic difference, to coincide with evolutionary difference. If anything, the evidence is that such measures are impossible. Hence, although "species are made by God, higher taxa are made by man."

Conclusion

Ghiselin and Hull are surely right when they argue that we must break with Aristotelian essentialism in biology. After Darwin, such a position is otiose. But they go too far when they deny that biological species are natural kinds of any sort. They are such kinds, and the reason why it is reasonable for us to accept them as such is that same reason which makes us think any scientific claim goes beyond the merely hypothetical. It is because species are consilient.

Acknowledgments

A version of this paper was given at a conference on Natural Kinds, sponsored by Simon Fraser University, February 1983. The following friends have read and criticized (sometimes extensively criticized) that version: Michael Ayers, Art Caplan, Michael Ghiselin, Vernon Grant, Marjorie Grene, David Hull, James Lennox, Elisabeth Lloyd, Ernst Mayr, Alex Rosenberg, Laurence Splitter, Paul Thompson. I am grateful also to an anonymous referee of this journal for constructive comments.

Notes

1. In my view, most of the modern supporters of natural kinds end up somewhere to the right of Aristotle (e.g. Kripke 1972, Putnam 1975, Wiggins 1980). Frankly, I am not sure how far these modern thinkers really intend their ideas to apply to biology, since they generally do not bother to refer to the works of practising taxonomists, and at times show an almost proud ignorance of the organic world. Any comments I have to make against Aristotle apply equally against them. Dupré (1981) shows how ignorant most modern philosophical thinkers are about biological reality.

2. Other critics of the s–a–i thesis include Caplan (1980, 1981) and Kitts and Kitts (1979). Unfortunately, these critics revert to a modern-day, genetic, Aristotelian essentialism. I find myself agreeing with much in Hull's (1981) spirited response to them.

3. Could spatiotemporal contiguity alone count as the criterion of individuality? We surely think of the planet Earth as an individual on these grounds. But, while this may be true, we do not think of Earth as a *biological* individual, which notion is the focus of the s–a–i thesis. Incidentally, however, given plate-tectonic theory and the consequent claims about Earth's organization, a case might be made for Earth's geological individuality, transcending mere spatiotemporal contiguity.

4. One does get cooperation between organisms. But, the point is that ultimately, biology regards it as "enlightened self-interest." Hence, at root we have tensions—separate reproductive strategies—between organisms. At times, for instance where mates are involved, these tensions break right out. See Trivers (1971), Wilson (1975), Barash (1977), Clutten Brock (1982), and Ruse (1979b), for more details.

5. An escape would be to embrace the neo-saltationary theory of "punctuated equilibrism," supposing that one gets periods of stasis, followed by abrupt switches from one species to another. See Eldredge and Gould (1972). The fears just expressed vanish. Wake (1980) and Mishler and Donoghue (1982) note just how tied up the s–a–i thesis is with this theory, and significantly the s–a–i thesis has been embraced enthusiastically by Eldredge (1985). But, there are serious queries about the position. See Gingerich (1976, 1977); Maynard Smith (1981); and Ruse (1982) for an overview.

References

Arnold, A. J. and Fristrup, K. (1982): The theory of evolution by natural selection: a hierarchical expansion. *Paleobiology*, 8, pp. 113–29.

Ayers, M. R. (1981): Locke versus Aristotle on natural kinds. *Journal of Philosophy*, 78, pp. 247–72.

Beatty, J. (1982): Classes and cladists. *Systematic Zoology*, 31, pp. 25–34.

Beckner, M. (1959): *The Biological Way of Thought*. New York: Columbia University Press.

Brandon, R. and Burian, R. (1984): *Genes, Organisms, Populations*. Cambridge, Mass.: MIT Press.

Caplan, A. (1980): Have species become declassé? In P. Asquith and R. Giere (*eds*.), *PSA 1980*, 1, pp. 71–82. East Lansing: Philosophy of Science Association.

Caplan, A. (1981): Back to class: a note on the ontology of species. *Philosophy of Science*, 48, pp. 130–40.

Dawkins, R. (1976): *The Selfish Gene*. Oxford: Oxford University Press.

Dawkins, R. (1982): Replicators and vehicles. King's College Sociobiology Groups (*eds*), *Current Problems in Sociobiology*, pp. 45–64. Cambridge: Cambridge University Press.

Darwin, C. (1859): *On the Origin of Species*. London: John Murray.

Darwin, F. (1887): *The Life and Letters of Charles Darwin, Including an Autobiographical Chapter*. London: Murray.

Dobzhansky, Th. (1951): *Genetics and the Origin of Species*, 3rd ed. New York: Columbia University Press.

Dobzhansky, Th. (1970): *Genetics of the Evolutionary Process*. New York: Columbia.

Dobzhansky, Th. *et al.* (1977): *Evolution*, San Francisco: W. H. Freeman.

Dupré, J. (1981): Natural kinds and biological taxa. *Philosophical Review*, 90, pp. 66–90.

Eldredge, N. (1985): *The Unfinished Synthesis*. New York: Oxford University Press.

Eldredge, N. and Gould, S. J. (1972): Punctuated equilibria: an alternative to phyletic gradualism. In T. J. M. Schopf (*ed*.), *Models in Paleobiology*. San Francisco: Freeman, Cooper.

Endler, J. A. (1977): *Geographic Variation, Speciation, and Clines*. Princeton: Princeton University Press.

Ghiselin, M. (1966): On psychologism in the logic of taxonomic controversies. *Systematic Zoology*, 15, pp. 207–15.

Ghiselin, M. (1969): *The Triumph of the Darwinian Method*. Berkeley: University of California Press.

Ghiselin, M. (1974a): A radical solution to the species problem. *Systematic Zoology*, 23, pp. 536–44.

Ghiselin, M. (1974b): *The Economy of Nature and the Evolution of Sex*. Berkeley: University of California Press.

Ghiselin, M. (1981): Categories, life, and thinking. *Behavoral and Brain Sciences*, 4, pp. 269–313.

Ghiselin, M. (1987): Species concepts, individuality, and objectivity. *Biology and Philosophy*, 2, pp. 127–44.

Gingerich, P. D. (1976): Paleontology and phylogeny: patterns of evolution at the species level in early Tertiary mammals. *American Journal of Science*, 276, pp. 1–28.

Gingerich, P. D. (1977): Patterns of evolution in the mammalian fossil record. In A. Hallam (ed.), *Patterns of Evolution, As Illustrated by the Fossil Record*, pp. 469–500. Amsterdam: Elsevier.

Gould, S. J. (1979): A quahog is a quahog. *Natural History*, 88, pp. 18–26.

Grant, V. (1981a): *Plant Speciation*, 2nd ed. New York: Columbia University Press.

Grant, V. (1981b): The genetic goal of speciation. *Biologisches Zentralblatt*, 100, pp. 473–82.

Hempel, C. G. (1952): *Fundamentals of Concept Formation in Empirical Science*. Chicago: University of Chicago Press.

Holsinger, K. (1984): The nature of biological species. *Philosophy of Science*, 51, pp. 293–307.

Hull, D. L. (1965): The effect of essentialism on taxonomy: two thousand years of stasis. *British Journal for the Philosophy of Science*, 15, pp. 314–26, 16, pp. 1–18.

Hull, D. L. (1975): Central subjects and historical narratives. *History and Theory*, 14, pp. 253–74.

Hull, D. L. (1976): Are species really individuals? *Systematic Zoology*, 25, pp. 174–91.

Hull, D. L. (1978): A matter of individuality. *Philosophy of Science*, 45, pp. 335–60.

Hull, D. L. (1979): The limits of cladism. *Systematic Zoology*, 28, pp. 417–38.

Hull, D. L. (1981): Kitts and Kitts and Caplan on species. *Philosophy of Science*, 48, pp. 141–52.

Johanson, D. and Edey, M. (1981): *Lucy: The Beginnings of Humankind*. New York: Simon and Schuster.

Johanson, D. C. and White, T. D. (1979): A systematic assessment of early African hominids. *Science*, 203, pp. 321–30.

Kitcher, P. (1984): Species. *Philosophy of Science*, 51, pp. 308–35.

Kitts, D. B. and Kitts, D. J. (1979): Biological species as natural kinds. *Philosophy of Science*, 46, pp. 613–22.

Kripke, S. A. (1972): Naming and necessity. In D. Davidson and G. Harman (eds.), *Semantics of Natural Language*, pp. 253–355. Dordrecht: Reidel.

Lande, R. (1980): Genetic variation and phenotypic evolution during allopatric speciation. *American Naturalist*, 116, pp. 463–79.

Leplin, J. (1984): *Scientific Realism*. Berkeley: University of California Press.

Levin, D. A. (1979): The nature of plant species. *Science*, 204, pp. 381–4.

Levin, D. A. (1981): Dispersal versus gene flow in plants. *Annals of the Missouri Botanical Garden*, 68, pp. 233–53.

Lewontin, R. (1974): *The Genetic Basis of Evolutionary Change*. New York: Columbia University Press.

Locke, J. (1975): *An Essay Concerning Human Understanding*, P. H. Nidditch (*ed.*). New York: Oxford University Press.

Maynard Smith, J. (1981): Did Darwin get it right? *London Review of Books*, 3(11), pp. 10–11.

Mayr, E. (1942): *Systematics and the Origin of Species*. New York: Columbia University Press.

Mayr, E. (1963): *Animal Species and Evolution*. Cambridge, Mass.: Belknap.

Mayr, E. (1969): *Principles of Systematic Zoology*. New York: McGraw-Hill.

Mayr, E. (1976): Is the species a class or an individual? *Systematic Zoology*, 25, p. 192.

Mayr, E. (1982): *The Growth of Biological Thought*. Cambridge: Harvard University Press.

Mishler, B. D. and Donoghue, M. J. (1982): Species concepts: a case for pluralism. *Systematic Zoology*, 31, pp. 503–11.

Putnam, H. (1975): The meaning of meaning. In H. Putnam, *Mind, Language, and Reality*. Cambridge: Cambridge University Press.

Quine, W. V. (1969): Natural kinds, in *Ontological Relativity and Other Essays*. New York: Columbia University Press.

Rosenberg, A. (1980): *Sociobiology and the Preemption of Social Science*. Baltimore: Johns Hopkins University Press.

Ruse, M. (1973): *The Philosophy of Biology*. London: Hutchison.

Ruse, M. (1976): The scientific methodology of William Whewell. *Centaurus*, 20, pp. 227–57.

Ruse, M. (1980): Charles Darwin and group selection. *Annals of Science*, 37, pp. 615–30.

Ruse, M. (1981): What kind of revolution occurred in geology? P. Asquith and I. Hacking (*eds.*), *PSA 1978*, 2, pp. 240–73. East Lansing: PSA.

Ruse, M. (1982): *Darwinism Defended: A Guide to the Evolution Controversies*. Reading, Mass.: Addison-Wesley.

Schlesinger, G. (1963): *Method in the Physical Sciences*. New York: The Humanities Press.

Simpson, G. G. (1961): *Principles of Animal Taxonomy*. New York: Columbia University Press.

Sober, E. (1980): Evolution, population thinking and essentialism. *Philosophy of Science*, 47, pp. 350–83.

Splitter, L. (1982): *Natural Kinds and Biological Species*. Unpublished Oxford D. Phil. Thesis.

Stanley, S. M. (1979): *Macroevolution, Pattern and Process*. San Francisco: W. H. Freeman.

Van Valen, L. (1976): Ecological species, multispecies, and oaks. *Taxon*, 25, pp. 233–9.

Wade, M. J. (1978): A critical review of the models of group selection. *Quarterly Review of Biology*, 53, pp. 101–14.

Wade, N. (1979): Supreme Court to say if life is patentable. *Science*, 206, p. 664.

Wade, N. (1980a): Supreme Court hears argument on patenting life forms. *Science*, 208, pp. 31–2.

Wade, N. (1980b): Court say lab-made life can be patented. *Science*, 208, p. 1445.

Wake, D. B. (1980): A view of evolution. *Science*, 210, pp. 1239–40.

Whewell, W. (1840): *The Philosophy of the Inductive Sciences*. London: Parker.

Wiggins, D. (1980): *Sameness and Substance*. Oxford: Blackwell.

Wiley, E. (1978): The evolutionary species concept reconsidered. *Systematic Zoology*, 27, pp. 17–26.

Wiley, E. (1980): Is the evolutionary species fiction?—A consideration of classes, individuals, and historical entities. *Systematic Zoology*, 29, pp. 76–80.

Wiley, E. (1981): *Phylogenetics: The Theory and Practice of Phylogenetic Systematics*. New York: John Wiley.

Wilson, E. O. (1975): *Sociobiology: The New Synthesis*. Cambridge, Mass.: Belknap.

Chapter 17

Species Concepts, Individuality, and Objectivity

Michael T. Ghiselin

Many years ago I published a paper in *Systematic Zoology* entitled "On Psychologism in the Logic of Taxonomic Controversies" (Ghiselin 1966). It was there that I first brought up the point that biological species are not classes, but individuals. This thesis was long rejected as counterintuitive, until it was arrived at, on the basis of independent lines of reasoning, by David Hull and Mary Williams. Although still controversial, it has been widely accepted, and widely discussed, by biologists, and has recently attracted considerable attention from professional philosophers (Holsinger 1984, Kitcher 1984, Sober 1984). Some other points which I raised in that paper have received less attention, particularly the difficulties with similarity as a basis for classification, and "psychologism" as an undesirable feature of systematics. Such topics are very important, for they bear upon efforts to develop alternative definitions of the species and other categories. In this paper I will emphasize the differences between "biological" species concepts, as advocated by Dobzhansky and myself (less consistently by Mayr), and "evolutionary" species concepts advocated by Simpson, Wiley, and Van Valen. Actually these terms are not altogether fortunate, since either concept might be called "biological" or "evolutionary." The real issue is whether species should be conceived of, respectively, as reproductive communities or as ecological entities. At a more general level, I suggest that the biological species concept provides the basis for a fundamental integration of biology with the rest of science, and argue that there is no objection to it that would not equally apply to such basic terms as "atom," "molecule," and "cell."

Different Kinds of Groups

In order to make this essay intelligible to a broad audience, it will help to reiterate what we mean in saying that species are individuals (see also Hull 1976, 1978; Ghiselin 1974a, 1981). *Individuals* are single things, including compound objects made up of parts—such as ourselves, and also every cell and atom in our bodies. Such parts need not be physically connected—a baseball team is an individual made up of players. Individuals each have a definite location in space and time. In general they are designated by proper names—such as "Ernst Mayr" or "Canada." *Classes*, on the other hand, are spatially and temporally unrestricted, and their names may designate any number of objects—including none at all. The only thing the members of a class have to share is the criteria of membership—usually what are called the "defining properties." Both classes and individuals have "elements" or "subunits," but the relationships are not the same. Individuals are "parts" of larger individuals. (John is part of his family.) They are "members" of classes. (John is male.) Classes are not parts of anything, though they can be included in larger classes. (The sexes include male and female.) In general one can tell if a thing is a part of an individual or a member of a class by virtue of the fact that parts are not "instances." For example, we do not say "This thumb is a Michael Ghiselin," or "Ontario" is a "Canada." To some people it is not obvious that it is equally wrong to say "Trigger is an *Equus cabalus*."

In biological classification we have two kinds of groups: *categories* and *taxa*. Categories are classes, taxa are (or can be) individuals. Compare:

Biological Hierarchy

Categories	Taxa
Family	Hominidae
Genus	*Homo*
Species	*Homo sapiens*

Political Hierarchy

Categories	Taxa
National State	U.S.A.
State	California
County	San Francisco County

Thus, in taxonomy it is clear that we have *both* classes and individuals. Individual species are populations. Individual higher taxa are branches of the phylogenetic tree—chunks of a genealogical nexus. At least they are if we chose to classify things that way. Some groups, called "artificial" taxa, have to be viewed as classes (such as the warm-blooded animals, or Haematothermia = Aves + Mammalia).

General Implications

From such simple considerations, a great deal follows. For example, evolution is possible. If species were not individuals, they could not evolve. Indeed, they could not do anything whatsoever. Classes are immutable, only their constituent individuals can change. "National state" (a class) cannot wage war—but Canada (an individual) has waged war. Individual species may be able to do things other than evolve. They can speciate, become extinct, and compete, but perhaps not much else. This is a very important point, one to which Eldredge (1985) has devoted an entire book. That species are individuals means that they cannot be defined, in the sense of listing properties they simply must have—but they can be described (see Ghiselin 1984). This of course has profound implications for the role taxonomic groups play in the thinking of biologists.

But perhaps the most important implication of the individuality of species thesis is that it holds out the prospect that we can develop a single body of knowledge for the entire universe. We can have one science and one philosophy of science. This possibility has been rejected by many authors, including Mayr (1982) and other eminent evolutionists, on the grounds that there are no laws of nature in biology. It was the notion of Smart (1963) that biology is not a science because there are no laws for *Homo sapiens* that led Hull to realize that species are individuals. Of course there are no laws for taxonomic groups, but there are no laws for individuals in physics, either. Laws are generalizations about classes of individuals. We therefore must look for biological laws that generalize about classes of species and classes of other individuals. It is ironic that Mayr (1982), who denies that there are any important laws in biology, devoted much of a brilliant career to defending a law of allopatry in speciation (see Mayr 1963). The law says that under ordinary conditions, speciation does not occur without an initial period of extrinsic isolation, such as a geographic barrier. If biology is to be a science, it needs both a body of descriptive facts, and a series of high-level generalizations. In other words, it needs both history and laws. Astronomy provides just such descriptive facts, and physics the laws of nature. In biology, the historical data are supplied by taxonomy, the laws of nature by evolutionary theory. Thus, in principle, there is nothing but the particular subject-matter to differentiate the physical from the biological sciences.

Some opponents of the thesis that species are individuals insist that there must be some sort of "essence" underlying the "form" which purports to be the subject-matter of taxonomy. Others have argued that if we accept it, then morphology cannot be the kind of nomothetic science that crystallography and chemistry are. A particularly good example from the recent anti-Darwinian literature is Webster (1984). And of course they are right, but this only means that their efforts to find "nomothetic" alternatives to Darwinism are futile. On the other hand, many who have been seeking to develop a better theory of macroevolution take the individuality of species as one of their fundamental premises (Eldredge and Cracraft 1980, Vrba 1974). In general it seems that those who are trying to relate evolutionary history to the underlying causal mechanisms accept the individuality of species. Those whose approach to evolution is ahistorical or who eschew the study of mechanisms are less sympathetic to it, if not downright hostile.

On Objectivity

By clearly distinguishing between the historical and the nomothetic aspects of biology, between individuals and classes, it will be easier to make biology a "hard" science. But that is not enough. How do we differentiate between what is, and what is not, science? One way is in terms of objectivity (see also Ridley 1985). Objectivity relates very nicely to the topic of "psychologism" earlier alluded to. Traditionally it has been discussed under the rubric of "natural" and "artificial" systems. In 1966 I exemplified "artificial system" by "a ranking of inkblots in the order of their obscenity." A natural system is something we discover, not something we create. Darwin (1859, 411) probably had something of the sort in mind when he wrote that the natural system "is evidently not arbitrary like the grouping of the stars in constellations." A better word than "arbitrary" would have been "subjective." A host of authors have, indeed, denied that there is any such distinction. They have asserted that a classification is "a construction of the intellect," something "merely for the sake of convenience," and so forth. When species were conceived of as classes such opinion seemed not unreasonable. After all, individuals are "concrete," classes "abstract," and perhaps classes might be viewed as something "mental." Now that species are conceived of as individuals, they have to be absolutely concrete, and must be viewed as no more intellectual constructs than organisms are. Some people have tried to argue that an entity is a class or an individual depending upon how we consider it. But if this were so, the ability of an organism to develop or of a species to evolve would depend upon someone's thought processes. In some cases efforts to treat species as conceptual have been based upon "phenomenalism." According to one version, what we are supposed to classify is not organisms or populations, but sense-impressions!

  Evidently such arguments appeal to persons with a certain kind of personality structure. According to Jung's (translation 1971) classical theory of psychological types, we can divide people into introverts and extroverts. Introverts organize their lives in relation to the subject, extroverts in relation to the object. It has been shown that different endeavors attract different psychological types—professional psychologists generally classify themselves as introverts (Shapiro and Alexander 1975). The importance of an objective approach in the sciences has been particularly well argued by psychologists (Brunswick 1952).

On the other hand, the subjective aspect is indeed important in taxonomy; not, however, in classification, but rather in identification. Simpson (1961) made this point quite effectively, although he confused matters by saying that we classify groups not individuals, for some groups are individuals. When we identify objects, we relate them to a preexisting system—as by dumping corpses into bins. Finding out the real, underlying order—classification in the strict sense of that word—is quite a different matter. Unfortunately our educational routine is so arranged that everybody is taught to identify, but virtually nobody is taught to classify, and then only at a late stage. In chemistry courses we were all taught to identify elements—but not to invent the periodic table. In biology everybody learns how to key out an organism—but not to revise a taxon. The few who do learn to classify have already been prejudiced by the experience of identification, which therefore becomes a stereotype, or Platonic Idea, of classification, the basis for a travesty of how objects are classified by scientists. Such a travesty is almost universally taken for granted in accounts of how we do it, whether presented by philosophers, or by taxonomists of whatever school. Namely, we are told that classification is somehow "based upon" characters. Of course, this is true in the trivial sense that counting scales and measuring apertures provides useful data. But this does not mean that sorting corpses into bins on the basis of shared attributes constitutes the entire rationale of all classification systems. In other words "observed traits of specimens" ≠ "evidence." I have repeatedly offered arguments and counter examples (Ghiselin 1966, 1969a, 1969b, 1970; Gosliner and Ghiselin 1984). Systematic biology ought to base its generalizations on the kind of historical reconstruction that has been general practice in geology ever since the time of Lyell, in which hypothesized sequences of events are evaluated according to how well they accord with the known laws of nature. And in fact the best workers, beginning with Darwin, have done so routinely. For example, vestigial organs have to be treated as something being lost, not as something preparing to become functional in the remote future. With a few noteworthy exceptions such as a new book by Ridley (1985) such operations have been studiously ignored by theoreticians of taxonomy.

Contrary, therefore, to what is generally asserted, I maintain that a scientific classification is based upon an understanding of the objects classified, and that any characters are therefore epiphenomenal. I hope that what I say will seem so obvious that people claim never to have believed otherwise. Of course, a classification can be based upon a *misunderstanding* of the objects classified, but this only means that we must have an objective criterion of whether the classification be true or false. One kind of psychologism results when we equate ontology with epistemology, and it is to be avoided here. Epistemologically, a natural system is based upon whatever scientific evidence legitimizes it. Ontologically, a natural system is based upon the objective reality to which it corresponds. And by an understanding, I mean a scientifically legitimate theory, not a mental condition, or what some philosophers (in the tradition of the southwest German school of neo-Kantianism) have referred to as *Verstehen*. To be more explicit, scientific classifications are etiological, or causal, not phenomenal, or based upon superficial appearances. In scientific medicine, diseases are classified upon an etiological basis—by what causes them, sometimes the agent, sometimes the physiological effects. They are diagnosed on the basis of symptoms, but these symptoms are not defining of the disease. This same distinction is evident in biological taxonomy: we too call the analogue of the "symptoms" a "diagnosis," and not a "definition" (Ghiselin 1984). And again, I stress that the "symptoms" are not exhaustive of the evidence, which includes experiments, theories, and anything else germane.

The causes upon which etiological classification is based generally fall under two major headings: history and law. This implies that the groups correspond to individuals such as the French language, *Homo sapiens*, or the Palaeozoic on the one hand, and to classes, such as homeotherms, chlorine, and competition. The individuals are held together by physical or other forces, or at least have a common origin, while the classes behave in the same way because they are subject to the same laws of nature. The very fact that we recognize that the order in taxonomy is an historical one clearly shows that the evidence is not exhausted by "characters." So does the fact that our interpretations are influenced by such truisms as the point that the common ancestor of a group of lineages must have existed in a restricted position in space and time.

Biological Species

I now propose to develop the thesis that classification is based upon an understanding of the objects classified by reference to familiar examples, getting to species in due course. We may begin with the periodic table of the elements, which as we all know consists of classes of elements, and treats each element as a mass noun, though atoms are obviously the individuals in the system. Larger groups such as the halogens include smaller ones such as chlorine. This periodic table provides a very powerful summary of chemical knowledge because it summarizes the important chemical properties, and can be related to the structure of the atoms, and not because of what the objects classified look like.

Some matter, but not all, is incorporated in atoms, a point to which I shall return. Some atoms form parts of molecules, some molecules form parts of larger wholes such as organisms. This gives us a familiar hierarchy, which we now need to examine more closely:

Species ⎤
...   ⎬ Population
Deme ⎦
Organism
Cell

...

Molecule
Atom

Observe that entities can be ranked at more than one level (as in a unicellular organism). Also, "population," as the term is used here is a class of classes (levels), with "species" ranked highest and "deme" ranked lowest. ("Population" has other senses, for example, it may be equivalent to "deme.") It is obvious that different kinds of objects are ranked at each level. We should say a little about what kinds of objects these are.

Atoms and molecules are structural units. They have structure. Cells and organisms are organizational units. They are organized. Of course, cells have structure, and some molecules are organized too. At the populational level, we also find organized units, but of a different kind. (In this discussion I will not attempt the formidable task of defining "structure" or "organization.") The organismal level can be defined in terms of physiological autonomy, the cell as the minimum unit capable of having such autonomy. Can we treat populational units the same way we did the lower ones? Can we bring the definition of "species" in line with the definitions of the lower units? I think we can, but before I do, it will be necessary to say a bit about the theory of definitions, which becomes more difficult here.

Generally a definition is understood to be the criteria that determine whether a name is to apply to a given object or class of objects. Sometimes this is done by giving the extension—enumerating all the members of the class. I can do this in principle for "element"—listing "hydrogen, helium, ..." But generally, we call for an intensional definition—a list of the properties necessary and sufficient for the name to apply: a molecule is a group of atoms united by a continuous series of chemical bonds. (Individuals have to be defined "ostensively"—by "pointing"—for they have no defining properties whatsoever.)

There is another notion about definitions, which is that we are trying to define "concepts." The term "concept" is most problematic. In some cases it is tainted with psychologism, as when concepts are equated with our "ideas" about things. With respect to species, however, we have an important issue, because one might define the term in more than one way, and yet have it refer to precisely the same class of objects. This is one sense of "concept." Thus we might get "genetical" and "evolutionary" definitions that are equivalent, in the sense that the entities with a certain genetical structure are precisely those that evolve. The problem here is that "species" is defined in the context of a body of evolutionary theory, just as "molecule" is defined in a way that presupposes a lot of chemical theory. The terse "definitions" in glossaries and textbooks rarely if ever do full justice to the criteria of usage applied by scientists in thinking and communicating. An essay, or even a book, may not suffice. My position here is akin to the virtual truism that "species" is a theoretical term. However, one would be hard pressed, in science, to find any word the definition of which is totally free of theoretical content.

Another notion that should be mentioned here to clarify my position is Locke's distinction between "nominal" and "real" essences. My views are similar in some respects, but not others. In the first place, I do not believe in essences, or in "real definition." Definitions are all nominal in the sense that we define names and not the things named. I distinguish three levels at which definition occurs, the first two of which roughly correspond to Locke's nominal essences. In the first place we have "diagnosis," which is not definition proper. In the second we have definition in the sense of a minimal set of criteria necessary and sufficient for the name to apply. Finally, we have the deepest level, what might be called a full "explication" of the term, providing a complete set of rules for how it is used in discourse. It would appear that some people have this deepest level in mind when they speak of defining concepts. It does not seem necessary to invoke essences here, as is sometimes done in the theory of "natural kinds." The deepest level is simply a group of facts, laws, and principles, from which the others may be derived. When one discovers these facts, laws, and principles, one has not discovered the essence or definition of what the name designated, but merely put one's self in a position to structure one's language in an appropriate way. The development of evolutionary biology did not lead biologists to discover what known entities called "species" were. Rather, it was found that the groups traditionally recognized could be identified as a collection of artificial assemblages and different kinds of populations. We have chosen to use the word "species" to designate one such kind of population. Here, as elsewhere, we scientists do not attach a name to a class, then discover the defining properties which are its essence, but rather redefine our terms as knowledge advances. Therefore the view of Kripke (1980) and his followers (see Schwartz 1977) that natural kinds terms are, like proper names, "rigid designators," should be dismissed as nugatory, and with it the accompanying essentialism.

We may also "conceive" of the same object or group of objects from different points of view. Now a point of view is neither true nor false, but it can be misleading or inappropriate for science. One point of view that virtually all of us would reject is the mystical point of view, a good example of which is the "quinary" system, a numerological approach popular early in the nineteenth century, which arranged everything in circles grouped in fives. But a fair number of reputable scientists advocate what may be called a "subjective" point of view in the sense already discussed earlier. Sometimes this takes the form of a "phenetic" species definition—the subjective notion of "degree of similarity" being treated as if it corresponded to some objective fact. In another form we get Tate Regan's aphorism that "A species is whatever a competent systematist says it is." A more recent example is Mishler and Donoghue (1982, 492) who deny that the biological species concept "will yield the same sets of organisms that would be recognized as 'species' by a competent taxonomist, or by a person in the street." A competent taxonomist, by a definition other than theirs, will of course see things quite differently than will a child on the street. Analogy with science in general shows the fallaciousness of the argument. We accept the heliocentric model of the solar system, not the geocentric model of the universe, in spite of what seems reasonable to nonscientists. Chemists do not put sucrose together with sugar of lead.

The position taken by many who advocate a subjective species concept might be labelled "pragmatic authoritarianism"—words are defined in terms of what is good for the experts. It is claimed, especially by certain botanists, that the biological species definition is somehow "impractical." The facts do not bear out these claims. Indeed the facts have been widely misrepresented. The biological species definition turns out to be fully applicable to those plants in which species actually do exist. Some people just feel disinclined, say, to synonymize a lot of oaks. The only relevant scientific facts are that sometimes populations diversify a lot before they speciate, and others are hard to tell apart when they have speciated. Therefore doing taxonomy well often requires a lot of work. If one is lazy, one may not feel inclined to do the work. If one is incompetent, one may not succeed. If one is dishonest, one may not wish to admit that one does not know all the answers. Therefore, a species is, by definition, whatever some expert finds it expedient to label with a specific epithet. That subjects differ in their ability or inclination to do cytology, experiments, electrophoresis, biogeography, or any number of other tasks, necessitates that such definitions will be as diverse, and as idiosyncratic, as human personalities. The experts will disagree, not because they differ upon a scientific issue, but because they are not engaged in science at all.

Some authors have argued for "pluralism" in this connection (Mishler and Donohue 1982, Kitcher 1984). In effect this means that one can pick and choose among a variety of criteria, such as reproductive isolation, and similarities and differences in this, that, and the other. But we are not told how to make the criterion of membership be an objective one. Such pluralism does not characterize such terms as "atom" and "molecule." It has been argued (Kitcher 1984) that the intension of "gene" is not monolithic. It has been broken down into such entities as cistron, muton, and recon. But the analogy here is false. The situation is more like that in population biology, where "population" means a variety of things, including species and deme. There is nothing analogous to a subjectively-defined class of similars in genetics. "Gene" has always designated a class of functional individuals, even when these have been hypothetical. In the case of species, the pluralists ask us that it designate not just a range of classes, but an incoherent mixture of classes and individuals. It is like defining "nation" in such a manner that the French nation means Frenchmen, plus some people who speak French, plus those with a French physiognomy, plus people who drive Renault automobiles et cetera ad nauseum.

From an objective, theoretical point of view, we might characterize the objects that fall under different levels according to what those objects do. Atoms may enter into chemical reactions, and become parts of molecules. Organisms do neither of those things, but may reproduce and engage in social behavior. Evolution is possible at the population level. But we need to restrict ourselves to a particular *kind* of population, namely, a whole integrated by sexual reproduction. (Yes, there are evolutionary changes in lineages of asexual organisms, and there are evolutionary changes in such things as languages and other cultural wholes.) Sexual populations, or reproductive communities, consist of populations and subpopulations, the largest of which are species, the smallest demes. We can, therefore, define "species" as the class whose members are the largest such units. And we do. Yet we can equally well define "species" by saying that species are by definition the populations that speciate (Ghiselin 1969, 1974a). This definition may seem circular, but it does not have to be. In theory at least, one can explain what a population is, and how they speciate, without ever having used the word "species." Therefore we can conceive of the same class of objects from two different points of view, and have quite different "defining properties" for it. In the context of evolutionary theory, the two are perfectly interchangeable. Both are "biological," or "evolutionary" species concepts, insofar as the same individuals participate in two important evolutionary processes: they become transformed, and they speciate.

We have yet a third way of formulating what is fundamentally the same species concept. This is to say that species are those individuals that have to evolve independently of each other. For this to happen, it is a necessary condition that they form separate reproductive units, and a sufficient condition that they have speciated. Again, the same basic group of propositions about biology is being invoked, at least implicitly. By the same token, we can also specify what properties of a species would be sufficient for speciation to have occurred. This was the basis of Mayr's (1940 and later) formulations of the biological species definition: "groups of actually or potentially interbreeding natural populations which are reproductively isolated from other such groups." But one might equally well formulate one's definition from the point of view of some other feature of the very same populations. I (Ghiselin 1974a, 538) did this using reproductive competition as the defining property: "the most extensive units in the natural economy such that reproductive competition occurs among their parts." It was felt that this definition had the advantage of not having to invoke such dispositional properties as "potentially interbreeding." (One encounters similar problems with various social groups—for example, a class that is not in session.) Also it focuses attention upon the evolutionary process, selection, that is so basic to the theory.

Others have preferred to emphasize what happens to genes. Dobzhansky (1935) deserves much of the credit for relating biological species to modern genetical theory. However, genetics has introduced a great deal of confusion, because of an unfortunate habit of overemphasizing its significance. This has led to a mistaken view that biological species definitions are "genetical." Actually, speciation can occur without genetical change, as when isolating mechanisms are the result of learned behavior. Another misconception has been that species are classes, which, by definition, share a certain degree of "genetical similarity," whatever that is supposed to mean. Some authors have treated species as if they were classes of populations, rather than populations that may contain smaller populational units. A species might be reduced temporarily to just one organism. Van Valen (1976, 235) wrongly emended my 1974 definition to read "the most extensive units in the natural economy such that reproductive competition [for genes] occurs among their parts." I had explicitly stated that by "reproductive competition," I meant that process which we observe in natural and sexual selection. It is not a competition "for genes" but investment of resources so as to maximize reproductive success, or Darwinian fitness. If it is "for" anything, it is "for" the ability to contribute most to the ancestry of subsequent generations. By definition it has nothing to do with interspecific competition, contrary to what Van Valen asserts.

Therefore, the definitions thus far considered may all be considered interchangeable verbal formulas defining the same class of entities, albeit from somewhat different points of view. Again we have just one "concept." There have been many objections to this "biological" species concept, but these can be answered by means of straight forward counter-examples. Among the most popular has been the point that not every organism falls under a species. In particular, asexual lineages do not form reproductive populations, and have to be considered "pseudospecies." It is sometimes said that a species definition which included all organisms would be better, because it would be "more general." True, but is it always desirable to maximize the generality of a term? If so, "virgin," ought to include those who have copulated as well as those who have not. Scientific classifications quite generally omit certain objects. Not every elementary particle in the universe is part of an atom. Not every part of an organism is a cell or part of one. And not every organism is part of an organization or society of a given kind. We may compare species to corporations, trade unions, or churches. A church is an organization, but not everybody belongs to one. "Religion" is more general than "church," but the former is not necessarily organized. One believes in a religion, one belongs to a church. Likewise, we ought not to conflate economic roles with economic organizations. The people who earn their living as barbers are one thing (a class); those who belong to the barbers' union form another (an individual). If one does not belong to the union, one need not pay dues, but it may be harder to get work. Similarly, organisms that are parts of species have to pay the "cost of meiosis" in consequence of their sexuality—but for some mysterious reason they seem quite prosperous.

Evolutionary Species

It is at precisely this point that we must take issue with the advocates of the so-called "evolutionary species concept." They try to define "species" in terms of "evolutionary role," or "niche." As a result, they confound professions with organizations. Thus a business firm, for them, would have to include those who had once worked for that firm, but had quit, and gone into private practice. Indeed, the firm might have long since been liquidated. In effect they are trying to have species be two quite different kinds of things at once. On the one hand they want species to be individuals—so they can evolve. On the other hand they want them to be classes of "ecologically similar" organisms. There are good metaphysical reasons why this will not succeed very well. If anything is to evolve, or do anything else, it has to be an individual—but an organization plus its former parts is just an historical unit, and cannot function as a whole either. Furthermore, an individual remains the same individual, irrespective of its activities. One does not become a different organism when one ceases to be a student and becomes a teacher. If, following Darwin, Elton, and Gause, we treat a niche as a "place in the economy of nature," it should be clear that where an object is located does not affect its being that object, irrespective of whether the place is a geographical or an economic one.

The simplest version of the ecological criterion occurs in Mayr's (1982, 273) latest emendation of the biological species definition: "A species is a reproductive community of populations (reproductively isolated from others) that occupies a specific niche in nature." Actually Mayr rejects the ecological criterion as defining, but applies it to asexual clones and the like. In effect he is conferring a kind of "honorary" status on things that don't fit in. (Rather like an "honorary virgin!") Mayr is justified in emphasizing the fact that species must occupy niches, but to say that a species occupies a specific niche is a truism, rather like adding "occupies a domicilary location" to the definition of "home."

The most influential version of the evolutionary species definition is that of G. G. Simpson, who writes (1961, 153), "An evolutionary species is a lineage (an ancestral-descendant sequence of populations) evolving separately from others and with its own unitary role and tendencies." The use of singular expressions ("a lineage," "its," and "unitary role") suggests that Simpson was conceiving of species as individuals. He also says that they can change roles, but must have one role at a given time. But do the asexual organisms form a lineage? Why not call them several lineages? And how does one decide how much similarity there must be in the "role" ("whole way of life")? He doesn't really tell us.

Wiley's (1978, 1981) formulation modifies that of Simpson. As Wiley (1981, 25) puts it, "An evolutionary species is a single lineage of ancestor-descendant populations which maintains its identity from other such lineages and which has its own evolutionary tendencies and historical fate." He adds: "Identity is a quality that an entity possesses which is a by-product of its origin and its ability to remain distinct from other entities." He lists that which confers identity—the ability of organisms to recognize each other, similar niches, and "phenotypic or genotypic similarity." In effect he is saying that the elements of such species are "similar" one way or another. Evidently he wants these objects somehow to be "the same thing," but in what sense? When we speak of two or more individuals being identical, we usually mean that they share all the properties of some class. Two individuals cannot be absolutely identical, for that means that they are the same individual, not two, as is the case of the Morning Star and the Evening Star. So when we speak of the identity of a lineage or a species to itself, we are only repeating the point that it is one whole. Therefore Wiley is treating a whole lineage as if it were something more than the totality of descendants of an ancestor, or rather as less, because if some of those descendants become somehow different, they would not be parts of that whole. But he defines "lineage" in a strictly genealogical manner, as "holophyletic" units—i.e., ones that incorporate all of the descendants of the common ancestor. Thus, his species can be "paraphyletic"—i.e., they can leave out some of the descendants of the common ancestor. This means doing precisely what, as a good cladist, he tells us one ought not to do. What makes an entity a whole is not "identity," in Wiley's sense of mere distinctness from other things, but "integrity," or "integration." Wiley (1981) rightly asserts that such integration is a necessary condition for a group to do anything. Clearly, however, mere "similarity," be it genotypic, phenotypic, or whatever, does not integrate a group. According to my analysis, entities may be divided into classes and individuals. Wiley (1980) split "individual" into "individual" and "historical entity." By this he implied that integration is a necessary condition for individuality, whereas I say that it is sufficient, but not necessary. Be this as it may, his treatment of species as if they can be integrated wholes, merely historical entities, a mixture of the two, or even parts of what I call individuals, is incoherent and contrary to the more fundamental principles upon which the two of us agree.

Van Valen (1976, 333) writes that "A species is a lineage or a closely-related set of lineages, which occupies an adaptive zone minimally different from that of any other lineage in its range and which evolves separately from all lineages outside its range." He should have said that a species is *either* a lineage which occupies an adaptive zone minimally different from that of any other lineage in its range, and which evolves separately from all lineages outside its range, *or* a closely-related set of lineages which *occupy* an adaptive zone minimally different from that of any other lineage in *their* range and which *evolve* separately from all lineages outside *their* range. This rewording gives the game away. Van Valen was trying to make "species" be two different kinds of things at once.

But this raises a very interesting issue. What is the connection between the taxonomic hierarchy and ecological classification? Basically, there is no particular connection, though there are diverse correlations (Eldredge 1985). Lineages and populations diversify through time, and tend to occupy different niches. But closely related organisms can have very different niches, distantly related ones virtually identical niches. Leaving aside the problem of the subjectivity of "amount of difference," it may be said that there is no clear limit to the amount of difference that can be built up within a species. Darwin (1859, 424) drew attention to the dwarf males of some cirripedes—an extreme case of sexual dimorphism. Two species can easily occupy identical niches when living in different places, and even when living in the same place, if certain unusual condition are met. Van Valen (1976) wants to make the properties of other species in the range give the amount of difference. But note what happens when the local biota changes. We obviously have a rubber yardstick here. Likewise Shaposhnikov (1984) attempted to argue that species are neither classes nor individuals but "systems"—whatever that is supposed to mean. Evidently he intended to treat them as "superorganisms," something that most of us would reject as bad metaphysics, if he means that species must therefore have adaptations. (For a general discussion of the superorganism notion see Ghiselin 1984b.) Shaposhnikov (1984, 1) says "A population is a group of individuals in a particular ecosystem whereas a species is a set of populations bound to a set of similar ecosystems." In effect he says that a species is a class of populations and organisms that are similarly adapted. So it all boils down to shifting from morphology, to genetics, and, as a last resort, to ecology, as a basis for defining "species" as classes of similars.

It would seem that species do very few things, and most of these are not particularly relevant to ecology. They speciate, they evolve, they provide their component organisms with genetical resources, and they become extinct. They compete, but probably competition between organisms of the same and different species is more important than competition between one species and another species. Otherwise, they do very little. Above the level of the species, genera and higher taxa never do anything. Clusters of related clones in this respect are the same as genera. They don't do anything either.

The shift toward defining species as a class of ecologically-similar organisms is an act of desperation, after the failure of efforts to define that category in terms of morphological, and then genetical, similarity. When, I repeat, we say that two individuals are identical, we mean that they share all of a certain *specified set* of properties. It is literally meaningless to say that two objects are "just plain" identical. There must be at least one thing not in common to them, if they are two individuals. In some cases by "identical" we really mean indiscernible, to us. But this is purely subjective and the criteria of identity are provided, if only implicitly. Now, similarity between two individuals mean that they share *at least some* of a specified set of properties. Identity is the limiting case. Apart from that specified set, it is nonsensical to say that two objects are similar. I can prove that any two objects in the universe are similar. My telephone number and Mt. Everest are similar, in that both are mentioned in this sentence. Two objects are objectively similar, insofar as the specified set of common properties is not a creation of the subject. Water is objectively similar to ammonia in containing hydrogen. Ammonia is subjectively similar to mushroom soup in that I don't like the taste of either. That water and ammonia contain hydrogen is a fact about those substances, how they taste is a fact about me. Many statements about the purported objective similarity of groups of objects are really statements that actually contain a subjective component. If I ask someone to sort flowers according to color patterns, he probably will not do much with ultraviolet data.

It has repeatedly been presupposed that there exists a real set of attributes called "overall similarity," but this proposition has insuperable difficulties. For one thing, the various components would have to be commensurable, for another we would have to scale them, and find a way to mix qualities and quantities in a meaningful way. Often people think they are measuring "overall similarity" when they actually are doing something quite different. If we are doing molecular phylogenetics, we can trace changes, stepwise, from a common ancestral form. There is a general rule that as time passes the proportion of homologous sites that are identical decreases. This legitimizes DNA × DNA hybridization techniques. However, in different lineages the changes will be qualitatively different: substituations, deletions, duplications, inversions, etc. The technique works because just one class of properties is being measured—the proportion of identical sites—and that happens to be a function of time elapsed since common ancestry.

When we move from mere molecular structure to trying to compare ecological properties of entire taxa, we get the same basic problem with a vengeance. Taxa differ ecologically from one another in various ways, and these are not fully commensurable. Consider, for example, the cnidarians with alternation of generations. In some cases we have medusae ("jellyfish") and polyps living in quite different places, and with different ranks assigned to synonymous taxa developed for the two stages of life history. In some cases the medusa is lost, in others the polyp. In many groups of marine invertebrates, a pair of "cryptic species" will occupy indistinguishable niches as adults, but one will have a larva, the other will not. How are we to decide whether the niches are minimally different? To this we may add the point that a species may itself remain unchanged, while the environment around it changes. Thus extinction of one species can readily advance another to the position of "top predator."

For any number of such reasons, there is no hope for treating species as classes of ecological similars. Species are important in ecology, because they are fundamental reproductive units, nothing more, nothing less. Ecology needs to generalize about reproduction, and has a legitimate place for species and classes of species. But it also needs to generalize about other processes, and ought to use such class terms as "primary consumer" and "homeotherm." Probably counting taxa of any rank is not the appropriate way to analyze diversity.

Furthermore, even though organisms are organized into species, they are also organized into other kinds of units, some of which are of considerable importance in ecology. An organism can be part of only one species, but it can be part of many kinds of social and ecological units as well. These include such things as families, societies, symbiotic unions, communities, and physically-constrained parts of the habitat. The very heterogeneity of such units precludes there being any monolithic hierarchy such as that we find when passing from species downward, through organism, cell, molecule, and atom. There is structure here, but it is an economic structure, with all sorts of units engaging in a wide variety of economic activities. So if one wants to fit species into an ecological context, one has to treat them on an individual basis, deriving their ecologically interesting features through observations upon all sorts of particulars. In other words ecology may need a lot more descriptive natural history and taxonomy than some people would hope.

Conclusions

The analogy with physics and astronomy may be of some help here. Astronomy has its structural units—galaxy, star, planet, satellite, etc. That an object is classified as a planet tells us something about its position relative to other objects, but it does not tell us much else. Thus the fact that a given body is a planet, and a satellite of a star, tells us how it relates to certain other cellestial bodies. But it does not tell us how big it is, or how many moons it has, if any. Some of the planets in the Solar System are smaller than some of the moons of Jupiter and Saturn, for instance. By the same token, there is no reason to expect the rank of a taxon to tell us much about its important ecological properties. These, like the mass and position of a celestial body, have to be provided by naturalists. This does not mean that ecology will never develop the analogue of celestial mechanics. Rather, the laws of ecology are one thing, the particulars of evolution are another, and to know either it is crucial that we not confuse the two.

Acknowledgments

Terrence M. Gosliner, David L. Hull, Ernst Mayr, Michael Ruse, Francesco M. Scudo, and E. O. Wiley advised me on drafts of the manuscript. Support of the John D. and Catherine T. MacArthur Foundation is gratefully acknowledged.

References

Brunswick, E., 1952, *The Conceptual Framework of Psychology*, Chicago University Press, Chicago.

Darwin, C., 1859, *On the Origin of Species by Means of Natural Selection, or the Preservation of Favoured Races in the Struggle for Life*, John Murray, London.

Dobzhansky, T., 1935, "A Critique of the Species Concept in Biology," *Philosophy of Science* 2, 344–355.

Eldredge, N., 1986, *Unifinished Syntehsis*, Oxford University Press, New York.

Eldredge, N., and J. Cracraft, 1980, *Phylogeneic Patterns and the Evolutionary Process: Method and Theory in Comparative Biology*, Columbia University Press, New York.

Ghiselin, M. T., 1966, "On Psychologism in the Logic of Taxonomic Controversies," *Systematic Zoology* 15, 207–215.

Ghiselin, M. T., 1969a, *The Triumph of the Darwinian Method*, University of California Press, Berkeley.

Ghiselin, M. T., 1969b, "Non-phenetic Evidence in Phylogeny," *Systematic Zoology* 18, 460–462.

Ghiselin, M. T., 1970, 'Models in Phylogeny', in T. J. M. Schopf, (ed.), *Models in Paleobiology*, Freeman and Cooper, San Francisco.

Ghiselin, M. T., 1974a, "A Radical Solution to the Species Problem," *Systematic Zoology* 23, 536–544.

Ghiselin, M. T., 1981, "Categories, Life, and Thinking," *Behavioral and Brain Sciences* 4, 269–313. [With Commentary.]

Ghiselin, M. T., 1984. 'Definition,' Character,' and Other Equivocal Terms," *Systematic Zoology* 33, 104–110.

Gosliner, T. M. and M. T. Ghiselin, 1984, "Parallel Evolution in Opisthobranch Gastropods and its Implications for Phylogenetic Methodolgy," *Systematic Zoology* 33, 255–274.

Holsinger, K. E., 1984, "The Nature of Biological Species," *Philosophy of Science* 51, 293–307.

Hull, D. L., 1976, "Are Species Really Individuals?," *Systematic Zoology* 25, 174–191.

Hull, D. L., 1978, "A Matter of Individuality," *Philosophy of Science* 45, 335–360.

Jung, K. G., 1921 (translation, 1971), *Psychological Types*, Princeton University Press, Princeton.

Kitcher, P., 1984, "Species," *Philosophy of Science* 51, 308–333.

Kripke, S., 1980, *Naming and Necessity*, Basil Blackwell, Oxford.

Mayr, E., 1963, *Animal Species and Evolution*, Harvard University Press, Cambridge, Mass.

Mayr, E., 1982, *The Growth of Biological Thought*, Harvard University Press, Cambridge, Mass.

Mishler, B. D. and M. J. Donoghue, 1982, "Species Concepts: A Case for Pluralism," *Systematic Zoology* 31, 491–503.

Ridley, M., 1985, *Evolution and Classification: The Reformation of Cladism*, Longman, London.

Schwartz, S. P. (ed.), 1977, *Naming, Necessity, and Natural Kinds*, Cornell University Press, Ithaca.

Shaposhnikov, G. Ch., 1984, "Aphids and a Step toward the Universal Species Concept," *Evolutionary Theory* 7, 1–39.

Simpson, G. G., 1961, *Principles of Animal Taxonomy*, Columbia University Press, New York.

Smart, J. J. C., 1963, *Philosophy and Scientific Realism*, Routledge and Kegan Paul, London.

Sober, E., 1984, "Sets, Species, and Evolution: Comments on Philip Kitcher's Species," *Philosophy of Science* 51, 334–341.

Van Valen, L., 1976, "Ecological Species, Multispecies, and Oaks," *Taxon* 25, 233–239.

Vrba, E., 1984, "Patterns in the Fossil Record and Evolutionary Processes," in M. Ho and P. T. Saunders (eds.), *Beyond Neo-Darwinism: An Introduction to the New Evolutionary Paradigm*, Academic Press, London.

Webster, G., 1984, "The Relations of Natural Forms," in M. Ho and P. T. Saunders (eds.), *Beyond Neo-Darwinism: An Introduction to the New Evolutionary Paradigm*, Academic Press, London.

Wiley, E. O., 1978, "The Evolutionary Species Concept Reconsidered," *Systematic Zoology* 27, 17–27.

Wiley, E. O., 1980, "Is the Evolutionary Species Fiction?—A Consideration of Classes, Individuals, and Historical Entities," *Systematic Zoology* 29, 76–80.

Wiley, E. O., 1981, *Phylogenetics*, Wiley, New York.

Chapter 18

Species, Higher Taxa, and the Units of Evolution

Marc Ereshefsky

Biologists draw a number of distinctions between species and higher taxa. For instance, a common distinction found in the literature is that species are units of evolution, or evolutionary units, while higher taxa are not (see Mayr 1982, Wiley 1981, Ghiselin 1987, and Eldredge and Cracraft 1980). Another popular distinction is that species are individuals and real entities, while higher taxa are historical entities and less real (see Eldredge and Cracraft 1980, Wiley 1981 for the individual/historical entity divide; see Eldredge and Cracraft 1980, Simpson 1961 for the real/less real divide). In brief, many biologists believe that species are concrete entities that play an active role in the evolutionary process whereas higher taxa are merely an epiphenomenon of that process.

For my part, I am hesitant to adopt this general distinction. I am skeptical of the arguments that species but not higher taxa are evolutionary units. Furthermore, I do not think that higher taxa are any less real than species or that most species fall into a different ontological category than higher taxa. Despite my hesitancy over these distinctions, I still think that there is a divide between species and higher taxa. It is just that the divide is more subtle than many have claimed.

While the bulk of this chapter will examine the arguments given for the above distinctions, it will also investigate several controversies on which those distinctions depend. For example, an argument for species but not higher taxa being evolutionary units relies on the assumption that species must be groups of interbreeding organisms. And the claim that species but not higher taxa are individuals turns on the assumption that species are indeed individuals. Both of these assumptions will be reviewed in this chapter. Another issue which the distinction between species and higher taxa depends upon is the nature of evolutionary units. Though the phrases "evolutionary unit" and "unit of evolution" are frequently found in the literature, there is little agreement on their meanings. An attempt will be made here to provide some resolution to their meanings.

The next section of this chapter will examine the argument that species but not higher taxa are evolutionary units because only the former can be groups of interbreeding organisms. The third section will review other arguments for species but not higher taxa being evolutionary units. And the fourth and fifth sections will respectively address whether the concepts of individuality and realism distinguish species from higher taxa.

Many biologists believe that higher taxa have an inferior role to that of species in the evolutionary process. The main question to be addressed here is whether such a ranking is justified.

Evolutionary Units and Reproductive Units

The idea that species are groups of interbreeding organisms, separated from all other such groups, is well entrenched among biologists. Some even claim that this idea highlights the divide between species and higher taxa and that it explains why the former but not the latter are evolutionary units (see Ghiselin 1987, Eldredge and Cracraft 1980, and Mayr 1970). For example, Eldredge and Cracraft (1980) write,

> For organisms among which there is at least occasional sexual reproduction, this unit would conform to the reproductive concept of species. We are led to the ineluctable conclusion that species, when conceived as reproductive units, are the units of evolution (pp. 89–90).

> That taxa of categorical rank higher than species do not exist in precisely the same sense as do species is crucial. . . . What all taxa, from species up through kingdoms, do share is presumed descent from a single ancestral species. What they do not share are similar reproductive patterns (p. 249).

> [T]here is nothing more to macroevolution than species, inasmuch as taxa of higher rank than species do not exist in the same sense as do species, and thus can in no way be construed as evolutionary units. . . (p. 327).

According to Eldredge and Cracraft, species but not higher taxa form groups of interbreeding organisms (I will call such groups "reproductive units"). Only reproductive units can be evolutionary units. Hence species but not higher taxa are evolutionary units.

The same argument is found in Ghiselin (1987). Ghiselin writes,

> Species are those individuals that have to evolve independently of each other. For this to happen it is a necessary condition that they form separate reproductive units, and a sufficient condition that they have speciated (p. 137).

> It would seem that species do very few things. . . . They speciate, they evolve, they provide their component organisms with genetical resources, and they become extinct. . . . Otherwise they do very little.

> Above the level of the species, genera and higher taxa never do anything. Clusters of related clones in this respect are the same as genera. They don't do anything either (p. 141).

For Ghiselin, the evolutionary unity of a species, that is, its being a distinct species, requires its members to be reproductively connected. Furthermore, what primarily distinguishes higher taxa and clusters of related clones from groups of organisms which Ghiselin takes to be species is that the latter and not the former are reproductive units. Thus species, as reproductive units, can evolve and be evolutionary units. But since higher taxa and clusters of related clones are not reproductive units, they cannot evolve and be evolutionary units.

In this section I want to examine the above argument that species but not higher taxa are evolutionary units because only the former are reproductive units. More specifically, I want to evaluate the premise that evolutionary units must be reproductive units. Accordingly, I will review two interpretations of "evolutionary unit" to see if either of them requires evolutionary units to be reproductive units. In the course of this review I will argue that the first interpretation does not require evolutionary units to be reproductive units. Furthermore I will point out that a number of biologists doubt that the second interpretation requires evolutionary units to be reproductive units.

Before conducting this review, it may be useful to get a better idea of what Eldredge and Cracraft and Ghiselin mean by "reproductive unit." In their first quotation, we see that Eldredge and Cracraft are interested in groups that have "at least occasional sexual reproduction." In other words, they take reproductive units to be groups of organisms which are actually interconnected by sexual activity. Such interconnection can range from that found within a well-integrated deme, to that which results from occasional migration between the subpopulations of some species. In a similar vein, Ghiselin (1974, 538) describes species as "the most extensive units in the natural economy such that reproductive competition occurs among their parts." Reproductive competition requires the members of a species to interact. So reproductive units for Ghiselin are not merely groups of sexual organisms, or organisms which have the potentiality to sexually interact; they are groups of organisms which actually sexually interact.

The first notion of evolutionary units I would like to consider is found in Rosenberg (1985). Rosenberg writes, "[T]o describe the units of evolution, we coin the biological neologism 'clan'.... A clan is a set of biological entities and all the descendants of the members of the set" (1985, 139).[1] According to Rosenberg, an evolutionary unit, or a clan, is a monophyletic taxon. In this chapter, I will use the term "lineage" to denote such entities. Some authors (for example, Hull 1980) use the term "lineage" to denote just single descendent-ancestor sequences, that is, single branches of a phylogenetic tree. In this chapter, however, I will use the term to denote both single descendent-ancestor sequences and groups of such sequences which share a common and unique origin.

In Rosenberg's description of evolutionary units, we find the requirement that evolutionary units must consist of organisms that are connected by heredity relations. As we shall see throughout this chapter, this requirement is found in all descriptions of evolutionary units. I assume the reason for this is that evolutionary explanations, as a type of explanation, require such heredity connections. When Darwin wanted to explain the distribution of the different types of ogranisms in the world he posited the hypothesis of evolution (Sober 1984, 21). According to that hypothesis, the distribution of biological types is explained by the passing down and subsequent alteration of traits. This paradigmatic type of explanation is subsequently employed by evolutionary theorists to explain the distribution of traits among the organisms of a lineage, whether the lineage is a phylum, a species, or a local population. In other words, evolutionary units must be groups of organisms which are connected by heredity relations simply because that is how post-Darwinian evolutionary theory explains the distribution of biological phenomena.

Turning to the main question of this section, must evolutionary units, as lineages, consist of subpopulations that exchange genetic material through gene flow? On the face of it, this conception of what it is to be an evolutionary unit does not require the existence of gene flow between a unit's members. All such units need do is display a pattern of descent by modification. So the only process requirement this conception of evolutionary units places on such units is the existence of heredity processes within them. Nevertheless, it would be well to point out that a change in the gene frequencies of a lineage does not occur unless some process is causing such a change. In answering whether evolutionary units must be reproductive units, we need to see if the processes causing such change require evolutionary units to be reproductive units.

There are a number of processes that can cause a lineage to evolve: selection, mutation, random drift, and recombination. If a lineage is to evolve by organismic selection, the following three factors must be present: the organisms within a lineage must vary in their traits; that variation must cause differential survival and reproduction among the organisms; and their traits must be heritable.[2] Selection may cause lineages to evolve by working at other levels of biological organization than that of the organism, but I will not take up that issue here.

Must a lineage that evolves as the result of organismic selection be a reproductive unit? I do not think so. Imagine a local population of asexual plants in which half the plants have a tolerance to high temperatures and the other half does not. In addition, suppose that having a tolerance to heat is heritable, and that the temperature of the zone where that population is found is rather high. As long as there are no forces countering the effects of selection for heat tolerance, the next generation of that population will have a higher frequency of genes for that trait. Moreover, we can imagine this selection process going on for a number of generations. In brief, a population or a lineage can evolve by selection without being a reproductive unit. (The same case can be made for lineages consisting of reproductively isolated groups of sexual organisms.)

Lineages consisting of asexual organisms and lineages consisting of reproductively isolated groups of sexual organisms can evolve by other processes than selection. A change in the gene frequency of such lineages can occur because a mutation arises within their organisms or as the result of random drift. Furthermore, recombination can occur within sexual organisms that belong to lineages consisting of reproductively isolated populations. (Though the occurrence of recombination in the organisms of a lineage does not change the gene frequency of that lineage, it allows the formation of new genotypes in it and thus is a source of variation.)

In sum, those processes that can cause a lineage to evolve do not require such lineages to be reproductive units. Recall the main question of this section, namely, must evolutionary units be reproductive units? If we follow Rosenberg's suggestion that evolutionary units are just lineages which evolve, then evolutionary units need not be reproductive units.

Some authors, however, have suggested that there is more to being a unit of evolution than merely being a lineage. For example, Williams (1985, 584–585) aligns evolutionary units with the Darwinian subclans of her axiomatization of evolutionary theory. A Darwinian subclan is not merely a lineage, but a lineage of organisms "which is held together by cohesive forces so that it acts as a unit with respect to selection" (Williams 1970, 357; also see 1985, 582, 584–585). The same conception of evolutionary units is found in Wiley (1981, 25) and Simpson (1961, 153). And Hull also suggests that such units may be more than just lineages. For example, Hull writes,

> [A]sexual species and monophyletic higher taxa are much in the same position. Both possess at least one of the characteristics necessary to function as units of evolution—continuity in time—but doubt exists if they possess sufficient unity and, if they do, how this unity is maintained (1976, 184).

Thus a number of authors think that a unit of evolution is a lineage that has "evolutionary unity," "cohesiveness," or "coherence." Unfortunately the nature of such unity or coherence is far from clear. Nevertheless a few observations can be made concerning its nature. First, when Hull (1976),

Williams (1985), and Wiley (1981) claim that evolutionary units have a certain cohesiveness, they allow that one of several processes (for example, gene flow, genetic homeostasis, or exposure to common selection regimes) may cause such cohesiveness. Second, when Hull (1978), Williams (1985), and Wiley (1981) maintain that evolutionary units have coherence they are not asserting that the members of an evolutionary unit share an essential trait. Third, such unity does not require the members of an evolutionary unit to have some uniformity over time, since, according to Hull (1976, 182) evolutionary units have the capacity to evolve indefinitely. What is left, and what I take to be the sort of cohesiveness the above authors are alluding to, is some sort of uniformity among the members of an evolutionary unit at a time. And over time, this uniformity may be in the form of stasis or it may be uniformity in change.

Returning to the main question of this section, we need to see if the above conception of evolutionary units requires such units to be reproductive units. More specifically, we need to ask if a lineage's having some sort of evolutionary uniformity requires those lineages to be reproductive units.

Numerous biologists hold that many species, and thus evolutionary units, consist of subpopulations that do not exchange genetic material through gene flow (see for example: Ehrlich and Raven 1969, 1230; Wiley 1981, 36–37; Eldredge and Gould 1972, 114). In fact, a number of authors believe that *most* species are distinct evolutionary units despite their lacking the cohering effect of gene flow (see for example: Ehrlich and Raven 1969, 1231; Lande 1980, 467; and Grant 1980, 167). Thus numerous authors believe that many if not most species need not be reproductive units.

There are three reasons why these biologists are led to this belief. First, empirical studies indicate that many sexual species consist of subpopulations that do exchange genetic material through gene flow. Second, empirical studies in the lab and in the field show that even the presence of gene flow within some groups of organisms may not cause those groups to be distinct evolutionary units. And third, most biologists recognize some groups of asexual organisms as distinct species or evolutionary units, yet the members of such groups obviously do not exchange genetic material through gene flow.

These considerations have led many biologists to investigate other processes besides gene flow that may cause species to be distinct evolutionary units. For example, some biologists have suggested that the members of a species may contain similar homeostatic genotypes (see Mayr 1970, Ehrlich and Raven 1969, and Wiley 1981). Such genotypes could cause the organisms in a species to produce the same basic phenotype despite the occurrence of mutations or variation in the environment. It has also been proposed that a species may maintain its unity by having its organisms exposed to similar selection regimes (see Lande 1980, Mishler and Donoghue 1982, and Ehrlich and Raven 1969). So not only do a number of biologists recognize that there are evolutionary units that are not reproductive units, but they have posited alternative processes that can be used to explain why such evolutionary units need not be reproductive units.

How does the claim that evolutionary units must be reproductive units fare on the assumption that evolutionary units are lineages with some sort of uniformity? According to the biologists just mentioned, such uniformity is not restricted to reproductive units. Moreover, there may be processes other than gene flow that cause such uniformity. Thus, according to a number of biologists, the assertion that evolutionary units must be reproductive units cannot be substantiated by the second conception of what it is to be an evolutionary unit.

In summary, we have looked at two proposals concerning what it is to be an evolutionary unit. According to these proposals, evolutionary units are mere lineages or they are lineages with some sort of uniformity. In the first case, I have argued that being a mere lineage does not require the existence of gene flow between the members of such units. In the second case, we saw that numerous biologists present several reasons for doubting that lineages with some sort of uniformity must be reproductive units. Recall that Eldredge and Cracraft (1980), and Ghiselin (1987) present the following argument: Only reproductive units can be evolutionary units; species but not higher taxa are reproductive units; hence species but not higher taxa are units of evolution. The preceding examination of two conceptions of evolutionary units should give us reason to doubt the premises of this argument. Consequently, the alleged evolutionary unit divide between species and higher taxa is not established (at least according to the numerous biologists cited) by which entities are and are not reproductive units.

Other Constraints on Evolutionary Units

In the previous section, I examined the argument that species but not higher taxa are evolutionary units because only the former are reproductive units. I would now like to look at two other arguments for species but not higher taxa being evolutionary units.

One of those arguments involves the claim that species but not higher taxa have ongoing processes. Wiley (1981), for example, writes,

> Cohesion in a species is maintained by reproductive ties (in the case of sexual species), and evolutionary stasis (asexual and sexual species), and similar responses of the component organisms of the species to

extrinsic factors of evolution. In contrast, there is no active cohesion within a natural supraspecific taxon because it is comprised of individual evolutionary units which have the potential to evolve independently of each other.... [N]atural supraspecific taxa have only a historical continuity of descent from a common ancestral species. In other words, species show both historical and ongoing continuity whereas supraspecific taxa have only historical continuity. These important distinctions result in a simple characterization of species and higher taxa; species are the units of evolution, and higher taxa containing more than one species are not units of evolution (1981, 75).

Thus according to Wiley, species but not higher taxa have the "ongoing" or "active" processes of gene flow, genetic homeostasis, and exposure to common selection pressures. The existence of such processes in species causes them to have "ongoing continuity." On the other hand, higher taxa lack such processes; thus they do not have any "ongoing continuity." As a result, species but not higher taxa are the units of evolution.

I have the following objection to this argument: I am skeptical of the claim that species and higher taxa are distinguished by the former but not the latter being exposed to ongoing unifying processes. Of course, it is commonly held that gene flow is a process that works among the subpopulations of a species but not among the different species of a higher taxon. However, in the previous section we saw that a number of biologists believe that many species consist of subpopulations that are not connected by gene flow. Thus according to those biologists, gene flow is not a process that distinguishes many species from higher taxa. But what about the other two unifying processes Wiley claims are found in species but not higher taxa? Should Wiley assume that the processes of genetic homeostasis and exposure to common selection regimes are unique to species?

I think Wiley makes this assumption too quickly. Genetic homeostasis, for example, may play a role in unifying some higher taxa. At least one author has made this suggestion. In explaining why one taxon of sibling species has less morphological diversity than another, Mayr maintains that the genetic homeostasis in one taxon may be stronger than it is in the other (1970, 35−36). In making this observation, Mayr is asserting that there are ongoing homeostatic processes among the organisms of these taxa. In addition, he is asserting that such a process can cause one of those taxa to have less morphological diversity, that is, more evolutionary unity, than the other.

There are plausible reasons for speculating that taxa higher than species may be subject to such unifying homeostatic processes. All the species in a taxon share a common ancestry, and this may cause their organisms to have some common genetic constraint on their characteristics. Whether there are such constraints in higher taxa, and how strong those constraints are, is ultimately an empirical matter. The point here, however, is that Wiley is too quick to rule out the existence of such processes in higher taxa.

I would also like to argue that Wiley is too quick to rule out the possibility that the members of a higher taxon may be exposed to similar selection regimes. Consider the ground finches and the large insectivorous tree finches of the Galapagos Islands. Each of these groups of birds is a taxon. And according to Lack (1953), the major difference between the species within each of these groups is the size of their beaks. This difference has been interpreted as an adaptation to their species-specific foods and has caused Lack to point out that their niches vary in the food items their birds consume. But besides that variation, the niches associated with the species within each group are pretty much the same. If this is the case, then it is implausible to assert that the species in each taxa do not share some sort of common selection regime. I am fairly confident that the same case can be made for other higher taxa as well.

In brief, Wiely should not foreclose the possibility that higher taxa, like species, can have the ongoing processes of genetic homeostasis and exposure to similar selection regimes. As we have already seen, a number of biologists believe that many if not most species lack the cohering effect of gene flow. Thus we have reason to believe that none of the ongoing processes Wiley cites distinguish all species from higher taxa. In turn, we have reason to doubt Wiley's claim that species but not higher taxa are units of evolution because only the former are exposed to such processes.

There is one last argument for species but not higher taxa being evolutionary units that I would like to consider. According to Mayr (1970, 1982), and Eldredge and Cracraft (1980), species but not higher taxa are evolutionary units because only the former are the source of evolutionary change. To better appreciate what this might mean, let's turn to Mayr's, and Eldredge and Cracraft's descriptions.

According to Mayr,

> The origin of new higher taxa and of all evolutionary novelties utlimately goes back to a founder species. The species, therefore, is the basic unit of evolutionary biology (1982, 296; also see 1970, 373–374).

Similarly, Eldredge and Cracraft write,

> In terms of the Linnaean hierarchy, there is nothing more to macroevolution than species, inasmuch as taxa of higher rank than species do not exist in the same sense as do species, and thus can in no way

be construed as evolutionary units; rather they are expressions of the
branching pattern produced by many speciation events through time
(1980, 327; also see 250).

Thus these authors provide the following argument for species but not
higher taxa being the units of evolution: Most evolutionary differences
arise during speciation events. Speciation events occur in species and not
higher taxa. So species but not higher taxa are the true nexus of evolutionary change. Hence species but not higher taxa are the units of evolution.

This is a nice argument, but it is vulnerable to the following charge: If
higher taxa are not evolutionary units because speciation events do not
occur in entire higher taxa, then a similar case can be made against species
being units of evolution. Consider Mayr's (1970) model of allopatric speciation. According to that model, speciation occurs when a population
becomes isolated from the main body of its species. Because such a population is both genetically isolated and relatively small, selection pressures
may cause it to radically diverge from the rest of its parental species. Thus
such a population may undergo what Mayr calls a "genetic revolution" and
become the founding population of a new species. The relevant point here
is that such speciation events do not occur in entire species but only in their
founding populations. (Gromko and Bradie 1987 make a similar observation.) As we just saw, Mayr and Eldredge and Cracraft argue that higher
taxa are not evolutionary units because speciation events do not occur in
entire higher taxa. However, the same argument counts against species
being units of evolution as well: Just as speciation events do not occur in
entire higher taxa, speciation events do not occur in entire species either.
Given the criterion that evolutionary units are the nexus of speciation
events, species are no more evolutionary units than higher taxa are.

In summary, we have seen three arguments for species but not higher
taxa being evolutionary units: Wiley's process argument; Mayr's and
Eldredge and Cracraft's speciation argument; and the reproductive unit
argument presented in the previous section. I have maintained that none of
these arguments show that species but not higher taxa are evolutionary
units. As a result, doubt should be cast on the claim that a major distinction
between species and higher taxa is that the former but not the latter are
evolutionary units (Mishler and Donoghue 1982 express a similar doubt).

More importantly, this analysis reveals that the distinction between
species and higher taxa may be of a different sort than is usually maintained
in the literature. In the above arguments, we see that the distinction
between species and higher taxa is based on the idea that certain processes
occur only in species. More specifically, the above arguments hold that
gene flow occurs in species but not in higher taxa, that other ongoing
unifying processes occur in species but not in higher taxa, and that specia-

tion occurs in species but not in higher taxa. Despite these claims, the discussion in this and the previous section suggests that the difference between species and higher taxa is not their being exposed to different processes, but their being exposed to mostly the same processes to a different degree. Let me explain.

As we have seen, a number of authors believe that many if not most species lack the unifying effect of gene flow. Such species, they suggest, may be caused to have their own evolutionary uniformity as the result of genetic homeostasis or exposure to similar selection regimes. These two processes, as I have suggested, may give higher taxa some sort of evolutionary unity as well. If many species lack gene flow, then perhaps higher taxa and many species are exposed to the same types of unifying processes. If that is the case, then the difference between species and higher taxa is not so much their being exposed to different types of processes, but the different degree of exposure they have to those processes. Of course, deciding whether this is in fact true is in part an empirical matter. Nevertheless, I think that the arguments presented here suggest that we depart from the commonly held process distinction and consider the distinction I have introduced.

This suggestion may draw the following criticism: If there is no process distinction between species and higher taxa, and the distinction between those categories is only a matter of degree, then species and higher taxa do not exist as distinct categories. In other words, it might be thought that if the boundary between species and higher taxa is vague, then the distinction between those categories is an illusion.

I do not think the above suggestion implies that the divide between species and higher taxa is in some sense unreal. Think of the analogous situation with the distinction between being bald and not being bald. The borderline between being bald and not bald is undoubtedly vague, nevertheless we believe that there is a distinction between the two. The same goes for oxygen and nitrogen (see Sober 1980). Though there are discrete jumps on the periodic table between the atomic numbers 14 and 15, there is a period of time when atoms transmuting between those elements have an indeterminate atomic weight. In other words, the boundary between having the atomic number 14 and the atomic number 15 is vague. Nevertheless, we still think that nitrogen and oxygen are distinct categories.

In brief, I suspect that the divide between many empirical categories, categories which we accept as real categories, is vague, and that such vagueness is a fact of nature.[3] If that is the case, then my suggestion that the divide between species and higher taxa is vague should not cause us to dobut the existence of those categories.

Ontological Distinctions

Another distinction drawn between species and higher taxa is that species but not higher taxa are individuals. For instance, Wiley (1980, 78; 1981, 74ff.) writes that species are individuals, while higher taxa are historical entities. This distinction is found in Eldredge and Cracraft (1980, 90, 275) as well. And Mayr (1987, 166) adopts it, but with a twist; while Mayr agrees that higher taxa are historical entities, he thinks that species are populations and not individuals.

In what follows I will argue that the individual/historical entity distinction does not signal a true divide between species and higher taxa. Instead, I will contend that higher taxa and many species fall into the same ontological category, namely that of being a historical entity. This point can be brought out through a brief analysis of the recent debate over the ontological status of species.

This debate started with reasons for why species are not natural kinds. The traditional conception of kinds holds that the members of a kind must share a kind-specific essence. In other words, it requires the existence of a property possessed by all and only the members of a kind and which is useful in explaining the other necessary properties had by the members of that kind (see Sober 1980 and Dupré 1986 for an elaboration of this latter point). The traditional account also maintains that the names of kinds are the predicates found in laws of nature. Since such laws are supposed to apply universally, the account holds there can be no spatiotemporal restrictions on the members of a kind.

Many authors have argued that species do not fit this description of kinds. For example, Ghiselin (1974) and Hull (1965, 1976, 1978), among others, have insisted that there are no interesting biological properties that all and only the members of a species must have.[4] Furthermore, Sober (1980) has maintained that species essentialism is both theoretically unnecessary and at odds with post-Darwinian evolutionary theory. Another argument against species being kinds is the one used by Hull to show that species, unlike kinds, consist of members that are spatiotemporally restricted. Hull (1976, 1978) argues as follows: Species are entities that are capable of evolving by selection. Such evolution requires the organisms of a species to be connected by parent-offspring relations. These relations, in turn, require the organisms of a species to be spatiotemporally connected. As a result, species, unlike kinds, consist of members that are spatiotemporally connected and thus spatiotemporally restriced.

This last argument not only casts doubt on species being kinds, but it has led some authors to think that species are individuals. For example, Rosenberg (1985) and Ghiselin (1987) contend that the mere spatiotemporal continuity of species suffices to show that species are individuals. Agreement on this, however, is not universal. Both Hull (1976, 1978) and Williams (1985) believe there is more to being an individual than being a spatio-temporally continuous entity. Hull writes,

> [I]ntegration by descent is only a necessary condition for individuality, it is not sufficient. If it were, all genes, all organisms and all species would form but a single individual. A certain cohesiveness is also required... (1976, 183).

Similarly, Williams (1985, 581) suggests that a lineage's being spatio-temporally continuous does not suffice to make it an individual; she adds that it must be cohesive with respect to natural selection as well.

Nevertheless, Williams (1985, 583ff.) and Hull (1976, 183–184; 1978, 627ff.) maintain that species are individuals because they believe that species are spatiotemporally continuous and cohesive entities. It should be noted that the cohesiveness Hull and Williams attribute to species is just the one we saw earlier in the discussion of evolutionary units. Again, the claim attributes no essential properties to the members of a species, merely some sort of uniformity to them. Hull (1976, 1978) provides no further information about the nature of this uniformity. Williams, however, describes a group of organisms as being cohesive when its members react in a relatively similar fashion to similar selection pressures (see Williams 1970, 356–357).

According to Hull (1976, 1978) and Williams (1985), several processes can cause cohesiveness in species. Both Hull (1976, 183; 1978, 631) and Williams (1985, 584) suggest that gene flow may be a process that can cause species to be cohesive units. But as we saw earlier, numerous biologists believe that many if not most species lack the cohering force of gene flow. For instance, Ehrlich and Raven write,

> Our suspicion is that, eventually, we will find that, in some species, gene flow is an important factor in keeping populations of the species relatively undifferentiated, but in most it is not (1969, 1231; also see Grant 1980, Lande 1980).

In accordance with such considerations, Hull (1978, 630–631) and Williams (1970, 356–357; 1985, 384) suggest that species lacking adequate gene flow may be cohesive wholes because of genetic homeostasis or exposure to similar selection regimes.

I will grant that those species that are caused to be cohesive by gene flow may be individuals. But I doubt that species lacking the cohesifying effect of gene flow are individuals. It is true that the members of the latter species are spatiotemporally connected to a common ancestor. And perhaps the cohesiveness found among the members of such species is due to similar kinds of processes working on those members, namely similar selection regimes or homeostatic genotypes. Nevertheless, individuality seems to require more than spatiotemporal continuity and cohesiveness due to similar but independent processes. It seems to require that the parts of an individual be causally connected in some appropriate fashion as well.

I would like to put forth the following suggestion: An entity is an individual only if its being that entity requires some appropriate causal connection between its parts. Furthermore, it is the theory governing that entity (if such a theory exists) that determines whether its parts must be causally connected and in what manner they must be causally connected.[5] This suggestion gains support when one examines those entities, both in and outside of science, that generally are thought to be individuals. Take for instance an ordinary cup. According to physics and chemistry, cup parts do not form a single cup unless they are causally connected by certain electrostatic forces. The same consideration, I suspect, applies to whether the entity is an organism, a country, or a solar system. In contrast to individuals, when one examines those entities that generally are thought to be *non*individuals, the theories governing those entities do not require their constituents to be causally connected. Take for example the natural kind, gold or all the bullets shot in World War II. Nothing in the theories governing these entities require their constituents to be causally connected.

This causal requirement on individuality has the following consequence for the ontological status of species. Those species that owe their evolutionary unity—that is their being distinct species—to gene flow may be individuals. Those species that lack adequate gene flow, but maintain their unity through genetic homeostasis or exposure to common selection regimes, are not individuals. If, as numerous authors argue, many species lack the cohering effect of gene flow, then the causal requirement I am proposing implies that many species are not individuals.

Ruse (1987) and Guyot (1987) have used similar arguments to show that species are not individuals. They also think that such arguments lead to the conclusion that species are natural kinds. I disagree. As we saw earlier, species are spatiotemporally continuous entities and they lack species-specific essences. Because of this, I agree with Hull and Ghiselin that species are not kinds. If species are not kinds and those species lacking gene flow are not individuals, what are we then to make of their ontological status?

I propose that such species are merely historical entities, akin to Wiley's (1981) description of higher taxa (Mishler and Donoghue 1982 make a similar suggestion). According to Wiley (1981, 74ff.) a higher taxon consists of species that are historically connected to a common ancestral species, yet the species within such a taxon lack any active cohesion between them. In other words, a higher taxon for Wiley is a spatiotemporally continuous entity whose members are not causally connected in any biological manner. This is analogous to the situation faced by many species: Their subpopulations have a common ancestor, yet their subpopulations are not causally connected in any biological manner either. In sum, some species may be individuals, but many species are merely historical entities. I believe that this result provides a more accurate description of the ontological status of species than has generally been offered in the literature.

Besides clarifying the ontological status of species, this result casts doubt on the distinction introduced at the beginning of this section. Recall that Wiley (1980, 1981), Eldredge and Cracraft (1980), and Mayr (1987) contend that species are individuals (populations in Mayr's case), while higher taxa are historical entities If many species are not individuals, then this division does not separate many species from higher taxa. In fact, the above result suggests that many species and higher taxa fall into the same ontological category, that of being merely historical entities.

Species, Higher Taxa, and Realism

There is one other alleged distinction between species and higher taxa I would like to briefly consider, namely, that species are real and higher taxa are not. This distinction amounts to no less than the claim that species exist in nature whereas the existence of higher taxa is in some way mind dependent. Hennig (1966, 78) cites a number of authors who held this view in the first half of this century. And such claims are found in Simpson (1961, 57), Mayr (1969, 91), and Eldredge and Cracraft (1980, 249–250, 327).

Why would one think that higher taxa are less real than species? According to the last four authors, it is because species evolve, yet higher taxa do not. In other words, as Mayr (1982, 296), and Eldredge and Cracraft (1980, 249–250, 327) put it, it is because species but not higher taxa are evolutionary units. The distinction that species but not higher taxa are evolutionary units is also the basis on which Wiley (1981, 75) and Eldredge and Cracraft (1980, 275) make the claim that species but not higher taxa are individuals. Likewise, Hull (1976, 183–184) maintains that species are individuals because they are evolutionary units, and higher taxa would be individuals if they were evolutionary units (Hull leaves this latter point unresolved).

In sections 2 and 3 of this chapter we saw several arguments for species but not higher taxa being evolutionary units. These arguments are all based on the contention that certain processes occur in species but not in higher taxa. For example, it is argued that only species have the cohering effect of gene flow, that only species have ongoing unifying processes, and that species are the locus of speciation events. In each case, I have responded that such process distinctions do not divide species from higher taxa: both species and higher taxa can lack gene flow, both can be exposed to ongoing unifying processes, and neither are the locus of speciation events. In sum, the process distinctions argued for in the literature do not show that species but not higher taxa are evolutionary units. As a result, claims concerning the reality of species and unreality of higher taxa based on the evolutionary unit divide should be viewed with suspicion. The same applies to the argument that species but not higher taxa are individuals because only the latter are evolutionary units.

Perhaps doubt over the existence of higher taxa comes from a different source. According to Hull (1988), most systematists do not use any explicit method for the recognition and ranking of higher taxa, and those who do must choose from principles that lead to the construction of quite different classifications. Doubt over the existence of higher taxa may be due to doubt over the inference procedures systematists use to construct represen- tations of those taxa. If that is the case, then skepticism concerning the existence of higher taxa is the result of mistaking an epistemological problem for an ontological problem.

The same problem infects our classifications of species; there are a number of species concepts that lead to the construction of quite different classifications of species. Yet despite this problem, the degree of skepticism concerning the existence of species is much less. Why this is, is no small question. It might have something to do with our ability to easily recog- nize nondimensional species (see Hull 1988). Putting considerations con- cerning the human perspective aside, there is very little in the evolutionary process that demands that we treat species and higher taxa as differently as some have claimed.

Notes

The author thanks David Hull, John Kirsch, Ernst Mayr, and Elliott Sober for their comments on earlier drafts of this chapter. Financial support for this chapter was provided by North- western University in the form of a postdoctorate fellowship.

1. The term "clan" is from Mary Williams' (1970) axiomatization of evolutionary theory. As we shall see, Williams thinks Darwinian subclans (another type of entity in her axiomatization), not clans, are the units of evolution.
2. A *ceteris parbius* clause needs to be added to these conditions: selection causes a lineage to evolve only if there are no forces counteracting its forces.
3. This is not to say that the categories, or the kinds, of nature do not have essences. It may be the case, as Sober (1980) has suggested, that there are kinds with correspondingly vague essences.
4. Kitcher (1984) argues that the members of a species have essences because there are properties all the members of a species must have. Even if Kitcher were correct in showing that species have necessary properties, this would not be enough to show that they have essential properties—essential properties are necessary *and* sufficient proper- ties. See Ereshefsky 1988 for details.
5. This type of suggestion is not a new one among philosophers. Shoemaker (1979), Armstrong (1980), and Slote (1979) have all proposed similar causal requirements on individuality. See Ereshefsky 1988 for a review of such requirements.

References

Armstrong, D. (1980), "Identity Though Time," in P. Van Inwagen (ed.), *Time and Cause*. Dordrecht: D. Reidel, pp. 67–78.

Briggs, D., and Walters, S. (1984), *Plant Variation and Evolution*. Cambridge, England: Cambridge University Press.

Dupré, J. (1986), "Sex, Gender, and Essence," in French, P., Uehling, T., Jr., and Wettstein, H. (eds.), *Midwestern Studies in Philosophy X*, Minneapolis: University of Minnesota Press, pp. 441–457.

Ehrlich, P., and Raven, P. (1969), "Differentiation of Populations," *Science* 165:1228–1232.

Eldredge, N., and Cracraft, J. (1980), *Phylogenetic Patterns and the Evolutionary Process*. New York: Columbia University Press.

Eldredge, N. and Gould, S. (1972), "Punctuated Equilibria: An Alternative to Phyletic Gradualism," in T. Schopf (ed.) *Models in Paleobiology*. San Francisco: Freeman, Cooper and Company, pp. 82–115.

Ereshefsky, M. (1988), "The Ontological Status of Species: A Study of Individuality and its Role in Evolutionary Theory," Ph.D. thesis, University of Wisconsin.

Ghiselin, M. (1974), "A Radical Solution to the Species Problem," *Systematic Zoology* 23: 536–544.

Ghiselin, M. (1987), "Species Concepts, Individuality, and Objectivity," *Biology and Philosophy* 2:127–143.

Grant, V. (1980), "Gene Flow and the Homogeneity of Species," *Biologisches Zentrablatt* 99:157–169.

Gromko, M., and Bradie, M. (1987), "Species Problems and Population Solutions." Paper presented at the 1987 Summer Conference in the History, Social Studies, and Philosophy of Biology. Blacksburg, Virginia.

Guyot, K. (1987), "Specious Individuals," *Philosophica* 37:101–126.

Hennig, W. (1966), *Phylogenetic Systematics*. Urbana: University of Chicago Press.

Hull, D. (1965), "The Effect of Essentialism on Taxonomy," *The British Journal for the Philosophy of Science* 15:314–326.

Hull, D. (1976), "Are Species Really Individuals?" *Systematic Zoology* 25:174–191.

Hull, D. (1978), "A Matter of Individuality," *Philosophy of Science* 45:335–360. Reprinted in Sober, E. (ed.) *Conceptual Issues in Evolutionary Biology*. Cambridge, Mass.: MIT Press.

Hull, D. (1980), "Individuality and Selection," *Annual Review of Ecology and Systematics* 11:311–332.

Hull, D. (1988), "Common Sense and Scientific Classifications," unpublished manuscript. Department of Philosophy, Northwestern University.

Kitcher, P. (1984), "Species," *Philosophy of Science* 51:308–333.

Lack, D. (1953), "Darwin's Finches." Reprinted in Wilson, B. W. (ed.) *Birds*. San Francisco: Freeman.

Lande, R. (1980), "Genetic Variation and Phenotypic Evolution during Allopatric Speciation," *American Naturalist* 116:463–479.

Mayr, E. (1969), *Principles of Systematic Zoology*. New York: McGraw-Hill.

Mayr, E. (1970), *Populations, Species, and Evolution*. Cambridge, Mass.: Harvard University Press.

Mayr, E. (1982), *The Growth of Biological Thought*. Cambridge, Mass.: Harvard University Press.

Mayr, E. (1987), "The Ontological Status of Species: Scientific Progress and Philosophical Terminology," *Biology and Philosophy* 2:145–166.

Mishler, B. and Donoghue, M. (1982), "Species Concepts: A Case for Pluralism," *Systematic Zoology* 31:491–503.

Rosenberg, A. (1985), *The Structure of Biological Science*. New York: Cambridge University Press.

Ruse, M. (1987), "Biological Species: Natural Kinds, Individuals, or What?" *British Journal for the Philosophy of Science* 38:225–242.

Shoemaker, S. (1979), "Identity, Properties, and Causality," in French, P., Uehling, T., Jr., and Wettstein, H. (eds.) *Midwestern Studies in Philosophy VI*, Minneapolis: University of Minnesota Press, pp. 321–342.

Simpson, G. (1961), *The Principles of Animal Taxonomy*. New York: Columbia University Press.

Slote, M. (1979), "Causality and the Concept of 'Thing'," in French, P., Uehling, T., Jr., and Wettstein, H. (eds.) *Midwestern Studies in Philosophy VI*, Minneapolis: University of Minnesota Press, pp. 387–400.

Sober, E. (1980), "Evolution, Population Thinking, and Essentialism," *Philosophy of Science* 47:350–383.

Sober, E. (1984), *The Nature of Selection*. Cambridge, Mass.: MIT Press.

Wiley, E. (1980), "Is the Evolutionary Species Fiction?" *Systematic Zoology* 29:76–80.

Wiley, E. (1981), *Phylogenetics: The Theory and Practice of Phylogenetic Systematics*. New York: Wiley and Sons.

Williams, M. (1970), "Deducing the Consequences of Evolution," *Journal of Theoretical Biology* 29:343–385.

Williams, M. (1985), "Species are Individuals: Theoretical Foundations for the Claim," *Philosophy of Science* 52:578–590.

Acknowledgments

I Biological Concepts

1. "Species Concepts and Their Application." From chapter 2 of *Populations, Species, and Evolution*, Cambridge: Harvard University Press (1963). Reprinted by permission of the publisher and the author. Copyright © 1963, 1970 by the President and Fellows of Harvard College.

2. "The Biological Species Concept: A Critical Evaluation." From *American Naturalist* (1970), 104, pp. 127–153. Reprinted by permission of the publisher and the author.

3. "Differentiation of Populations." From *Science* (1969), 165, pp. 1228–1232. Reprinted by permission of the publisher and the author. Copyright © 1969 by the AAAS.

4. "Ecological Species, Multispecies, and Oaks." From *Taxon* (1976), 25, pp. 233–239. Reprinted by permission of the publisher and the author.

5. "The Evolutionary Species Concept Reconsidered." From *Systematic Zoology* (1978), 27, pp. 17–26. Reprinted by permission of the publisher and the author.

6. "Species Concepts and Speciation Analysis." From R. Johnston (ed.), *Current Ornithology* (1983), 1, pp. 159–187, New York: Plenum Press. Reprinted by permission of the publisher and the author.

7. "Species Concepts: A Case for Pluralism." From *Systematic Zoology* (1982), 31, pp. 491–503. Reprinted by permission of the publisher and the author.

8. "The Recognition Concept of Species." From E. Vrba, (ed.), *Species and Speciation* (1985), pp. 21–29. Pretoria: Transvaal Museum Monograph No. 4. Reprinted by permission of the publisher and the author.

9. "The Meaning of Species and Speciation: A genetic perspective." From Otte and Endler (eds.), *Speciation and its Consequences* (1989), pp. 3–27, Sunderland Mass.: Sinauer Assoc. Reprinted by permission of the publisher and the author.

II Philosophical Implications

10. "The Effect of Essentialism on Taxonomy: Two Thousand Years of Stasis." From *British Journal for the Philosophy of Science* (1965), 15, pp. 314–326, 16, pp. 1–18. Reprinted by permission of the publisher and the author.

11. "Speaking of Species: Darwin's Strategy." From D. Kohn (ed.), *The Darwinian Heritage* (1985), pp. 265–281. Princeton: Princeton University Press. Reprinted by permission of the publisher and the author. Copyright © 1985 by Princeton University Press.

12. "Evolution, Population Thinking, and Essentialism." From *Philosophy of Science* (1980), 47, pp. 350–383. Reprinted by permission of the publisher and the author.

13. "A Radical Solution to the Species Problem." From *Systematic Zoology* (1974), 23, pp. 536–544. Reprinted by permission of the publisher and the author.

14. "A Matter of Individuality." From *Philosophy of Science* (1978), 45, pp. 335–360. Reprinted by permission of the publisher and the author.

15. "Species" *Philosophy of Science* (1984), 51, pp. 308–333. Reprinted by permission of the publisher and the author.

16. "Biological Species: Natural Kinds, Individuals, or What?" From *British Journal for the Philosophy of Science* (1987), 38, pp. 225–242. Reprinted by permission of the publisher and the author.

17. "Species Concepts, Individuality, and Objectivity." From *Biology and Philosophy* (1987), 2, pp. 127–143. Reprinted by permission of the publisher and the author. Copyright © by D. Reidel Publishing Company.

18. "Species, Higher Taxa, and the Units of Evolution." From *Philosophy of Science* (1991), 58, pp. 84–101. Reprinted by permission of the publisher and the author.

Index

Index